Statistical Analysis for Education
Psychology Researchers

To my wife Diane

Statistical Analysis for Education and Psychology Researchers

Ian S. Peers

 The Falmer Press

(A member of the Taylor & Francis Group)
London • Washington, D.C.

UK   Falmer Press, 1 Gunpowder Square, London, EC4A 3DE
USA   Falmer Press, Taylor & Francis Inc., 1900 Frost Road, Suite 101, Bristol,
PA 19007

First published in 1996

The author has made every attempt to obtain all the necessary permissions, should any have been omitted we will do our best to correct this at reprint stage.

A catalogue record for this book is available from the British Library

Library of Congress Cataloging-in-Publication Data are available on request

ISBN 0 7507 0506 x paper

Jacket design by Caroline Archer

Typeset in 10/12pt Times by
Graphicraft Typesetters Ltd., Hong Kong

Printed in Great Britain by Biddles Ltd, Guildford and King's Lynn on paper which has a specified pH value on final paper manufacture of not less than 7.5 and is therefore 'acid free'.

Contents

List of Figures

List of Tables

Appendix – List of Figures and Tables

List of Statistical Symbols

α The level of statistical significance selected. If you select $p = 0.05$ you are setting a 5% probability of making a Type I error, that is, a 5% chance of rejecting a null hypothesis when it is true.   11

α_i Fixed effect of the ith treatment in a statistical model for ANOVA e.g.

$$y_{ij} = \mu + \alpha_i + \varepsilon_{ij}$$ 80 and 314

a_i Random effect of the ith treatment in a statistical model for ANOVA   80

β The probability of making a Type II error, that is, the chance of not rejecting a null hypothesis when it is not true.   115

$\beta_0, \beta_1, \ldots \beta_n$ Population regression weights (parameters) in a statistical model for regression e.g.

$$y = \beta_0 + \beta_1 x_1 + \varepsilon$$

β_0 is a constant in the above linear model.   255

$b_0, b_1, \ldots b_n$ Sample regression statistics (sometimes called partial regression coefficients) in a regression equation e.g.

$$\hat{Y} = b_0 + b_1 x_1$$

b_0 is a constant in the above regression equation.   256

$1-\beta$ The power of a statistical test, that is the probability of rejecting a null hypothesis when the null hypothesis is not true.   114 and 115

$\chi^2_{(v)}$ Chi-squared statistic with corresponding 'v' degrees of freedom (v represents the appropriate degrees of freedom on which the value of Chi-square is evaluated).   94 and 168

$\chi^2_{(FR)}$ Friedman's Chi-square statistic.   244

CI   Confidence interval.   102

n_{C_r}	Binomial coefficient which refers to r successes in n trials.	98
df	Degrees of freedom.	70
ε	Random error term in a statistical model for regression.	255
ε_{ij}	Random error term for the *jth* observation in the *ith* treatment in an ANOVA statistical model.	314
η	Greek letter eta, population median.	192
$F_{(v_1, v_2)}$	F-ratio or F statistic with associated v_1 and v_2 degrees of freedom.	320
H	Kruskal-Wallis test statistic.	236
H_0	Statistical or null hypothesis.	112
H_1	Alternative or research hypothesis.	112
K	Kappa statistic, index of agreement.	31
MS	Mean square term (sum of squares/df).	267
μ	Population mean.	76
N or n	Sample size (number of observations in a sample).	68
n'	Harmonic mean of two samples.	140
ϕ	Phi coefficient.	174
π	Population proportion.	94
p	Sample proportion.	94
p	Probability of obtaining a particular value for a test statistic. If we state that $p \leq 0.05$ this implies that the probability of obtaining such a test statistic value by chance alone is less than or equal to 1 in 20.	110
Q	Cochran Q statistic.	199
Q_1	Lower quartile or 25th percentile in a distribution.	57
Q_2	Median, second quartile, or 50th percentile in a distribution.	57
Q_3	Upper quartile or 75th percentile in a distribution.	57
ρ	Rho, general notation for a population correlation.	208
ρ_s	Spearman's population rank order correlation.	211
r	Pearson (sample) correlation.	208
r_s	Spearman's (sample) rank order correlation.	211

List of Formula

Acknowledgments

The Author and Publisher would like to thank the following for the kind permission to reproduce some of the material produced in this book:

Appendix A4, Table 4, page 387-8, Critical value of U in the runs test for testing randomness is taken from table G by Siegel, S. and Castellan, N. J. (1988) *Nonparametric Statistics for the Behavioral Sciences*, 2nd edition, New York, McGraw-Hill.

Appendix A4, Table 6, page 390, Critical values for the Kruskal-Wallis ANOVA by ranks statistic h is taken from table O by Siegel, S. and Castellan, N. J. (1988) *Nonparametric Statistics for the Behavioral Sciences*, 2nd edition, New York, McGraw-Hill

Preface

In writing this book I have particular readers in mind: Postgraduate research students or researchers who do not have a mathematical or statistical background but who want to *understand* and *use* statistics. This book provides an introduction to the use of statistical tests and has three main aims. First, to help readers learn statistical concepts, to think statistically and thereby become a more astute consumer of research papers and reports. As consumers of research, they will want to *understand* statistics as they appear in other researchers' reports, theses and so on. The second aim is to enable potential producers of statistics to become judicious users of them. Producers of statistics will need to *choose and apply* appropriate statistical tests to a wide range of research problems typically encountered by social science researchers. A further aim of this book is to help researchers use statistical software effectively. The present-day researcher has a number of sophisticated computer programmes available for data analysis. Examples of the SAS[1] system programming language are used to show how data is entered into a proprietary package and how this data is then analyzed. Printouts of results are illustrated with interpretive comments and where appropriate suggestions for further analysis.

Put simply this book is intended to help non-mathematical researchers to understand statistical ideas, to apply statistical thinking to research design, to choose and use appropriate statistical procedures and to interpret their own or other researchers' data analysis. Those readers wishing simply to confirm an appropriate statistical procedure for their research problems should refer directly to the fifth chapter in the book.

The approach adopted in this book is based on ten years' experience of teaching statistics to research students. My past students have been my most valuable critics and my present students continue to be my guide as to what works and why. Based on their evaluations this book is grounded on three general premises. To use statistics appropriately one has to understand basic concepts of research design and probability. Appropriate use requires judgment which develops with experience. There is no substitute for practical use of statistics with real data for those seeking to enhance their understanding and polish their skills of analysis and interpretation.

An understanding of key concepts can be obscured by unnecessary formulae and accordingly these have been kept to a minimum, and where used are explained in full. Statistical tests are introduced using description and examples from the literature of Psychology and Education. Understanding is thereby facilitated by familiarity with the general kinds of research questions and issues discussed. The text is judiciously punctuated with questions that encourage reflection.

New statistical concepts are distinguished from other concepts and these ideas are related to real research examples drawn from the literature. This practical orientation helps to relate statistical ideas to the use of statistics in real life research problems. Choice of appropriate statistical procedures and skill in analysis and interpretation are developed through an awareness of what other researchers do and by practice in application. Each statistical test is explained with a worked example. Excerpts from papers, reports and theses are used as illustrative material throughout.

Note

1   SAS is the registered trademark of SAS Institute, Inc Cary, NL, USA.

Chapter 1

Statistics and Research Design

In everyday use the word *statistics* has two meanings. In one sense it refers to the way we collect, analyze and interpret numerical facts which are termed **data**. Second, statistics are in themselves the raw numerical data resulting from observations or measurements, or are the results of calculations derived from such data. The term *statistical analysis* is often used and in general this may refer to the **descriptive** use of statistics to present and summarize data, or it may mean the way in which these statistics are used to make statistical inferences. This is the process whereby statistical information obtained from a sample is used to draw conclusions which have wider applicability than solely to the sample of observations or measurements obtained and is referred to as the **inferential** use of statistics.

Statistical inferences are described in terms of **probability**; the likelihood or chance in the long-run of occurrence of an event. In statistical jargon an event means any outcome(s) from among a set of all possible outcomes. The concept of probability is used in **statistical modelling** which compares patterns of variability and frequency of outcomes in real data with the idealized frequency of outcomes that would be expected from a statistical probability model. We can think of such a probability model as a mathematical representation to describe and predict phenomena such as patterns and relationships in data and outcomes of experiments. Interpretation of the fit or match of data to a particular statistical model can provide insight into the phenomena being investigated.

Data, however, do not interpret themselves and may be meaningless unless descriptive statistics are used to arrange numbers into a coherent and more meaningful summary of information. Inferential statistical techniques are the tools which can then be used to analyze data, answer specific questions, draw trustworthy conclusions and thereby gain information which might not be apparent from an initial scrutiny of data.

In this chapter we begin by emphasizing the importance of statistical thinking in research design and then go on to examine the role which statistics plays in the planning and data collection stages of a study. Next, we review the general principles and distinguishing features of survey and experimental designs and then present statistical guidelines which can be referred to during the design stage of a study or which can be used in the assessment of research papers, reports and manuscripts.

1.1 Why Consider Research Design in a Text About Statistics?

It is important to appreciate that statistics is much more than a collection of techniques for data analysis. Statistical ideas can and should be used to advantage in the design and data collection stages of a study. A well designed study that has generated reliable data but which has been poorly analyzed can be rescued by appropriate reanalysis. A poorly designed study, however, that has generated data of dubious quality, is beyond redemption, no matter how sophisticated the statistical analysis.

Use of Statistical Ideas in Research Planning

Sample size and statistical power

When planning a survey or an experiment a common problem for researchers is the determination of sample size or number of subjects in experimental groups. It is possible to estimate the number of subjects required either in a sample survey or in experimental design so that sample or treatment differences would be detected at a specified **significance level**. The significance level of a statistical test is the likelihood of concluding there is a difference (rejecting a hypothesis of no difference) when in fact there is a difference (the hypothesis of no difference is refuted). The estimation of sample size is achieved through statistical power analysis. Given certain assumptions, a statistical test is said to be powerful if it is able to detect a statistically significant difference should one exist (statistical power analysis is considered in Chapter 5). The point of doing a power analysis for a research plan based on a particular sample size is that if the design turns out to have insufficient power, that is one is unable to detect any statistically significant difference, then the researcher can revise the plan. One option would be to increase the sample size. There are other options, including, at the extreme, dropping the proposed study. Clearly, as little can be done after data has been collected, consideration of sample size and statistical power is crucial at the planning stage.

It should also be emphasized that statistical significance does not always imply educational significance. For example, a small gain in maths scores after an experimental maths programme may be statistically significant but may be considered to be of no educational importance. The researcher in planning an evaluation of this maths programme would have to determine what maths gain score would be considered a significant educational gain and design a study to be able to detect this magnitude of treatment effect.

Validity and reliability of measurement

Attention should be given to the construction of measuring instruments like questionnaires and sociometric indices. A common problem encountered with self-completion questionnaires is missing responses, often referred to as 'missing data'.

The best answer to this particular problem is to have none. If you do have missing data, this often tells you as much about the design of your questionnaire as the knowledge, opinions or thoughts of the respondent. The pattern of missing responses is also informative. Descriptive analysis of pilot study data may reveal selective non-response or indeed returned blank questionnaires for certain individuals. It is therefore sensible to spend time at the planning stage considering strategies to ensure complete responses and subsequently to complete a pilot study.

If there are problems with the specific method that generates the data, such as, ambiguous questions, then the data will not be valid. That is, the data will not be trustworthy because we have not measured what we think we have measured. In this case the questionnaire is said to have poor **construct validity**. Messick (1989) suggests that construct validity encompasses three other forms of validity often referred to in the measurement literature as content, concurrent and predictive validity. A questionnaire survey that has dubious construct validity is also likely to yield erroneous conclusions about differences that appear in the sample data. Researchers refer to the issue of drawing false conclusions from statistical tests of differences or relationships as a problem of **statistical conclusion validity**. Cook and Campbell (1979) suggest it is appropriate to establish whether differences or relationships exist before considering the magnitude or strength of any effects. Another aspect of statistical conclusion validity is the **reliability** of measurement, the idea that consistent results will be given by a measurement instrument when a subject is measured repeatedly under near identical conditions. Lack of reliability increases the amount of observed variation which has the effect of making it more difficult to detect significant covariation among variables. Larger sample sizes can, to some extent, compensate for this increase in variability of measures. However, as Henry, (1990) comments, 'to compensate for the inflation of the variance [variability of observations] due to the lack of reliability of the instrument, it must be recognized and accounted for early in the design process' p. 13.

Procedures for data collection

Data generated in a quantitative investigation should be the product of a research design, which is a plan specifying what information will be collected, how this will be done and how it should be analyzed. Quantitative studies such as surveys and experiments, if systematically planned, should make use of the idea of **chance** when data is collected because the role that chance plays in data generation influences the trustworthiness of any statements we make about research findings. For example, chance is involved when selecting subjects for a survey or allocating subjects to an experimental group. If data are collected in a systematic rather than in a haphazard way then knowing the role that chance plays in generating the data allows valid conclusions to be drawn about your results – or the results of others.

A **random sampling** procedure is often used in survey design. This means choosing subjects at random from a defined population. When random sampling is used each member of the target population has a known chance of being selected for the sample. In experimental research the principle of **randomization** is used as a means of assigning subjects to treatment groups on the basis of chance. Random assignment, which should not be confused with random sampling, is intended to produce experimental groups that are similar in all respects prior to any treatment. The randomization process, which does not mean a haphazard one, uses the laws of chance to assign subjects to treatment groups in a way which eliminates any systematic differences that might exist among subjects.

Whereas survey methods vary, for example, postal self-completion, class administered questionnaires, telephone, interview and observational surveys, the one feature most are likely to share is the need to obtain a sample. A survey sample is usually intended to represent the population from which it is drawn. If the sample is faulty or is not designed to be representative, then it is not reasonable to generalize beyond the achieved sample. This presents the researcher with a problem of **external validity** or **generalizability**. The ability to generalize findings relates to the definition of the population of interest, the sampling method used and the validity and reliability of measurement.

Sources of variability

A good sample design will minimize the amount of variability in observations or measurements to an acceptable level given the purpose and required precision of a survey or experiment. Variability is inherent in measurements on subjects. For example, consider a teacher who selects a sample of school children and measures for each child his or her assertiveness behaviour using the School Motivation Analysis Test (SMAT instrument described by Boyle and Houndoulesi, 1993) and then estimates an average assertiveness score. If on the following day the teacher repeats the testing, it is very likely that the two measurements for each child will vary as will the two averages of the first and second set of measurements. Such variability may be due to random variation in measurement, a real change in the children's assertiveness (a dynamic trait) or a combination of both.

In designing a survey to estimate teenagers' assertiveness, for example, consideration should be given to three potential sources of variability or error. The full inventory has 190 items, and some students may become bored or tired and not answer all items. This would introduce a **measurement error** which is an example of **nonsampling bias**. If the teacher had selected a **non-probability** sample that is a non-random sample, then the sample may not be representative of all teenagers (not every teenager would have an equal or known chance of being selected). This would introduce a **selection bias** and is an example of **sampling bias**. Finally any sample is subject to **sampling error** or sampling variability. Put simply this means that any particular sample average, given certain assumptions, will vary from another independent sample average. This idea of a distribution of sample averages and how it relates to sampling error will be explored in Chapter 4. The implication for planning is that the precision of a sample statistic such as an average assertiveness score is related to sampling error. In fact the precision of a sample statistic decreases as sampling error increases. Sampling error is influenced by sample size and variability of what is being measured in the population, in this case assertiveness. In this example, the smaller the population variability in assertiveness (more homogeneous) the smaller will be the sampling error; this will provide a more precise average assertiveness score. Larger sample sizes also reduce sampling error, which is one reason why larger samples are preferable to smaller ones. 'Small' in survey and experimental research is generally taken to mean less than 30 subjects, but this is only a guideline. Generally for both experiments and surveys more subjects are better than fewer subjects up to a point. The more subjects that participate in an experiment, the more it is likely that randomization to treatment groups will be effective. Consequently, on average groups will be similar because any individual differences among subjects will be averaged out by the random allocation of subjects to groups.

Choice of statistical tests

After data collection, descriptive statistics are used to summarize data. The research questions addressed and the nature of the data will influence the choice of summary statistics. For example, if more scores are at one extreme rather than in the middle of a distribution, the median may be a more appropriate measure of central tendency than the average. If differences between mean scores are to be estimated then the laws of chance may be used to say whether differences among the means of treatment groups are **statistically significant** and to indicate whether differences are too large to be attributable to chance alone. Thought should also have been given to appropriate analyses at the planning stage. A common significance test for comparison of two independent groups is the independent t-test, which makes certain assumptions about how data is generated: the sampling, how the data is measured and the variability of the data (these considerations are discussed in Chapter 8). In other studies, for example, in the evaluation of a maths programme it may be more appropriate to measure individual change, that is the difference between *before* and *after* scores. The important statistic in this example would be the mean of the difference scores (after 'minus' before) rather than the difference between means of independent groups.

Being a critical research consumer

Most empirical researchers will be consumers of research reports and papers. It is necessary to be able to discern good studies from poor ones, to be able to identify limitations in design and interpretation and hence judge the dependability of conclusions. As we will see in later chapters, not all studies published in educational research journals meet the statistical standards that we might expect, therefore publication should not be seen as a guarantee of quality and trustworthiness. The novice researcher may find this difficult to believe but as researchers become more experienced and knowledgable they also become more critical and rely more on their own judgments than on the judgments of others.

Whenever we encounter research findings we need to consider their trustworthiness. A particular sample statistic such as the sample average may be calculated and used to estimate the mean for the population from which the sample was drawn. As one particular sample average is likely to vary from a second independent sample average, even if exactly the same procedure for selection and calculation is used (all sampling results are subject to sampling errors), then the laws of chance can be used to provide an estimate of precision or a confidence interval for the obtained sample average. When reading a research report we should consider the confidence intervals around any sample statistics given. It is good practice to report the confidence interval or to give sufficient information for the confidence interval to be calculated (see Chapters 6 and 8).

Survey research is seldom confined to drawing conclusions only about the subjects in an achieved sample. Even if this is intended, often implicit generalizations will be made, if not by the researcher then by the research consumer, to the parent population, or to similar subjects. In this case the trustworthiness of the results will depend not only upon the precision of the sample statistic but also on the extent to which the picture given by the sample represents the situation in the population. Clearly the survey design, that is how the data were measured, collected and recorded, will influence estimates of precision and the veracity of any generalizations. A good research report would provide information on all important aspects of the study design and data collection procedures. An informed reader can then judge whether or not the results claimed are reasonable.

Similarly, the validity of experimental conclusions will need to be judged against the extent to which results are attributed solely to the causes identified in the experiment. Again the laws of chance are involved. They allow the outcomes of an experiment to be explained by taking into account what outcomes would be expected by the laws of chance alone. Observation of differences among treatment groups which are too large to be attributable to chance alone are said to be **statistically significant**. Data which is generated from an experiment is the product of an experimental design. The quality of that design, the adequacy and accuracy of data measurement and recording procedures, the effectiveness of randomization of subjects to treatment groups, and the choice of the number of subjects or treatments will influence the validity of experimental results.

The most important overall message to be gleaned thus far is that consideration of statistical principles is crucial to good research design and that statistical ideas are involved as much in data collection as in data analysis. Any data analysis will be influenced by the method of data collection. For example, if data are collected in a haphazard way then it may not be worth spending any time on data analysis. Clarity of purpose and statistical awareness at the design stage of a study should lead to the avoidance of typical problems such as small numbers of observations, missing responses for key variables, large sampling errors, and unbalanced experimental designs. These problems make any subsequent analysis and interpretation more difficult and possibly less powerful. Do not leave consideration of data analysis until after data has been collected. It may be too late at this stage to rectify a fundamental design problem which would render impossible the answering of the research question you had in mind.

1.2 Surveys

Many studies are labelled as surveys, ranging from Charles Booth's classic poverty surveys of the working-class population of London (Booth, 1889–1902) to modern day Gallup Polls, Government Surveys (General Household Survey, Labour Force Survey, Family Expenditure Survey, British Household Panel Study, Child Development Study, Youth Cohort Study) and opinion and market research surveys. Surveys are usually designed to collect data from a **population** of interest. A population in a statistical sense refers to a complete set of subjects, values or events that have some common characteristic. In many survey designs the population of interest – all those to whom you would like to generalize your findings – may be indeterminable in number or impossible to enumerate. In this sense the term population is a theoretical concept because all members could never be observed or counted. Most surveys involve the selection of samples, unless they are censuses or total population surveys. A **sample** is usually a collection of subjects, values or events which is finite in size, therefore quantifiable, and represents a subgroup of a population. The idea of sampling is to use characteristics of a selected sample to infer properties of the **population** from which the sample was drawn. Rarely is it feasible or necessary to include the total population of interest in a study.

Surveys may be classified in at least two ways based on how data is collected and when data is collected. These are not the only ways to classify survey research but they are convenient ones. From a methodological standpoint survey data may be collected by questionnaire, interview or observation. As well as method, the time when data is collected may be used to distinguish among survey type. In a cross-sectional study the sample would consist of different subjects representing all relevant subgroups in a population measured at one moment in time. In a longitudinal study the sample may consist of one group of subjects who are studied over time and each subject may be measured more than once.

Longitudinal surveys can be subdivided into studies which look backward in time, **retrospective studies** and those which look forward, **prospective studies**. Retrospective studies determine the effect of exposure, retrospectively, on an outcome of interest. For example, a researcher may set up a retrospective longitudinal survey to investigate bullying in school. A sample of school children would be selected and then divided into two groups on the outcome of interest. Here one group would consist of children who report that they have been bullied in school and the other group would comprise those children who say they have not been bullied. A potential *exposure effect* such as type of school attended, public or state school, is then determined retrospectively by examining the proportions of children in each school type who were bullied. This design is also called a **causal comparative survey** design because it attempts to determine the causes or reasons for existing differences between groups of individuals, in this case those children bullied and those not. The inference in this example would be that school type leads to the observed differences in bullying. Both the outcome, bullying, and the suggested causal factor, school type, have already occurred and are studied retrospectively.

Causal comparative research is distinguished from experimental research because variables are not under the control of the researcher and effects or outcomes are observed and possible causes sought. In experimental research causal factors are deliberately manipulated with the intention of observing particular outcomes. In causal comparative research suggested causal factors, such as the type of school, could not be manipulated because they have already occurred. Caution should be used when interpreting causal relationships from causal comparative studies. Such studies may lead to the setting up of 'true' experimental designs.

In prospective studies, subjects would be grouped according to exposure or some other factor and individuals would be followed up and outcomes of interest observed. In the bullying example, two groups of children, those attending public schools and those attending state schools, would be followed up over a number of years and the proportion of those who report being bullied would be observed at different points in time in both groups. The National Child Development Study (NCDS) is an example of a longitudinal prospective survey. This study is intended to follow the lives of individuals living in Great Britain who were born between the 3rd and the 9th of March 1958. Obstetric data was collected from the first sample of approximately 17,000 children. The first follow-up of these children took place in 1965 and this gave the study its name, the NCDS. A second follow-up was in 1969 when the children were aged 11, and futher observations occurred in 1974, 1981 and 1991.

An alternative approach to describing surveys is to focus on purpose. Surveys may be primarily descriptive or explanatory. In a descriptive survey a sample would be drawn from a defined population with a view to *describing* prevalence (total number of occurrences), incidence rate (new occurrences in specified time period) or, for example, what subjects think or feel about an issue, such as the Gallup Polls. In an explanatory survey the purpose and subsequent analysis would focus on *explaining* interrelationships between or among phenomena.

Sampling

Selection of a sample is an integral part of most survey designs. Samples may be characterized as one of two main types, **probability samples**, sometimes called random samples, where every member of the population has some probability of being selected for the sample (not necessarily equal probability) and **non-probability samples** in which some section of the population may not be represented (non-random). Statistical techniques for estimating precision of sample statistics which are based on probabilistic reasoning should be used cautiously with non-probability samples. Examples of non-probability sampling approaches include:

- Convenience   subjects selected on basis of availability
- Quota   subjects sampled in proportion to population proportions on key variables
- Purposive   subjects selected on the basis that they are known to have certain attributes

- Dimensional   subjects selected to represent similar or dissimilar dimensions
- Snowball   subjects identified by sample members
- Critical case   subjects selected that will give an overall assessment

The degree of representativeness of a sample depends upon how the sample is selected. If the population was not carefully specified or a non-probability sampling procedure was used then a non-representative sample may be drawn and one's confidence in estimating characteristics of the target population from the selected sample would be limited.

Survey and correlational studies are generally characterized by the absence of planned change and control of variables. They cannot therefore show cause–effect relationships. In these studies variables are not manipulated and it is unwise to attribute causality to variables that change jointly or **covary**. Variables are said to covary if, say, high values on variable 'A' are associated with (but do not cause) high values on another variable 'B' or, alternatively, if lower values on variable 'A' are associated with (but do not cause) higher values on variable 'B'. **Correlation** is a special case of covariation when the degree of relationship between two variables is expressed on a common scale of measurement or standard scores (see Chapters 7 and 8). If values of two variables covary in survey and correlational designs then the relationship is said to be **concomitant** rather than causal. Covariation of two variables in surveys could be attributed to a common third variable, the effect of a number of confounding variables or causation. Only an experimental design would be able to establish causation as an explanation for the observed covariation. Correlational surveys are designed with the specific purpose of gaining insight into the extent of the relationship between two or more quantifiable variables and in this sense are distinct from typical self-report questionnaires or observational studies. If variables are found to be related or correlated then scores on one variable may be used to predict scores on another variable. This would be an example of a prediction study. A researcher, for example, may be interested in whether A-level grades predict degree performance. The variable predicted, in this example degree performance, is called the **criterion** or **response variable**. The variable(s) upon which the prediction is made are called **predictor** or **explanatory** or **independent variables**. See for example the study described by Peers (1994). The most common failings in survey designs are i) the use of non-probability and non-representative samples of subjects when the researcher wishes to generalize findings to a wider population and ii) small sample sizes which provide imprecise sample statistics with large sampling errors.

Example 1

A research student was interested in investigating provision and practice for staff development in secondary schools. This is an extract from the student's research plan.

> The overall purpose of the study will be to inform national policy on staff
> development in secondary schools. As part of the study a structured interview

schedule will be designed to determine what principals think of school-based staff development, the importance they attach to it and their willingness to involve themselves in staff development. Information will also be collected on respondents' age, sex, years of experience in post and academic qualifications. A sample of 15 principals, personally known to the researcher, in one of four geographical regions will be selected for inclusion in the study.

Given the purpose of the study, this was not an appropriate design. A probability-based sampling strategy would have been preferable, possibly using region as a stratification factor. This involves taking a random sample from each of the four regions (the stratification factor). The number of interviews would need to be increased if the sampling error were to be kept to a reasonable level. The sampling design chosen, a non-probability convenience sample, may also introduce bias into the study. It is possible that colleagues would give favourable responses. Any generalizations beyond this convenience sample would not be reasonable and therefore the main purpose of the study would not be addressed.

This example illustrates the importance of matching design and methods to research purpose. It also demonstrates the value of planning prior to data collection. Given the problems identified with this design a number of alternatives exist:

- Use a probability sampling strategy and increase sample size, that is the number of interviews, to obtain reasonable precision on the most important variables.
- Use the convenience sample but change the aims of the study from descriptive to explanatory. For example, research questions might include exploration of relationships between principals' attitudes and involvement in staff development and the gender, age, job related experience and academic qualifications of staff.
- Use a probability sampling strategy with a survey questionnaire. Either develop or choose an appropriate attitude questionnaire and follow up selected respondents with interviews for validation of attitude responses and additional in-depth information.

At the design stage of a survey it is useful to consider:

- purpose of the study, whether it is intended to answer specific questions or is exploratory;
- target population and any subpopulations of special interest;
- variables of most interest;
- appropriateness of data collection procedure;
- type of sampling and sample size;
- whether analysis is likely to be descriptive or analytical.

Example from the Literature

Cullingford (1994) surveyed 370 7–11-year-old children's responses to advertisements on TV. Data was collected by lengthy semi-structured interviews. Descriptive statistics were used to show that 75 per cent of 7-year-old children when asked whether their favourite advertisements were true answered that they were. This was compared with 90 per cent of 11-year-old children who, in answering the same question, said that the advertisements were not true. In the interviews children were given a chance to reflect upon their responses and the author goes on to say that whereas the 7-year-olds' *first* response was that the adverts were true, because the products existed, their *second* response (presumably on reflection) was that adverts were essentially fantasy. Similarly, the 11-year-olds' *first* response was to say the adverts were fantasy, and their *second* response was to say that they were a fantasy about a real thing so were true. The author concludes that interviews allow in-depth exploration of answers and children show a clear shift in explaining their responses at the age of eight. The shift is in the order of their responses, putting greater emphasis on social awareness rather than on pragmatic facts.

1.3 Experimental Research

Experimental research is distinguished from non-experimental research by the critical features of **manipulation** and **control** of variables to determine cause and effect relationships. Researchers select and manipulate **independent variables** (sometimes called explanatory variables) to observe the effect they have on **response variables** (sometimes called dependent variables). Whereas in a general sense a **variable** represents a property or characteristic of an object which varies from one object to another, when designing a study researchers make distinctions among different types of variables depending on the role they play in a study. For example, in one experimental study the variable 'degree classification' may be the response variable or outcome variable of interest. In another regression study degree classification may represent an explanatory or independent variable such as in predicting the starting salary of a first job.

The essence of experimental design is a research situation in which at least one independent variable is deliberately manipulated or varied by the researcher with the purpose of observing the effect this has on at least one response variable. Other variables which could influence the response variable are controlled. Variables can be controlled by three main strategies, singly or in combination: allocation of subjects to conditions, holding variables constant and statistical control (adjustment). Good experimental design should allow a situation to be set up so that plausible alternative hypotheses can be ruled out. The extent to which plausible alternatives have been explained or ruled out, a cause and effect can be implied, i.e., 'X' was responsible for 'Y', and **internal validity** has been established.

A variable which is not effectively controlled and which changes along with the independent variable may account for an alternative explanation of the observed experimental effect. This is called a **confounding variable** and it confounds or confuses the effect of the independent variable on the response variable. This would threaten any causal inference and hence any internal validity of an experiment. In many experimental studies we may want to make statements about effects that apply beyond the particular situation studied. This raises the question of **external validity,** the extent to which the study findings can be generalized from the particular experimental setting to other similar settings.

Example 2

A researcher may be interested in the effectiveness of different ways of teaching vocabulary to 6-year-old children. Three teaching methods could be compared: silent reading of a story by children, story-telling by a teacher and storytelling by a teacher which is also enhanced by pictures. *Teaching method*, an independent variable, could be manipulated by the researcher, and pupils would be **randomly** assigned to one of three independent teaching method groups. Sometimes groups in an experiment are referred to as **treatments.** Randomization means that each pupil has an equal probability of being assigned to any treatment.

If different teachers were involved in each teaching method group, then any effect of teaching method may be confounded by *teacher effects* see Figure 1.1.

Treatment (Group)

Silent reading	Storytelling	Storytelling enhanced by pictures
Teacher 1 (35 pupils randomly assigned to treatment)	Teacher 2 (35 pupils randomly assigned to treatment)	Teacher 3 (35 pupils randomly assigned to treatment)

Figure 1.1: Effect of teacher confounded with treatment (group)

It is possible that one of the teachers was more enthusiastic than the others and that this was responsible for the results. One way to control for this confounding effect is to hold the confounding variable teacher constant, that is to use one teacher for all three methods. Any effect of teacher would be equally represented in all treatment groups, see Figure 1.2.

Treatment (Group)

Silent reading	Storytelling	Storytelling enhanced by pictures
Teacher 1 (35 pupils randomly assigned to treatment)	Teacher 1 (35 pupils randomly assigned to treatment)	Teacher 1 (35 pupils randomly assigned to treatment)

Figure 1.2: Effect of teacher controlled

The researcher may believe, based on previous studies, that storytelling enhanced by pictures is a more effective method of teaching vocabulary than either of the other two methods. It is posited that pictorially enhanced storytelling will have a greater effect on pupils' vocabulary acquisition, measured by a score representing correct understanding of a number of target words. This vocabulary score is known as the **dependent** or **response variable** because these response scores are dependent on the experimental manipulation of teaching method, the independent variable.

A **factor** is a discrete or categorical variable which is used to define experimental groups. In the teaching methods experiment because there are three **experimental** or **treatment** method groups, these different groups correspond to **levels** of the factor teaching method. Here there are three levels of the factor. In this example the three levels of the factor teaching method are deliberately selected or **fixed** by the researcher and this is known as a **fixed-factor** or **fixed-effect** design. Another way a factor could be fixed is by natural circumstances not under the direct control of the researcher. Such a factor could be sex. In both the fixed-effect example of teaching method and the fixed-effect sex, any experimental manipulations would be the same in any replications of the experiment because they are fixed and do not change randomly from one replication to another. Note, however, that we could only draw general conclusions from the methods experiment to sets of the three methods used and not from any other methods of teaching vocabulary. In some circumstances it may be appropriate to select the levels of a factor at random from a population of treatments or levels. This is known as a **random effects design**. For example, a random sample of three ways of teaching vocabulary could have been selected and methods selected may include peer teaching, storytelling and silent reading in the reading corner. Given the random process whereby the teaching methods were selected it would be unlikely that the same methods would be selected in a replication of the experiment. Note, however, that we could draw more general conclusions about the effectiveness of teaching methods if our experimental design were based on a random effects design. If data from a fixed-effect design were analyzed by *analysis of variance* procedures this would be referred to as a **fixed-model ANOVA**. The term **One-way ANOVA** may also be used to refer to analysis of a one-factor design even though it has in this case three treatment levels. Analysis of a random effects design would be referred to as a **random-model ANOVA**. This distinction between random and fixed effects designs is important because it influences the choice of denominator *error term* in the *F* test (see for example Chapter 8).

The term *subjects* usually refers to individuals taking part in an experiment. All subjects who are allocated to a particular level of treatment within a factor are referred to as being in a **cell** in the experimental design. In the fixed-effects teaching methods example all subjects allocated to the storytelling experimental **condition** would belong to one cell. This would be a **one-factor** experimental design. Experimental designs are more efficient (more powerful for the same number of subjects) if the designs are balanced which means having equal numbers of subjects in each cell of the design. A one-factor fixed ANOVA design could be extended if pupils were classified by sex, thus introducing a second factor. If every level of every factor is crossed with every level of every other factor, this is called a **completely crossed factorial design** and is an example of what is called a **two-factor design**. In the methods by sex experiment this would be a **3 × 2 factorial design** with six cells (see Figure 1.3).

Factor 1: Sex   Factor 2: Method

	Level 1 (Silent reading)	Level 2 (Storytelling)	Level 3 (Storytelling enhanced by pictures)
Level 1 (female)	Cell 1	Cell 2	Cell 3
Level 2 (male)	Cell 4	Cell 5	Cell 6

Figure 1.3: Two-way (unrelated) completely crossed factorial design (one-factor 'sex' with 2 levels and one-factor 'method' with 3 levels)

The term **two-way ANOVA** may be used to refer to analysis of the two factors. It is possible to have an experimental design with both fixed and random effects. This is known as a **mixed-model design.**

In the example of a two-factor experimental design, methods by sex, if the researcher examines only differences among the three teaching methods, ignoring the other factor, sex, this is looking at the **main effects** of teaching method. The researcher may then decide to look at the other main effect in this design, sex, ignoring any effects of teaching method. If the researcher were to look at the effect of a factor at one level of another factor, for example, to compare differences among three teaching methods (teaching methods factor) for females only (at one level of factor, sex), this is looking at the **simple effects** for females. If the effects of one factor are different at different levels of the other factor then an **interaction** between the two factors is said to exist. For example, if the differences in vocabulary score due to teaching method were much greater for males than females then an interaction exists between the factors teaching method and sex (interaction effects are explained in Chapter 8).

All the examples referred to thus far are examples of **between subject designs** because different subjects appear in each cell of the experimental design, which is the same as different subjects being allocated to each combination of experimental conditions. When the experimental design requires the same subjects to be included under more than one treatment combination, this is referred to as a **repeated measures design.**

Example 3

Involvement of friends and relations in the completion of a hearing handicap inventory (HHI) prior to rehabilitative audiological assessment and hearing aid fitting is believed to increase clients motivation to use a hearing aid. A research student wanted to know whether clients who used the HHI were on average well motivated to use their hearing aid. The researcher chose to investigate this question for her thesis study. She decided to do a survey to study the impact of the pre-assessment HHI on clients' motivation to use their hearing aids.

The first 15 clients who were scheduled to attend a hearing aid centre were sent a brief explanatory letter and the HHI with their appointment card. They were asked to bring along the completed inventory to their appointment. The next 25 clients scheduled to attend the clinic received a brief explanatory letter inviting them to participate in the study to form a comparison group. They did not receive the HHI.

At the clinic assessment, clients in both groups completed a motivation questionnaire relating to their use of hearing aids. A motivation score was computed for each client. The researcher expected there to be a statistically significant difference in mean motivation score in favour of the HHI group. After data had been collected the researcher sought advice on which statistical test to use.

The study in Example 3 is an experiment and not, as the researcher thought or intended a survey. It is an experiment because the clients, the experimental subjects, had something done to them. The intention was to observe a response and attribute cause and effect relations. In a survey the subjects in a sense are passive, that is they are not exposed to treatments. The intention is usually to estimate a population characteristic, in this example clients' average motivation to use their hearing aids.

The experimental design chosen did not address the original research question, and in any case has a number of design flaws which render any subsequent analysis at best tenuous. Some of the problems with this design include:

- no random allocation of subjects to experimental groups;
- no inclusion or exclusion criteria specified, that is control for potentially confounding influences, such as previous hearing aid users, stroke patients, age of clients;
- no control over the intervention, that is how the HHI was used by clients;
- not a balanced design, that is unequal numbers of subjects in the two groups;
- no mention of what would be a meaningful difference in average motivation scores, that is the magnitude of the expected effect.

This example illustrates the importance of considering statistical principles at the design stage. Here thought should have been given to questions such as:

- How many individuals do we need in total for this study?
- How will individuals be selected to participate?
- How many individuals should be allocated to each experimental group?
- How will individuals be allocated to experimental groups?

These questions involve the idea of chance. Provided a study is designed systematically we know the role that chance plays in the generation of data. This enables assumptions to be made, such as the equivalence of experimental groups before any treatment. Prior to data analysis and preferably prior to data collection, consideration should be given to the general issue of how data will be collected. In Example 3 an unbalanced design is used; a balanced design would have been better. Balanced designs are the most efficient, because they have most statistical power for a given number of subjects. Statistical power in experimental research is the chance of detecting a treatment difference should one exist. To maintain the same statistical power, the total number of subjects in an unbalanced design needs to be greater than in a balanced design.

Summary

It is important to stress that at the design stage before you collect any data – or if given data before you begin analysis – use your *judgment* to consider the *context* which generated the data. For example, certain questions might usefully be asked: Were the data collected to answer a specific question or for some other reason? How were subjects included in the study? What exactly was observed, counted or measured? How was measurement carried out and was it valid and reliable? What are the sources of error? Put simply, you should assess the quality and structure of the data. Statistical guidelines are presented in Figure 1.4 as a summary of the main points covered in this chapter. The last two points in these guidelines relate to more detailed statistical concepts which will be covered in later chapters. The guidelines should not be seen as definitive but as an *aide-mémoire* to important aspects of statistical design that should be considered when planning an empirical quantitative study.

1. Is the purpose of the study clear? e.g., *Is it exploratory, predictive, causal?*
2. Are the proposed method(s) commensurate with the main aims of the study? e.g., *Is probability sampling to be used so that generalizations can be made?*
3. Are criteria specified for recruitment of subjects? e.g., *What is the sampling frame, who is included and who is excluded?*
4. How will subjects be selected or allocated to groups? e.g., *Will there be random/ non-random sampling, randomization, comparison groups not randomly allocated (nonequivalent groups)?*
5. Are procedures for data generation clearly specified? e.g., *Will questionnaires be constructed and if so are they valid and reliable or will fidelity of treatments in experimental designs be checked?*
6. Have sample size and power been considered? e.g., *What is the expected magnitude of effect and is the design sensitive enough to detects this?*
7. Is the design efficient? e.g., *Is the design balanced, is sampling error reasonable and will precision be adequate, have potential sources of error been identified?*
8. What strategies will be used to deal with missing or incomplete data? e.g., *Are missing and not applicable responses distinguished in data coding?*
9. Are proposed statistical procedures appropriate? e.g., *Have levels of measurement, data distributions been checked and transformations been considered?*
10. If inferential tests or estimation of parameters are intended has an underlying statistical model been specified? e.g., *Have model assumptions such as homogeneity of variance for ANOVA been checked?*

Figure 1.4: Statistical guidelines for planning a quantitative study

Chapter 2

Measurement Issues

Educational researchers are often interested in students' knowledge, abilities, aptitudes or personality characteristics. Many of these variables are not directly observable and this creates particular measurement problems, which is an important consideration for researchers reviewing other researchers' studies or designing their own study. Fortunately, many measurement procedures, such as intelligence tests, tests of reasoning, or tests of verbal ability have been developed and evaluated and are accessible to researchers. Whereas these tests and scales can be applied in many research contexts, the proper use of these techniques requires an understanding of the fundamentals of measurement and familiarity with statistical ideas which underpin test design and interpretation of test data. Important concepts to be introduced or reinforced in this chapter include classification and measurement, validity, reliability, criterion and norm-referenced tests and standard error of measurement scales.

This chapter begins by considering measurement issues in education and the classification and measurement of statistical variables, and goes on to consider properties and assumptions of measurement scales, practical measurement decisions faced by researchers, statistical ideas underpinning the use of psychological tests and scales and finally concludes with advice on choosing a standardized test and interpreting test and scale scores.

2.1 Measurement in Educational Research

Many observations in education can be described in comparative assessments such as 'this group is better at reading than that group', 'this child's verbal reasoning ability is well above average for his or her age', or 'this child's work is not good enough'. Statements such as these require judgment. One application of statistics in education is in the use of numerical characteristics to replace such wordy descriptions and thereby to put data into a context in which its meaning can be better evaluated and communicated. Put simply, measurement means the rules that are used to assign numbers to statistical variables. That is the process whereby particular properties or attributes of a variable are given a numerical value. Educational researchers, whatever their interest, will invariably be concerned with measurement; either how to measure variables in their own study or how to interpret other researchers' measurements.

A **statistical variable** is one which is measured or enumerated (counted).

When interest focuses on physical measurements, such as the height or weight of an individual, the indications as to what should be done and what measurement scales should be used are obvious. In educational research, however, the measurement of statistical variables such as *attitude score*, *verbal reasoning scores* and *achievement scores* is not so obvious. When designing a study a researcher has to operationalize abstract ideas or concepts of interest. For example, a consideration of the concept of self-image includes defining the term and how it will be observed or measured so that numerical values for the constructed statistical variable self-image can be recorded. A student's self-image cannot be measured directly as can, for example, his or her height. Instead it is measured indirectly by the researchers' constructed variable. The extent to which constructed variables do actually measure the concept of interest, which in this instance is that of self-image, is referred to as the **construct validity** of the measure. This idea was referred to in Chapter 1.

It is important to recognize that measurement, in this example, relates to an attribute of the student which is abstract. Measurement in education is a means whereby abstract attributes are quantified and used to describe, for example, the amount of self image, ability, achievement, or understanding possessed by an individual. The development of educational and psychological measures with construct validity presents a challenge to educational researchers.

Whenever an attribute is quantified, that is when a number is used to quantify the amount or type of an attribute (variable of interest), then the statistical variable so formed is classified according to the following convention:

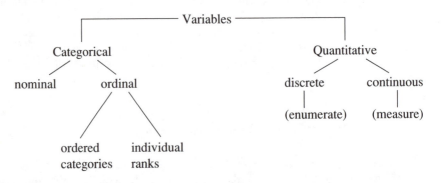

As a discerning parent what variables might you consider important in choosing a new secondary school for your daughter?

The following variables might be included in a check list when visiting the school:

- Distance from home (kilometres)
- Whether sibling attends the school (yes/no)
- State of school buildings (general appearance of buildings is excellent, average, poor)
- Position of school in Education Authority league tables of school examination results (e.g., 1, 33, 56)
- Denomination of school (e.g., Roman Catholic, Jewish, Church of England)

- Average turn-over time for staff (time staff remain in post in months)
- Number of pupils in sixth form (e.g., 120)

Each of these variables represents a property or characteristic of a school which is likely to vary from one school to another. Variables may represent characteristics of objects (such as schools), or attributes of individuals (height, sex and exam score) or other entities.

Numbers are used to represent properties of variables and impart information about them. When used in this way the values associated with each variable are called data. One such piece of information is a **datum**. Many observations in education involve categorizing and measuring data. An important first distinction to make when examining data is to decide whether observed quantities have been obtained by **enumeration** (which is categorical or frequency data) or by **measurement** (which gives quantitative data). This distinction has important implications for the choice of statistical methods used.

Categorical Variables

When observations are categorized, they are not merely placed indiscriminately into categories; qualitative judgments based on similarities and differences are made. Numbers which are used in a qualitative way have no more than a labelling role. A number used in a categorical labelling role carries no implied order, amount or quantity and is used simply as a description. For example, each school might be categorized by religious denomination: 1 representing Roman Catholic; 2 representing Jewish; 3 representing Church of England; etc. Numbers are used here to label observations about the categories of schools. The **category variable** in this case 'school denomination', is referred to as a **nominal** variable. This qualitative use of numbers is the most limited form of data classification. It simply takes advantage of the property of identity, and the assignment of numbers is arbitrary. The only rule to apply is that objects must be assigned to categories on a logical basis. For example, Jewish schools do not belong to the same denominational class of schools as Roman Catholic schools. The fact that Roman Catholic schools are assigned a value of 1 and Jewish schools a value of 2 is purely arbitrary and these numbers cannot be used in any meaningful mathematical way.

Whereas 'sibling attends the school' and 'state of buildings' are also categorical type variables, the latter variable is different from the other nominal variables because it implies ordering of qualitative difference. A school may be judged according to how much (more or less) repair work is required. 'State of buildings' is an **ordinal** variable. If schools were classified as belonging to one of the three ordered categories of state of buildings (excellent, average, poor) then this would be an example of an **ordered category** type of variable with the number 1 perhaps representing an 'excellent condition' category, 2 representing an 'average condition' category and 3 a 'poor condition' category. The assignment of numbers to categories in this instance reflects the order of the qualitative difference.

The statistical variable 'position of school in league tables of school examination results' is an ordinal variable of **individual rank** type, rather than of category rank type, because each school has an individual ranked position (or possibly a joint ranking). A school's individual ranked position might, for example, be based on the percentage of 15-year-old pupils achieving 5 or more GCSEs at grades A to C. Every school could be listed in order using the percentage of achievers as the criterion. For example, in November 1994, the School League Table of Examination results was published. Selecting at random Bolton Education Authority in the NW of England, and excluding maintained special schools and independent schools, the school in the Authority with the lowest rank position had a percentage pass rate of 21 per cent and the school which was ranked the highest had a percentage pass rate of 66 per cent.

In this example, numbers are used to label and to rank in order individual schools. Ranking of individual schools in this way necessitates the availability of examination information from each and every school. Similar to ordered categories, the numbers assigned to individually ranked schools serve as labels and show only differences in qualitative order.

What do you think the statistical variable 'position of school in league table', based on the percentage of 15-year-olds achieving 5 or more GCSE passes at grade C or better, is meant to measure? What do you think about the construct validity of this measure?

It is possible that examination passes are thought to be a measure of school performance. If this is the case one should consider precisely what is being measured or counted and then ask yourself what other factors might account for the number of examination passes in a school.

A non-exhaustive list is as follows:

the ability of pupils on entering the school;
the number of pupils entered for exams and the number of exams taken;
the comparability of exams in terms of difficulty;
the effectiveness of teaching;
the school examination policy, for example, a school that only enters pupils
who are thought to have a good chance of obtaining at least a grade C.

As numbers are assigned to individual schools on the basis of ranked position, these numbers should only be used in certain ways. For example, **non-parametric** or distribution free statistics should be used rather than **parametric** statistics. These terms will be explained in more detail in later chapters. For the time being, it is sufficient to consider non-parametric statistics as statistical procedures which do not depend upon certain distributional and measurement assumptions. Non-parametric statistics are often used when data are considered to be categorical, that is when statistical variables are at the nominal or ordinal level of measurement or when a data distribution is not equally dispersed around its mid-point.

Ranking scores is a simple procedure which sometimes causes confusion. Scores are ranked in terms of their size, which establishes their relative location.

Each score is assigned a rank of 1, 2, 3, 4, 5, etc, in order of its magnitude. It does not matter whether the smallest score is given the highest or lowest rank unless the value has some intuitive meaning. For example, a rank position of 1st in a school league table makes most sense if it is related to the school which has the best examination pass rate. Sometimes schools may achieve the same examination pass rate. When this occurs the schools share a ranked position. If two schools have the same pass rate they are both assigned a rank, but this rank is calculated as the average of the ranks that each of the schools would have occupied.

To use a simplified example, consider the following list of numbers of A-level passes achieved at one sitting for 10 schools:

School	A	B	C	D	E	F	G	H	I	J
No. of A-level passes	29	18	0	56	52	60	18	52	85	52

To make these data more meaningful they are first displayed in a table in order of magnitude with the highest rank placing given to the school with the greatest number of A-level passes.

Table 2.1: Ranking of A-level passes by school

School	Number of A-level passes	School rank
I	85	1
F	60	2
D	56	3
E	52	5
H	52	5
J	52	5
A	29	7
B	18	8.5
G	18	8.5
C	0	10

The three schools with 52 A-level passes in Table 2.1 would have been assigned ranks 4, 5 and 6 because they came after rank score 3 and are the next three possible ranked places. It would be unfair to give either school E, H or J a higher ranked position because they all obtained 52 A-level passes. These schools are therefore given the average of the three ranks, i.e., 5. When scores are equal they are referred to as tied scores. Similarly, the two schools with 18 A-level passes are given a rank of 8.5, the average of the two ranks 8 and 9.

Quantitative Variables

Up to now the use of numbers for categories and ranks only has been considered. Numbers, however, can also be used quantitatively to measure amount. Technically, measurement is when numbers are assigned to data according to a set of logical rules. Numbers when used for measurement make use of the logical properties of the number system and therefore can be manipulated mathematically.

The number system is entirely logical and numbers are unique, in the sense that no two numbers are exactly identical. Numbers also have the properties of order, additivity and can be subtracted, multiplied or divided. Whenever numbers are manipulated they result in new unique numbers. For example, the subtraction of one particular number from another particular number always yields a unique number. The usefulness of numbers in measuring phenomena is dependent upon properties that apply to the phenomena. It is not essential that a measurement scale has all the properties of numbers, but the more properties that apply to a measurement scale, the more useful that scale because of the more precise interpretation of meaning.

Similar to the way in which qualitative observations are subdivided, quantitative observations are often subdivided into two types, discrete and continuous measurements. **Discrete measurements** are those for which possible values are distinct and clearly separated from one another: for example, the school variable 'number of pupils in sixth form'. It is impossible to have 43.5 pupils. Discrete measurements are usually counts which must comprise of positive whole numbers called **integers**.

Continuous measurements are those which can, at least in theory, assume a continuous and uninterrupted range of values. Examples include the variables 'distance from home to school in kilometres' and 'the average point score of pupils aged 16, 17 or 18 entered for 2 or more GCE A-levels or AS equivalent'. This latter example is in fact one of a number of criteria used in the compilation of national school league tables.

2.2 Properties of Measurement Scales

In many texts **measurement scales** are referred to and four scales of measurement are generally distinguished: nominal; ordinal; interval; ratio. Nominal and ordinal scales of measurement equate to categorical classification. Interval and ratio are true scales of continuous measurement.

Nominal Scale

The **nominal** scale is used to label and hence classify observations into categories. The procedure adopted for forming categories should be: well defined, mutually exclusive and exhaustive. Numbers should not be used mathematically. Frequency counts may, however, be compiled for different categories. When frequency counts on two or more qualitative variable are tabulated the frequency table produced is called a **contingency table**. Data in the contingency table may be treated statistically, for example, by use of the Chi square test (see Chapter 6).

Ordinal Scale

The **ordinal** scale incorporates the properties of the nominal scale, labelling and classification, and in addition introduces the meaning of order – either through ordered categories or individual ranks. Numbers are used as labels in ordinal scales and do not indicate amount or quantity. It should not, therefore, be assumed that intervals between numbers are equal. For example, if a teacher places pupils in rank order in terms of their maths achievement scores, from the pupil with the highest score to the pupil with the lowest score, then it cannot be assumed that the difference in maths ability between pupils ranked 2nd and 3rd is the same as that between the pupils ranked 1st and 2nd. Moreover, it cannot be supposed that the pupil ranked 1st in the class has three times as much maths ability as the 3rd ranked pupil. Statistical tests that are based on ordinal type data include Spearman's Rho and Wilcoxon Mann-Whitney (see Chapter 7). These tests are frequently used with higher levels of measurement (interval and ratio) and the data are then ranked.

Interval Scale

An **interval** scale, in addition to labelling and ordering has the essential requirement of equality of units of measurement. That is, a given numerical distance on an equal interval scale of measurement, is associated with the same empirical distance on a real continuum. Interval scales are amenable to certain mathematical manipulations, such as addition (and subtraction). One limitation of the equal interval scale of measurement is that it has no absolute zero point. Numbers cannot therefore be multiplied or divided. Many educational tests and psychological measures such as IQ, provide data that achieve or approximate to this level of measurement.

Ratio Scale

The highest type of measurement is a **ratio** scale. This scale has all the properties of an interval scale but also has a meaningful absolute zero point where zero means no part at all of the quantity being measured, for example, a weight of 0 kg means no weight (mass) at all. Ratio scales of measurement are almost exclusively confined to use in physical sciences. Most statistical tests that can be used with ratio scales can also be used with equal interval scales so the distinction in applied statistics is not as important as is often emphasized.

Example 1

It was mentioned earlier in this chapter that a school's individual rank position in the national school league tables might, for example, be based on the percentage of 15-year-old pupils achieving 5 or more GCSEs at grades A to C. To show how conclusions derived from data are dependent upon measurement assumptions, an example based on the schools' league table of examination results is described. For the time being it can be assumed that league position is meant to reflect the schools' academic standing based on examination results. The school which is first in the league would be considered to be the most academic school and the school which is last would be considered to be the one demonstrating least academic excellence.

If four schools were selected at random from the national school league table where a ranking at the top of the league, that is 1st position, indicates the best exam performance

School	League Position (Based on GCSE exam performance)
St. James RC	(45th)
Gill Road	(55th)
Mount Secondary	(65th)
St. John Moore	(90th)

with which of the following statements would you agree?

A   Do you agree that St. James' RC School has twice as good an exam performance as St. John Moore's School? The St. John Moore School position is twice that (90th) of St. James' (45th) in a league in which 1st position indicates a best exam performance.

B   Do you agree that the difference in academic excellence between Mount Secondary School and Gill Road School is the same as the difference in academic excellence between St. James RC School and Gill Road School? There are only 10 league places separating Gill Road School from both the Mount Secondary School and St. James RC School.

C   Do you agree that St. John Moore School is lowest in academic excellence, that Mount Secondary School is second, that Gill Road School is next, and St. James RC School is the best in terms of academic excellence? It should be observed that St. John Moore School has the lowest individual rank position of all four schools because lower rank positions are indicated by larger numbers, in this instance 90th position (the top of the league is 1st rank position). Similarly, Mount Secondary is ranked second from bottom or 65th, Gill Road School is ranked third from bottom or 55th and St. James RC, which has the smallest rank number 45th, is the highest individually ranked school.

D   Do you agree that whereas all four schools differ in academic excellence, you cannot say anything about their relative levels of academic excellence? The ranked positions of the schools shows only that the schools are not all of the same academic standard.

These four statements correspond to four different assumptions about the relationship between the results of the measurement and the variable that is being measured. Statistical tests incorporate similar assumptions so it is important to understand these assumptions. What are they?

If you agree with statement A, you are assuming that a rank position score in the school league table is measured on a **ratio scale**.

If you agree with statement B, you are assuming that rank position in the school league table is measured on an **interval** scale. Unlike ratio measurements, a score of 0 does not imply absence of exam performance but you are assuming that it is as easy to move 10 rank positions at the top of the league as it is from lower down the league table, that a given interval or one rank position represents an equal amount of academic excellence.

If you agree with statement C, you are assuming that individual rank position is measured at an **ordinal level**. You can say nothing about the size or amount of the difference between two rank positions. Equal differences between rank positions do not correspond to equal differences between amounts of academic excellence. You can only infer that some schools are better or worse on the characteristic being observed – the school's academic excellence in this instance.

If you agree with statement D, you are assuming that academic excellence is measured at a **nominal level**. You are willing to place the four schools in different categories of academic excellence but are unwilling to state which school has a better or worse academic performance.

Many educators would not agree with the initial assumption that number of examination passes is indicative of a school's academic excellence. However, if you accept this contentious idea then agreement with statement C and the measurement assumption of individual ranked scores would seem most appropriate. Many educators, because of the problems of construct validity, would be happier with statement D because it makes the fewest measurement assumptions. It does, however, also tell us the least about the schools.

2.3 Practical Decisions about Measurement

Should an underlying continuum exist theoretically, it does not necessarily mean that it can be measured. Such measurement depends upon the availability of a suitably sensitive or refined measurement device. For example, common constructs such as attitudes and motives may be measured by scoring individual responses on a rating scale, from say 1 to 5. Here it would be assumed that individuals vary continuously along a continuum but on which one can not make direct refined measurements. Discrete measurements are therefore used by which individuals score either 1 or 2 or 3, etc. It is further assumed that individuals who score, 2 on a 5-point attitude scale are distinguishable only by the fact that subjects having a similar quantity of the attribute also score 2 and these subjects differ in amount of attitude from those who score 1, 3, 4 or 5.

Measurement assumptions for psychological and educational tests and scales are different from those appropriate to physical measures such as height and weight (measured on ratio scales). These different measurement assumptions lead to different conclusions. For example, zero marks on a test of science knowledge may not mean that the person tested has no science knowledge (probably the test is inappropriate for that individual). It would, however, be valid to conclude that a measurement of zero metres means no height. Whereas it would be valid to conclude that the difference between a child that is 1.0m tall and another that is 1.25m tall is the same as the difference between a child that is 0.75m tall and another that is 1.0m tall, it may not be valid to conclude that a person who scores 4 on a 5 point attitude scale has twice as much attitude compared to a person who scores only 2 on the same scale.

Different measurement assumptions, for example, the distinction between discrete and continuous measurements, are often over emphasized and certainly are not always clear. This ambiguity between discrete and continuous measures seldom matters given that the same statistical methods can often be used for both types of measurement, particularly if the discrete measurement scale has fine gradations and care is taken when interpreting the results.

Attaining at least interval levels of measurement for tests and scales is a measurement and interpretation problem and not a statistical one. Statistics deals with numbers whereas the researcher has to deal with the properties underlying any numerical measurements. For example, interval level measures are often tacitly assumed, even when it is obvious that it is not realistic to do so. Subsequent statistical analysis may then yield numbers which in themselves are numerically correct. It is the consumers of statistical data, who have to, as Hayes (1981) comments, 'judge the reinterpretability of the numerical results into a valid statement about properties of things' (p. 64).

The researcher may interpret results as real quantities of an attribute, or simply as test scores, leaving readers to judge their meaning. In either case, this amounts to a problem of interpretation and not of statistics. It is quite possible for statistical procedures to produce correct numbers but ones which have no meaning whatsoever because little thought has been given to what is being measured and what are appropriate levels of measurement. Some statistical measures do lend themselves to nominal and rank order levels of measurement (for example, see Chapters 5, 6 and 7). Researchers should use these procedures if they have serious doubts about their measurement assumptions. The simple message here is that one should not neglect measurement issues, but at the same time, one should not be over concerned about attaining interval levels of measurement for tests and scales. The tacit assumption of interval level of measurement is often reasonable provided interpretations are judicious.

2.4 Psychological Tests and Scales

Psychological testing is a form of measurement and many tests relating to learning are concerned with measures of mental processes, such as intelligence, motivation, aptitude, knowledge and understanding. These tests are referred to as cognitive and attainment tests and are frequently employed by teachers and educational psychologists. Another category of tests concerned with, for example, an individual's feelings, attitudes, personality, creativity, anxiety or identity status are generally referred to as affective or personality type tests.

In practice, none of these psychological constructs can be measured directly. Instead, psychological tests have been designed which produce either quantitative scores or some qualitative diagnostic outcome. In essence, one measures what people say about their feelings, mental states, traits, behaviours and what they know. These statements, which are usually assessed on a quantitative scale, provide raw scores which are often manipulated using statistical techniques. Psychological test procedures may be designed for either individual or group administration. If individual test procedures are used, different test materials are administered.

Criterion and Norm Referenced Tests

Psychological and, particularly, attainment tests can be categorized by the way in which meaning is given to the raw scores. If the questions in a test represent specific material, such as specified knowledge or skills, and the overall test is designed to show or describe what an individual knows or can do, then this is called a **criterion referenced** test. This category of tests has a long history in the United States where they are called *content referenced* or *domain referenced* tests. Criterion tests were developed to evaluate objective based curricular programmes of study. The content of such tests would be directly related to the objectives of a programme of study and to the criteria by which these objectives could be judged to have been met. Test scores would indicate what had or had not been achieved in a specified domain or following a specified programme of study. More recently this path has been followed by the national curriculum development and testing programme in the United Kingdom.

The other major category of tests based in the psychometric or psychological measurement tradition are **norm referenced** tests. The emphasis in this type of test is on relativity of an individual's overall score. An individual's score is interpreted relative to those of other individuals. A normative test score provides an indication of an individual's standing relative to other individuals, for example an individual's IQ (intelligence quotient) score. Such a score would be interpreted by comparing it with those of a representative sample of individuals. The researcher has to decide what is meant by representative. Usually this refers to individuals of similar age, gender and perhaps ethnicity. Representative sets of scores for defined groups of individuals, for example, age group 6–7 years, are usually presented in a test standardization manual and are referred to as tables of **norms**. Many norm tables present information about the standard reference group as the percentage of individuals in the reference group who score lower than the particular individual's test score to which reference is being made. Standard reference scores presented in this way are called percentile norms.

As with a standardized test score from a normative test, a single attainment mark from an educational test seldom has an absolute meaning. The significance of a datum point (single mark) can best be interpreted in the context of other marks or scores and in that sense is relative. These other marks may represent other pupils' scores on the same test or an average normative reference score for a particular age group. A single datum point or achievement score for a pupil acquires meaning only when it is interpreted together with other data such as achievement scores obtained by individuals on the same test or when compared with achievement norms. To help assess the relative importance of a particular datum point or score one can examine a data set graphically, paying particular attention to both the spread of scores and summary measures of central tendency such as a mean or median. Measures of spread or dispersion and central tendency are examples of **descriptive statistics** and are helpful when summarizing a distribution of scores. Any individual score can then be compared with the average for that score.

Choosing a Standardized Test

Most of the tests referred to so far are existing tests which have been carefully developed and evaluated – what are called 'off the shelf' tests. Helpful sources of information about these tests are the Buros Mental Measurement Yearbooks produced about every five years and test publishers' catalogues. Standardized, 'off the shelf' tests are published with norm tables and validity and reliability coefficients. Choice of a test should relate to the variables and underlying constructs one wishes to measure. One should consider both the characteristics of the test, the characteristics of the testees and how the test information will be used – to show change, for selection or prediction. For whatever purpose a test is selected, it should be valid and reliable. If a normative test is used it should have adequate norms, and if a criterion test is used the test content should be relevant to the purpose of testing, for example, in the case of an achievement test, it should be relevant to learning objectives. A good test manual should provide most of this psychometric information. A straightforward guide to selecting the best test is given by Kline (1990) and a clear description of how to measure performance and use tests, including advice on test construction and interpretation is given by Morris, Fitz-Gibbon and Lindheim, 1987.

Interpretation of Validity and Reliability

Arguably, the most important aspect of a test or scale is its validity (see Chapter 1). Here the earlier description of validity is elaborated upon to determine whether a test measures what it is supposed to measure and to include the idea of justification of inference. For example, it might not be known precisely what a test or scale is measuring, but there might be independent evidence that if the test is used for selection or prediction, the test scores are known to be related to a criterion of interest. It might be, for example, that a potential employer asks job applicants to complete a computer programming aptitude test knowing that high scores on the test are related to job success. Here, the validity of the inference (generalization) justifies the appropriateness of the test. It was noted in Chapter 1 that construct validity encompasses other forms of validity. These other forms of validity, concurrent, predictive and content validity are described briefly below.

    Content validity is a descriptive indication (not given as a statistic) of the extent to which the content of the test covers all aspects of the attribute or trait of interest.

Predictive validity is usually measured by a correlation coefficient such as the Pearson Correlation Coefficient 'r' which has possible values ranging from -1 through 0 to $+1$. Higher correlation coefficients indicate better validity. The predictive validity of a test is the extent to which the test score predicts some subsequent criterion variable of interest. For example, the predictive validity of A-level examinations is the extent to which A-level scores achieved by candidates predict the same candidates' subsequent degree performance. In this example, A-level score is the predictor variable and degree performance is the criterion variable. As it happens, on average, the predictive validity of A-levels is poor, with r being about 0.3 (Peers and Johnston, 1994). Some authors claim, for example, Kline (1990), that any correlation greater than 0.3 is an acceptable coefficient for predictive validity of a test. This seems rather low, and only about 10 per cent of variation in the criterion variable would be accounted for by a predictive test with such a low validity coefficient. It is suggested that the minimally acceptable coefficient should be nearer 0.4. An obvious question to consider is, whether a test that accounts for only a small proportion of variation in the criterion is of any use as a predictive test? Again this judgment needs to be made by the researcher.

Concurrent validity is similar to predictive validity but both the predictor and criterion tests are taken at the same time. If an end-of-course mathematics achievement test was constructed by a teacher and given to a group of students and at the same time a standardized numeric ability test was administered, the correlations between the two test scores would provide a measure of the concurrent validity of the mathematics achievement test. It is suggested that correlations of at least 0.5 are required for acceptable concurrent validity.

Construct validity embodies both content and concurrent or predictive validity. It represents all the available evidence on the trustworthiness of a test. Strictly, validity and trustworthiness refer to the inferences drawn from a test rather than to a property of the test itself. Whenever validity coefficients are given, sample sizes on which the validity coefficients were based should be checked. Sample sizes of at least 100 are required for satisfactory validity.

Another important aspect to consider whenever choosing a test is **test reliability**, or the consistency of a test (see Chapter 1). Whenever one obtains educational or psychological test scores such as aptitude, personality, intelligence or achievement measures, these are what are called **observed scores**. These observed scores can be thought of as consisting of two parts, a **true score** component reflecting the amount of attribute of interest and a nuisance or **error component** which reflects various sources of error, such as measurement error, transcription error, anything in fact which is not the true score component. It can be stated that:

Observed score = true score + error score

The reliability of an observed measurement depends upon the relative proportions of the true score and error score components. When the error portion is large in comparison to the true score, the reliability is low. To increase test reliability all sources of error should be reduced. As with validity, measurement reliability is given by a reliability coefficient which is often presented as a correlation coefficient, '*r*'. Unlike a Pearson correlation coefficient which can range from −1 to +1, the reliability coefficient ranges from zero, total absence of reliability, to +1, perfect reliability. An obvious question to ask, but not easy to answer, is how large is a good reliability coefficient if the maximum is $r = +1$. Instruments designed to measure attitudes and personality traits (affective type tests) tend to have lower coefficients than measures of achievement or cognitive ability (cognitive type tests). For affective type tests coefficients as low as $r = 0.7$ are acceptable whereas carefully constructed and standardized cognitive tests would be expected to have coefficients above $r = 0.9$.

There are three general types of test reliability measures, **internal consistency**, **stability** and **equivalence**, each appropriate for different circumstances. These reliability coefficients are summarized in Table 2.2.

Table 2.2: Reliability coefficients

Coefficient of reliability	What is measured	Comment
Internal consistency	Extent to which all test items measure the same construct.	Reliability of a scale can generally be increased by increasing the number of items in a scale and by decreasing their homogeneity, that is the interrelatedness of items.
Split half measured by the Pearson correlation '*r*'.	Two scores are calculated for each person on a test. The Pearson correlation between these scores on each half of the test gives a measure of internal consistency.	This procedure effectively reduces the number of items on a test by 50 per cent. The Spearman-Brown Prophecy Formulae can correct for this (see Cronbach, 1990).
Cronbach's Alpha	A measure based on the ratio of the variability of item scores to the overall score variability.	Requires that all test items have equal variability, that all items are equally interrelated and that a single construct is measured.
Kuder-Richardson K–R 20	A measure of the ratio of item variability to total score variability. Equivalent to Cronbach's Alpha but modified for dichotomous scoring.	Equivalent to Chronbach's Alpha, and requires the same assumptions. Used when items are scored dichotomously, i.e., 1 or 0. The K–R 21 is a simplified version of the K–R 20 formulae but makes the additional assumption that all items are of equal difficulty.
Stability	The correlation between measurements taken on two occasions.	Not useful for attributes that are unstable, e.g., measures such as anxiety.

Table 2.2:   Cont'd

Coefficient of reliability	What is measured	Comment
Test-retest measured by an appropriate correlation coefficient, e.g., Pearson '*r*' or rank correlation.	Correlation between scores on the same test administered on two separate occasions. If the time interval between testing is no longer than 2 weeks this is often called **coefficient of dependability** (see Cattell et al., 1970).	Always tends to over-estimate test reliability.
Equivalence **Alternate form** measured by an appropriate correlation.	The correlation between scores on parallel tests. Correlation between two parallel forms of the same test (different items in each test) given on two separate occasions. May be called **coefficient of equivalence**.	Parallel forms of a test eliminate possible memory effects and also have the advantage of covering an entire domain of interest because more items are used.
Inter-rater measured by suitable statistics: per cent agreement, Kendall's coefficients of concordance *W*, and Kappa *K*.	The equivalence of independent observer rates judgments of an attribute or behaviour.	The effect of agreements by chance can be corrected by use of the Scott (1955) coefficient.

The Standard Error of Measurement of a Test

The idea of sampling error or sampling variability was introduced in Chapter 1. We now consider extending this idea to look at the **standard error** of any set of measurements. Expressed simply, the variability of a set of measures is called its **standard error of measurement** (s.e.m.), and represents an index of how widely measures vary. The larger the variability, the larger the s.e.m., the less accurate is the measure. The idea of standard error is a very important statistical concept which will appear on many occasions throughout this book. This concept of standard error applies to sample statistics, as well as to scale measures and test scores. For example, a sample average has a standard error, that is the **standard error of the mean**. This idea was presented in Chapter 1 where it was called the sampling error (variability) of a sample average.

To review, suppose there was a large population of school children – over 1000 – and a random sample of 20 children was taken, it would be possible to calculate the average or mean reading score for this sample of 20 children. Call this figure *mean 1*. We could continue taking random samples of 20 children calculating the mean of each sample until there were 100 sample means. There would now be, $mean_{(1)} \ldots mean_{(100)}$, and the mean of these 100 sample means would be a reasonable estimate of the population mean reading achievement. Each of the sample means would of course vary to some extent around the true population mean and this variability of the sample means or sample averages is the standard error of the mean. This gives an indication of the size of the error one is likely to make if any one sample mean is used to estimate the population mean.

As with the standard error of the mean, a measurement scale or test also has a standard error and is simply called the standard error of the test or scale score. This is often reported in test manuals. It represents the accuracy of a test score: the larger the standard error of measurement for a scale, the less accurate is the scale in measuring the construct of interest. This measurement is provided so that researchers and other test users do not place undue significance on small differences in test and scale scores. Often one wishes to establish that there is a certain degree of confidence correctly called a 'confidence interval'. It is introduced in Chapter 4.

The standard error of measurement (s.e.m.) of a test and the test reliability (r_{tt}) are closely related:

(s.e.m. of test)^2 = (variability of observed scores) $\times$ (1 − test reliability)

In notational form, the relationship between s.e.m. and test reliability is,

s.e.m.$^2 = \sigma^2(1 - r_{tt})$

where: s.e.m. is the standard error of measurement of the test

σ^2, is a Greek letter, sigma squared, the variance of the total scores on the test. Variance (variability of scores) is explained in Chapter 3.

r_{tt} is the reliability of the test, that is a correlation coefficient.

The s.e.m. of a test is often more informative than the reliability of a test because test reliability is likely to change when the test is administered to different groups (groups are likely to have different variances) whereas s.e.m. is less likely to change from group to group (Cronbach, 1990).

A note of caution is introduced at this point. Most of what has been stated about reliability and standard errors so far applies to all raw test scores and to some standardized test scores. Whenever raw scores are changed or transformed, caution is required in the interpretation of any statistics that are the results of computations done with these transformed scores. Further discussion of this topic is delayed until Chapter 5.

Summary

Measurement is the process of representing quantitative variables with numbers. It is an essential component of educational and psychological research because constructed variables such as aptitude, motivation, anxiety and knowledge cannot generally be observed or measured directly. Instead tests and scales which are indirect measures of underlying attributes, predispositions and concepts are used. The number system used in quantifying test and scale scores in itself is entirely logical. It is the application and interpretation of numbers based on certain measurement assumptions which are often questionable, and at worst the system is not even considered by researchers.

Assessment of a test's validity and reliability and standard error of measurement enables a researcher to make judgments about the appropriateness and consistency of measures and hence their trustworthiness. Validity should be seen more as an issue of validity of inference or generalizability rather than as a property of a scale *per se*. It is the appropriateness of the interpretation of measurement results which is important. Researchers and other readers may over-interpret results, that is, generalize findings beyond the context of a particular study. Researchers when writing reports and papers should be aware of this and use coefficients of validity, reliability and standard errors when reporting data derived from tests and measurement scales.

One point often overlooked is that validity and reliability are not synonymous; it should be realized that valid measures are likely to be reliable but reliable measures may not always be valid. For example, a clock may be reliably five minutes fast, but it is not giving you the true time. Similarly a measurement scale may be consistent in measuring something it was not designed to measure.

Finally, for a more detailed discussion of educational measurement the reader is referred to Ebel and Frisbie's (1986) text on *Essentials of Educational Measurement*, and useful reviews of criterion and norm referenced testing are provided by Pilliner (1979) and Murphy and Torrance, (1988). An accessible and introductory guide to the use of psychological tests is The British Psychological Society's *Psychological Testing Guide* (1990) which contains an introduction to testing, practical advice on what to look for in tests and further information on how to proceed.

Chapter 3

Initial Data Analysis

This chapter introduces the important, but often overlooked, topic of initial data analysis (IDA). The aim of IDA is to process data so that its quality can be assessed before any further analysis is undertaken. There are three basic steps in IDA, **data processing**, **data scrutiny and 'cleaning'**, and **data description**. Data processing involves coding and entry of the data into a data set with a format suitable for subsequent exploratory analysis. Data scrutiny and cleaning means checking on the quality and structure of data and correcting any errors due to recording and processing. Data description involves summary and display of the main characteristics of data distributions.

It is crucial to know the integrity of your data and to be confident that any data recording and processing errors have been identified and remedied. Simple frequencies, that is score counts for variables and range statistics, minimum and maximum values, will reveal any odd data values. A listing of cases will enable those cases with odd values to be checked against raw data as recorded on questionnaires or coding sheets. After data processing and cleaning, underlying distributions of variables may be examined using data visualization techniques. The main features of the data can then be summarized using appropriate descriptive statistics and possible statistical models identified.

Concise and simple data presentation is essential for communication of research findings. Examples include: barcharts, stem and leaf and box and whisker plots, histograms and frequency tables. These represent a few of the many possible data visualization and presentation techniques available, most of which are illustrated in later sections of this chapter.

3.1 Data Processing

After having collected or been given some data preliminary considerations should include:

- Close examination of what exactly has been measured, that is, number of observations and number of variables. You should also consider whether numbers used for statistical variables represent nominal, ordinal, interval or ratio levels of measurement. It should be stressed that taking numbers at face value without consideration of how the data were obtained can lead to wasted time in data processing and at worst misleading results.

Also check whether the variable measured is appropriate for the construct of interest. For example, the construct 'social class' may have been measured by asking respondents what newspapers they read regularly. Certain newspapers are given scores which are equated with higher or lower social classes. You should ask yourself whether this measure of social class is likely to have any construct validity.

This initial scrutiny of the raw data provides a second opportunity, the first being at the design stage, to consider whether all the data collected are required for subsequent statistical analysis. It is remarkable how often researchers collect information which is not central to the purpose of an investigation. It is preferable to have a smaller amount of data of high quality than a large amount of 'dirty' data, that is data which is incomplete or illegible.

- Once the criteria of utility and appropriateness have been established it is advised to consider exactly how data were recorded. Ask yourself, were questions ticked or circled by respondents? Were numeric values entered by the researcher? Consistency is important. For example, either integers (whole numbers) should be used throughout (don't change from case-to-case) or values should be recorded to the same number of decimal places. Make sure you can distinguish between **missing values** – no value recorded, **out of range values** – a value recorded but known to be impossible, and for questionnaire data, **'don't know'** and **'not applicable'** responses.

  Beware of problems when data from different sources are combined into one data set. The same variable may have been measured in different ways, for example, by asking slightly different questions or recording to a different number of decimal places.

- Consideration of what roles variables have in the overall study design is important. For example, whether a nominal variable was used as a stratifying factor in a sample design or whether a continuous variable will be turned into a categorical variable and used for stratification. A stratification variable or **stratifying factor** is a variable that is used to separate the target population into a number of groups or strata where members of each strata have a common characteristic, such as stratification of postgraduate students by fee-paying status, stratum i)UK fee-paying status; and stratum ii)Overseas fee-paying status.

  Similarly, a variable may be used as a controlling factor in an experimental design, as a covariate, or as a blocking variable in a factorial design. The variable acting as covariate would need to be a continuous measure and the blocking variable a categorical variable. In some designs it is important to distinguish between response (outcome) variables and explanatory (independent) variables. In a regression design, 'A-level points score' may be an explanatory variable and 'degree performance' the response variable (sometimes called the criterion variable in regression analysis). More complex experimental designs, such as repeated measures and nested designs, may require the data to be entered in a particular format. You should consult appropriate manuals, such as SAS or SPSS Procedure Guides, for the statistical analysis procedure that you are using.

Coding data

After preliminary considerations you should decide how data will be coded so that it can be analyzed. The initial data analyses should enable obvious errors, omissions, or odd values which may be errors or valid outlying values to be identified. Thought should be given to the choice of the variable format. That is whether the value for a variable is numeric or character and the number of columns that each variable occupies.

It is helpful, for each data set, to construct a data coding sheet which contains the following summary information: name of researcher, data set name, date collected, and total number of cases/individuals. For each variable the following information is required:

- full variable description;
- short variable name (up to 7 characters for use in statistical programmes);
- column format for variable (number of columns needed including a column, if required, for the decimal point);
- possible variable range (minimum and maximum values);
- values for missing data (Full-stop (.) for missing numeric values and a blank for missing character variables – these are the SAS system default values);
- it may also be helpful to have 'labels' for nominal variables. For the variable religion, 1 = Jewish; 2 = Roman Catholic; 3 = Church of England; for the variable sex, 0 = Male and 1 = Female.

Example 3.1

Data collected by psychologists who were investigating the relationship between children's reasoning ability, age and social class (SES), is shown in Table 3.1.

Table 3.1: Data for children's age, reasoning ability and social class

Case	Age (yrs)	Sex	SES	Raven Score (reasoning)
Henry Forbes	7	0	1	1
Joyce Bishop	9	1	2	1
Jane Hopper	.	1	1	2
John Kylivee	10	0	1	9
Louise Green	7	1	1	6
Jenna Maccoby	9	1	1	3
Justin Langholm	8	0	1	1
Heather Lochlin	7	1	1	1
Sian Jones	10	1	.	1
Susan Ishihara	11	1	2	1

If the data on children's reasoning ability is to be analyzed using statistical programmes such as SAS or SPSS, it needs to be coded, that is numbers need to be
assigned to particular values of variables. A coding sheet to accompany the children's
reasoning ability data set is shown in Figure 3.1.

It is preferable if each case has a unique numeric case identifier – case number,
patient reference number, or hospital number. This number may be generated by the
researcher, or existing case numbers may be used provided they are unique. If you are
creating two or more data sets for the same individuals the case identifier should be
the same so they can be easily combined if required. A unique numeric case identifier
simplifies editing of the data should any cases be identified which have odd or out of
range values. SAS is particularly flexible when it comes to importing, exporting or
combining data sets.

Particular care should be taken with the coding of nominal variables and missing data. Categorical variables which are nominal serve to label values only and are
therefore arbitrary. In this example, the variable gender is coded 0 for male and 1 for
female and socioeconomic status coded 1 for low SES, and 2 for high SES. Numeric
values used in this way act simply as labels and should not be used in any subsequent
computations as they would give nonsense results. It is suggested that missing data
is coded as a period (full stop) (.) for a numeric variables and a blank space for character variables. These are the SAS default options. The advantage of using these default
options is that no additional definition of missing values is required (unless you choose
to specify types of missing or non-valid data). Similarly, if different categories of
missing data are to be coded, 'don't know', 'not applicable', and 'not valid' then these
should be assigned numeric values which are treated as indicators and should not be
used in a numeric way in analyses (you may of course wish to count them).

RESEARCHER: Joan Baron   D/O/C: 29/11/94
DSN: 'Child1.dat'*   NUMBER OF CASES = 10

Variable	Variable Name	Format	Column Begin	Column End	Var Range	Code Miss
Case id	caseid	3	1	3	1–10	.
Age in years	ageyrs	2	5	6	5–11	.
Sex	sex	1	8	8	0–1	.
SES	ses	1	10	10	1–2	.
Raven score	raven	1	12	12	1–7	.

*Note the data set has been given a name DSN = child1.dat, the .dat
extension is used throughout this text to denote a data file.

Figure 3.1: Coding sheet for children's reasoning ability data set

---

Once data has been coded (often questionnaires are designed pre-coded so that
data can be entered directly from the questionnaire without first having to enter it
onto a data coding sheet) it is then entered into a computer data file. There are two
options for this stage of data entry:

- Use of a dedicated (belonging to a particular statistical software programme)
  data entry programme to create a specially formatted data file, for example,
  use of SAS/INSIGHT programme editor or SPSS data editor.

- Use of a DOS Text editor (or similar editor) to produce an ASCII text file containing all the data.

The second option is illustrated here because it is of more general utility. The advantage with creating an ASCII text file for your data is that you produce an exportable data file that can be read by most statistical programmes and spreadsheets. Some statistical analysis packages have their own dedicated data entry programmes. These are useful if you intend using just that particular software package (although some do have facilities for producing ASCII text data files). A specially formatted data file produced by a dedicated data entry programme can only be used by that particular software package. An SPSS data file cannot be read directly by SAS or ML3E statistical programmes. In addition, use of dedicated data entry programmes requires you to have to learn another set of data entry instructions.

Saving Data in a Computer Data File

Data in a computer data file are usually arranged in a matrix consisting of rows and columns. For each subject or case, there is one row or line of data (it is possible to have more then one row of data per case). The columns of data represent variable(s). Usually there is more than one variable, in which case it may be helpful to separate different variables by a blank column. This format facilitates checking of the data file. When there are many variables it is better to omit the blank space because more variables can then be fitted onto one line. However, it is not a problem if there are more variables than there are spaces on a line. The recommended maximum is 72 columns of data per line. This suggested restriction is so that a whole row of data can be seen on a computer screen at once. Individual cases need not be limited to the 72 columns. If a case consisted of 130 columns of data the first 72 characters would occupy the first 72 columns on line one of a data file and the remainder of 58 characters would occupy the first 58 columns on the second line of the data file. Similarly, the second case would occupy lines three and four, in this example there would be two lines of data per case. Appropriate data format statements could be given to ensure that SAS or SPSS reads two lines of data per case.

Example 3.2

An ASCII data file for the children's reasoning ability data set, DSN = child1.dat, is shown in Figure 3.2. This data was entered with a DOS text editor. Any text editor that can produce an ASCII text file would however be suitable. (Beware, some text editors add control characters to the end of a file and this can cause problems when the text data file is read by your statistical analysis programme).

We can see that there are 10 rows in the data file child1.dat, one row per case, hence 10 cases are represented. For each case there are 5 variables, each variable is separated by a blank column. The first variable, here 'caseid' always occupies columns 1–3. A blank column separates this variable from the second variable, 'ageyrs' which always occupies columns 5–6. The variable 'sex' occupies column 8, the variable 'ses' occupies column 10, and the variable 'raven' occupies column 12. If we count 'caseid' as the first variable, then the first case has a value of 001 for the first variable, a value of 07 for the second variable, 0 for the third, 1 for the fourth and 1 for the fifth.

```
001 07 0 1 1
002 09 1 9 1
003  . 1 1 2
004 10 0 1 9
005 07 1 1 6
006 09 1 1 3
007 08 0 1 1
008 07 1 1 1
009 10 1 . 1
010 11 1 2 1
```

Figure 3.2:   Example of a data file, data set child1.dat

The illustrated data set in Figure 3.2 is an example where a **fixed format** data entry procedure is used, that is, a fixed number of columns specified for each and every variable. This gives a fixed number of columns in total per case. Variable formats are possible but tend to be problematic when data sets are combined. Generally it is advisable to use a fixed format.

Data Verification

After data has been coded, typed into a suitable editing or data entry package and saved as a data file the next step is data verification. This means the data input procedure is checked for transcription errors. If possible, the data should be re-entered and any differences between the two versions of the data set identified and checked against the original data. A convenient procedure in SAS is PROC COMPARE which compares the values of variables in two data sets and can provide information on differences found for each observation and the number of variables in both data sets that were found to have unequal values.

The SAS System

In the following section the basic structure of the SAS system (Statistical analysis system) is introduced and the use of the SAS procedure PROC COMPARE to verify a data set is illustrated for the PC version of SAS.

The SAS system, which is available on mainframe and personal computers, is a software system for the modification and statistical analysis of data. A great advantage of the SAS system is its dual function of offering both extensive 'off the shelf' statistical procedures and a high-level programming language capability. This later facility means that virtually any manipulation and analysis of data is possible thereby making the SAS system a very flexible and powerful data analysis system.

Statistical analysis of data using the SAS system usually takes place in three simple steps: a data step, a procedure step and an output step. First you create a SAS data set from your own raw data. This is the DATA step. You then analyse your data using any of the appropriate statistical procedures. This is the procedure or PROC step. Finally the results of your analysis are produced and directed to an appropriate location such as your monitor screen or a computer file. This is the output step. Schlotzhauer and Littell (1987) provide a straightforward guide to elementary statistical analysis using the SAS system. Spector (1993) presents a very readable problem-based introduction to programming using the SAS language.

SAS Data Step

Any data that is to be analyzed using SAS software, for example, the data set on children's reasoning ability (see Figure 3.2), has to be turned into a SAS data set so that the SAS system recognizes it. This simple procedure is called the DATA step. It has three parts:

- The DATA statement which assigns a name to the SAS data set.
- The INFILE statement which tells SAS software where the ASCII data file is located.
- The INPUT statement which describes the data format. It declares variable names, assigns variables as either numeric or character and tells SAS where the variables are to be found (usually by column locations).

An example DATA step for the childrens reasoning ability data set, child1.dat (see Figures 3.1 and 3.2) is shown:

```
data child1;
    infile 'a:child1.dat';
    input caseid 1-3 ageyrs 5-6 sex 8 ses 10 raven 12;
```

The SAS data set created is called *child1*. This SAS data set name is specified in the first line of SAS code. The data on children's reasoning ability is located in a file called 'child1.dat' on a disk in the directory a: (specified in the second line of SAS code). The first variable is called *caseid*. It is numeric and the data values are to be found in columns 1 to 3 inclusive. If any variable was a character variable then a dollar sign '$' would need to be placed after the variable name (leave a blank space between the variable name and the dollar sign). The second variable is called *ageyrs*, is numeric and the data values are to be found in columns 5 and 6. The other variables are formatted in a similar way.

SAS Procedure Step

The statistical procedure illustrated here is PROC COMPARE. This procedure matches variables and observations in what is called the base data set, here child1.dat, with the same variables and observations in a comparison data set, in this example child2.dat. The raw data was first entered using a DOS text editor into the data set child1.dat. The data was then re-entered and saved as child2.dat. Both ASCII data sets as entered are shown below:

```
Data:child1.dat      Data:child2.dat
001 07 0 1 1         001 07 0 1 1
002 09 1 9 1         002 09 1 9 1
003  . 1 1 2         003  . 1 1 2
004 10 0 1 9         004 11 0 1 9
005 07 1 1 6         005 07 1 1 6
006 09 1 1 3         006 09 1 1 3
007 08 0 1 1         007 08 0 1 3
008 07 1 1 1         008 07 1 1 1
009 10 1 . 1         009 10 1 . 1
010 11 1 2 1         010 11 1 2 1
```

To use a SAS procedure simply add the appropriate procedure to the SAS programme (colloquially termed a SAS job) after the DATA step, for example,

```
data child2;
     infile 'a:child2.dat';
     input caseid 1-3 ageyrs 5-6 sex 8 ses 10 raven 12;
proc compare data=child1 compare=child2;
  run;
```

A SAS programme that uses the procedure PROC COMPARE is presented in Figure 3.3. The PROC COMPARE statement is used here to check that the two data sets, child1.dat and child2.dat, are the same.

```
0001 options nodate;
0002 data child1;
0003    infile 'a:child1.dat';
0004    input caseid 1-3 ageyrs 5-6 sex 8 ses 10 raven 12;
0005
0006 data child2;
0007    infile 'a:child2.dat';
0008    input caseid 1-3 ageyrs 5-6 sex 8 ses 10 raven 12;
0009
0010 proc compare data=child1 compare=child2 transpose nolistequal nosummary;
0011 title 'PROC COMPARE OUTPUT';
0012 run;
```

Figure 3.3: Example SAS programme using PROC COMPARE

Each line of the example programme in Figure 3.3 is explained in the following section. Line numbers have been added to this programme to aid explanation, these should not be included in your programme (although there is a screen option to turn line numbers on – type 'nums on' on the command line, see options in the appropriate SAS Language guide).

Line 0001 contains OPTION statement an NODATE, which tells SAS not to print the date and time at the top of each page of output.

The first DATA statement, line 0002, tells SAS to create a SAS data set called 'child1'. You can call your SAS data set anything you like provided the name has no more than 8 characters. You should notice that this SAS statement ends in a semicolon (;). All SAS statements must do so. For examples, look at each statement in the programme.

In line 3 the INFILE statement is used to tell the SAS system where to find the external ASCII data file. Here the file is on the a: directory and is called 'child1.dat'. Line 4 of the programme is the format statement for the variables. There are 5 variables, 'caseid' in columns 1–3, 'ageyrs' in columns 5–6, 'sex' in column 8, 'ses' in column 10, and 'raven' in column 12. If this fixed format is used, all cases must have the these variables in the same column positions in the ASCII data file.

Lines 6–8 of the programme have the same function as lines 2–4 but this time the child2.dat data file is read into the SAS system. In this example there are two data steps because we have entered two data files (in any session, SAS can handle more than one data file but by default always refers to the last named data set unless an alternative data set name is specified).

Line 10 is the PROCEDURE step. PROC COMPARE checks the two SAS data sets, child1 and child2.

A TITLE is given to the programme output in line 11. Finally, a RUN statement is used in line 12. This tells the SAS system to execute the statements contained in the SAS procedure. To actually run the job and submit the data for analysis you can use the SUBMIT command on the command line or the F8 key in SAS versions 6.10 and 6.08 (or the F10 key in SAS version 6.04). Depending on the particular procedure you choose and on your SAS configuration, output is sent to the output window where it can be viewed and printed.

SAS Output

When a SAS programme is submitted a LOG file is created, and the results of the analysis are produced in an OUTPUT file. Note, the statistical output appears by default in an output screen (it can be routed direct to a printer or a computer file). The LOG and OUTPUT files resulting from the PROC COMPARE statement are shown in Figures 3.4 and 3.5.

```
0001 NOTE: Copyright(c) 1989 by SAS Institute Inc., Cary, NC USA.
0002 NOTE: SAS (r) Proprietary Software Release 6.08 TS404
0003 Licensed to UNIVERSITY OF MANCHESTER, Site 0020900316.
0004
0005 NOTE: AUTOEXEC processing beginning; file is
     C:\SASWIN\AUTOEXEC.SAS.
0006
0007 NOTE: Libref MYLIB was successfully assigned as follows:
0008 Engine:        V608
0009  Physical Name: A:\
0010
0011 NOTE: AUTOEXEC processing completed.
0012
0013 1     options nodate nonumber;
0014 2     data child1;
0015 3         infile 'a:child1.dat';
0016 4         input caseid 1-3 ageyrs 5-6 sex 8 ses 10 raven 12;
0017 5
0018
0019 NOTE: The infile 'a:child1.dat' is:
0020  FILENAME=a:\child1.dat,
0021  RECFM=V,LRECL=132
0022
0023 NOTE: 10 records were read from the infile 'a:child1.dat'.
0024  The minimum record length was 12.
0025  The maximum record length was 12.
0026 NOTE: The data set WORK.CHILD1 has 10 observations and 5 variables.
0027 NOTE: The DATA statement used 3.83 seconds.
0028
0029 6     data child2;
0030 7         infile 'a:child2.dat';
0031 8         input caseid 1-3 ageyrs 5-6 sex 8 ses 10 raven 12;
0032 9
0033
0034 NOTE: The infile 'a:child2.dat' is:
0035     FILENAME=a:\child2.dat,
0036     RECFM=V,LRECL=132
0037
0038 NOTE: 10 records were read from the infile 'a:child2.dat'.
0039  The minimum record length was 12.
0040  The maximum record length was 12.
0041 NOTE: The data set WORK.CHILD2 has 10 observations and 5 variables.
0042 NOTE: The DATA statement used 0.33 seconds.
0043
0044 10    proc compare data=child1 compare=child2 transpose nolistequal
0045 nosummary;
0046 11        title 'PROC COMPARE OUTPUT';
0047 12    run;
0048 NOTE: The PROCEDURE COMPARE used 0.66 seconds.
```

Figure 3.4: Log file for the PROC COMPARE programme

```
0001                      PROC COMPARE OUTPUT
0002
0003                      COMPARE Procedure
0004          Comparison of WORK.CHILD1 with WORK.CHILD2
0005                        (Method=EXACT)
0006
0007              Comparison Results for Observations
0008
0009    _OBS_1=4 _OBS_2=4:
0010    Variable     Base Value       Compare        Diff.       % Diff
0011      AGEYRS      10.000000     11.000000     1.000000    10.000000
0012
0013    _OBS_1=7 _OBS_2=7:
0014    Variable     Base Value       Compare        Diff.       % Diff
0015      RAVEN        1.000000      3.000000     2.000000   200.000000
0016
0017 NOTE: Values of the following 2 variables compare unequal:
     AGEYRS RAVEN
```

Figure 3.5: Output for the PROC COMPARE programme

Interpretation

It is recommended practice to always consult the Log file first to check whether there are any errors attributable to mistakes in the analysis programme (variables you think you may have created but have not, or errors due to mistyping of variables or commands). If there is a programme compilation error, SAS provides a diagnostic note of this in the log file. For example, the following is a portion of a log file with a diagnostic error.

```
0018 ERROR: Physical file does not exist, a:\child1.day.
0019 NOTE: The SAS System stopped processing this step because of errors.
0020 WARNING: The data set WORK.CHILD1 may be incomplete. When this step
0021 was stopped there were 0 observations and 5 variables.
```

Here SAS is saying that the data file 'child1.day' does not exist on a:. When entering the programme the name of the data file was mistyped as 'child1.day' instead of 'child1.dat'. This lead to a critical error and no output was produced. This however is not always the case. Sometimes an error is not critical and output is produced but is not likely to be correct or what you intended.

Once the log file has been checked the output should be consulted, see for example, Figure 3.5. Lines 1–5 simply describe what procedure was used and what data sets were compared. Line 9 identifies a mismatch for observation 4, in this example this coincides with case number 0004 in both data sets. In lines 10–11 the mismatch is identified for the variable AGEYRS and the values in the base data set (child1) and the compare dat set (child2) are given. The absolute and percentage differences are also given. A similar description is given for the variable RAVEN in lines 14–15. Finally, a summary of all the mismatches is given in line 17.

In this example the researcher would need to check in both ASCII data sets, observation 4, here case number 4, to establish which if any of the data sets has the correct value for this variable. The original raw data would need to be consulted to identify the source of the error, whether the wrong value was entered on the first data entry in CHILD1.DAT or at the second data entry stage when CHILD2.DAT was created. The same procedure would be followed for case 7, this time examining the variable RAVEN.

3.2   Data Cleaning

After data verification and editing of any data input errors, the next step is scrutiny of the data structure and checking of any out of range or spurious data. To do this a listing of the data and a simple frequency count for all variables are required.

Data Listing and Frequency Count

A data listing is simply a print out of the raw data held in the ASCII data file which has been read into a SAS data file in a DATA step. A data listing is produced by the SAS procedure PROC PRINT. Scrutiny of the listing enables you to be certain that the data you are about to analyse is what you think it is.

A frequency count of all variables should be checked against the coding sheet for any odd or out of range values. This can be done using PROC SUMMARY. Three simple checks will suffice:

1   Check the number of observations. Sometimes data is typed in twice or a datum point may be omitted.
2   Check whether the maximum and minimum values are what you might expect. For example, consulting the coding sheet in Figure 3.1, you would not expect a score of 8 on the RAVEN variable because the valid score range is 1–7 and missing data is coded (.). This procedure is called checking out of range values and will identify impossible values.
3   Check for cases which have missing values for variables. Missing values usually have their own special value indicator such as a period (.) for numeric values and a blank space for character values. These are the default missing data codes in SAS. Most statistical analysis packages allow

you to specify different missing value indicators for different variables. If the data set is complete, each variable should have one of the following; an allowable valid response, an impossible out-of-range response, or a missing response.

Example 3.3

SAS programmes for a data listing and a frequency count, using the children's reasoning ability data set, child1.dat, are shown in Figures 3.6 and 3.8. Output from these two programmes are illustrated in Figures 3.7 and 3.9. The data listing resulting from the PROC PRINT is self explanatory (see Figure 3.7). You should compare this output with the original ASCII data file shown in Figure 3.2. The only difference is the column headed OBS (Observation number). SAS adds this.

Output resulting from the PROC SUMMARY, illustrated in Figure 3.9, requires some explanation. The title is in line 0001, and in lines 0003 to 0010, for each variable, is a listing of the number of valid cases (N), the number of cases with missing data (Nmiss), and the minimum and maximum values. If these values are compared with what is expected (see data coding sheet, Figure 3.1) it is evident that each variable has 10 observations, and two variables (AGEYRS, SES) have missing data. There are also out-of-range values for the variables SES and RAVEN. The actual case(s) which have these out-of-range values would need to be located in the data listing, Figure 3.7.

From this listing it can be seen that case 2 has an out-of-range value of 9 for the variable SES and case 4 also has an out-of-range value of 9 for the variable RAVEN. The two cases with missing data are case 3 (variable AGEYRS) and case 9 (variable SES). These out-of-range values should be checked against the original data to see whether they are transcription (copying) or recording errors. In the original data (see Table 3.1), case number 2 had a valid response of 2 for the variable SES but this has been transcribed wrongly when input to the data file 'child1.dat'. In Figure 3.2 it appears as the value 9. Whereas for case number 4, the response value of 9 for Ravens's score is a recording error. After close scrutiny, data should be edited if appropriate. In the next section suggestions for dealing with missing data are given and later in this chapter use of a check programme is illustrated which is a more systematic way of checking for out-of-range and missing data values than using a frequency count.

```
0001 options nodate nonumber;
0002 data child1;
0003    infile 'a:child1.dat';
0004    input caseid 1-3 ageyrs 5-6 sex 8 ses 10 raven 12;
0005 proc print;
0006 title 'Data listing for data=child1';
0007 run;
```

Figure 3.6: Example SAS programme to produce a data listing, for the data child1

```
0001                    Data listing for data=child1
0002
0003       OBS       CASEID      AGEYRS       SEX        SES       RAVEN
0004
0005        1          1           7           0          1          1
0006        2          2           9           1          9          1
0007        3          3           .           1          1          2
0008        4          4          10           0          1          9
0009        5          5           7           1          1          6
0010        6          6           9           1          1          3
0011        7          7           8           0          1          1
0012        8          8           7           1          1          1
0013        9          9          10           1          .          1
0014       10         10          11           1          2          1
```

Figure 3.7: SAS output from PROC PRINT, for the data child1

```
0001 options nodate nonumber ;
0002 data child1;
0003     infile 'a:child1.dat';
0004     input caseid 1-3 ageyrs 5-6 sex 8 ses 10 raven 12;
0005 proc summary print n nmiss min max;
0006 var caseid—raven;
0007 title 'Number of valid cases, missing, max & min for data=child1';
0008 run;
```

Figure 3.8: Example SAS programme for a frequency count using PROC SUMMARY

```
0001   Number of valid cases, missing, max & min for data=child1
0002
0003   Variable      N      Nmiss       Minimum          Maximum
0004   - - - - - - - - - - - - - - - - - - - - - - - - - - - - - - -
0005   CASEID       10        0       1.0000000       10.0000000
0006   AGEYRS        9        1       7.0000000       11.0000000
0007   SEX          10        0       0                1.0000000
0008   SES           9        1       1.0000000        9.0000000
0009   RAVEN        10        0       1.0000000        9.0000000
0010   - - - - - - - - - - - - - - - - - - - - - - - - - - - - - - -
```

Figure 3.9: SAS output from PROC SUMMARY, data=child1

Dealing with Missing Data

Large data sets, especially if collected by survey questionnaire methods, inevitably have missing data values. However, this problem is not confined to survey research. In experimental designs participants may become tired, bored or simply uncooperative. If data is missing, the researcher must decide what to do. It is sensible to follow the suggestion given by Chatfield (1993), namely, identify first why a value is missing. The seriousness of missing data depends upon why it is missing and how much is missing. An initial distinction would be whether missing responses were random or systematic. Examples of systematic missing responses include censoring or truncation of data perhaps because a respondent refuses to answer personal questions or a subject may withdraw part way through an experiment.

How do you know whether missing data is random? Tabachnick and Fidell (1989) suggest you should check for this. Essentially this involves scrutiny of the data to identify any patterns in missing values. One approach other than simply looking for patterns in the raw data is to draw a missing (denoted by '.') valid (denoted by blank '+') table for all levels of the suspect variable against other variables of interest. Initially it may be more informative to examine the presence/absence of missing data than to be concerned with the amount.

If missing data does appear to be non-random then those cases with missing data should be retained for further investigation. If missing data seems to be random then two general options exist, either estimate missing values or delete cases or particular variables that have missing data (an alternative to deleting a case is to just drop the missing variable for a particular analysis).

How do you decide which of these two strategies to adopt?

The most radical procedure is to drop any cases with missing data. This is the default option in many statistical programmes. If missing data are scattered at random throughout cases and variables, dropping a large number of cases with any missing data may result in loss of a substantive amount of data. The consequence of losing cases is more serious in some research designs, for example, balanced experimental designs with small numbers of subjects, than in large survey designs where a margin for data loss is designed into the sampling strategy. In these circumstances it may be preferable to estimate missing values provided it makes sense to do so.

Deleting cases is advised when only a few cases have missing data. Dropping variables but retaining cases is an alternative but is generally only suitable when the variable is not critical to the analysis.

Another alternative to deleting cases or dropping variables is to substitute missing values with 'best estimates'. In general there are five options ranging in degrees of sophistication. These are substitute a missing value with:

1   a best guess;
2   the overall mean for that variable;
3   a relevant group mean;
4   a regression equation based on complete data to predict missing values;
5   a generalized approach based on the likelihood function.

Advice on using each of these options is:

1   Do not use at all.
2 and 3 Do not use with binary data. For example, if the variable sex was

coded 0 for female 1 for male, it would not make sense to substitute a proportion because this represents the overall mean on that variable. Using the overall mean for a variable reduces the variability (variance) of that variable especially if there is a large amount of missing data. This is because the substituted mean is closer to itself than to the missing value (unless the missing value was the same value as the overall mean). A reduction in variability of a variable has the effect of reducing the correlation that variable has with other variables (see Chapter 8). The net effect of many missing data substitutions would be to reduce any underlying correlation between variables. This could have a dramatic effect in some statistical procedures such as factor analysis.

4   Is only useful when other variables in the data set are likely to predict the variable(s) with missing values, the dependent variable. If there are no suitable independent (predictors) then use of option 2) or 3) is probably best.

5   Rather sophisticated and generally not necessary. It makes use of the iterative two-step, expectation, maximization (E–M) algorithm to derive maximum likelihood estimates for incomplete values (see Little and Rubin, 1987, for details and limitations).

Spurious values, that is values that are extreme but plausible i.e. within the allowable range are more problematic than gross errors and need to be checked very carefully. Extreme data values which are possible but not consistent with the remaining data are called **outliers**. An outlier may be an error or a valid and influential observation. For example, caseid 5 in the child1 data set on children's reasoning ability has an outlier observation for the variable Raven (see Figure 3.7). The value of this observation is 6 which is within range (1–7) but very different to the other data (twice as large as the next nearest valid value). You may think that Caseid 4 has an outlier observation for the same variable, here the Raven score is 9. However, this is an out-of-range value.

Both of these examples pose a dilemma, What should be done?

If the raw data had been checked and recording, transcription and typing errors had been eliminated, the Raven value of 9 could be coded as a missing observation. However, the Raven value of 6 is within range and, provided similar editing and transcription checks had been made, I would suggest repeating any analyses with and without this value in the data set. Provided interpretation of the findings were not radically different for both analyses then it is not crucial whether or not the value is counted as valid or is treated as missing. If, however, different conclusions are drawn depending upon whether or not this variable is counted as valid, then this is an example of an **influential observation**. You should interpret such data with care as the influential observations may represent a different population to the majority of observations.

It is of paramount importance to begin your data analysis with data whose structure you know and understand and in which you have confidence. The trials and tribulations of collecting, coding and entering data can only be appreciated by experience.

These simple steps of data processing and data cleaning are an essential pre-requisite to data description and subsequent analysis. Despite this, it is a neglected topic and taken for granted in most statistical texts. Any data errors attributable to processing errors or recorded out-of-range values would render subsequent analysis invalid. Gross data errors are likely to be identified at the early editing stage. It is possible, however, that some errors will remain undetected. It is important therefore to build into subsequent analyses diagnostic procedures to guard against erroneous data points unduly influencing your analysis.

3.3   Describing Distributions

After data processing, editing and cleaning, the final stages of IDA are data description and formulation of an underlying statistical model for the data. The main purpose of data description is to present essential and important features of the data usually in tables, graphs and charts. Space is limited in journal articles and final reports and besides many readers find it difficult to process large amounts of detailed data. Usually required are a small number of tables which convey a concise summary of the important aspects of the data and perhaps a graph or chart to convey information visually.

Displaying Data Distributions

Charts, data plots and tables are the most common ways of displaying data. Charts and data plots in particular are an excellent means of data visualization, and a way of identifying particular features and patterns of variation in data.

Example 3.4

Educational researchers were interested in the relationship between university students' A-level achievements and their degree performance. Part of a data set obtained from a study of university entrants is shown in Table 3.2. All students who entered a UK university in 1988 were included in the study, but the data shown is only for those students, in four separate disciplines, who graduated with a first class honours degree.

In Table 3.2 data is listed for 8 cases. There are 7 variables in the data set and a description is as follows:

Variable	Description
SUB	Subject studied at university
SEX	Gender of candidate
CASENO	Unique ID of candidate
DEGP	Degree class obtained (Ist class only, coded as I/5)
ASCORE1	Total A-level points score (A = 5, B = 4, C = 3 etc)
NUMV	Number of A-levels obtained
AGEY	Age in yrs of candidate at start of course

The full data set is presented in Table 1, Appendix A1.

You may recall that when beginning an analysis with data like that presented in Table 3.2, preliminary considerations should include clear identification of what variables have been observed or measured, the level of measurement of each variable and whether there is any variation in the values of each variable. Depending upon the level of measurement of the variables there are a number of options for displaying visually data distributions.

Table 3.2: Details of first class honours graduates

OBS	SUB	SEX	CASENO	DEGP	ASCORE1	NUMV	AGEY
1	Phys.Sci/5	F	302	I/5	7	3	18.7500
2	Phys.Sci/5	M	303	I/5	14	3	18.7500
3	Phys.Sci/5	M	320	I/5	15	3	18.2500
4	Phys.Sci/5	M	321	I/5	12	3	20.3333
5	Phys.Sci/5	M	329	I/5	11	3	19.0000
6	Phys.Sci/5	M	330	I/5	9	4	18.7500
7	Phys.Sci/5	M	331	I/5	14	4	19.0833
8	Phys.Sci/5	M	367	I/5	20	4	18.6667

Bar charts, stem and leaf plots, relative frequency tables and pie charts are most often used to depict **categorical** data and **quantitative discrete** (count) data. Grouped relative frequency tables, stem and leaf plots, histograms, box and whisker plots and scatter plots are most often used to display **quantitative continuous** data.

Although it is suggested in many introductory statistical texts that a pie chart can be used to display percentages and count data, this method of data display is seldom seen in journal articles. It is usually more difficult to compare angles and sectors of a pie chart than heights or lengths of bars in a bar chart. The use of pie charts is therefore not recommended.

The relationship between level of measurement and possible data display method for the A-level data set is shown in Table 3.3.

Table 3.3: Relationship between variable level of measurement and method of data display

	Category nominal (Binary)		Category ranked (Ordinal)		Quantitative continuous (interval/ratio)	
	SUB	SEX	DEGP#	ASCORE1	NUMV	AGEY
Data display:						
Bar chart	+	+		+	+	
Stem and leaf plot	+	+		+	+	+
Box and whisker plot				+*		+
Frequency table	+	+		+	+	+
Histogram						+

+ denotes an appropriate method of data display
+* denotes appropriate for continuous variables but can be used with discrete variables which have many distinct values
# in this example, because there is no variation in the value of DEGP, none of the methods of data display would be appropriate

Bar Charts

Bar charts can be constructed to summarize information about qualitative variables. A **frequency bar chart** shows the number of observations that fall into each category of the qualitative variable. **Relative frequency bar charts** show the proportion or percentage of the total number of observations that fall in each category of the qualitative variable and are useful when comparing data distributions which have different numbers of observations.

Example 3.5

The distribution of number of A-levels that 1st class honours graduates had obtained on entry to university is shown in Figure 3.10, as a vertical bar chart, and following this is a horizontal bar chart for the variable subject of study. These bar charts were produced by the following SAS code:

```
proc chart;
    vbar numv /discrete; /* Vertical bar chart */
    title 'Frequency of number of A levels for 1st class honours graduates';
run;

proc chart;
hbar sub /discrete; /* horizontal bar chart */
title 'Frequency of 1st class honours graduates by subject of study';
run;
```

The discrete option is used after the vbar/hbar statements to tell SAS to produce a bar chart with a bar for each value (category) of the specified variable. Whenever a categorical variable with numeric values (nominal/ordinal) or a quantitative discrete variable (count) is used the discrete option is useful.

Frequency of number of A levels for 1st class honours graduates

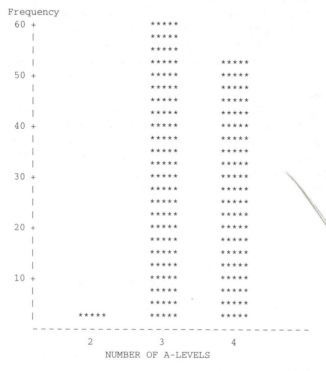

```
         Frequency
            60 +                        * * * * *
                |                       * * * * *
                |                       * * * * *
                |                       * * * * *        * * * * *
            50 +                        * * * * *        * * * * *
                |                       * * * * *        * * * * *
                |                       * * * * *        * * * * *
                |                       * * * * *        * * * * *
            40 +                        * * * * *        * * * * *
                |                       * * * * *        * * * * *
                |                       * * * * *        * * * * *
                |                       * * * * *        * * * * *
            30 +                        * * * * *        * * * * *
                |                       * * * * *        * * * * *
                |                       * * * * *        * * * * *
                |                       * * * * *        * * * * *
            20 +                        * * * * *        * * * * *
                |                       * * * * *        * * * * *
                |                       * * * * *        * * * * *
                |                       * * * * *        * * * * *
            10 +                        * * * * *        * * * * *
                |                       * * * * *        * * * * *
                |                       * * * * *        * * * * *
                |         * * * * *      * * * * *        * * * * *
                - - - - - - - - - - - - - - - - - - - - - - - - - - - - - -
                             2             3                4
                              NUMBER OF A-LEVELS
```

Frequency of 1st class honours graduates by subject of study

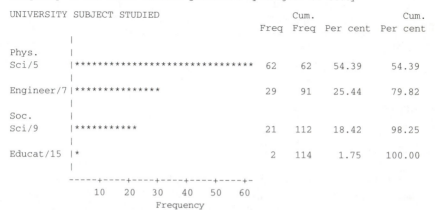

UNIVERSITY SUBJECT STUDIED		Freq	Cum. Freq	Per cent	Cum. Per cent
Phys. Sci/5	|******************************	62	62	54.39	54.39
Engineer/7	|***************	29	91	25.44	79.82
Soc. Sci/9	|***********	21	112	18.42	98.25
Educat/15	|*	2	114	1.75	100.00

```
        -----+----+----+----+----+----+-
            10   20   30   40   50   60
                      Frequency
```

Figure 3.10: Vertical and horizontal frequency bar charts

Interpretation

The **frequencies** of 114 first class honours graduates who obtained either 2, 3 or 4 A-levels are shown in the vertical bar chart and the same students by subject of study are presented in the horizontal bar chart. In both charts a bar is shown for each category of the qualitative variable, NUMV or SUB. The number of graduates in each category is proportional to the height or length of the bar. In the horizontal bar chart the category variable, SUB, is shown here on the vertical axis. The length of each horizontal bar corresponds to the number or frequency of graduates who obtained a first class degree in a particular discipline of study. Here, simple visual inspection shows that a larger number of graduates in physical sciences gained a first class degree compared with graduates in education.

Closer scrutiny of the horizontal bar chart shows that approximately 25 per cent (29) of graduates who obtained a first class degree graduated in engineering compared with only 18 per cent (21) in the social sciences. The highest percentage of first class graduates came from physical sciences (54 per cent, n = 62). Note it is good practice, whenever percentages are used, to provide the base figure on which the percentage is based here 100 per cent = 114. The width of the bars has no significance in a bar chart (unlike in a histogram – see later).

Stem and Leaf Plot

A stem and leaf plot is a useful way of looking at the shape or pattern of a distribution as all data values are shown for a variable.

Example 3.6

A stem and leaf plot for the variable ASCORE1 (A-level points score) from the student A-level data set is shown in Figure 3.11. These plots can be drawn easily by hand. In the example shown, the first two columns of figures form the *stem* and the adjacent row of figures form the *leaves*. Look for example at the highest stem value of 20. Moving along the leaf it can be seen that in this data set there are 17 values of 20 (17 zeros). Consider another example at the other extreme end of the distribution, one student had a total A-level score of only 7 points and two students had a score of 8 points. The plot in Figure 3.11 was produced by the SAS procedure UNIVARIATE using the option PLOT.

Appropriate SAS code would be:

```
proc univariate plot;
        var ASCORE1;
run;
```

By default in SAS you multiply the stem and leaf value by 1 unless the output indicates otherwise. This explains why the lowest value in the ASCORE1 distribution is 7. The stem value is 7 and the leaf value is 0 written as 7.0, this becomes $(7.0 \times 1) = 7$.

```
Stem   Leaf                                            #
  20   00000000000000000                  ·          17
  19   0000000000                                    10
  18   00000000                                       8
  17   000                                            3
  16   0000                                           4
  15   000000000000000000                            18
  14   00000000000                                   11
  13   0000000000000000                              16
  12   0000000                                        7
  11   000000000                                      9
  10   000000                                         6
   9   00                                             2
   8   00                                             2
   7   0                                              1
```

Figure 3.11:   Stem and leaf plot of the variable ASCORE1 (Total A-level points score)

It is possible when plotting a stem and leaf plot to split the stems in two thereby showing the distribution in more detail. Look, for example, at the distribution of the variable **AGEY** (age in years) in Figure 3.12.

```
Stem   Leaf                                                     #
  27   2                                                        1
  26
  26
  25
  25
  24
  24   2                                                        1
  23
  23
  22
  22
  21   8                                                        1
  21   1                                                        1
  20   667789                                                   6
  20   112333                                                   6
  19   555556666667889                                         15
  19   00000000011111112223344444                              25
  18   55556666666677777888888888888899999                     36
  18   11222222222223333444                                    20
  17   8                                                        1
  17
  16   8                                                        1
```

Figure 3.12:   Split stem and leaf plot for the variable AGEY (age in years)

Interpretation

The youngest student is 16.8 years and is represented by a stem of 16 and a leaf of 8. There are 114 values in the distribution (the sum of the number of values in each leaf). The middle value in the distribution or **median** is between the 57th and 58th value, counting up from the lowest value of 16.8. When, as in this case, there is an even number of data values, the middle value is taken as the average of the two centre values. This gives an approximate median for the distribution. When counting either up from the bottom or down from the top be careful to count from the correct end of the leaves. For example, in order, the three lowest values in the distribution are 16.8, 17.8 and 18.1.

There are more precise methods of estimating the median but this method is adequate and seldom differs very much from more precise procedures. In this example, the 57th value is 18.9 and the 58th value is also 18.9. The median is therefore (18.9 + 18.9)/2 = 18.9. A stem and leaf plot seldom appears in journal articles probably because it is seen more as a heuristic device to examine the shape of distributions and to arrive at a 'feel' for the data. A particular advantage with this plot procedure is that it allows a quick and easy calculation of the quartiles of a distribution, that is the lower quartile or 25th percentile, the median or 50th percentile and the upper quartile or 75th percentile. Quartiles and their use in describing the characteristics of a distribution are referred to in a later section (3.4).

Box and Whisker Plot

An effective way to compare distributions of continuous (interval or ratio) data is with a box and whisker plot. Strictly, the plot is appropriate for continuous data only but is often used with count data provided there are a reasonable number of distinct data values. The main discriminatory features of a box and whisker plot are the length of the box from top to bottom and the length that the whiskers extend from the ends of the box.

To understand the significance of a box and whisker plot you first have to be familiar with **percentiles**. A percentile is a measure of relative standing in a distribution of scores.

Often in psychology and education we are concerned with comparing individual scores either for different students or for the same student on different tests. If you want to make a comparison of a student's performance on two different tests you need a measure of relative standing on each of the tests. That is, a student's test score relative to the distribution of scores for all other students who completed the test (or whatever reference group is appropriate). The percentile rank provides a convenient measure of relative standing in a group.

To calculate a percentile, data values or scores are arranged in ascending order of magnitude using for example a stem and leaf plot. The required per cent is then counted up from the smallest score or data value. The 0th percentile is the smallest score in the distribution, the 25th percentile is a score which is larger than 25 per cent of the total distribution of scores, put simply 25 per cent of scores would lie at or below the 25th percentile. The 50th percentile or median is a score which is larger than 50 per cent of the scores in the distribution, half the scores are below the median and half are above. The 75th percentile is the score which is larger than 75 per cent of scores, or in other words, 75 per cent of the scores would fall at or below it. The 100th percentile is the largest score in the distribution.

The **lower quartile**, Q_1, is simply the 25th percentile in a distribution. Similarly, the **median** or Q_2 is the 50th percentile, and the **upper quartile**, Q_3 is the 75th percentile. The distance between Q_1 and Q_3 is called the interquartile range and contains 50 per cent of all values in the distribution.

Example 3.7

A box and whisker plot next to a stem and leaf plot for the variable ASCORE1, from the student A-level data set, is shown in Figure 3.13.

The significance of the quartiles when plotting a box and whisker chart now becomes apparent. The bottom and top of the box in a box and whisker plot correspond to the lower quartile and the upper quartile respectively. Thus the length of the box, $Q_3 - Q_1$, gives a visual image of the spread of the middle 50 per cent of scores in the distribution. Here 50 per cent of scores are in the range 13 to 18, and we can say that the interquartile range is $(18 - 13) = 5$ A-level points.

The heavy line in the middle of the box with an asterisk at each end marks the 50th percentile or MEDIAN, here Q_2 is 15. The + sign indicates the mean and in this example it is approximately 15, the same as the median because the + lies on the median line.

Whiskers usually extend from the quartiles up to a distance 1.5 times the interquartile range, here up to $(1.5 \times 5) = 7.5$ points below Q_1 or 7.5 points above Q_3, or to the most extreme points within this range, $(Q_1 - 7.5)$ or 5.5 to $(Q_3 + 7.5)$ or 25.5. The most extreme values in this example are 7 and 20. Data values more extreme than 1.5 times the interquartile range would be plotted with either a zero or an asterisk. If the extreme value is between 1.5 and 3 times the interquartile range a zero is used as the plotting symbol. If a value is greater then 3 times the interquartile range then an asterisk is used to plot the data value. These are the SAS default values. Other statistical computing packages may have different options and may calculate the quartiles in a slightly different way. Any differences are however likely to be small.

```
Stem  Leaf                           #          Boxplot
  20  00000000000000000             17            |
  19  0000000000                    10            |
  18  00000000                       8         +------+
  17  000                            3         |      |
  16  0000                           4         |      |
  15  000000000000000000            18         *--+--*
  14  00000000000                   11         |      |
  13  0000000000000000              16         +------+
  12  0000000                        7            |
  11  000000000                      9            |
  10  000000                         6            |
   9  00                             2            |
   8  00                             2            |
   7  0                              1            |
```

Figure 3.13: Box and whisker plot for the variable ASCORE1, total A-level score (stem and leaf plot adjacent)

Grouped Frequency Table

In large data sets with continuous variables a grouped frequency table may be used to obtain a general picture of data distributions. For example, look at the values of the variable AGEY (Age in years) in Figure 3.12. It is difficult to discern any pattern in the distribution of ages. Rearrangement of the data in a grouped frequency table may provide a clearer picture of the distribution of ages.

With so many data values a frequency distribution constructed by counting the number of cases observed at each age value would be no more informative than looking at an ordered list of individual ages. It is often more convenient in these circumstances to group the data values and to record the frequency within each group, called a **class interval**. The only difference between a frequency distribution which has grouped data and one that does not is that rather than having frequencies for each possible data value the data values are grouped into class intervals and frequencies are stated for each class interval.

In addition to a simple frequency count for each class interval, the relative number or percentage of observations that fall into each class interval are reported. These are called **relative frequencies** and are expressed as percentages. The percentage for a given class is obtained by dividing the class frequency by the total frequency of data values for all classes. The sum of the relative frequencies should be 100 per cent; this provides a quick check for any errors. The advantage of a relative frequency distribution is that it expresses the pattern of scores in a way that does not depend on the specific number of cases observed at each score value or interval of score values.

Example 3.8

To obtain a grouped relative frequency table for the variable AGEY in the A-level data set use the following SAS code:

```
proc format;
value clasfmt
16.5-18.5 = '17-18'
18.5-20.5 = '19-20'
20.5-22.5 = '21-22'
22.5-24.5 = '23-24'
24.5-26.5 = '25-26'
26.5-28.5 = '27-28';
run;
proc freq;
   tables agey;
format agey clasfmt.;
run;
```

The format procedure when used in this way automatically changes overlapping range values to be noninclusive, the first occurrence is included and the second occurrence is excluded. Your output should look similar to Table 3.4. A glance at this table reveals there are 114 observations (cumulative frequency total) which tallies with the expected number of cases, the minimum value would be located in the class interval 17–18 and the maximum value found in the interval 27–28. You can also see that the largest percentage of students, 68.4 per cent, is in the age range 19 to 20 years. The one observation in the interval 27–28 would appear to be an outlier.

Percentages ought not to be used with small numbers because a small change in the number of cases brings about an apparently large change in percentage points. Percentages or relative frequencies are particularly useful when looking at two or more distributions with different numbers of data points in each distribution. It is then as if the distributions each had 100 scores.

Tables are so often used in journal articles and reports to present data or summary statistics, a few comments are included here on clear presentation. First, provide a clear explanatory title including units of measurement if appropriate. Arrange the table so that columns are longer than the width of rows, it is easier to look down a column than to scan across a row. Round the numbers to an appropriate number of decimal places, seldom more than two, and arrange the data in an appropriate natural order or in order of size. Avoid footnotes if possible. Finally, you should summarize, in a brief paragraph, the main patterns and features of the data illustrated in the table.

Table 3.4: Grouped relative frequency table for the variable age in years

| | | AGE IN YEARS | | |
AGEY	Frequency	Percent	Cumulative Frequency	Cumulative Percent
17–18	26	22.8	26	22.8
19–20	78	68.4	104	91.2
21–22	8	7.0	112	98.2
23–24	1	0.9	113	99.1
27–28	1	0.9	114	100.0

In constructing Table 3.4 two related decisions have to be made. Namely, the number of class intervals and the width of each class interval. Usually the number of class intervals is between 5 and 20 depending upon the number of cases. Generally, the smaller the number of cases, then the fewer class intervals should be used. Too many class intervals will not summarize the data and too few may not describe the data accurately. You should choose natural intervals whenever possible. To estimate an approximate number of class intervals, divide the range of the distribution by a selected interval width so that you arrive at a number of intervals somewhere in the range 5 to 20.

The **inclusive range** of a distribution is the maximum data value minus the minimum data value +1. The range for the 114 ages recorded in Figure 3.12 is 11.4 (27.2 − 16.8) +1.

If an interval width of 5 was chosen this would give 11.4/5 = 2.28 or 3 class intervals rounded up to the nearest integer. This is too few. Suppose an interval width of three is selected then the range of 11.4 will be covered by 11.4/3 = 3.8 or 4 class intervals rounded up to the nearest integer. Looking at the age distribution in Figure 3.12 most of the ages are between 18 and 20, and 4 class intervals would only be acceptable if the data were more evenly distributed. This is not so here, 4 intervals would not show enough detail in the middle of the distribution where values are bunched. It should however be borne in mind that a class interval frequency table presents a summary of the data distribution and judgment should be used in choosing either sufficient class intervals to show any variation or to use an alternative data display method. In this example I suggest using a stem and leaf plot if a visual impression of the data distribution was required. For illustrative purposes a grouped frequency table will be constructed with 6 class intervals. This is based on an interval width of 2, 11.4/2 = 6 to the nearest integer.

The next step is to determine the first interval, and the upper and lower **stated limits** for the interval. All subsequent intervals can then be completed and frequencies and relative frequencies for each class interval evaluated.

The first interval must obviously contain the minimum data value in the range. It is desirable to ensure that the minimum data value in a distribution is evenly divisible by the width of the interval. Since in Figure 3.12 the minimum value of 16.8 is evenly divisible by 2 we can select the **lower stated limit** of the lowest class interval to be 17, and the **upper stated limit** of the first class interval would be 18.

It may seem odd that the lowest interval begins at the stated limit of 17 when there is one data value of 16.8, and that the size of the interval 17–18 is 2 and not 1. If however, the integer intervals are listed, there are 2 of them, e.g. 17 and 18. The stated limit of 17 has a *lower real limit* of 16.5 and an *upper real limit* of 18.5. The width of the class interval is determined by subtracting its lower real limit from its upper real limit. So, the class interval of 17–18 is (18.5 − 16.5) = 2. The stated limits and real limits are shown diagrammatically in Figure 3.14.

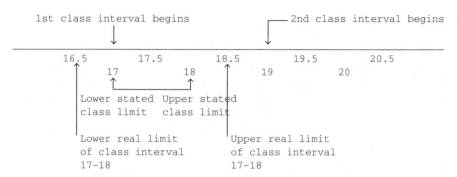

Figure 3.14: *Stated limits and real limits for the two lowest score intervals in Table 3.4*

The **format** procedure in SAS is a convenient way of specifying ranges of variables (see Example 3.8). The procedure automatically changes overlapping range values to be noninclusive. For example, if the variable AGEY had a value of 18.5 then this value could be part of the first class interval, 16.5 to 18.5, or part of the second class interval 18.5 to 20.5. SAS would automatically include the first occurrence of 18.5 (in the first class interval) and exclude the second occurrence of 18.5 (from the second class interval).

Sometimes it is useful to calculate the **mid-point** of a class interval as this may be used to plot frequency histograms. This is the exact centre of the interval, that is half way between an interval's real limits. The mid-point of an interval can be calculated by adding half of the size of the class interval to the lower real limit of the interval. The mid-point of the lowest interval, 17–18, in Table 3.4 is $(18.5 - 16.5)/2 + 16.5 = 17.5$.

Histogram

A histogram is similar in some respects to a bar chart, it has bars which represent the relative values of a variable. However, it is unlike a bar chart in three important ways. The horizontal scale is continuous, in a bar chart it is discrete. The width of a bar or block in a histogram, unlike in a bar chart, is important for interpretation. In a histogram the bars are usually of constant width representing equal intervals on the continuous scale. A bar chart usually has a bar width of unity but this has no interpretative meaning. It is actually the area in each histogram bar that is crucial for interpretation. The area is clearly related to the width of each bar. The height of a bar in a histogram may represent either a frequency or a percentage.

Example 3.9

Figure 3.15 shows a histogram for the variable age in years (AGEY) from the A-level data set.

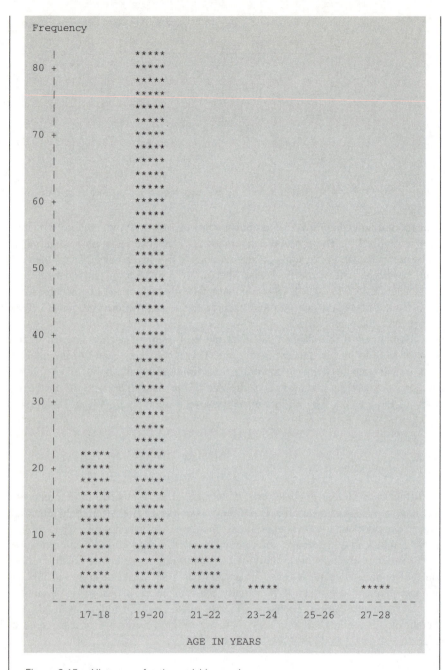

Figure 3.15: Histogram for the variable age in years

The SAS code that produced the histogram in Figure 3.15 is:

```
proc format;
    value clasfmt
      16.5-18.5 = '17-18'
      18.5-20.5 = '19-20'
      20.5-22.5 = '21-22'
      22.5-24.5 = '23-24'
      24.5-26.5 = '25-26'
      26.5-28.5 = '27-28';
run;

proc chart;
    vbar agey / midpoints=17.5 19.5 21.5 23.5 25.5 27.5;
format agey clasfmt.;
run;
```

The class intervals are set up using PROC FORMAT, and the mid-points option is used to specify the mid-points of each bar. For example, the mid-point for the interval 27–28 is $(28.5 - 26.5)/2 + 26.5 = 27.5$.

The horizontal axis shows the class intervals which are centred on the mid-point values of each class. The vertical axis shows the frequency or number of observations in each class interval. Clearly the majority of subjects were in the age range 19–20 years.

Univariate and Multivariate Analyses

When a data distribution for one response variable of interest is displayed this is called a **univariate** distribution; **univariate statistics** describe essential features of the distribution such as the mean and the standard deviation. These summary statistics are introduced in a later section.

Univariate statistical analysis does not imply analysis involving only one variable, there may be one or more independent variables, as well as the response variable of interest. For example, a researcher may want to investigate differences, in final examinations performance, among different groups of candidates. The response variable, performance in final examinations, (continuous dependent variable) may be explained by a candidate's age (classified as mature candidate, not mature) and gender. Analysis of variance (ANOVA), which is a classical example of a univariate statistical analysis, may well be an appropriate statistical procedure to use. This would still be a univariate analysis because the research question relates to whether there are any differences between groups with respect to a single response variable.

When the joint distribution of two continuous variables is shown, for example in a scatterplot, this is called a **bivariate distribution**. Calculation of statistics to assess the degree of relationship between two variables, neither of which is deemed to be a response (outcome) variable, would be an example of a bivariate statistical analysis. Univariate analysis is, in fact, a special case of a more general statistical model. The ideas underpinning univariate analysis can be extended to the analysis of two or more variables. Analysis of multiple response variables which may be related is called **multivariate analysis**. The response variables may be substantively different from each other, for example, overall performance in final examinations could be one response variable and a second, may be salary in first year of employment. Number of A-levels (categorical) could be an independent variable. A multivariate analysis of variance, **manova**, may be an appropriate way to analyse data structured in this way. Response variables do not have to be different in kind, they may be substantively similar but measured on a number of different occasions, such as exam performance at the end of years one, two and three. This is a special case of multivariate analysis called repeated measures analysis. In summary, whenever a simultaneous single analysis is performed with multiple dependent variables (instead of two or more univariate analyses on each dependent variable) then a **multivariate analysis** should be used.

The above examples of multivariate analysis are more concerned with testing inferences than data exploration. Other forms of multivariate analysis which are useful if a researcher is interested in the wider perspective of how observations on several variables may be related include principal component analysis, cluster analysis, and correspondence analysis. Multiple regression analysis, although usually presented in text books as a way of evaluating the effect that independent variables have on the prediction of a response variable, can be used in an exploratory way to identify which independent variables are important (i.e. have explanatory power).

3.4 Descriptive Statistics

An important part of IDA and data description is the use of summary statistics to characterize important features of a distribution. Three essential descriptive statistics which help describe a data distribution are measures of central tendency or position, measures of shape, and measures of dispersion (spread).

Measures of Central Tendency

Common statistics which identify the centre of a distribution include the **mode**, the **median**, and the **arithmetic mean**. Less common measures of centrality are the **weighted mean**, the **trimmed mean**, and the **geometric mean**.

The **mode** is the most frequently occurring value in a distribution. In the following distribution of 10 values,

2 15 9 2 18 14 0 6 11 3,

the mode is 2. In a grouped frequency distribution the class interval which has the largest frequency (largest number of values) is called the **modal interval**. Looking at Table 3.4 the modal class interval is 19–20.

The **median**, you may recall, is the 50th percentile or the middle value in a set of observations ordered in magnitude. In an ordered series which has an odd number of values the median is the middle value. In an ordered series which has an even number of values,

0 2 2 3 6 9 11 14 15 18,

the median is the average of the middle two values. In this example the median is between the 5th and the 6th values ie $(6 + 9)/2 = 7.5$.

The **arithmetic mean** is equal to the sum of values in a distribution divided by the total number of values. For the following 10 numbers,

2 15 9 2 18 14 0 6 11 3,

the arithmetic mean is:

$(2 + 15 + 9 + 2 + 18 + 14 + 0 + 6 + 11 + 3)/10 = 80/10 = 8$.

The mean is sometimes called the first moment. This terminology stems from mechanics where the first moment corresponds to the centre of gravity of a distribution of mass. The mean corresponds to the centre of a distribution.

The three measures of central tendency, mode median and mean will suffice for the majority of situations you are likely to encounter. There are however two situations when an arithmetic mean may not be appropriate. When all the values in a distribution do not have equal importance or when we want to compute an overall mean from two samples combined. Values may not have equal importance if, for example, some values have been measured more precisely. In these circumstances we should give relatively more weight to the more precise values.

When combining values from two or more samples the arithmetic mean would be misleading unless the samples to be combined were of equal size. Each sample that is combined should be weighted by the number of observations in the sample. This is because a sample mean's reliability is in proportion to the number of values in the sample. Smaller samples are less reliable than larger samples and should therefore be given less weight in calculation of an overall mean. Consider one sample with 10 observations,

2 15 9 2 18 14 0 6 11 3,

and a second sample with 5 observations,

17 6 21 16 15.

The **arithmetic mean** for sample one is $80/10 = 8$, and for sample two is $75/5 = 15$. You may think that the overall mean is simply the average of both sample means i.e., $(15 + 8)/2 = 11.5$. However, this is incorrect because equal weight is given to both samples when sample one has twice as many observations as sample two.

The **weighted mean** for the two samples is, the sum of, each sample mean multiplied by its appropriate weight, all divided by the sum of the weights.

$$\text{Weighted mean is } \frac{(8 \times 10) + (15 \times 5)}{(10 + 5)} = 155/15 = 10.3$$

This value of 10.3 is the same value you would obtain if you treated the 15 observations as one sample. Combining the two sample means without weighting them resulted in a higher value of 11.5 compared with the weighted mean of 10.3. The overall mean was pulled upwards by the relatively larger mean of the smaller sample.

The **trimmed mean** may be used with large samples and is similar to the arithmetic mean but has some of the smallest and largest values removed before calculation. Usually the bottom and top 5 per cent of values are removed and the mean is calculated on the remaining 90 per cent of values. The effect is to minimize the influence of extreme outlier observations in calculation of the mean.

The **geometric mean** is useful for calculating averages of rates. Suppose a new house dwindles in value to 95 per cent of its original value during the first year. In the following year the value reduces to 90 per cent of the value it had at the beginning of the second year and in the third year the value reduces still further to 80 per cent of the value it had at the beginning of the third year. The average rate of decrease in value over the three-year period that would result in the same value of the house at the end of the three years is given by the geometric mean of the three rates.

This can be evaluated as $rate_1 \times rate_2 \times rate_3 = 95 \times 90 \times 80 = 684000 = rate^3$, so rate = cube root of $684000 = 88.1$ per cent.

A general notation is the nth root of the product (multiplication) of the values. The n refers to the number of values, for example, two values would be the square root of the product of the two values. A simplified way of calculating the geometric mean is to take the antilogarithm of the mean of the natural logarithm of the rates.

Logarithms to the base e, denoted as $\log_e x_i$ (where x_i is any positive real number) is called a natural logarithm. For example, $\log_e 2$ is $= 0.693$. The geometric mean of the three rates, 95 per cent, 90 per cent and 80 per cent is $= (\log_e 95 + \log_e 90 + \log_e 80)/3 = 13.436/3 = 4.479$. The antilogarithm of this value is $= 88.1$.

Measures of Shape

The shape of a distribution is often compared to what is called a **normal distribution**. This is actually a mathematically defined theoretical distribution for a population which when drawn is characterized by a number of properties:

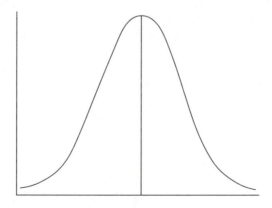

Figure 3.16: Theoretical normal distribution curve

- The curve is unimodal, it is smooth, has one highest point which is in the centre of the distribution.
- The mode, median and mean all have the same value and indicate the centre of the distribution.
- The curve is characteristically bell-shaped. The highest point of the curve is in the centre and the tails extend out both sides of the centre to the ends of the distribution in a smooth fashion.
- The curve is symmetric. If the curve were folded in half at the centre, the left side would be a mirror image of the right side.

The normal distribution is useful for not only providing a standard against which other empirically derived distributions can be compared, but it also plays a very important role in inferential statistics. The reason is because many naturally occurring phenomena, such as height or weight of subjects, approximate to a normal distribution in the population. Many statistical tests assume values in a data set represent a sample from a population which has an underlying normal distribution.

When looking at a data distribution it is sometimes difficult to judge how non-normal the data is. Two measures of shape sometimes help, these are **skewness** and **kurtosis**.

Skewness is an index of the extent to which a distribution is asymmetrical or non-normal. (Recall a normal distribution is perfectly symmetrical.) A skewed distribution departs from symmetry and the tail of the distribution could extend more to one side than to the other. This would indicate that the deviations from the mean are larger in one direction than the other. If the **tail** of a distribution extends to the **right** it has a **positive skew** (think of positive as being on the right side). The mean is pulled to the right of the median. If the **tail** of a distribution extends to the **left** it has a **negative skew** (think of negative to the left side). The mean is pulled to the left of the median.

Positive tail to right (right skew)
positive skewness coefficient

Mode < Median < Mean

Negative tail to left (left skew)
negative skewness coefficient

Mode > Median > Mean

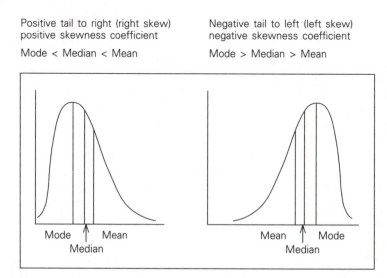

Figure 3.17: Positively and negatively skewed distributions

A simple procedure for calculating a sample coefficient of skewness is given by, $3 \times ((\text{mean} - \text{median})/\text{standard deviation})$. SAS uses a slightly more complex formula, when samples are large estimates produced by the two procedures are usually very similar.

No matter which coefficient is used the interpretation is the same. If a distribution is symmetrical, skewness is close to zero. If a distribution is right skewed it has a positive skewness coefficient and if left skewed a negative coefficient. Caution is required when interpreting skewness coefficients especially when samples are small, <30 observations. Knowledge of the skewness coefficient does not provide any information about the shape of a curve, at best it gives an indication, provided the curve is unimodal, of how asymmetrical the distribution curve is.

A fourth moment about the mean is sometimes used as an index of shape, this is **kurtosis**. This shape coefficient reflects the 'heaviness' of tails of a distribution and in a normal distribution has a value close to zero. Heavier tails are indicated by positive values of the coefficient and lighter tails have negative coefficients. Kurtosis, similar to skewness, is an unreliable estimator of the corresponding population parameter when samples are small. In small samples, you should pay attention only to large values of these coefficients.

Measures of Dispersion

To describe a distribution we need a measure of spread or dispersion of values as well as measures of central location and shape. Common statistics which indicate the dispersion of values are the **range**, **inter-quartile range**, and the **standard deviation**. Less common is the **coefficient of variation**.

The **range** (non inclusive) is the difference between the largest and smallest values in a distribution. It is simple to calculate and easy to interpret.

A measure of dispersion which conveys more information about the spread of scores is the **inter-quartile range**. This is the difference between the third and first quartiles $(Q_3 - Q_1)$. See the box and whisker plot presented in Figure 3.13 and following text for interpretation of the interquartile range.

The stem and leaf plot provides a convenient way of finding not only the median but also the upper and lower quartiles of a distribution. Recall, to find the median you count up from the lowest value (or down from the highest) until you reach the middle value in the distribution. This is the median. If there are two values in the middle because there are an even number of observations, the averages of the two centre values is taken. If we say the number of values from the most extreme value is called the depth, and n is the total number of observations, in the sample the following general rule can be used to calculate the median.

When n is odd the median is the unique values at, $1/2(n + 1)$.

When n is even the median is average of the two values at depth $1/2n$.

To illustrate this look again at Figure 3.12. Here n is 114. Since this is an even number we locate the two values at depth $1/2 \times (114) = 57$. We count 57 values from the lowest value. The 57th value is 18.9. The 58th value is 18.9, which is the same as counting 57 values from the highest value. The two centre values are therefore 18.9 and 18.9. The median is the average of these two values which is 18.9. This agrees with our earlier calculation.

To find the quartiles we use a similar approach which is described in detail in the Open University Statistics in Society course text Unit A1, (Open University Press, 1986). The method is summarized here. The lower quartile is found by counting up from the lowest value a defined number of places. This is the depth of the lower quartile. The depth of the upper quartile is found in the same manner but counting down from the highest value. What we have to find is the correct depth. The depth will be approximately at 1/4 of n, the number of values in the distribution. The precise value will depend upon whether n is exactly divisible by 4. A general rule for calculating the quartiles is:

When $n/4$ is not an integer, the quartiles are the values whose depth is the next whole number larger than $n/4$.

When $n/4$ is an integer, the quartiles are the average of the two values at depth $n/4$ and depth $(n/4 + 1)$. The upper quartile is found by counting down from the highest value and the lower quartile is found by counting up from the lowest value.

How do we interpret the interquartile range, how large is large?

The inter-quartile range only really makes any sense when it is compared to the median and when the number of values in the distribution is known.

To calculate the lower quartile for the data shown in Figure 3.12 we first need to divide n, that is 114 by 4. This gives the value 28.5 which is not an integer. We next identify the next whole number larger than 28.5, that is 29. The quartiles are at the 29th value in from the extremes of the distribution. The lower quartile is therefore 18.6 and the upper quartile is 19.8. This simple method gives similar results to more exact methods, the more precise values calculated in SAS are, Q_1 =18.6, and $Q_3 = 19.5$.

The most widely used measure of dispersion is the **standard deviation**. This statistic measures the dispersion of scores around the mean. If all the values in a distribution were the same, each value would equal the mean, there would be no dispersion and none of the values would deviate from the mean and the standard deviation would be zero. The more values that deviate from the mean, that is the greater the variation around the mean, the greater is the value of the standard deviation.

A sample standard deviation is calculated by finding the deviation of each score from the mean, that is by subtracting the mean from each score. If each deviation from the mean is then squared, add up all the squared deviations and then divide by the number of values in the distribution less 1, we have calculated a statistic called the **variance**. Unfortunately, the variance is in squared units (re-member we squared the deviations of each value from the mean) and is therefore not in the same units of measurement as the data. To return to the original units of measurement we need to take the square root of the variance, this new statistic is the **standard deviation**.

Instead of explaining in a verbose way how to calculate the standard deviation we can express these arithmetic manipulations succinctly using a kind of shorthand or algebraic notation. If you are unfamiliar or cannot remember how to use notation, a brief review is presented in Appendix A2. If you have difficulty with the following calculation you should read through this appendix. The following formulas differ from the explanatory ideas just described because these formulas are easy to use with a pocket calculator. Whichever computational method is used the results will be the same.

Sample Variance and Standard Deviation:

The variance, S^2 of n observations $x_1, x_2, \ldots, x_n$ is

$$\left(\frac{\sum x_i^2 - \dfrac{(\sum x_i)^2}{n}}{n-1} \right) \qquad \text{**Sample Variance-3.1**}$$

The standard deviation, S, is the square root of the variance.

$$\sqrt{\left(\frac{\sum x_i^2 - \dfrac{(\sum x_i)^2}{n}}{n-1} \right)} \qquad \text{**Sample Standard Deviation-3.2**}$$

Degrees of Freedom

You may wonder why the denominator (bottom number) is $n-1$ in the formulae for both the variance and the standard deviation. The standard deviation represents the average deviation of each value form the mean. When we compute an average we divide by n, the sum of all the values. For the standard deviation we divide by $n-1$ because the sum of the deviations, (mean $- x_i$) always equals 0. If you think about this, the last deviation can be found when we know the first $n-1$ deviations because all deviations sum to 0. Only $n-1$ of the squared deviations can vary freely (the last one is fixed) and we therefore take an average by dividing the total by $n-1$. We call the number $n-1$ the **degrees of freedom** (df) of a statistic.

Non-statisticians generally find degrees of freedom a difficult concept to understand and given its importance in design and statistical analysis it is worth explaining this idea in more detail. The meaning is best illustrated by considering further examples. First, it is important to realize that every statistic has a certain number of degrees of freedom associated with it. For example the mean, $\overline{X}$ has n degrees of freedom. If we look at the formula for the mean:

$$\overline{X} = \frac{\Sigma x_i}{n}$$ *Sample Mean 3.3*

we can consider which components in this formula can vary at all, and which cannot.

The sample size, n, does not vary. It is a fixed value for the sample. The scores x_i may well vary, and take on different individual values. Thus the individual scores, x_i *are free to vary*.

Each x_i score could assume any possible value, and knowing the values of all but one score does not tell us the value of the last score. If there are five scores and we know four of them, (2,5,3,7,?), there is no way for us to determine the value of '?'. We must know the individual values of the x_i, and the total number, n, of all x_i scores to calculate the mean. In this sense the *degrees of freedom for the statistic x is simply n*. It is a fixed value, the number of scores.

Now consider a more complicated example, degrees of freedom for the sample variance. An explanatory formula for the sample variance S^2 is (we would usually use formula 3.1 for computational purposes):

$$S^2 = \frac{\Sigma(x_i - \overline{X})}{n - 1}$$

Again, consider which components in this formula can vary and which cannot. The sample size, n, does not vary. It is a fixed value for the sample. The mean, $\overline{X}$, does not vary. It is also a fixed value for the sample. The deviations between each x_i score and the mean $(x_i - \overline{X})$ *are free to vary* and take on different values depending upon the individual x_i scores in the distribution. The question is, How many of these $(x_i - \overline{X})$ scores are free to vary? The answer to this gives the degrees of freedom for the sample variance.

The answer is all but one $(x_i - \overline{X})$ scores are free to vary. This is because the sum of the deviations of scores about their own mean is always zero, $\Sigma(x_i - \overline{X}) = 0$ If you know $n-1$ of these deviations, you can always determine the last one because its value is such that the sum of all deviations is zero.

Consider for example the distribution of scores (3,7,11). The mean is 7. Look what happens if any two of the deviations $(x_i - \overline{X})$ are computed:

x_i	$\overline{X}$	$(x_i - \overline{X})$
3	7	−4
7	7	0
11	7	?
		$\Sigma(x_i - \overline{X}) = 0$

The third deviation must be +4 because the sum of the deviations from the mean is always zero.

In this sense the last deviation is not free to vary. Knowing $n-1$ of the deviations, the last deviation can be determined. Therefore only $n-1$ deviations are free to vary and take on any value. Thus, the number of degrees of freedom for the sample variance (and the sample standard deviation) is df = $n-1$, where n is the number of x_i scores in the sample (sample size).

Interpretation of Quantiles

Most computer statistical packages are able to provide a range of data plotting facilities and descriptive statistics. PROC UNIVARIATE in SAS provides comprehensive summary statistics which are divided into four sections, moments, quantiles, extremes and if appropriate, missing values.

Consider once again the A-level data set. To obtain descriptive statistics for the variable age in years the following SAS code is submitted:

```
proc univariate;
   var agey;
run;
```

The VAR statement lists the variables to be summarized. The output produced by this code is as follows:

```
Variable=AGEY              AGE IN YEARS
                            Moments

       N              114           Sum Wgts       114
       Mean           19.1769       Sum            2186.167
       Std Dev        1.180186      Variance       1.392839
       Skewness       3.601622      Kurtosis       20.44996
       USS            42081.29      CSS            157.3908
       CV             6.154207      Std Mean       0.110535
       T:Mean=0       173.4924      Pr>|T|         0.0001
       Num ^= 0       114           Num > 0        114
       M(Sign)        57            Pr>=|M|        0.0001
       Sgn Rank       3277.5        Pr>=|S|        0.0001

                        Quantiles(Def=5)

     100% Max          27.16667     99%            24.25
      75% Q3           19.5         95%            20.75
      50% Med          18.91667     90%            20.33333
      25% Q1           18.58333     10%            18.25
       0% Min          16.75        5%             18.16667
                                    1%             17.83333

     Range             10.41667
     Q3-Q1             0.916667
     Mode              18.75

                           Extremes

          Lowest     Obs                  Highest     Obs
        16.75      (       95)        20.91667 (         69)
        17.83333 (         56)        21.08333 (         15)
        18.08333 (        106)        21.75    (        104)
        18.08333 (         29)        24.25    (        112)
        18.16667 (         72)        27.16667 (        108)
```

Output in each of the sections headed moments, quantiles, and extremes is explained below:

Moments

N   is the number of observations with non-missing values for the variable being summarized here AGEY.

Mean   is the arithmetic average. Here the mean age is 19.1769 years. This value is a case of spurious accuracy. Computation of the mean has introduced more apparent accuracy than there was in the original data. In reporting this result the age should be rounded or cut to one decimal place, i.e., 19.2 years. You should always be consistent when rounding data for reporting and either round up to the next nearest decimal place or round down, but do not round up on one occasion and down on another. The mean is not the best summary statistic of central location because the distribution is positively skewed, see positive skewness and kurtosis. Also the mode (18.8) < median (18.9) < mean (19.2).

Std Dev   is the standard deviation. This indicates the amount of dispersion about the mean, but is easier to interpret than the variance (also a measure of dispersion about the mean) since the units of measurement for the standard deviation are the same as those for the data. In this example the standard deviation is 1.2 years. If the data had been approximately normally distributed we could have used the standard deviation to estimate that the middle 68 per cent of observations would fall between 18.0yrs and 20.4yrs, that is within plus or minus 1 standard deviation from the mean. This is an example of use of one of the inferential properties of the normal distribution. We will look at this in more detail in a later chapter.

USS   is the uncorrected sum of squares and is given by:

$$\Sigma w_i x_i^2$$

Unless specified otherwise the weight w is 1. We will mention sums of squares in later chapters.

CV   is the coefficient of variation. This is a less common descriptive statistic which compares the dispersion of observations with their magnitude. It is calculated as S/mean*100 (S is the sample standard deviation, see Table 3.5. Unlike the standard deviation, it is a unitless measure of relative variability which is sometimes useful when variables with different dimensions are being compared, for example, weight in kilograms and weight in pounds.

Similar to the standard deviation, a low value of this coefficient indicates greater precision or less variability in observations. However, this judgment is only helpful when there is another measure of the coefficient with which to compare. If all sample values are multiplied by a constant CV remains unchanged.

T:Mean = 0   is the value of the t test statistic for the null hypothesis that μ (population mean) = 0yrs (in this example clearly a silly hypothesis to entertain). It is calculated as:

$$t = \left(\overline{X} - \mu_0\right)/\left(S/\sqrt{n}\right)$$

which is the difference between the sample mean and the hypothesized population mean divided by the estimated standard error of the mean. You can base a decision rule on the t statistic:

if $t < -1.98$ decide on H_1 (Alternative hypothesis: $\mu < 0$)
if $-1.98 \leqslant t \leqslant 1.98$, reserve judgment
if $t > 1.98$, decide on H_2 (Alternative hypothesis: $\mu > 0$)

The value 1.98 is obtained from a table of Student's t distribution to give a significance of 5 per cent (two-tailed test) for 113 $(114 - 1)$ df. In this example the value of the t statistic is 173.5, so you reject the null hypothesis and conclude that the sample mean is not zero, and that in the population, the mean age of first class honours graduates is not zero. Clearly this is a meaningless test in this example but it may be useful in some applications.

The probability, P, associated with the t statistic is given in the column next to the t value.

Sgn Rank   is the signed rank statistic, computed as:

$\Sigma r_i^+ - n(n + 1)/4$, *where r_i^+ is the positive rank of $|x_i|$, where $|x_i|$ means the absolute value of x_i.*

It is similar to the t statistic and is used to test the hypothesis that the median = 0. This test is only valid if the distribution is symmetric. In this example the (Wilcoxon) Signed Rank test would not be valid. The sign test should be used.

M(Sign)   is the sign test and is evaluated as M(Sign) = p−$(n/2)$, where p is the number of values greater than 0 and n is the number of non-zero values. Here the median sign test, M(Sign) = 114 − 114/2 = 57. This statistic tests the null hypothesis that the population median is zero. Associated with the statistic is the probability of obtaining a sign statistic the same as or greater than the observed sample value. In this example we can reject the null hypothesis and conclude that the population median is not zero.

Num ^=0   is the number of values not equal to zero.

Sum   is the sum of weights. Weights are assumed to be 1 unless
Wgts   defined otherwise.

Sum   is the sum of scores (values).

Variance is a measure of variability about the mean. When the values are
          scattered widely about the mean the variance is large. It is only
          ever zero if all the values are the same. It is evaluated as:

$$\Sigma(x_i - \overline{X})^2/d$$

          where d is the specified df which depends on whether a popu-
          lation or a sample variance is estimated.

CSS   is the sum of squares corrected for the mean. It is calculated as
          the variance but not divided by d (df).

Std Mean is the standard error of the mean. This is calculated as $\left(S/\sqrt{n}\right)$.

Quantiles

This section includes a selection of percentiles including the median and the upper
and lower quartiles, the interquartile range ($Q3$–$Q1$), the non-inclusive range, and
the mode. In this example the distribution of scores is unimodal. The mode unlike
the mean and sometimes the median represents an actual value in the distribution.
The mean in contrast represents a point on the distribution of values.

Extremes

The five lowest and highest values in the distribution are displayed along with
corresponding observation numbers.

3.5   Statistics as Estimators

Whereas this chapter is concerned with initial data analysis, in choosing appropriate
descriptive statistics we should consider the purpose of a study and pay particular
attention to the inferences that may be required to answer particular research questions. In designing a study we tacitly acknowledge that it is not feasible to measure
the entire population of interest, instead we draw a sample from the population. Our
basic research question may, for example, be concerned with the average A-level
points score in the population of first class honours graduates. What we have is an
average score for the obtained sample. To answer our research question we need
to infer from our sample average what the population mean is likely to be. We use
statistical inference to do this.

We generally use descriptive statistics such as the sample mean and variance
to **estimate** the corresponding population parameter. When descriptive sample

statistics are used to yield estimates of yet other statistics that describe properties of populations, this is referred to as **estimation**.

Characteristics of samples are called **statistics** and the comparable measures in a population that these statistics estimate are called **parameters**. By convention, and to help distinguish between sample statistics and population parameters, sample statistics are designated by Latin letters and population parameters are designated by Greek letters. For example: a sample average is denoted by 'x-bar', written as $\overline{X}$, and the comparable population parameter is symbolized by the Greek letter μ (mu). It may help you to remember, that P's go together e.g., 'Population Parameters', and S's go together e.g., 'Sample Statistics'. This terminology and notation is summarized in the following table.

Table 3.5: *Names, notations and explanatory formulas for summary measures of populations and samples*

	Name	Notation	Read as	Formulas
		Summary Measures		
Sample statistics:	Average	$\overline{X}$	x-bar	$= \dfrac{\Sigma x_i}{n}$
	Variance	S^2	S-squared	$= \dfrac{\Sigma(x_i - \overline{X})^2}{n-1}$
	Standard deviation	S	S	$= \sqrt{\dfrac{\Sigma(x_i - \overline{X})^2}{n-1}}$
Population parameters:	Mean	μ	mu	$= \dfrac{\Sigma x_i}{n}$
	Variance	σ^2	sigma squared	$= \dfrac{\Sigma(x_i - \mu)^2}{n}$
	Standard deviation	σ	sigma	$= \sqrt{\dfrac{\Sigma(x_i - \mu)^2}{n}}$

Note: these are explanatory formulas and are not necessarily the formulas that would be used for computational purposes.

It is necessary to use the notion of **expectation** when considering relationships between samples and populations because the expectation of a sample statistic is used to estimate the corresponding population parameter. Sometimes a population parameter is simply the expected value of the corresponding sample statistic. This is the case with the mean. In notational form this is $\mu = E(\overline{X})$ and in words this states that the population mean is equal to the expected value of the sample average. Here the sample average is an **unbiased point estimator**. A non-mathematical explanation of expectation is that if samples were to be repeatedly drawn at random many times from a population (with replacement) then the average of these sample averages would equal the population mean. That is in the long run the average of these sample averages is the expected value, $E(\overline{X})$.

When choosing a statistic as an estimator of a parameter four properties are desirable.

- The statistic should be **unbiased**. An unbiased statistic is an estimator that has an expected value equal to the parameter to be estimated. The sample mean is an unbiased estimator of the corresponding population parameter.
- The statistic should be **efficient**. An efficient statistic is one that is a better estimator in all respects than any other statistic. Both the median and the mean are unbiased estimators of the population parameter μ, but the mean is more efficient. If we select repeated random samples of equal size from a defined population and plot the averages of each sample and the medians of each sample we would find that the averages cluster closer around the population mean than do the medians. The sample average is therefore more efficient because any average is, in the long run, more likely to be closer to the population mean than a sample median.
- The statistic should be **sufficient**. A sufficient statistic is one which uses the maximum amount of relevant sample information. The sample range uses only two values in a distribution whereas the variance and standard deviation uses all the values. Similarly the mean uses all the values but the mode uses only the most common observations. The mean and variance are more sufficient statistics than the mode and range.
- The statistic should be **resistant**. A resistant statistic is the degree to which a statistic is influenced by extreme values in a distribution. As we have mentioned the mean is greatly influenced by extreme values whereas the median is relatively uninfluenced. The median is more resistant than the mean.

You might think that all sample statistics are unbiased estimates of their corresponding parameters but this is not true. The sample variance and standard deviation are biased estimates of their respective population parameters. That is why the denominators in the formulae 3.1 and 3.2 are corrected by subtracting one from the sample size, i.e., $n-1$. This is the degree of freedom associated with the statistic. One degree of freedom is lost for every parameter estimated from sample data and one degree of freedom is gained for every independent observation. These are important considerations when designing studies and choosing possible statistical models. We will return to these issues when we consider regression and analysis of variance.

Deciding which Summary Measure to Use

We now have considered descriptive statistics for measures of central tendency and measures of dispersion. At this point you may well be wondering which statistic to use and when. When choosing a statistic you should consider: the properties of the statistic as an estimator, that is whether the statistic is a biased, efficient, sufficient and resistant estimator; level of measurement of a variable; and subsequent inferential analyses.

Measures of central tendency

The sample mean is generally more widely used as a descriptive statistic than either the median or the mode. The mean is unbiased, efficient, sufficient but not resistant. The median is also unbiased, sufficient but less efficient than the mean. It has the advantage however of being more resistant than the mean. It is often stated in statistical textbooks that the mean should not be used with nominal or ordinal data. This is not true. For nominal data which has values 0 and 1, (say females are coded 0 and males 1) then the mean is simply equal to the proportion of males in the distribution. The mean may even be used with ordered categorical data. An implicit assumption however would be that the change from say 1 to 2 would be the same amount as the change from 2 to 3. Should this assumption seem unrealistic do not use the mean.

In my view the mean is used more often than it should be and is widely mis-understood. Chatfield (1993) illustrates misunderstanding about the mean by reference to, 'the apocryphal story of the politician who said that it was disgraceful for half the nation's children to be under average intelligence' (p. 33). When the mean is used it should be accompanied by the standard deviation.

The mean should not be used when a distribution is skewed, instead use the median and interquartile range. Another situation when the mean should not be used is when data is censored. Educational researchers frequently ask whether and if so when events occur. For example, in a study of teachers' careers, the response variable of interest might be 'survival time', that is how long it is before a teacher quits teaching. A problem is that, no matter how long a follow-up study lasts, some teachers may not quit teaching. These observations are **censored**, the researcher does not know when, if ever, the teacher will quit teaching, in that sense the data is incomplete. For discussion of alternative strategies to summarize survival time data see a paper on discrete-time survival analysis by Singer and Willett (1993).

Measures of dispersion

The range is influenced by the sample size and interpretation is problematic. The sample standard deviation and variance are biased (but can be adjusted by appropriate df) and sufficient but are not resistant statistics. The interquartile range is more resistant than either the standard deviation or variance but is less efficient. The standard deviation is most useful with approximately normal data; when data is skewed, the interquartile range is more appropriate.

3.6 Statistical Models

Whereas the primary aim of IDA is to describe and summarize data a secondary aim is to suggest an appropriate underlying statistical model for the data which will form the basis of subsequent inferential statistical analysis. I follow Chatfield's thinking here (Chatfield, 1985) and stress that IDA may be all that is required particularly if the entire population of interest is analyzed rather than a sample. Another situation when IDA would suffice is when data is of such poor quality that further inferential analysis would not be justified, for example, when it was evident that there were non-random errors. Sometimes visual scrutiny of the data and descriptive analysis is so clear-cut that further inferential statistical analysis is unnecessary. If none of the above situations arise then the researcher should indeed consider what statistical models might be appropriate for further data analysis.

A **statistical model** is a mathematical representation of the relationship between variables in a population of interest or a mathematical expression for the shape of an underlying population distribution of a variable. In reality, there may or may not be a relationship between variables in a defined population. Similarly, a particular variable which has the values 0 or 1, where 1 denotes 'treatment success' and 0 denotes 'treatment failure' may or may not follow an underlying distribution such as the binomial distribution or binomial model. (The binomial model, see Chapter 6, depends on the underlying treatment success rate in the population of interest. If this were to change the binomial model would not be appropriate.) We collect data, usually by sampling from the population, to see if the data fits our simplified statistical model. If the data does not fit the model, we change the model not the data.

As a further illustration consider once again the example of the vocabulary teaching methods experiment introduced in Chapter 1, Example 2. You may recall from this earlier teaching methods example that the researcher's basic question was concerned with vocabulary acquisition in a population of 6-year-olds, not simply vocabulary acquisition in the sample itself. The use of sample statistics to estimate corresponding population **parameters** (properties of populations rather than samples) is central in this way to experimental design and statistical analysis.

We could argue that the vocabulary scores are subject to random, unsystematic variation which makes them appear very much like random observations on a response variable. The population formed by such a distribution of random observations is *not* real, but can be thought of as a hypothetical population which would be generated. We could put forward a statistical model to account for and explain this random variation. The question we would need to consider is, Does this model yield an account of relationships in the data? In other words, Does our data fit our statistical model?

To interpret data we search for patterns. Any systematic effects such as those attributable to teaching method may be blurred by other more haphazard variation. A statistical model contains both **systematic** and **random** effects. We can say that a general probabilistic statistical model has two components, a deterministic or effect component which represents the effects of variables in the model and a random or error component which allows for random fluctuation of the variables in the model.

The value of a statistical model is that it should suggest a simple summary of the data, using parameters, in terms of both systematic effects and random effects. The problem then is to look at the data using IDA and decide what model may best describe and account for observed variation and in particular what model reduces the amount of error variation.

A relatively simple family of statistical models which allows for systematic and error or random variation is known as the **general linear model**. Put simply this states that values of a response variable are given by the weighted sum of independent variables specified in a model plus a term standing for error. In equation form this can be stated as,

$y_{ij} = \mu_i + \varepsilon_{ij}$, where y_{ij} is the value of the jth observation from the ith treatment, μ_i is a constant representing the mean treatment score for the population and ε_{ij} is a randomly fluctuating error term. This model is sometimes called the 'means model' because it accounts for the overall mean treatment effect and underlying variation only.

It is possible to formulate a linear model for the one-factor vocabulary teaching methods experiment introduced in Chapter 1. Recall this was a fixed-effects model with three conditions or levels of treatment. This is important in specifying the statistical model. The statistical model for this design would be:

$y_{ij} = \mu + \alpha_i + \varepsilon_{ij}$, where $i = 1$, 2 or 3 representing the effects of one of the treatments, so y_{ij} is the observed value for an individual j in the ith treatment group, μ is a constant or mean response in the population and ε_{ij} is the deviation from the mean treatment response for the jth individual in the ith treatment (the error term). This error term is assumed to have a normal distribution. This model is sometimes called an 'effects model' because it accounts for various treatment effects.

This statistical model implies that any score can be decomposed into three parts, one component μ which is constant over all observations and treatments, a **fixed treatment effect** α_i making the same contribution to all vocabulary scores in a given treatment group and an error component that will differ both between treatment groups and also within treatment groups. If a random effects design was used then the fixed treatment effect α_i would be replaced by a **random treatment effect** a_i representing the effect of the ith treatment (teaching method) which would be sampled at random from a population of teaching methods. This statistical model, sometimes referred to as a **structural model**, states, for example, that an individual in the enhanced storytelling method group (say method group 1) has a vocabulary score which is represented by the mean vocabulary score of the population, μ, plus any difference between this population mean and the mean score for all pupils exposed to method group 1, the treatment effect α_i, plus any difference between the individuals score and the contribution of the treatment effect.

Summary

The foregoing chapter should have impressed upon you the importance of IDA. By now you should also realize that the choice of descriptive statistics and data display methods is not always as straightforward as it seems. You should by now be in a position to know how to describe and summarize a data set and make a preliminary decision about whether further inferential statistical analysis is justified.

Case Study

A research student collected data on secondary school pupils attributions about chance, mathematical self-concept and mathematical achievement as well as background information about what class and maths set they were in. A self-completion questionnaire was used and 227 useable scripts were returned by teachers to the researcher. Two class teachers (57 student questionnaires) did not return any questionnaires.

Four attribution statements in the questionnaire included: 'Winning the national lottery depends on chance', 'Getting a 6 on a normal dice depends on knowing how to throw the dice', 'Your success in life depends on chance' and 'If it rains in Manchester a week from today this is just a matter of chance'. Each statement was given a score of 1 to 5 where 1 represents strongly disagree, 3 represents undecided and 5 represents strongly agree.

Four statements used to assess mathematical self-concept included: 'I can learn mathematics if I work hard', 'I am as talented in mathematics as other pupils in my class', 'I just cannot learn mathematics', and 'No matter how much I try I shall have problems learning mathematics'. A mathematics achievement test was specially constructed, based on relevant sections of the mathematics national curriculum. The normative test contained 30 items designed to have different facility indices (easiness levels). Scores could range from 0–30. The data coding sheet is shown in Table 3.6. and the data set, Main.dat, is given in Table 2, Appendix A1.

Table 3.6: Coding sheet for data set on school children's mathematical self-concept and mathematical achievement

Researcher:					D/O/C: 16/05/94	
DSN: Main.dat					Number of cases = 227	
Variable	Variable Name	Number of Columns	Column Begin	Column End	Range of Variable	Missing Data
Case id	caseid	3	1	3	1–127	.
Classroom	class	1	4	4	1–9	.
Maths set	set	1	5	5	1–6	.
Attribute1	attb1	1	6	6	1–5	.
Attribute2	attb2	1	7	7	1–5	.
Attribute3	attb3	1	8	8	1–5	.
Attribute4	attb4	1	9	9	1–5	.
Self-concept1	selfc1	1	10	10	1–5	.
Self-concept2	selfc2	1	11	11	1–5	.
Self-concept3	selfc3	1	12	12	1–5	.
Self-concept4	selfc4	1	13	13	1–5	.
Maths score	score	2	14	15	1–30	.

The raw data as presented for analysis is shown in Table 2, Appendix A1.

Task

The initial task facing an investigator would be to perform an initial data analysis.

The first step is to scrutinize the data, assess its structure and to reflect on the data collection procedure. You should then summarize the data in a form suitable for presentation in a journal article and comment on any special features of the data. This task is intended to be carried out using a computer.

The first part of this task has been completed and is intended to illustrate the use of the COMPARE programme.

Data processing and cleaning

Looking at the data as presented, it is a little messy. See Table 2, Appendix A1. This data needs 'cleaning-up'. Notice missing data has been coded as character (.). Missing data and spurious values can be checked by using PROC SUMMARY to produce a frequency count; an example of the output from this procedure is shown in Figure 3.9. The procedure PROC SUMMARY enables any **numeric** variables with missing or out-of-range values to be identified. A listing of the data is then used to find those case numbers (caseid) corresponding to the variables with spurious values. Once a particular caseid is identified this can be used to check data values on the data listing against original data.

This process of identifying out-of-range values and corresponding caseids can be considerably speeded-up and completed in one step using the SAS programme Check.job given in Figure 1, Appendix A3. This programme produces, for all numeric variables (except caseid), a listing of caseids which have out-of-range values and missing data. It prints the caseids against each corresponding variable with missing or spurious data. Once caseids with missing or out-of-range values are identified, see Figure 3.18, these values can be checked against original data.

```
        Case identifiers with out-of-range values or missing data
                    for each numeric variable
            variable
            name            <min         missing        >max
            ATTB1            .            202            .
            ATTB2            37           .              .
                            151           .              .
                             .           188            .
                             .           202            .
                             .           221            .
            ATTB3            .            .              82
                            134           .              .
                             .            .             157
                             .           194            .
                             .           202            .
                             .           225            .
```

variable name	<min	missing	>max
ATTB4	118	.	.
	.	.	151
	.	176	.
	189	.	.
SCORE	.	.	3
	.	188	.
	.	191	.
	.	194	.
	.	200	.
	.	201	.
	.	207	.
	.	208	.
	.	.	210
	.	214	.
	.	220	.
	.	221	.
SELFC1	.	.	44
	.	.	86
	.	115	.
	162	.	.
	181	.	.
	189	.	.
	.	191	.
SELFC2	154	.	.
	157	.	.
	.	194	.
	.	202	.
SELFC3	154	.	.
	190	.	.
SELFC4	154	.	.
	163	.	.
	207	.	.

Figure 3.18: SAS output from the programme check.job. (Missing and out-of-range values are printed)

Once data has been cleaned and processing errors checked, descriptive analysis can begin. You should comment on the data collection procedure and construct appropriate charts and plots to help you:

- identify outliers;
- identify any pattern in missing data;
- identify the shape of distributions;
- summarize each variable using appropriate descriptive statistics;
- present a summary of the data in the form of frequency tables that would be suitable for inclusion in a journal article.

Further considerations:

- How have you dealt with missing values and does this affect your data summary?
- How have you rounded your summary statistics for presentation in tables? What element of accuracy is implied?
- Are you able to describe in a paragraph the main features of the data?
- What appear to be the most important statistics?

By simply looking at the data distributions does there appear to be any association between variables? To answer this you will need to compare a set of boxplots, for example, a series of boxplots showing maths set against the four different variables of self-concept (SELFC1 to SELFC4).

Chapter 4

Probability and Inference

In this chapter basic statistical concepts involved in the design and subsequent data analysis of empirical investigations are introduced. These ideas are considered in the context of planning and implementing a quantitative empirical research study. Unlike in the previous chapter where we explained that the purpose of initial data analysis was to describe and summarize data, in this chapter we will focus on another aspect of statistical analysis, namely, how statistics can help answer specific research questions and provide evidence on the trustworthiness of our conclusions.

Two of the most important statistical ideas which are central to the use of statistical tests and indeed are fundamental to the empirical research process are **probability** and **statistical inference**. These statistical ideas play an essential role when a researcher's interest turns from describing data to answering more specific research questions.

4.1 Research Process

A good way to begin an empirical investigation is with a research question, for example:

- 'Do teachers' expectations of students' abilities influence students' performances?'
- 'Is illness perceived by young children as a form of punishment?'
- 'Are secondary school pupils' academic achievements in the most part determined by their academic performance in primary school?'

Selection of focused research question(s) and definition of a population of interest is the first step in what is typically a four-stage empirical research process. The statistical concepts of probability and inference, which are often not explicitly recognized as part of the research process, are introduced in the context of these four stages of research, see Figure 4.1.

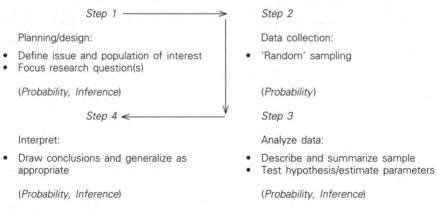

Figure 4.1: Overview of the empirical research process

Generally our research questions refer to whole populations of interest, such as all teachers, all young children, all secondary school pupils. However, after having specified a population (step 1), it is often impossible to collect data for the whole population of interest. Instead, a sample from the population is selected (step 2). A wise researcher should give careful thought to the kind of statistical inference(s) required to address the research question(s) at the planning and design stage, that is *before* data is collected.

You may recall from the previous chapter that initial data analysis of the achieved sample is the first phase in our overall data analysis strategy. We used graphical techniques and summary statistics to describe our sample data and to identify underlying data distributions and possible statistical models (step 3). In so doing, we were preparing for the next phase of analysis which involves more formal procedures of statistical inference.

Fundamentals of Inference

The idea of **statistical inference** is involved whenever we go beyond the numeric findings obtained from sample data to suggest what the situation is, or what would happen, in the parent population. There are two aspects to statistical inference – estimation and hypothesis testing. Whereas both hypothesis testing and estimation make use of the same concepts: sample, statistic, population and parameter, fundamentally they address different questions.

Estimation addresses the question, 'What is the value of a population parameter?'. For example, what is the mean maths achievement score in the specified population?

Hypothesis testing addresses the question, 'What is the probability or likelihood that the population parameter is equal to a specified value?' For example, what is the probability that the mean maths achievement score is 100? A test of significance is used to assess the strength of evidence against the hypothesis (step 3). The central tenet of our research question(s) is usually concerned not so much with the findings from a particular sample *per se*, but rather with generalizing these findings beyond the immediate experimental or survey setting (step 4).

You should by now be convinced of the central role that statistical inference has in quantitative research. Statistical inference is, however, not an end in itself but is simply an aid to decision making in uncertain circumstances. Information in the form of data is collected, sample statistics are then calculated and used in a formal way in what is called estimation and hypothesis testing. The confidence we have in a sample estimate, or the strength of evidence we have against a hypothesis is evaluated by this formal process. The researcher can then draw conclusions based on the outcome(s) of statistical test(s) and the strength of evidence for or against a hypothesis.

Probability: Its Role in Research

The idea of probability is central to the process of statistical inference. Whenever a sample is selected an element of uncertainty is introduced. This uncertainty is a consequence of not collecting information from the whole population, but relying instead on information contained in a sample. This degree of uncertainty is numerically expressed as a **probability** or the likelihood of occurrence of an event.

Probability can generally be thought of as the study of patterns of chance events and is based on the idea that certain phenomenon are random. Statistics are calculated from sample data and may be used not only to summarize data but also to assess the strength of evidence provided by sample data in favour of an assertion or statement about circumstances in the population, the hypothesis. Provided data is produced by a random process (step 2), then the sample statistics themselves, such as an average or a proportion, can be thought of as random variables which obey the laws of probability. We can, therefore, use the language of probability to make statements about the likelihood of outcomes such as the difference between averages or the strength of a relationship between two variables. We can in effect say how likely we would be to observe a given outcome simply by chance.

We actually observe these outcomes in our sample only. However, because sample statistics are estimators of corresponding population parameters, and also because they behave in a probabilistic way, we can use statistical inference to draw conclusions about circumstances in our population of interest.

A sample which has been produced by a random process is called a **probability sample** and subjects or sample values will be independently drawn from the population. This means the chance that one subject has been sampled is not dependent on the chance that other members of the population have been or would be sampled. A major problem with many quantitative research designs is that non-probability samples are used.

A non-probability sample can arise when:

- you do not have a sample frame, essentially a list of every subject or value that is a member of the target population;

- not every member of the population has an independent chance of being selected;
- there is no underlying probability model specified, that is we cannot work out in advance of sampling the chance of any member of the population being selected. It is not necessary that all members of the population have an equal chance of being selected.

A probability model for the values of a variable in a population is a mathematical description or a kind of model for randomness which gives the probabilities for all possible values of the variable.

Example 4.1: Use of Non-probability Samples

Non-probability samples are usually not representative of the population of interest and generally, therefore, should not be used for statistical inference. In practice however they often are. For example, it is not uncommon in experimental designs that involve school children as subjects, to use for a sample those children that were nominated by their class teacher. Sometimes, for administrative convenience, an entire class is used as the sample, for example, a common programme evaluation design involves the administration of an appropriate 'before' and 'after' test to an entire class of children who are all programme participants.

Alternatively, teachers may *not* select pupils for participation in an experimental study on the grounds of chance alone; they may have other reasons for selecting pupils which the researcher may be unaware of, for example, a talkative child, a nuisance, or because a teacher thinks that a particular child will 'perform' best.

Considering a typical 'before' and 'after' design then if *all* participants in the programme were tested, they either represent the entire population of interest and therefore there is no need to use statistical inference, or as is often the case, it is not clear whom the population of interest is, in which case it cannot be a probability sample.

So, if in a journal article you read about a study which was similar to the 'before' and 'after' design mentioned above, how should you interpret the reported results of the statistical analysis?

In general we are asked to assume that we are dealing with a probability sample which is representative of an often undefined population. If this assumption is not reasonable, perhaps you are not convinced by the evidence provided by the author(s), then the statistical test(s) will be invalid, and there is a good chance the study conclusions will be also.

Linking Probability and Inference

A key link between the ideas of probability and statistical inference is the sample statistic, or more precisely, the sampling distribution of the sample statistic. The **sampling distribution** of any statistic is a distribution of the values of that statistic (not the raw scores) when separate independent random samples of equal size are drawn from the same population. The sampling distribution of a statistic is actually a probability distribution which describes the behaviour or likely values of a sample statistic in repeated sampling, provided the data are produced by a random process. This explains the importance of random sampling or randomization when collecting data. The term **probability distribution** has been slipped in here without explanation. We shall defer explanation until a later section, this should not affect your grasp of how the basic ideas of statistical inference and probability fit into the research process.

Estimation

Let us return again to the research process outlined in Figure 4.1. After having defined a population of interest and specified research questions in terms of the variables to be measured, the researcher then selects a sample, where possible a random probability sample, from the population of interest (step 2). Both the concept of probability and the idea of sampling variability are involved when a random sample is chosen from a population. *Sampling variability* is sometimes referred to as *sampling error* when referring to survey designs.

Random sampling in survey research is based on the idea of probability or chance, that is, in a random sample each member of the target population has a known chance of being selected into the sample. If an experiment was planned, the principle of randomization would be appropriate, (see, for example, experimental design in Chapter 1). When a researcher selects a random sample, calculates a statistic such as a mean and then goes beyond the descriptive function of the statistic to use it to determine the population mean, this represents another aspect of statistical inference called **estimation**. Put simply, estimation is when we use sample statistics to estimate the value of population parameters. The formulae we use to calculate the statistic is called the **estimator**.

For example, with reference to the research question at the beginning of this chapter about the relationship between academic performance in primary and secondary school, we could use a sample statistic the Pearson correlation, r (a measure of relationship between two variables), to estimate the population correlation, ρ (rho). Any one sample that is chosen randomly is very unlikely to be identical to another independent random sample selected from the same population. It follows that if, for example, correlations were calculated for two independent samples it is unlikely that they would be the same. This is because of sampling variability, also called sampling error (see Chapter 1, section 1.1). Sampling error is a feature of quantitative empirical research studies and this variability needs to be estimated so that we can tell how good an estimator any one sample correlation is. The sampling error or standard error of a statistic also plays an important role in some statistical tests for example the t-test.

Rather than using the statistic, r, to estimate the population correlation, we could use it to test a hypothesis, for example, 'Is the population correlation between primary and secondary school performance equal to zero?' Once again, using the idea of probability, we can state with a specified degree of certainty whether it is reasonable to believe that the population parameter is zero. We could of course propose that the population parameter is some other non-zero value. In reality the population parameter is likely to be some true non-zero value but we do not know this. The logic of hypothesis testing demands that we assume the population correlation is zero and that we accumulate evidence to refute this conjecture. The reason why we set about testing hypotheses in this strange and convoluted way will be explained in section 4.7 (hypothesis testing).

Interpretation of Statistical Analyses

The final stage in the research process is when the researcher interprets the statistical tests and draws conclusions about circumstances in the parent population based on sample data (step 4). You may not have consciously noticed but the four steps shown in Figure 4.1 are interdependent, and our interpretation is therefore based on what we know about each stage of the study. For example, the kinds of questions addressed will influence the nature of the variables; how they are operationalized (observed/measured). This in turn will influence, amongst other considerations, the size of the sample and how it is chosen. Sample size and level of measurement of variables are two important characteristics that influence the choice of a statistical test.

Interpretation of statistical results should also be related to limitations of the study design, for example, how confident are you that randomness was built into the design? Were there any sources of hidden systematic error (bias), for example, only certain ability groups of pupils were involved in a study? Was an experiment realistic – a referential communication task may be based on role play – is this something that 5- and 6-year-old children do very often? Are there any leading questions in a survey? You should of course relate your results to findings from similar studies.

As you may have guessed, the research process illustrated in Figure 4.1 is oversimplified. Important questions have been conveniently overlooked, examples include: How do you know when to reject a hypothesis? What happens if you reject a hypothesis when you should not? What is the chance of detecting a relationship or difference if one really exists? What is the chance of detecting a difference which does not really exist? How large should my sample be? Is variability in my sample important? How precise is my estimate and what confidence should I have in it? What statistical test should I use and why? Answers to these questions affect the confidence and trustworthiness that we have in any conclusions we draw.

I am sure you would like answers to these questions. We are, however, not quite at the point yet where such answers would be meaningful. These questions and similar issues are discussed in Chapter 5, 'Choosing a statistical test'.

Finally, it once again needs to be stressed that a statistical analysis plan should not be left until after data has been collected. The idea of statistical randomness should not just enter a study in a haphazard way, it should be deliberately planned into the research design if you intend to use inferential statistical tests. In the next section, the idea of probability and its role in the research process is explored in greater depth.

4.2 Statistical Probability

Statistical probability forms the basis of all tests of statistical significance. Probability is a way of assigning a number to the likelihood of the occurrence of an event or outcome. Put another way, probability is a way of measuring chance and allows us to place the likelihood of an outcome on a continuum ranging from certainty, which has a probability value of 1, to impossible which has a probability of zero. The closer a probability is to 1 the more certain is the occurrence of the event.

In statistics an **event** refers to an observable or measurable outcome of an 'experiment'. The term experiment is unfortunate because it does not mean an experiment in the sense of research design, rather it means a conceptual experiment in which something is done or observed and for which there are various possible outcomes. For example, the sex of a child at birth is an observable outcome, counting the percentage of 15-year-old pupils in a school who achieve 5 or more GCSE grades A to C is an observable outcome, the number of children who improve their reading skills in a reading recovery programme is an observable outcome, and improvement in a school's average A-level points score is a measurable outcome.

Most of these events or outcomes have a degree of uncertainty attached to them and could be considered to be random. We use the idea of a **random variable** to describe events of interest. For example, if we role two dice, a random variable could be the value we obtain when we multiply the two totals on the upturned dice, another random variable might be the value of the sum of the two scores on the upturned dice. If we administer a standardized maths achievement test to a class of 8-year-old school children, a random variable could be the value of one pupil's test score, yet another random variable could be the average test score for the class. The sex of a child, percentage of GCSEs and average A-level points score could all be random variables of interest. Use of the term **random variable** has gained such widespread use in probability theory it needs a mention here. The term **random** in this context does not mean outcomes that are equally likely as in the term **simple random sample** or **random selection**. It denotes a variable whose outcome is determined by an element of chance and has a degree of uncertainty associated with it. We can say the outcome of the experiment is not predictable but is one of many possible outcomes, each with a numerical value or probability.

Probability Models

One of the aims of educational and psychological research is to describe and predict the world in which we live and thereby gain an insight into all kinds of educational and psychological phenomena. One way to do this is by empirical quant-itative research. When we use statistical inference, we want to model our random experiments and to be able to give values to the probabilities associated with each outcome. To do this we construct a **probability model** which adequately describes that part of the world we are interested in.

It would be almost impossible to model the outcome of a single random event such as a birth, or a flip of a coin, or a single test score for an individual, because by its random nature the sex of a child at birth, whether a coin lands heads or tails, or an achieved test score is uncertain. However, in the long run, and provided the experiment is random, a pattern of outcomes is detectable. This predictable pattern is the basis of probability models and is the reason why we can use statistical inference and statistical tests. It may seem strange, but random uncertainty, in the long run, leads to predictability, and the long-run regularity of random phenomena can be described using a mathematical or probability model.

In the long-run refers to repeated flips of a coin, repeated births, repeated test scores, that is each experiment repeated many times under the same conditions. In many flips of a coin the proportion or **long-term relative frequency** of heads will approach 0.5, that is half of the outcomes will be heads and half will be tails.

Clearly not all situations of interest would lend themselves to this long-run interpretation. An individual usually only takes a test once, not repeatedly under the same conditions, and we could never observe an infinite number of flips of a coin. The best we could do would be to observe a very large number of flips of the coin. In these kinds of circumstances we make use of a **theoretical probability distri-bution**. That is a mathematically determined probability distribution, which describes the relative frequency of outcomes in an infinite number of experiments, each pos-sible outcome having a probability value on the scale 0 to 1. To be able to use the idea of probability and these expected long-term patterns, research designs have to have randomness or chance planned into them. For example, random sampling or randomization in experimental designs. Randomization is not designed into a study just to prevent bias, it is essential if statistical inference is used, that is, whenever we collect a sample of data, test a hypothesis using a test of statistical significance, and derive conclusions about a population of interest. Statistical inference relies on the laws of probability which in turn assume observations or random variables result from a random process.

4.3 Sampling Distributions

Probability theory allows us to describe mathematically the outcome of random events. One aspect of interest to statisticians is the behaviour of sample statistics and test statistics in the long-run. Provided data is generated by a random process, the values of sample statistics are random and we can use probability theory to describe how a statistic will vary with repeated samples of the same size from the same popu-lation. This idea of repeated sampling leads to the concept of the sampling distribution of a statistic. We can think of the **sampling distribution** of a sample statistic as the distribution of the values of that statistic over repeated samples of the same size from the same population. Although individual values of a variable may differ and individual sample statistics repeatedly sampled from the same population differ, it is perhaps by now no surprise that the sampling distribution of a sample statistic has a predictable and regular pattern. Statistical inference depends upon the predictable pattern of the sampling distribution.

Sampling Distribution of Test Statistics

Whereas each descriptive statistic, mean, proportion, median variance, etc., has its own sampling distribution, the shape of these distributions differ. Another group of statistics called test statistics also have unique sampling distributions. **Test statistics** such as t, F, and χ^2, are all associated with specific statistical tests and similar to the descriptive statistics, each has its own computational formulas and sampling distribution. Statistical tables shown in the appendix of many statistical texts are simply tables of expected outcomes or probabilities based on theoretical sampling distributions of descriptive statistics and test statistics.

Sampling distribution of the χ^2 statistic

If you are unfamiliar with hypothesis testing you might like to come back to this section after having read 'Hypothesis testing' (pp. 108–113). Consider the sampling distribution of the χ^2 statistic. This statistic is often used to answer questions of the type, 'Is there a relationship between two categorical variables such as school type and identity status?' For example, we may select a random sample of pupils and cross classify them on two variables to see whether there is a statistically significant association between school type, (one variable, two categories private or state), and the other variable, identity status, four categories; – achievement, moratorium, foreclosure and diffusion. In another type of design the χ^2 statistic can be used to compare the distribution of proportions in two populations. When there are two separate and independent random samples (sample size fixed by the research design) drawn from two populations, for example, boys and girls or state schools and private schools, a χ^2 test of homogeneity would be appropriate. Use of the χ^2 statistic in various research designs is discussed in Chapter 6.

A research question addressed by investigators might be: 'Is there a relationship between school type and identity status' (See for example, an empirical study by Roker and Banks, 1993). The corresponding null hypothesis would be that the population proportions in the four identity states is equal in the two populations of students (private/state school). The **Null Hypothesis** is a hypothesis of no difference and plays a crucial role in statistical analysis (it is sometimes called the statistical hypothesis). This is the same as saying the distribution of the population proportions, the parameter pi, π, is the same in each population. This is illustrated in Table 4.1.

Table 4.1: Table of parameter distribution for a two-way table

Outcome (rows)	Population (columns)	
	1 (Private)	2 (State)
Achievement 1	$\pi_{1(1)}$	$\pi_{1(2)}$
Moratorium 2	$\pi_{2(1)}$	$\pi_{2(2)}$
Foreclosure 3	$\pi_{3(1)}$	$\pi_{3(2)}$
Diffusion 4	$\pi_{4(1)}$	$\pi_{4(2)}$
Σ	1	1

Looking at Table 4.1, another way of stating the null hypothesis, H_0, is to say that the set of parameters in column 1 is the same as the set of parameters in column 2. In notational form:

$$H_0: \pi_{1(1)} = \pi_{1(2)}$$
$$\pi_{2(1)} = \pi_{2(2)}$$
$$\pi_{3(1)} = \pi_{3(2)}$$
$$\pi_{4(1)} = \pi_{4(2)}$$

You could obtain empirically the sampling distribution of the χ^2 test statistic when H_0 is true by drawing a very large number of pairs of random samples, a random sample for column 1 and a random sample for column 2, *but* all from one population. In this case the null hypothesis would have to be true because the population proportion who were at achievement status would be equal, ie $\pi_{1(1)} = \pi_{1(2)}$. The extent of any difference between sample proportions $P_{1(1)}$ and $P_{1(2)}$ would be attributable to sampling variability. The χ^2 statistic could be computed from sample data arranged in a two-way table similar to that shown in Table 4.1. If the sampling was repeated an infinite number of times, under the same conditions, we could plot all the values of the obtained χ^2 statistic. This would give the sampling distribution for χ^2 when H_0 is true for a fixed sample size. We could now select a random sample of data, the same sample size as before, compute a χ^2 value, and compare this with what we would expect from the sampling distribution. We could reject the null hypothesis if our χ^2 value was not what we would have expected when the null hypothesis is true.

One other point that is worth noting, is that there is not one χ^2 distribution, but a whole family of χ^2 distributions which are described by a single parameter, the degrees of freedom (see p. 70 for an explanation of this concept). Every time we change the degrees of freedom we have to use a different sampling distribution. Fortunately, theoretical sampling distributions have been evaluated for all reasonable degrees of freedom and these are the χ^2 tables often presented in the appendix of many statistical texts.

4.4   Discrete Random Variables

The way in which we assign probability to all possible outcomes of a random variable depends upon whether the random variable is discrete or continuous. This distinction is important because it will influence the choice of an underlying statistical model for the data.

A **discrete random variable** is one in which all possible values of the random variable take a countable value, for example, the number of girls in a year four class, the number of questionnaires returned in a survey, the number of experimental tasks you write into your research submission. It would not make sense to count half a person, a proportion of a questionnaire (unless this was part of the study design) or some fraction of an experimental task. The distinction between discrete and continuous is not always clear cut in practice. For example, someone with an average IQ may have a score of about 100 or 101 but not 101.5. IQ is therefore discrete in a measurement sense. It is, however, almost always treated as a continuous measure. The reason is because IQ is supposed to measure an underlying and theoretically continuous dimension of intelligence. Many readers will be aware that the meaning of intelligence and what IQ-like tests measure, has been, and still is an issue in which there is considerable debate.

The probability distribution of a discrete random variable (unlike a continuous probability distribution, see 'Continuous random variables', pp. 104–08), has a probability attached to each and every possible outcome. If we plot a probability distribution for a discrete random variable it is similar to a relative frequency bar chart. We met this in the previous chapter when describing distributions of variables. The only difference is that we replace the relative frequency of an outcome with a probability value.

Discrete Probability Distribution

Example 4.2:   The Binomial Probability Distribution

If we choose a simple random sample of 10 schools from the population of all secondary schools in a Local Education Authority and for each school we assigned it into a 'better' or 'worse' category, depending on the answer to the following question, 'Is the percentage of 15-year-old pupils achieving 5 or more GCSEs at grades A to C 'better' or 'worse' than the median national (population) pass rate of 39.9 per cent?' We may find that our sample of 10 schools has the following per cent pass rates (+ or – indicates whether it is better or worse than the national average):

19(–); 37(–); 52(+); 11(–); 13(–); 31(–); 100(+); 25(–); 41(+); 18(–)

When a discrete random variable is a count, X, of the 'successes' in n independent trials or observations which each has the same probability of success, it is said to be a **binomial random variable**. If we consider a sampled school that is above the median to be a success then an appropriate statistical model to describe the probability

---

distribution of the random variable (school= success/fail) is the binomial probability distribution, sometimes called the binomial model. This probability distribution enables determination of the probability for any number of successes r, $(r = 0,1,2 \ldots 10)$, in $n = 10$ schools provided they were selected at random.

We can use the binomial sampling distribution to answer questions like, 'Could it happen by chance that we obtain 3 schools in our sample that have above the national median pass rate?'

Pascal's Triangle

Pascal's triangle, named after the Mathematician Blaise Pascal who discovered it when he was only 16, is used to illustrate how probabilities can be calculated for a binomial variable. Let us consider selecting one school at random. This is equivalent to one flip of a coin. *What is the probability that the selected school lies below the population median? Think about the probability of obtaining a 'head' with one flip of a coin.* In both cases the answer is one-half.

Intuitively, it is easy to answer the question about flipping the coin. Assuming the coin is fair there is an even chance that heads will turn up. The reason why the probability that the selected school lies below the median is one-half is because by definition half the population lies below the median. Think about it this way, there are only two possible outcomes, the selected school is either below or above the population median (we are assuming for now that none of the schools sampled has a pass rate that is equal to the population median).

If we select 10 schools at random this is equivalent to flipping 10 coins. We can work out, for each school selected, the probability of falling above the national median pass rate in the following way. If one school is selected there is an even chance that it will be above, using (A) for above, or below, using (B) for below, the population median. If a second school is selected, there are four possible outcomes: both schools are above the median AA, the first school sampled is above the median and the second school sampled is below the median AB, the first school is below the median and the second school is above BA, and both the first and second schools are below the median, BB. If three schools were sampled, the possible outcomes are shown in Figure 4.2.

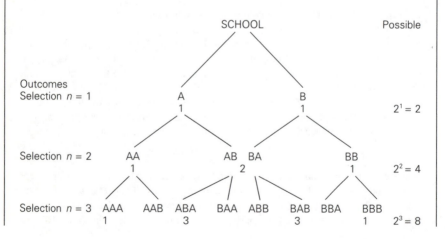

Possibility:	1 with *3* above	3 with *2* above	3 with *1* above	1 with *0* above	= 8
	AAA	AAB ABA BAA	ABB BAB BBA	BBB	
Frequency of possibility:	1	3	3	1	= 8
Probability: to 3 decimal places	1/8 0.125	3/8 0.375	3/8 0.375	1/8 0.125	= 8 = 1

Figure 4.2: Pascal's triangle of expected outcomes

If you look closely at Figure 4.2 you can see a pattern beginning to emerge. The total number of outcomes for each school selected (event) is raised by a power each time you move down a row. In the row for selection $n = 2$, the middle number in the row 1 2 1 is 2. This is obtained by summing $(1 + 1)$ from the row immediately above, row $n = 1$. This pattern can be extended indefinitely.

You should note, for a sample of n, there are $n + 1$ possible outcomes, i.e., if $n = 3$ there are 4 outcomes, 3 schools above the median, 2 schools above the median, 1 school above the median and 0 schools above the median. Also, the probability of each possible outcome is calculated by dividing the frequency of each outcome by the total number of possible outcomes. The probability of all outcomes sums to 1.

The last line of Figure 4.2 are the values of the PROBABILITY DISTRIBU-TION for the binomial variable with $n = 3$ and $p = 0.5$. It is analogous to the relative frequency distribution, if we replace relative frequencies with probabilities. This distribution could be plotted as a bar chart with 'bars' proportional in area to the probabilities. The total area of all the bars would sum to 1 which is the sum of all the probabilities. If we extend Pascal's triangle to a sample of ten schools, the probability distribution is shown in Table 4.2

Table 4.2: Probability distribution for a binomial sample of n = 10 with p = 0.5

Distribution	10A	9A1B	8A2B	7A3B	6A4B	5A5B	4A6B	3A7B	2A8B	1A9B	10B
Frequency	1	10	45	120	210	252	210	120	45	10	1
n above median	10	9	8	7	6	5	4	3	2	1	0
Probability	0.001	0.010	0.044	0.117	0.205	0.246	0.205	0.117	0.044	0.010	0.001

[$(n + 1)$ outcomes = 11, and a total frequency of $2^{10} = 1024$]

To answer the question at the beginning of this example, 'Could it happen by chance that we obtain 3 schools in our sample that have above the national median pass rate?' We can see from Table 4.2 that the probability of obtaining 3 schools above the median is 0.117, or approximately 12 per cent. This suggests that if we have chosen a random sample then we would expect by chance, 12 schools in every 100 to lie above the population median. The question now arises, '*What is the critical probability level below which we cannot accept that the outcomes would be expected to arise by chance alone?*'

This brings us to the problem of statistical significance and p values. We will deal with this when discussing hypothesis testing but for now we will make do with the generally accepted convention that if we obtain a probability of less than 0.05, written as $p < 0.05$ ($<$ means less than), then the results are deemed to be statistically significant and not to have arisen by chance.

Since the observed probability $p = 0.117 > p = 0.05$ we conclude that it is reasonable that these data represent a random sample of schools. If we had observed either 8 or more schools above the median, or 8 or more schools below the median, we would conclude that it would have been very unlikely to have obtained this kind of distribution by chance. We could then say that the schools did not represent a random sample of schools from the population.

The Binomial Model

A general statistical model that describes the probability of the number of successes r in a sample of size n is given by,

$$p = {}^nC_r \times p^r \times (1 - p)^{n-r}$$ **Binomial Probability** – 4.1

where: ${}^nC_r$ = the binomial coefficient and generally refers to r successes in n trials (events). Assume that we had selected another sample of 10 schools and found 7 had a pass rate below the national median. Using the general notation, $r = 7$, $n = 10$, in notational form ${}^nC_r = {}^{10}C_7$. To keep the notation simple, we will call below the median a success. Success could be defined as any outcome of interest, such as count of deaths in dead/alive, count of passes in pass/fail or count of yes in yes/no.

p^r = probability of success, here 0.5, raised to the power of the number of successes over all trials. In this example, $p^r = 0.5^7$

$(1 - p)^{n-r} = 1$ – probability of success in any trial, raised to the power of number of trials less number of successes. In this example, $(1 - p)^{n-r} = 0.5^{10-3}$

To answer the question 'Could it happen by chance that we obtain 7 schools in our sample that have below the national median pass rate?' we need to recognize that the underlying statistical model is a binomial model and evaluate formula 4.1:

$${}^{10}C_7 \times 0.5^7 \times 0.5^{10-3}$$

The first term is a combinatorial, ${}^nC_r$, that is the number of combinations of n things taken r at a time. This term is also known as the **binomial coefficient**. It is defined by,

$$\frac{n!}{r!(n-r)!}$$

where $n!$ is n factorial which is the product of all integers from 1 to n (note $0! = 1$ as does $1!$). We can now evaluate the binomial probability using formulae 4.1:

$$= \frac{10!}{7! \times 3!} \times (0.5^7) \times (0.5^3)$$

$$= \frac{10 \times 9 \times 8 \times 7!}{7! \times 3 \times 2 \times 1} \times (0.5^{10})$$

$= 10 \times 3 \times 4 \times 0.000976$ (7! cancels, 3 and 2 cancel)

$= 0.117$

We can say that the probability of choosing, at random, 7 schools out of 10 below the national median is 0.117. We can check this against the value derived from Pascal's triangle shown in Table 4.1.

Use of the Binomial Distribution in Research

Any data which is discrete and can be coded 0 or 1 such as success or failure, follow a binomial distribution provided the underlying probability of a success, π, does not change over the number of trials, n. Whereas the probability distribution is symmetric for a fixed sample size when $\pi = 0.5$, if π changes, for example, it reduces, the distribution also changes shape (it would become positively skewed). Knowing the underlying distribution of a discrete variable means we can estimate values and test hypotheses. Data in the form of frequencies, proportions or percentages is very common in education and psychological research and the variability of these sample statistics is very important in estimation and inference. Typically the kinds of questions a researcher might want to ask include:

'How much confidence can we have that a sample frequency or proportion represents the actual proportion in the population of interest?'

'Does the outcome of interest, such as number of successes, number surviving, pass rate or number of correct choices differ from what we would expect by chance?'

'Are the proportions of male and female truants in a school the same?'

Mean and Standard Deviation of a Binomial Variable

When a discrete random variable is a count of the successes in n independent trials which each have the same probability of success, we use the term **binomial variable**. We should realize that a binomial variable is a random variable or a statistic that is a count and therefore has a sampling distribution or probability distribution. For every count there is an associated probability. Just like distributions of variables described in Chapter 3 a binomial variable has a mean and a standard deviation. If we designate the count, X, of a binomial variable from a binomial population, in notational form $B(n,\pi)$, then the mean of the binomial variable is given by,

$$\mu_X = n\pi \qquad \textbf{Mean of a Binomial Variable} - 4.2$$

and the standard deviation is,

$$\sigma_X = \sqrt{n\pi(1 - \pi)} \qquad \textbf{Standard Deviation of a Binomial Variable} - 4.3$$

When π is not known it is estimated from the sample data as the number of successes divided by the number of trials. It is simply a proportion, $P = X/n$, where X is the count for the binomial variable and n is the number of trials or observations.

Example 4.3:   Mean and Standard Deviation of a Binomial Variable

The probability of a secondary school having an unauthorized absence rate $> 1\%$ is about $\pi = 0.5$. This is known *a priori*, based on Department for Education figures for the previous year. If we plan to select a simple random sample of 500 secondary schools, what will be the expected mean and standard deviation of the number of schools with unauthorized absence rates $> 1\%$?

An appropriate statistical model is the binomial probability model. Each school has a probability of 0.5 and the binomial population from which the sample is selected is B(500,0.5). The mean number of schools is evaluated using equation 4.2 for the mean of a binomial variable.

$$\mu_x = n\pi = (500).(0.5) = 250$$

We would expect to find 250 schools in our sample with unauthorized absence rates $> 1\%$, and using equation 4.3, the standard deviation would be:

$$\sigma_X = \sqrt{n\pi(1 - \pi)} = \sqrt{(500) \times (0.5) \times (0.5)} = 11.18$$

Sample Proportions and Percentages

Proportions and percentages are common in education and psychological research and the sampling distributions of these statistics allow researchers to make statistical inferences about proportions and percentages in the population.

Example 4.4:   Sample Proportions and the Binomial Distribution

Consider pupil performance on interpreting graphs. Swatton and Taylor (1994) report that 30 per cent (total $n = 60$) of age 11 pupils cannot correctly interpret graphs in which minor grid lines represent values other than 1 or 10.

Should we wish to estimate the proportion of age 11 pupils in the population who can not correctly interpret graphs with complex scales, that is estimate the proportion of 'successes' in the population, then we can use the binomial probability distribution provided we make a minor change to the data. In this example, do not confuse the term 'success' which relates to 'successes' & 'failures' in a binomial sample, with the idea of success meaning to be able to interpret graphs with minor grid lines.

A sample proportion does not have a binomial distribution because it is not a count. To estimate π, the proportion of 'successes' in the population, we simply restate the reported sample percentage as a count and use the sample proportion ($P = \text{count}/n$) as an estimator of π. The sample proportion, P is an unbiased estimator of the population proportion, π. More precisely, the mean of a sample proportion, μ_p of 'successes', say those children who can not interpret graphs, equals the population proportion of 'successes', π.

The population proportion, π, who can not correctly interpret graphs with complex scales is estimated by the observed proportion, $P = 18/60 = 0.3$. If the 60 pupils in the study are a simple random sample of age 11 pupils, then on average, we would expect 30 per cent of the population not to be able to interpret complex scales on graphs.

How confident should we be with the precision of this estimate?

To answer this question we turn to consideration of standard errors and confidence intervals, these are discussed in the next section.

4.5 From Sample to Population

Standard Errors

The standard deviation of a sampling distribution of a statistic is the **standard error** of that statistic. It follows that the standard deviation of the sampling distribution of a proportion is called the **standard error of a proportion**, represented as σ_p. Just as the sample proportion, P, is an unbiased estimator of the population proportion (π), the standard deviation of a sampling distribution of a proportion, $S_{(p)}$, is used to estimate the standard error of a population proportion, σ_p. The standard error of a statistic is an index of the precision of a parameter estimate.

The standard error of a proportion is evaluated as:

$$\sigma_p = \sqrt{\frac{P(1-P)}{n}} \qquad \text{\textbf{Standard Error of a Proportion} – 4.4}$$

Where P is the proportion of interest and n is the sample size.

Example 4.5:   Standard Error of a Proportion

The standard error of the observed sample proportion of age 11 pupils who cannot correctly interpret graphs with complex scales (see Example 4.4) is;

$$\sigma_p = S_p = \sqrt{\frac{P(1-P)}{n}} = \sqrt{\frac{(0.3)(1-0.3)}{60}} = 0.059$$

The standard error is an index of precision, that is an indication of the amount of error that results when a single sample statistic, here a proportion, is used to estimate the corresponding population parameter. The larger the standard error the less precise is an estimate. The standard error is related to both sample size and heterogeneity in the population. Larger sample sizes reduce the standard error; we divide by a larger denominator in equation 4.4. Greater heterogeneity in the population, that is a larger variance, increases the standard error. In this example, as the proportion of successes approaches 0.5, the numerator in equation 4.4 increases, thereby increasing the size of the standard error. As the population becomes more homogeneous, i.e., P tends towards 0 or 1, then sampling variability will reduce.

In planning a study consideration should be give to both sample size and the variances of important variables.

There is often confusion about whether a standard deviation or a standard error should be reported. This confusion generally stems from misunderstanding what a standard error is. The sample standard deviation is a measure of spread of raw scores and should therefore be reported, with the mean, when the purpose is to describe a data distribution. The standard error is an index of the precision of an estimated parameter and should be reported when the aim is to compare parameter estimates e.g., when comparing means for different treatment effects. You should put standard error bars and not standard deviation bars on a graph which compares treatment means.

Confidence Intervals

Estimation is when a sample statistic is used to estimate a population parameter; this is sometimes called **point estimation**. A **confidence interval** (CI) defines a range of values within which the parameter is likely to be found, this may be referred to as **interval estimation**. It is important to realize that it is the parameter which is fixed and the confidence interval which might vary from sample to sample. The idea of confidence is the proposition that the stated interval actually includes the population parameter of interest. A common confidence interval is the 95 per cent interval. We would expect the 95 per cent confidence interval, written as $CI_{0.95}$, to encompass the estimated parameter 95 times out of 100. We can also evaluate confidence intervals for the difference between two parameters, for example, the difference between two means.

In general a 95 per cent CI is defined as:

sample statistic $- 1.96 \times$ standard   to   sample statistic $+ 1.96 \times$ standard
error of statistic   error of statistic

The formula therefore for a $CI_{0.95}$ of a proportion is:

$$P - 1.96 \times \sqrt{\frac{P(1-P)}{n}} \quad \text{to} \quad P + 1.96 \times \sqrt{\frac{P(1-P)}{n}}$$

$CI_{0.95}$ **for a Proportion** – 4.5

Example 4.6: $CI_{0.95}$ **for a Proportion**

The $CI_{0.95}$ for the proportion of age 11 pupils who cannot correctly interpret graphs with complex scales, see Example 4.3, is;

$$0.3 - 1.96 \times \sqrt{\frac{0.3(0.7)}{60}} \quad \text{to} \quad 0.3 + 1.96 \times \sqrt{\frac{0.3(0.7)}{60}}$$

This gives a 95 per cent confidence interval for the population proportion π as 0.18 to 0.42, that is from 18 to 42 per cent. You may think this is rather a wide range for the possible values of π. To narrow the range a larger sample size would be required.

In the author's paper standard errors were not reported. When you evaluate a confidence interval you are in a better position to make a judgment about the author's conclusions. You should read the article for yourself.

In the previous example, individual pupils can either interpret graphs or they cannot. If they can, they are given a score of 1, and if they cannot, a score of 0.

Why then do individuals always have a score (1 or 0) which lies outside the 95 per cent confidence intervals of 0.18 to 0.42?

We should not forget that the confidence interval represents the probable limits around an AVERAGE number of pupils who can perform the task. We interpret the 95 per cent CI as inferring that if another random sample of sixty pupils were to complete the graphical task, then this sample would have an average proportion of success in the confidence interval 0.18 to 0.42.

You should be aware of one small problem when estimating confidence intervals for a discrete random variable. When the underlying distribution is binomial, probabilities of events can only change one whole unit at a time. Interpretation of the confidence intervals, however, is on a continuous scale. This does not present a problem when samples are large, that is when $n > 30$ or when the minimum value of P or $1 - P \leqslant 0.10$. With smaller samples a **correction for continuity**, $1/2n$ should be applied;

$$P - 1/2n + 1.96 \times \sqrt{\frac{P(1-P)}{n}} \qquad \text{to} \qquad P + 1/2n + 1.96 \times \sqrt{\frac{P(1-P)}{n}}$$

$CI_{0.95}$ for a proportion
with continuity correction – 4.6

This chapter has been 'heavy going' so we will pause at this point to sum up. If you have followed the story so far you will have an understanding of the tricky ideas of probability and statistical inference and how they relate to research design and statistical analysis. The next section extends these ideas to continuous distributions and introduces the formal procedure of hypothesis testing.

To summarize so far:

1   Data are summarized by statistics such as means, standard deviations, counts, percentages and proportions. Statistics are stochastic or random variables, provided data on which they are based have been generated by a random process.

2   Statistics can be considered to be random variables which follow the laws of probability. The variability of a sample statistic is shown in the sampling distribution of that statistic. Empirically, this is obtained by calculating the statistic for many samples of a fixed size, drawn at random from a specified population. In practice, with a finite population, the sampling distribution is described by a theoretical probability model.

3   The sampling distribution of a statistic is the link between probability and inference.

4 The sampling distribution of a statistic, just like a sample distribution of observations, has a mean and variance. The standard deviation of the distribution of a statistic is known as the standard error.

5 Sample statistics can be used to estimate corresponding population parameters. An index of the precision of the estimation is given by the standard error of the statistic. Standard errors are also used in calculating test statistics.

6 The 95 per cent confidence interval captures the true population parameter for 95 simple random samples out of a hundred (assuming the same *n* for each sample).

7 You cannot be certain of estimating a population parameter, the 95 per cent CI is not 100 per cent. There is a 5 per cent chance that the parameter of interest is not captured by the $CI_{0.95}$.

4.6 Continuous Random Variables

A continuous random variable denoted as *X*, can take any value in a range depending upon the sensitivity of the measuring instrument. A continuous probability distribution represents the distribution of probabilities assigned to an interval of a continuous random variable. The idea of a discrete probability distribution where the distribution can be represented by a bar chart, with each bar of unit width, and the height of bars representing the probability of outcomes for the discrete random variable, can be extended to a situation where the random variable is continuous. If you could imagine having a large number of bars with the mid-point of the top of each bar joined, then as the number of bars increases towards infinity, the line joining the tops of the bars would approximate closer and closer to a smooth continuous curve. As we near infinity the curve becomes a **normal curve** that is the normal curve becomes the limit of the binomial distribution. The normal curve is a continuous probability distribution. Other examples of continuous probability distributions include; *F*, *t* and χ^2 distributions.

With a continuous probability distribution probabilities are assigned not to discrete outcomes but to an area under the density curve. This area equals the interval between two values of the continuous random variable.

Normal Distributions

Many random continuous variables in the social sciences have an approximate normal distribution in the population. For example, if distributions of measurements of a person's height, weight and reaction times are plotted, they would approximate to a normal curve. Some psychological and achievement measures are specifically designed to have a normal distribution, for example, IQ and standardized achievement tests.

We can think of a normal distribution as either a model describing a probability distribution for a defined population or an empirically determined distribution.

The normal curve, more correctly termed a normal probability distribution, is important not only because many variables of interest are assumed to be normally distributed in the population, but also many statistical test procedures are based on the assumption of normality – *t*-test, *F*-test, and Pearson correlation. The sampling distributions of a wide range of descriptive and test statistics have a normal probability distribution. There is a probability theory in statistics called the **Central Limit Theorem** which describes the sampling distribution of the mean. The theorem states that as the size of a sample increases, the shape of the sampling distribution approaches normal *whatever* the shape of the parent population. The significance of this important theory is that it allows us to use the normal probability distribution even with sample means from populations which do not have a normal distribution. For example, binomial samples (counts, such as true/false) and proportions approximate a normal probability distribution when the sample sizes are large.

We can think of a normal distribution as a mathematical description of an idealized population with the following important characteristics:

- It is so large that for practical purposes it can be regarded as unlimited in size.
- Measurements must be on an interval or ratio scale and have at least an underlying theoretical continuous distribution.
- Values are symmetrically distributed about the mean.
- Values close to the mean occur relatively more frequently than those further away, the frequency falling off to a well defined bell-shaped curve.
- Measurement units can be standardized in terms of **standard deviation units** (measurement of spread about the mean) sometimes called Z-scores.
- About 68 per cent (68.26 per cent) of the measures in a normal distribution lie between −1.0 and +1.0 SD below and above the mean respectively. The mean is 0 if measures are standardized.
- About 95 per cent (95.44 per cent) of measures lie between −2 and +2 SDs below and above the mean.
- About 99 per cent (99.74 per cent) of measures lie between −3 and +3 SDs below and above the mean.

A common belief is that there is one normal curve. This is not so. There are many different normal curves, each particular one described by specifying two parameters, where the curve is centred, that is the mean μ, and how much the distribution spreads out about its centre, σ, the standard deviation. With a specified mean and standard deviation, the *probability* that a random continuous variable, X, with a particular value falls in a defined interval on the X axis, is equal to the area under the normal density curve. The vertical axis, is referred to as density, and is related to the frequency or probability of occurrence of the variable X.

The value of the mean μ, is the particular value on the X axis lying directly below the centre of the distribution. The value of the standard deviation σ, is at the point of inflection (where a curve turns up, if previous it was down) on the X axis.

Whenever we try to construct a table of normal distribution densities (probability values falling within a defined range) we have a problem because each normal distribution is dependent upon the particular μ and σ of the defining distribution. Rather than tabulate separate tables for each possible combination of μ and σ, statisticians have chosen a particular normal curve as a reference curve. This is the **standard normal** or Z **curve**. The normal distribution Z scores and associated probability values are shown in Table 1, Appendix A4. It has a mean μ of 0 and a σ standard deviation and variance of 1. In notation this is $N(0,1)$ where N refers to Normal and $0 = \mu$ and $1 = \sigma$. This may also be written as $N(\mu,\sigma^2)$.

Example 4.7:   Use of the Standard Normal Distribution to Describe Probabilities of Events

The following is the distribution of pulse rate for males in the author's statistics classes see Figure 4.3. The average pulse rate is 72 and the standard deviation is 12. For this example, consider these values to represent the population of all male students at the University of Manchester. We can use the sample mean and standard deviation to estimate the corresponding population parameters.

We want to know the probability of observing a male with a pulse rate of 96 or more, and the probability of observing a male student's pulse rate of 105 or more?

The standard normal distribution can be used to answer questions like those above. We would proceed by first transforming the distribution of pulse rate scores to a standard normal distribution, so we can use the normal deviate or Z tables. We want to be able to say that a score x_i from $N(72,144)$ is comparable to a score Z_i from $N(0,1)$.

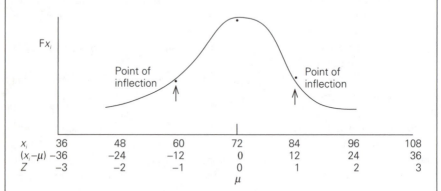

x_i	36	48	60	72	84	96	108
$(x_i-\mu)$	−36	−24	−12	0	12	24	36
Z	−3	−2	−1	0	1	2	3

Figure 4.3: Distribution of male pulse rates

We can use a linear transformation, that is subtract a constant from each score and divide by a constant. Look at the second row of scores $(x_i-\mu)$ in Figure 4.3. This distribution has a mean of zero. This distribution is transformed into a Z distribution by dividing $(x_i-\mu)$ by the σ of the original distribution.

$$Z = \frac{(x_i - \mu)}{\sigma}$$

Equation for Z score or deviate – 4.7

For a pulse rate of 84 then, $Z = (84 - 72)/12 = 1$.
For a pulse rate of 72 then, $Z = (72 - 72)/12 = 0$.

A linear transformation does not alter the shape of a distribution, that is the observations remain in the same relative position to each other. Therefore, if the shape of the distribution was not normal to begin with then the Z transformation will not normalize (in the sense of producing a normal distribution) the data.

The total area under the standard normal curve is 1 and that areas under the curve translate to probabilities. To find the area under the normal curve that is above two standard deviations, we would look for the area above $Z = 2$.

To answer the first question in Example 4.7, the probability of observing a male with a pulse rate of 96 or more, first convert 96 to a Z score giving the value +2.0 then go to the table of the normal distribution (Table 1, Appendix A4), and find the column headed Z. Move down this column until the value 2.0 is reached. Go along the row until under the column headed .00 (Z to two decimal places), the value is $p = 0.0228$. This means that 2.28 per cent of the area under the curve is beyond the Z value of 2, that is above two standard deviations. The larger portion to the left of Z comprises 97.72 per cent of the area under the normal curve. The probability of observing a pulse rate of 96 or more is therefore $p = 0.0228$.

To answer the second question, that is to find the probability of observing a pulse rate of 105 or more, we again transform this score into a Z score, $= 2.75$, and look up this value in the body of the normal distribution Table (Table 1, Appendix A4). The answer is $p = 0.0030$. The probability is very small, $p < .05$ (5 per cent). In fact, a Z score of only 1.65 would be needed to give a probability of $p < .05$. We would conclude that the male with a pulse rate of 105 is unlikely to have come from the same population of males because it is so different from the population mean of 72.

A Z score or standard score indicates where any particular score lies in relation to the mean score of its distribution. We can convert any raw score, x_i, into a Z score, all that is required is the mean and standard deviation of the distribution of scores. A Z score will show a score's relative position above or below the mean of a distribution of scores. Z scores may have negative values, namely all those below the mean. Since the normal distribution is symmetrical we can use it to evaluate negative Z scores. For example, the probability of a Z score < -2 is equivalent to the probability of a Z score of > 2, namely 0.0228.

Example 4.8:   Transforming Raw Scores into Z Scores

As part of a selection procedure a company requires graduates to take three tests consisting of Test 1, Numeracy; Test 2, Computer Programming Aptitude; and Test 3, Verbal Reasoning. Given the following test results for a candidate, and assuming a normal distribution for each of the test scores with mean and standard deviation given below, on which of the three tests did the candidate do best?

	Raw Score	Mean	S.D.
Test 1	22	12	4
Test 2	42	30	5
Test 3	110	100	15

The best score is on the numeracy test, (test 1) $Z = +2.5$

Example 4.9:   Setting Probable Limits Using Z

Rather than a tail area we may be interested in both directions of the distribution. If we wanted to know what are the pulse levels that are likely to be either larger or smaller than the values, we would expect for 95 per cent of all males sampled? Call these values the Lower and Upper probable limits. This is equivalent to finding the Z values for 5 per cent (100 per cent–95 per cent) of cases at the extremes of the distribution. By symmetry half of the area must be in each tail so we actually need the Z values for $p = 0.025$. The Z values are −1.96 and +1.96. You should check these values in Table 1, Appendix A.

These values can now be transformed into pulse rates by use of Equation 4.7 to determine a Z score.

$$-1.96 = \frac{\text{Lower limit} - 72}{12}$$

$$+1.96 = \frac{\text{Upper limit} - 72}{12}$$

Lower limit = $(12)(-1.96) + 72 = 48.48$

Upper Limit = $(12)(+1.96) + 72 = 95.52$

In other words, the upper and lower limits within which 95 per cent of male pulse rates would fall is between 48 and 96.

Probable Limits and Confidence Intervals

You should not confuse describing probable limits for an observation with the 95 per cent confidence interval of a sampling distribution. The former is concerned with locating the limits within which 95 per cent of **observations** fall and is descriptive. Confidence intervals are concerned with estimating unknown parameters and are inferential.

4.7   Hypothesis Testing

Another important use of the normal distribution is when testing hypotheses. We can test hypotheses about observations or statistics. If you have understood how the concepts of statistics, parameters and sampling distributions are used in estimation you should find the logic of hypothesis testing not too demanding. The thinking underpinning the logic of hypothesis testing is best illustrated with a specific example.

Example 4.10: Hypothesis Test about Proportions

Teachers in a Local Education Authority claim that the Authority is saving money by limiting the number of statemented children. They believe that the proportion of referrals that result in statements (an obligation for the Authority to provide special provision for a child) has reduced drastically and is now lower than the national average. As principal psychologist, you are sceptical about the teachers' claims and decide to investigate them.

You believe that the number of statements issued would have been much higher than they were if it were not for the new policy of supporting ordinary schools and thereby increasing their capability to manage pupils who have special needs.

Your working assumption is that the proportion of referrals that lead to statements will be no different from the national average. According to the Audit Commission Report, *Getting in on the Act*, in England and Wales about 13 per cent of referrals result in a statement being issued (Audit Commission Report, 1992). You decide to take a simple random sample of referrals over the last two years and identify the proportion that have resulted in statements being issued. The figure you obtain is 10.92 per cent.

The research question that you want to answer is: 'Is the proportion of referrals leading to statements in the local education authority statistically less than the proportion nationally (13 per cent)?' You begin the statistical investigation with a proposition or **hypothesis**; The proportion of referrals leading to statements in the LEA is equal to 13 per cent (the national figure).

This is a hypothesis of no difference, that is the proportion of referrals leading to statements in the LEA is the same as the national proportion. The hypothesis of no difference is also called a **null hypothesis** or a **statistical hypothesis**. The null hypothesis is a statement about the value of the parameter, π for the LEA population. If the null hypothesis is true, then the proportion of referrals leading to statements in the LEA would be the same as that throughout England and Wales. The null hypothesis is not usually explained in words in research journals, rather a special notation is used: H_0.

The **statistical** or **null hypothesis** is held to be tenable until such times as data collected from a sample yields results which suggest that it is no longer reasonable to believe the null hypothesis. Clearly there is a true value for π, the proportion of referrals leading to statements in the LEA and if the **null hypothesis** is true, this true value would equal 13 per cent. If the null hypothesis is not true, then the laws of logic suggest that π for the LEA population proportion of statements must equal some other value. Put another way if the null hypothesis is not true then some other **alternative hypothesis** must be true, the problem is we cannot know precisely what this alternative is. All we can say is that it is not 13 per cent.

Thus far three important ideas in hypothesis testing have been introduced. The statistical or null hypothesis of no difference, the alternative hypothesis, and the logic

---

> that connects them both. The law of logic says that if the null hypothesis is not true then some alternative hypothesis must be true.

You may be thinking, why do researchers use such a circuitous procedure when testing a hypothesis? That is why, when the question of real interest is the alternative hypothesis, do we pretend to believe its opposite, the null hypothesis, and hope this can be refuted so that we are then able to consider the alternate hypothesis as tenable? Put simply, why not test the alternative hypothesis directly?

There are at least three answers to these questions. Statisticians generally are very cautious and have over the years developed a tried-and-tested approach to making inferences about a population of interest. They work with the idea of a null hypothesis which describes the possible situation in the population. The accepted and proven convention is to assume that there is no difference between two parameters and to uphold this belief until we can provide evidence that it is no longer tenable. This indirect approach has worked well in the past and so it is used now.

A second and more brief answer is that the statistical inferences cannot prove anything, they can only provide evidence, in the form of probabilities, that a proposition is not reasonable. A third answer is that if we test the alternative hypothesis directly we would be in danger of selectivity, testing hypotheses which fit in with our thinking. That is certain evidence would fit in with our thinking and support our selected alternative hypothesis. In this situation negative evidence would have no effect because absence of proof (i.e., we don't test the hypotheses that are inconsistent with our beliefs) is not the same as proof of absence. Moreover logic would suggest that it is virtually impossible to prove absence of anything. The perceived wisdom is that it is better to assume absence of proof, i.e., null hypothesis, until we have positive evidence.

p-values and Statistical Significance

Statistical tests provide probabilities or p-values for test statistics. These probabilities indicate the likelihood that obtained results are chance differences or are significant differences. Results are interpreted by researchers as being statistically significant when differences between treatments or test scores are greater than would be expected by sampling error – a difference that is not attributable to chance alone. By convention, p-values that are less than 0.05 are generally regarded as statistically significant. A p-value of ≤ 0.05 derived from a statistical test represents the chance of observing the results (or more extreme results and consequent rejection of the null hypothesis), given that the null hypothesis is true. Recall we test the null hypothesis and this is why it is sometimes called the statistical hypothesis.

When we state that results are significant at $p \leq 0.05$ this implies that the conditional probability of obtaining such results simply by chance (given that H_0 is true) is less than or equal to 1 in 20 (or 5 in 100 – 5 per cent). In education and psychology by convention odds of 1 in 20 ($p \leq 0.05$) or 1 in 100 ($p \leq 0.01$) are used as the basis for rejecting a null hypothesis.

What p-values should count as significant is up to the researcher although there are conventions of 5 per cent and 1 per cent significance. The level of statistical significance selected by a researcher, called the ALPHA level, α, (usually 5 per cent or 1 per cent) should be distinguished from the p-value associated with a test statistic. This sometimes causes confusion when statistical packages are used because they often report the actual p-value for a statistical test rather than $p \leq 0.05$ or $p \leq 0.01$. The alpha level of significance chosen by the researcher, before the statistical hypothesis is tested, is compared with the p-value derived from the statistical test. If the obtained p-value for the statistical test is less than or equal to the chosen alpha level then the null hypothesis is rejected and the results are said to be significant at the chosen alpha level. You should remember that even when we say a result is statistically significant at the 1 per cent level, there remains a possibility that the result is a chance result, we are only 99 per cent certain and not 100 per cent certain.

It is this author's view that too much emphasis is placed on the use of p-values when testing hypotheses and publishing results. Statistical significance does not equate with educational or clinical significance. Moreover, the magnitude of any differences (or effect size – this is referred to in Chapter 5) is likely to be more informative than whether results are significant or not significant. An alternative strategy to simply reporting p-values as significant or not significant, is to use and report confidence intervals alongside p-values.

A confidence interval provides a range of plausible values in which the parameter of interest lies. Just as we can calculate a $CI_{0.95}$ for a parameter, recall in Example 4.6 we estimated $CI_{0.95}$ for the proportion of age 11 pupils who cannot correctly interpret graphs with complex scales, so it is possible to calculate a $CI_{0.95}$ for the difference between two sample proportions (which is the best estimate of the population difference in proportions). Just as the 5 per cent level of significance is generally used, so the $CI_{0.95}$ is commonly used although alternative confidence intervals can be constructed, for example, $CI_{0.99}$. When reporting results of hypothesis tests using confidence intervals the following should be included: sample estimates, confidence intervals, test statistics and associated degrees of freedom, and associated p-values. If a confidence interval of a difference excludes zero then this is evidence of a significant difference and will coincide with a significant p-value. The advantage of reporting a confidence interval is that it conveys a range of values for the population difference although the actual population difference is likely to be near the centre of the confidence interval. For an informative introduction to testing hypotheses using confidence intervals with worked examples, the reader is referred to Gardner and Altman's (1989) text *Statistics with Confidence*.

You may wonder why discuss hypothesis testing and p-values if confidence intervals are more appropriate? The answer is simple, reporting of p-values is so common that you need to grasp the fundamental idea to be able to evaluate reports and papers. Throughout the remaining chapters on inferential statistical procedures, in addition to p-values, wherever appropriate confidence intervals will also be used.

One-tailed and Two-tailed Significance Tests

The null hypothesis is always contrasted with an alternative frame of reference, called the **alternative hypothesis** (sometimes called the **research hypothesis**). This has the special notation H_1. Statistical significance tests can be either one-tailed or two-tailed depending on the nature of the alternative hypothesis. Consider the proportion of referrals that result in statements (Example 4.10), the null hypothesis is:

H_0: $P = \pi = 0.130$ (null hypothesis, P is the sample proportion)

Can you state three alternative hypotheses?

The three possible alternatives are:

- $H_1 : P \neq \pi$ (LEA proportion of statements is not equal to ($\neq$) the proportion in England and Wales)
- $H_1 : P > \pi$ (LEA proportion of statements is greater than ($>$) the proportion in England and Wales)
- $H_1 : P < \pi$ (LEA proportion of statements is less than ($<$) the proportion in England and Wales)

The first alternative hypothesis reflects the situation when a researcher is interested in testing whether the proportion of referrals is different from the national proportion, either less than or greater than. This is a two-tailed test because consideration is given to proportions both less than 0.130 (π) and greater than 0.130.

This last alternative reflects the teachers' opinions; they were concerned about the LEA proportion of referrals being *less than* the proportion in England and Wales. If the researcher were to just consider this possibility, $P < 0.130$, this would represent a one-tailed test since there would be no interest in values of $P > 0.130$.

Generally it is this author's advice not to use one-tailed tests unless there are compelling reasons to do so. The reason is that it is easy to introduce bias by making a choice prior to testing a hypothesis. The intention of hypothesis testing is not to test what is expected but to identify what is plausibly not true.

The idea of hypothesis testing is so important in quantitative research design and analysis that at this point it is helpful to pause and to recap the logic underpinning this approach. The idea is that we test for a statistically significant difference between two or more population parameters. Sample statistics are used as estimators and this explains why a null hypothesis may be stated as, 'there is no difference between sample A and sample B' or 'treatment C and treatment D are equally effective' or 'the proportion for the LEA is no different from the proportion for England and Wales'. Although we may be comparing sample statistics or a sample statistic with a known population parameter you should remember that a null hypothesis is a hypothesis about the situation in the population hence the importance of statistical inference, probability and sampling distributions.

In summary, the general approach to hypothesis testing is based on inference and is a way of deciding whether data are consistent with a null hypothesis. The usual steps in testing a statistical hypothesis are:

1 State the null and alternative hypotheses.
2 Decide whether a one- or two-sided (tailed) test is appropriate and state the significance level, alpha, of the test. Alpha is the level of probability for rejection of the null hypothesis, usually in social sciences $p \leqslant .05$). A one-sided test means that you are only concerned with one tail of the sampling distribution.
3 Calculate a **test statistic** and confidence interval from the data obtained in a sample.
4 Report whether the selected confidence interval excludes zero and compare the probability value associated with the test statistic with the chosen alpha level (e.g., $p \leqslant .05$). If the obtained p-value for the test statistic is less than or equal to alpha then this is evidence that the data are **not consistent** with the null hypothesis (the confidence interval will also exclude zero). You reject the null hypothesis and conclude that an alternative hypothesis is feasible. If the p-value associated with the test statistic is greater than alpha, then it is not reasonable to reject the null hypothesis and it remains tenable (the confidence interval will include zero).

4.8 Errors in Decision Making

Whenever we test a hypothesis we make a decision, either we make a decision to reject the null hypothesis or not to reject it. Consider, for example, a simple treatment effectiveness design where we have two groups, a treatment group – the reading recovery programme and a comparison group – with no special intervention. Further assume that the response variable of interest, reading score, is treated as a continuous variable. We could determine the effectiveness of the programme by comparing mean reading scores for the treatment and comparison groups. The null hypothesis we would tests is:

H_0: $\mu_t = \mu_c$

Type I Error

Suppose the population means really do not differ. In this case the null hypothesis would be true. If we performed a statistical test of the difference between two means, the correct finding would be to *fail to reject H_0* – we say we failed to attain significance in the statistical test at a given probability level. We conclude that it is tenable, the population means for the treatment and comparison groups do not differ. Put simply, the reading recovery programme had no beneficial effects. In reaching this conclusion the decision was that we failed to reject H_0. However, it is possible that just by chance the sample means differed substantially. The difference between the sample means may have been sufficiently large to lead us to reject H_0 even though the null hypothesis is tenable ($\mu_t = \mu_c$). In this case we would have taken the wrong decision or made an error in our decision making. If you reject the null hypothesis when you should not, that is, you conclude from a statistical test of the sample data that population means differ, (reject this null hypothesis) when in reality the population do not differ, you make what is called a **Type I Error**.

This idea is so important in hypothesis testing that we need to spend time thinking about it. Putting the same concept another way may help. If in reality the population means do not differ, H_0: $\mu_t = \mu_c$, the null hypothesis is true, then there is only one error that could be made in these circumstances.

What is it?

The *error* is to *incorrectly* reject a *true* null hypothesis, and conclude wrongly from the statistical test that the population means do differ. We make a **Type I Error**.

If a mistake is made it is in the decision making based on results of a statistical test of the null hypothesis. It is not a matter of probability whether population means actually differ – either they do or they do not (if we could access the entire population we could determine the parameters of interest and would not need a statistical test). A Type I error: occurs when the decision is to reject the null hypothesis when it is actually true. Diagrammatically this is shown in Figure 4.4. The significance level (p-value) chosen by a researcher equals the probability of making a Type I error, that is when the results of a statistical test lead to rejection of the null hypothesis given that the null hypothesis is true. The selected probability (or alpha level) is in fact a conditional probability. For discussion of this point see Dracup (1995).

Population Circumstances

Conclusion from statistical test:	Population means differ, i.e., H_0 is not true	Population means do not differ, i.e., H_0 is true
Significant difference (REJECT H_0)	Correct decision Power $p = 1 - \beta$	Type I Error Researcher sets $p = \alpha$ (alpha)

Figure 4.4: Statistical power and Type I error

There are two notable features about Figure 4.4. The idea of **statistical power** is introduced and alpha (α) is defined as the probability of occurrence of a Type I error. The probability of a **Type I Error**, α, is set by the researcher (usually at p $\leq$ 0.05). It is under the direct control of the researcher. The **power** of a statistical test is the probability of detecting a true difference should one exist, or put another way the probability of rejecting a null hypothesis given that it is false. The statistical power is not set directly by the researcher rather it is related to the chosen α. As alpha increases so the power decreases and vice versa.

Type II Error

Another way a wrong decision could be made is to *fail* to *reject* a null hypothesis that is in fact *not true*. Suppose in reality, μ_t does not equal μ_c, that is the population means do differ. In this case we could make a **Type II Error** if we do not reject H_0. The probability of a Type II error is denoted by beta (β). This is shown in Figure 4.5:

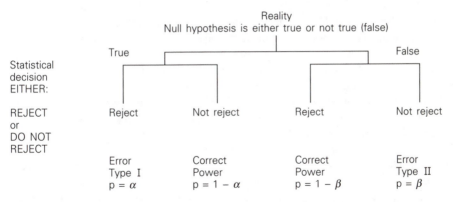

Population Circumstances

Conclusion from statistical test:	Population means differ, i.e., H_0 is not true	Population means do not differ, i.e., H_0 is true
No significant difference	Type II Error (Do not reject H_0) $p = \beta$	Correct decision $p = 1 - \alpha$

Figure 4.5: Type II error

The decision-making process following a statistical test of the null hypothesis is summarized in Figure 4.6:

Reality
Null hypothesis is either true or not true (false)

	True			False
Statistical decision EITHER:				
REJECT or DO NOT REJECT	Reject	Not reject	Reject	Not reject
	Error Type I $p = \alpha$	Correct Power $p = 1 - \alpha$	Correct Power $p = 1 - \beta$	Error Type II $p = \beta$

Figure 4.6: A summary of the possible outcomes of the decision-making process

4.9 Statistical Inference in Context

My reason for including this last section is to set the classic inferential, what may be called Fisherian (after the eminent statistician R.A. Fisher) hypothesis testing approach in the context of modern day use of statistics. The statistics of random sampling, survey and experimental design, probability theory, formal inference and test statistics, are what I call here, the Fisherian approach. The importance of this approach as Bartholomew (1995) notes is that much could be learned from little data provided attention was given to well designed studies. For this reason alone it is important that researchers should understand and be familiar with the Fisherian approach to statistical design and analysis and the debate that surrounds the different schools of inference.

Fisher Neyman-Pearson Debate

Statistical inference has a central role in hypothesis testing and thus far little reference has been made to different schools of inference. Fisher first put forward the idea that we can only show that a null hypothesis is likely to be false, we cannot prove that it is true. It follows from Fisher's reasoning that the only useful result is a significant result, i.e., rejection of the null hypothesis. In Fisher's view, a non-significant result, that is non-rejection of the null hypothesis, is of little value because there is not sufficient evidence to make a definitive decision (to reject the null hypothesis) therefore no decision should be taken until sufficient evidence (data) is available (to allow rejection of the null hypothesis). Put simply, Fisher's case would have been that decisions should be suspended until the null hypothesis can be rejected.

Neyman and Pearson adopted a more pragmatic approach to hypothesis testing. Their position was more action-oriented. They claimed that a null hypothesis should either be rejected or not rejected. The crucial difference between their approach and Fishers's position was that non-rejection should not imply suspended judgment and no consequent action. If the null hypothesis is deemed to be tenable, decisions should be taken as though the null hypothesis were true. Clearly, the consequences following a typical hypothesis test of the effectiveness of, for example, a reading recovery programme would depend upon whether a Fisherian or a Neyman-Pearson position were adopted. Should the null hypothesis of no difference between reading recovery intervention and control group not be rejected then from a Fisherian perspective no action would follow. There is not sufficient evidence to conclusively reject the null hypothesis and the intervention should therefore not be discontinued until there was sufficient evidence to reject the null hypothesis. From a Neyman-Pearson position, the intervention would be discontinued.

This debate presented here, in a somewhat simplified form, is essentially a debate about different schools of inference. However, it does illustrate the distinction between scientific and mathematical significance which is part of the long-standing tension in statistics between mathematics and applications (Efron, 1995).

Since the seminal work on inference in the 1930s by Fisher and Neyman-Pearson developments in experimental design, multivariate analysis and non-parametric procedures have advanced and spread into education and psychological research. However, the Fisherian approach is often not well suited to the analysis of many complex educational and psychological relationships which can be characterized as dynamic (as opposed to static) stochastic processes. Complex stochastic (statistical) models are required to model the complex social phenomena of the real world of schools, classrooms and learning environments; again advances have been made using approaches such as LISREL and Multilevel modelling.

More recent computational-intensive statistical techniques such as Logistic Regression, Gibbs Sampling, Jacknife and Bootstrap estimation procedures, to name a few, are procedures which are now available given the data handling capabilities of modern computers. However, these computer-intensive approaches are not well known and seldom used by educational researchers and have only recently been brought to the attention of psychologists (Robertson, 1991).

This section has provided the reader with a glimpse over the statistical horizon. Should one choose to begin this journey, a sound statistical grounding in the fundamentals of probability and inference is an essential prerequisite. Even if one is not interested in statistics *per se*, as social science researchers, basic numeracy and basic statistical awareness should form part of your tool kit as a competent researcher.

Summary

You should have by now a good grasp of the ideas of probability, inference and how they are used in estimation and hypothesis testing. This will equip you to tackle many statistical procedures. All that you need to determine when considering a statistical test are the following points:

- Choice of a possible underlying statistical model for the data:

  Ask yourself what are the important variables – are they random discrete or continuous variates?

- Consideration of the most appropriate test statistic:

  What aspect of the data am I interested in – mean, proportion, relationship?

- Identify the sampling distribution under the null hypothesis for the chosen test statistic:

  This is shown in statistical tables.

- Decide acceptable levels of probability for errors when drawing conclusions from a statistical test of the null hypothesis:

  Consider Type I and Type II errors.

- Consider whether the statistical test has sufficient power:

  Sample size, alpha, magnitude of effect that you want to detect, and variability of the statistical variable all affect statistical power.

In the next chapter we look more closely at choosing a statistical test and issues of statistical power.

Chapter 5

Choosing a Statistical Test

Having completed initial data analysis (IDA) you may now want to consider inferential statistical procedures. This stage of the analysis will be based on some kind
of probability model and will more than likely involve one or more statistical tests.
With a number of alternative statistical tests to choose from the new researcher is
often unsure about which test to use. A few general considerations will be presented first, then a strategy for choosing among the possible statistical tests will be
described and summarized in the form of a decision chart. Other considerations
such as statistical power and its relationship to statistical tests, alpha (Type I error),
sample size, effect size, and variance will be discussed, and the ubiquitous question
about sample size will be addressed. Examples of sample size and power calculations are presented. Finally, testing for normality of distributions is illustrated and
what to do when distributions are non-normal is considered.

5.1   General Considerations

The purpose of statistical inference and the use of statistical tests is to draw conclusions from sample data. When choosing a statistical test a number of matters
should be considered: how data was (will be) generated, the study design, measurement issues, distribution of response variable(s) in the population of interest, results
of IDA, specification of research questions and hypotheses to be tested, choice of
an underlying statistical model, specific statistical test assumptions. Regard should
also be given to statistical power and how this is related to the study design and
choice of statistical test(s). It is the author's belief that generally too much stress
is placed on hypothesis testing and the reporting of p-values (see comments in
Chapter 4). It is suggested, therefore, that emphasis be given to estimation and the
use of confidence intervals for reporting tests of significance (p-values should of
course also be reported).

How a Decision About Statistical Significance is Reached

Formal statistical inference used in hypothesis testing is based on probability theory.
A significance test is a test of a null hypothesis (hypothesis about population parameters), the strength of evidence against the null hypothesis is assessed using the

idea of probability. Probability theory is central to statistical inference and statistical tests because it enables the effect of chance variation to be accounted for in our decision making. Put simply, tests of significance are methods for assessing the strength against the null hypothesis and the strength of this evidence is given by the obtained p-value for the statistical test. The statistic that should be used in a hypothesis test or when estimating confidence intervals is the statistic that estimates the parameter of interest stated or implied in the null hypothesis.

Any particular parametric statistic will have a known sampling distribution. Possible values of the test statistic and associated probability of occurrence under the null hypothesis are usually tabulated in statistical tables. When data is analyzed and the computations yield a particular test statistic value, (sometimes referred to as the **observed test statistic**), this will have an associated probability of occurrence. This **observed probability** is compared with a pre-selected probability or alpha level, commonly called the **level of significance** of a test (generally 5% $p \leq .05$ or 1% $p \leq .01$).

Usually, if the observed probability, p, is $\leq$ the selected alpha level of probability (probability of making a Type I error, see Chapter 4) then the null hypothesis is rejected and statistical significance is attained. It is good practice to state confidence intervals, such as confidence intervals of a difference for a *t*-test, as well as the observed test statistic and associated probability level, and if appropriate, degrees of freedom.

As the formal process of inference is based on the sampling distribution of a chosen statistic, there should be an underlying statistical or probability model for the statistical test. For example, the normal probability distribution is a common statistical model that describes probability distributions of variables and is the basic probability model underlying a number of statistical tests. Statistical tests whose inferences are based on the normal distribution are called **parametric statistical procedures**. Inferences using parametric statistical procedures are only likely to be valid when *four* conditions are met:

- observations are independent;
- they are drawn randomly from a population;
- they have continuous levels of measurement (at least in theory);
- and the random errors associated with observations or measures have a known distribution, (usually normal).

The manner of sampling and level of measurement of variables in an empirical investigation therefore influences the validity of the underlying statistical model and hence the choice of statistical test. These three conditions mentioned above are a consequence of the **central limit theorem** (see Chapter 4).

Some statistical tests require that additional assumptions be met; these assumptions vary in number and degree. Moreover, there is much debate amongst statisticians as to the conditions under which particular assumptions are important. For example, amongst the most powerful statistical tests are the *t*- and *F*-tests. The *t*-test (for testing a hypothesis about the difference between two sample means) requires in addition to assumptions underlying the general parametric model, the condition that the populations from which the two samples are drawn should have similar variances (homogeneity of variances assumption, see *t*-test Chapter 8). Different statistical tests require different assumptions and the practical implications of these assumptions for research design and analysis are discussed in later chapters when each statistical test is introduced. Generally, the more extensive and the stronger the assumptions, the more powerful the statistical test. That is, the test is more likely to detect a true difference should one exist. (The statistical test is more likely to lead to rejection of the null hypothesis when it is false.)

What do we do if the general assumptions of the parametric model and or specific conditions of particular statistical tests are not met?

In the first instance we have to recognize when test assumptions are violated and be aware of the severity of the consequences of violating particular assumptions. This problem is dealt with in the sections describing particular test procedures. Assuming we believe distributional assumptions for a particular parametric test are not met then we can use other statistical test procedures called NONPARAMETRIC TESTS. These tests are sometimes called distribution-free tests because they do not make assumptions about the probability distribution of errors. These nonparametric tests have fewer and less restrictive assumptions. For example, when the underlying population distribution of a key variable is thought to be non-normal (i.e., when data is very skewed), or when measurement assumptions are not met, then a nonparametric test should be considered. The terms 'parametric' and 'nonparametric' are used in inconsistent ways (even among 'experts'). Nonparametric may refer to the use of statistical tests which make no assumptions about the distribution of errors (hence the term 'distribution free') or to the procedure of hypothesis testing based on distribution free inference (a hypothesis which does not make an assertion about a parameter). However, nonparametric test procedures are generally less powerful than comparable parametric tests (on average about 10–20 per cent less powerful). An alternative strategy to using nonparametric tests is to transform data to make it more normal. Procedures for checking normality of data distributions and transforming variables are discussed at the end of this chapter.

5.2 From IDA to Inferential Analysis

A quantitative study is often based on previous empirical studies and or theoretical considerations, either of which may suggest a possible class of statistical models for your data. The choice for the new researcher conducting his or her first study in education or psychology, is usually limited to three classes of models: the **general parametric model** based on the normal probability distribution, (associated parametric statistical tests might include *t*, *F*, Pearson *r*); the **binomial model** based on the binomial distribution (associated tests might include binomial and sign tests); and **distribution free procedures** (associated with nonparametric statistical tests). Other classes of models less frequently encountered include Poisson, Hypergeometric (discrete distributions) and Exponential, Gamma and Weibull (continuous distribution) models. These distributions and other complex multivariate and time series designs are beyond the scope of this text. The reader is referred to Manley (1986) for a non-mathematical introduction to multivariate statistical analysis and the text by Tabachnich & Fidell (1989) is an excellent practical guide to the use of multivariate analysis. A general introduction to time series designs is given by Chatfield (1984).

One purpose of IDA is, as Chatfield (1993) comments, 'to help you do a "proper" analysis "properly"' (p. 46). Even if a possible statistical model is identified *a priori* from previous theoretical or empirical considerations, IDA should be used to check the structure of the data and to identify whether variables are discrete or continuous and hence to confirm plausible underlying models, such as binomial, normal, bivariate normal (for correlations). It is good practice to use as much relevant data as possible and not to collapse variables and thereby transform them to lower levels of measurement.

Outlier observations can have a drastic effect on statistical tests. For example, *t*-tests are sensitive to extreme skewness and outlier observations especially with small sample sizes. When fitting data to a statistical model the effect of inclusion and exclusion of outliers should be checked.

Scatterplots of one variable against another will indicate, visually, the extent of relationship between two variables and whether it is linear (a straight line can be drawn through the cloud of points). Linearity is a necessary assumption for some statistical procedures, such as linear regression and correlation. Histograms and stem and leaf plots provide information on the distribution of variables and more sophisticated procedures for testing assumptions of normality, whether a variable is normally distributed in the population, are presented at the end of this chapter.

It is a common misunderstanding amongst new researchers that a criterion variable of interest has to be normally distributed in your achieved sample. For example, in a two sample *t*-test it is often believed that the criterion variable should be normally distributed in the two samples. This is not necessary. The general parametric model makes the assumption that the variable (or more accurately the errors) are distributed normally in the population (not necessarily in your sample). More important is homogeneity of variance in both samples.

Specific procedures for checking statistical test assumptions or more correctly, the assumptions underlying the probability model, are presented when use of the statistical procedures are introduced in the following chapters. For now it is sufficient to note that you should include checks for violations of assumptions in your inferential analysis. Checks on these assumptions can be considered as an extension of IDA and as a preliminary to inferential analysis. These checks usually take the form of residual plots. A residual represents the difference between an observed and an expected value based on the statistical model that is used.

Statistical test assumptions often have to be made by the reader in the absence of evidence presented by author(s). Given the robustness of parametric procedures this is not usually seen to be a problem. This view, however, is not without its critics and the issue of robustness is discussed in a later section. Regardless of whether or not you view many parametric tests as being robust, it is wise when interpreting results, to remember that the attained statistical significance (as stated in many articles and papers) is dependent upon the validity of the assumptions relating to the statistical model being used (not usually stated in journal papers). You should consider whether the underlying statistical model is appropriate, as well as the statistical power of the tests used. All too often assumptions are made implicitly which on closer scrutiny, for example, using IDA, would render the statistical tests invalid and the conclusions spurious. Examples that have appeared in the literature include: Reporting Pearson correlations when the relationship is clearly non-linear, or when variables are clearly categorical, reporting t-tests for independent samples when sample sizes are small, unequal and there are outlier observations. Another problem is performing statistical tests when they are simply not required. Perusal of the psychology and education periodicals indicates that it is rare for shape parameters (skewness and kurtosis) to be reported – a case of forgotten moments.

Results of the IDA will indicate when statistical tests are unnecessary. Typical situations would be when a whole population is assessed, when means of two large samples are identical, or when large samples of equal size have non-overlapping confidence intervals for the means when plotted. Other more critical situations would be when there was evidence of bias, outliers, and non-constant errors perhaps due to inadequate randomization or non-probability samples.

Generally one data set should not be used to both generate and test hypotheses. If the data set is of sufficient size it can be randomly partitioned into two equal data sets, a **training data set** and a **confirmatory data set**. The training set is used to generate hypotheses and the confirmatory set is used to test these hypotheses. It is always necessary to be aware that statistical significance does not equate with educational or clinical significance. The result of a statistical test is only an aid to decision making. For example, a significant mean difference of three points on a vocabulary acquisition test, between two groups, may not hold much educational significance when considered in the context of natural growth in vocabulary acquisition.

5.3 Choosing a Statistical Test

The problem for the new researcher when choosing a statistical test is lack of experience with applied statistical procedures. The reader may have studied an introductory course in statistics but will not have experience of applied methods. This chapter and indeed the whole book concentrates on, 'the when to do this or that . . . and why' rather than rote learning and computational detail. A series of choices when choosing a statistical test are presented and summarized in Figure 5.1. For those who want to check whether a procedure they have in mind is appropriate, they can go directly to Figure 5.1 (pp. 130–1) which is self explanatory. If you want to develop your applied skills then read through the following three-point rationale on which the decision chart shown in Figure 5.1 is based.

When deciding what statistical test to use, three interrelated issues need to be considered:

1   *Research question.* Is the main research question concerned with association/relationship, dependence/prediction between measures (same individuals), or comparison/differences between groups?
2   *Research design.* How many groups are there in the study and is there any relationship between them? For example, if there are two or more groups of data are they *related* or *independent*? If each set of scores is obtained from a different sample of subjects, the groups are independent. If different measures are obtained from the same group of subjects on two (or more) occasions, i.e. the same subjects take two or more tests, or subjects take the one test on two or more occasions, then the measures are related or dependent.
3   *Data distributions.* Are the distributions of the important variables discrete with inferences based on count data, for example, binomial, nominal or ranked data? Or are the distributions continuous, for example, normal, bivariate normal with inferences based on the normal distribution?

These three issues will now be appraised in more detail.

Research Questions

Correlation, relationship and association

In many research studies more than one research question is addressed, consequently more than one type of statistical test may be used. If the purpose of the study is to test for a relationship between observations or scores then correlation type statistics are used. Statistics about relationships are often called **correlations**. They are frequently used but generally not well understood. The concept of significance in correlation is not very helpful. Correlation represents a measure of the degree of closeness (co-relation) between two variables. The correlation coefficient provides an indication of the strength of the relationship. Even very weak correlations (small correlation coefficients) can be statistically significant with large sample sizes.

When data is category ranked, Spearman's Rho, r_s is an appropriate correlation statistic to use. When data is continuous and has an underlying normal distribution, the Pearson correlation r should be used. In both cases, the null hypotheses are:

H_0: $\rho = 0$, that is the population correlation (ρ, rho) is zero.

The one sample χ^2 (Chi square) **test of independence** (Goodness-of-fit test) is often considered as a correlation type statistic for nominal data. Goodness-of-fit refers to the extent to which observed frequencies correspond to expected frequencies. This test provides a measure of the degree of statistical independence of two variables, or put simply a measure of the relationship between two variables when data is categorical (two or more categories). This procedure is appropriate when one sample from a population can be cross classified into two or more categories on two variables. The null hypothesis is that the two variables are independent that is no relationship exists between them.

The $r \times 2$ sample χ^2 test of **homogeneity** is actually a test of the equality of the distributions of two sets of proportions (the distribution of proportions in each population for an example see Chapter 4 Table 4.1). It is appropriate when data is categorical. The null hypothesis is that the distribution of proportions is the same in each population. A two sample χ^2 refers to only two populations, the r refers to the number of categories or rows in an $r \times 2$ contingency table, and the 2 refers to the two populations.

Dependence and prediction

When the research question of interest focuses on prediction then a regression type analysis should be considered. The simplest form of statistical linear regression is when a response variable, Y, is dependent on a predictor variable X and both Y and X are continuous variables with a linear relationship. A regression equation can be used to predict the dependence of Y on X. The line which best represents the linear relationship between X and Y in the population can be described by two parameters: beta$_{(0)}$, (β_0) the intercept (value of Y when $X = 0$) and beta$_{(1)}$ (β_1) the regression coefficient, a measure of the slope of the regression line (change in Y per unit change in X). The parameters are estimated by the regression equation and hypothesis tests can be constructed for beta$_{(0)}$ and beta$_{(1)}$. Some introductory statistical texts state that the response variable in a linear regression has to be normally distributed; this is not strictly correct. The important assumption is that the residuals are normally distributed and independent (see Chapter 8). The response variable does not have to be normally distributed or even a continuous measure.

The idea of simple linear regression can be extended to find the best fitting statistical model that describes the relationship between a response variable and more than one predictor (explanatory independent) variable. This is called **multiple regression.** When the outcome variable is binary, then an appropriate underlying probability model is the logistic regression model. Not surprisingly the regression approach is called a logistic regression, predictor variables may be continuous or binary.

Differences between two samples

When a research study is designed to assess treatment effectiveness, probably the first statistic to come to mind is the *t*-test. This ubiquitous statistic is generally appropriate for two sample comparison designs (sometimes called two group comparison designs). Being a parametric statistical procedure, several assumptions have to be met before the *t*-test can be properly used (see Chapter 8). Another important consideration is whether the two-sample comparison is between independent or related samples. If a response variable such as height is measured for two independent samples of individuals, for example, boys and girls, then to test whether there was any statistically significant difference between the mean height for boys and the mean height for girls (a difference between two independent samples) an **independent *t*-test** could be considered. However, if a group of boys were weighed on two occasions, for example, before and after dieting, two measures are taken for the one group of subjects, then a **related *t*-test** (paired, repeated measures) should be considered, because the measures on the two samples of weights are related or correlated. An alternative design would be to match pairs of subjects on certain variables. For a matched subjects design the paired *t*-test should be considered. One advantage of the related *t*-test over the independent *t*-test is that statistical significance is attained, at a specified *p*-level, with a smaller difference between the two means (assuming other important attributes are equal). The null hypothesis for the independent *t*-test is that the two means are equal, $\mu_1 = \mu_2$, and for the related *t*-test the mean difference is zero, $\mu_1 - \mu_2 = 0$.

Should the independent *t*-test be considered inappropriate then an alternative nonparametric procedure is the **Wilcoxon Mann-Whitney test**. The null hypothesis is that the two samples have the same population distribution. An alternative nonparametric procedure to the repeated measures *t*-test is the **Wilcoxon Signed Ranks** test.

A nonparametric repeated measures test for change, when any change is indicated simply as + or −, is the **Sign test**. This test makes use of medians only, has only one distributional assumption, the response variable, which theoretically has a continuous distribution. The sign test provides an indication of only the direction of any difference, not a measure of any difference, between the two occasions. The null hypothesis tested by the sign test is that the median difference between two sets of scores is zero. Although theoretically the response variable should be continuous, because only the sign of any difference is used, the test can be treated as a binomial procedure hence its location in Figure 5.1.

The Wilcoxon signed ranks test is a more powerful repeated measures test than the sign test because it uses more information (more of the data), that is the ranked positions of individual scores, rather than just the medians of the distributions. Similar to the *t*-test it is a test of **no difference**. The null hypothesis is stated in terms of the sum of the positive ranks equals the sum of the negative ranks.

The two-sample **Proportions test** is a convenient test for the difference between two proportions or percentages. It is based on the binomial approximation to the normal distribution so a minimum combined sample size should be about 40 with a minimum of 20 in each group (two-sample test). The normal approximation is also less accurate as the proportion *P* in each group moves away from 0.5. The proportions test is much underused in educational research. A one-sample proportions test can be used when we want to make an inference for a single proportion − an unknown population proportion can be estimated from a sample proportion.

The **Binomial test**, similar to the sign and proportions tests, uses binomial data. Unlike these two tests, it is a single sample test, and one binomial population is classified into two groups. When this test is used, the two proportions (or percentages) should add up to 1 or 100 per cent (the total sample size). The binomial test is useful when we want to determine whether observed proportions − yes/no, male/female, etc. – differ from what would be expected by chance. When data is in a 2×2 contingency table and cell frequencies are small (< 5), **Fisher's extact test** should be considered.

Differences between three or more samples

When more than two samples are to be compared and the response variable is distributed normally then an ANOVA (Analysis of variance) type analysis should be considered in preference to a series of t-tests. Multiple tests on the same sample increases 'experiment-wise' error. The most common multiple sample comparison procedure (sometimes called multiple group comparison procedure) is the F-test. This is a parametric procedure with similar requirements to the t-test. The null hypothesis tested with the F-test is that the group means are equal, i.e., H_0: $\mu_1 = \mu_2 = \mu_3 \ldots = \mu_n$. Similar to the t-test there is a repeated measures ANOVA which also uses the F-test. In the related ANOVA unlike the independent ANOVA, variance in scores due to individual subjects can be treated as a separate source of error. This confers the same advantage that the repeated t-test has over the independent t-test. Nonparametric equivalents of the F-test are the **Kruskal-Wallis one way ANOVA** for independent samples, and the **Friedman's ANOVA** by ranks procedure for related measures. Both the Kruskal-Wallis and the Friedman procedures test the null hypothesis that the samples (or repeated measures) come from populations all with the same median, effectively one population. Both procedures require data to be ordinal (ranked).

When three or more samples are to be compared and data is in the form of counts (frequencies) then two parametric procedures should be considered. If the samples (three or more groups) are independent and interest is focused on association between different samples (groups) then an extension of the $r \times 2$ Sample χ^2 test of association, referred to as an **$r \times k$ Sample χ^2 test**, should be considered. When three or more related samples are to be compared on, for example a true/false or pass/fail basis, i.e., binomial data, then the **Cochran's Q-test** should be considered. It can be thought of as an extension of the two sample proportions test, the null hypothesis being that the proportions are equal in each group.

Research Design

Choice of an appropriate statistical test depends upon whether the samples of scores or observations are independent or related. Generally a related measures design is preferable to an independent samples (groups) design because statistically there are fewer degrees of freedom. Hence statistical significance is attained, at a specified p-level, with a smaller difference. Also a practical benefit is that fewer subjects are required and individual differences between conditions can be eliminated or accounted for. A disadvantage is the need to counterbalance possible order effects and the requirement for a wash-out period between measurement occasions. The effects of measurement or participating in an experiment may carry over to the second measurement occasion. There are some designs where independent samples have to be used, for example, in an investigation of differences between boys and girls in their coping skills in different social settings.

The number of samples (groups) in a design can become complex. Various combinations are summarized below. These descriptions are referred to in Figure 5.1.

One sample   when a single random sample of observations is obtained from a defined population.

Two sample   this design can take two forms:

- when two independent (separate and not related) random samples of observations are obtained from a defined population;
- when two samples of observations are obtained, but the two observations come from the same individuals (related).

Multiple samples (or multiple groups)

when there are more than two samples of observations. These designs can be split into two types depending upon the number of independent variables (factors):

- when there is just one independent variable (factor) with different levels (categorical) forming groups and one response variable;
- when there is more than one independent variable (factor) and one response variable, i.e., two independent variables with two or more levels (categorical) forming the groups. For example, a 2×2 design would be two independent variables each with two levels forming four groups.

Data Distributions

Data distributions can be classified into: i) binomial/nominal; ii) ranked; and iii) continuous. These distributions have different underlying probability models and can be thought of as three distinct classes of statistics. Here we group binomial and nominal as one category of discrete measurement although they have different underlying distributions, for example, binomial and χ^2 distributions. The remaining chapters in this book introduce various statistical tests and are sequenced on the basis of the type of inference and the type of underlying data distribution. Inferences about count data including binomial and χ^2 distributions are presented in Chapter 6. Inferences based on ranked data are presented in Chapter 7, and statistical inferences and associated test statistics based on the normal distribution are presented in Chapter 8.

When data is classified as binomial all data values are categorized into one of only two possible values, this is sometimes referred to as binary data. Nominal data is when data values can be classified into two or more groups. It can be thought of as an expansion of the binomial situation. A useful statistic for nominally classified data is the χ^2 statistic based on the χ^2 distribution. If a response variable is rank ordered, or the distribution of a continuous variable is asymmetrical, then the continuous variable can be treated as a ranked variable and nonparametric or distribution free statistics should be considered. This class of statistics makes very few distributional assumptions. All that is required for some tests is that scores can be identified as being different, other tests require that scores or values can be ranked. It is possible that scores may have a joint rank, in these circumstances the majority of tests do not include these tied scores in the computation of the test statistic. The value of initial data analysis in identifying possible underlying statistical models for the data can not be overemphasized.

In many circumstances, probably too many, data is assumed to be normally distributed. When this assumption is made, either implicitly or explicitly, then it follows that scores should have a mean and a standard deviation. If either a mean or a standard deviation does not make sense, for example, a standard deviation of 0.6 'blue eyes', then you are probably applying a continuous measure when you should not. Clearly blue eyes represents a discrete and probably nominal value. Apart from simple plots there are inferential procedures that can be used to check for normality assumptions. These are presented in section 'Checking for normality', p. 143.

Using the Statistical Test Decision Chart

The decisions chart shown in Figure 5.1 incorporates the three main criteria outlined in this section: **research questions**; **research design**; and **data distributions**. The chart can be thought of as a map with grid references consisting of statements about **study design** and **research questions** down the left hand side and statements relating to **inferences** and **data type** along the top of the chart.

To use the chart you should first consider the research design and research questions(s); decisions about these are located under the column heading **design** on the left of the chart. If you move down this column you are presented first with **one sample** (group) designs, subdivided into research questions about association/ relationships, differences and prediction, then **two sample** (group) designs and research questions related to comparisons/differences and associations. The final choice is between types of **multiple sample** (group) designs involving questions about differences and associations between samples.

Along the top of the chart under the general heading statistical inferences there are two main columns headed **count data** and **continuous data**. Inferences about count data are further subdivided into inferences relating to binomial/nominal data and inferences relating to ranked data. The three types of data distributions, binomial/nominal, rank and continuous normal correspond to three main classes of statistics mentioned in the previous section. For some designs these three types of data distributions are further divided into independent and related measures. This gives a total of six columns: binomial independent/related; ranked independent/ related; and continuous normal independent/related.

To decide on an appropriate statistical test start at the top of the left hand **design** column and move down this column until you reach a design and research question that is consistent with your study design. The type of independent vari-

	STATISTICAL INFERENCE ABOUT		
DESIGN:	**COUNT DATA**		**CONTINUOUS DATA**
One. Sample	*Binomial/Nominal*	*Rank*	*Normal*
Research Q: *Association/ relationship*	One sample χ^2 test of Independence (6.1) Phi Coefficient and Cramer's Phi (6.1)	Spearman's rank order r_s correlation (7.2)	Pearson correlation *r* (8.3)
Difference	Binomial test difference *between* 2 proportions (or %) (6.2)	One sample Runs test (7.3)	—
Research Q: *Prediction* (independent variable is continuous)	—	—	Linear Regression (Response variable is continuous (8.2))

Two. Sample	*Independent*	*Related*	*Independent*	*Related*	*Independent*	*Related*
Research Q: *Comparison/ differences*	Fisher's exact test (6.3) Proportions test* (6.4)	Sign test (6.5)	Wilcoxon M-W test (7.4)	Wilcoxon Signed Ranks test (7.5)	*t*-test (8.4)	*t*-test (8.5)
Association (class variable is discrete forming groups)	r × 2 sample χ^2 test of homogeneity (6.1)	—	—	—	—	—

Multiple Samples (groups) *1 Independent variable* (factor)

	Independent	*Related*	*Independent*	*Related*	*Independent*	*Related*
Research Q: *Differences between groups* (class variable is discrete forming groups)	—	—	Kruskal-Wallis One-way ANOVA (7.6)	Friedman ANOVA by Ranks (7.7)	One-way ANOVA (unrelated) (8.7)	One-way ANOVA (related) (8.8)

Multiple Samples (groups) *More than 1 independent variable* (factors)

	Independent	*Related*	*Independent*	*Related*	*Independent*	*Related*
Research Q: *Differences between groups* (class variable is discrete forming groups)	Cochran's *Q* test for > 2 proportions (6.7)	—	—	—	Two-way ANOVA (unrelated) (8.9)	Two-way ANOVA split-plot[†] (8.10)
Association (class variable is discrete forming groups)	r × k χ^2 test (6.6)	—	—	—	—	—

* Can be independent or related; (6.1) indicates Chapter and section in text; [†] Independent and related

Figure 5.1: *Decision chart for choosing a statistical test*

ables, continuous or discrete variables are also stated under the design column. Discrete independent variables are sometimes called class variables because they classify subjects into relevant groups for analysis.

You should then follow the row along and stop when the row intersects with an appropriate column heading relating to type of data and inference, for example, binomial/nominal; rank or normal data distributions. For some designs you need to choose between an independent or related measure for the response variable and also make a choice between discrete or continuous independent variables. At the beginning of each of the following chapters there is a summary of statistical tests included in that chapter.

Example 5.1:   Choosing an Appropriate Statistical Test

In part of a study designed to identify whether there were any differences between mathematics and verbal self-concept among Norwegian school children, Skaalvik and Rankin (1994), sampled 165 sixth grade boys and 191 sixth grade girls. An additional question addressed in the study was whether any differences in self-concept were gender related. Two of the scales developed and used in the study were the *Mathematics Self-Concept* (MSC) scale; self-perceived ability to learn mathematics, for example one item is 'I have high mathematics aptitudes', and the *Verbal Self-Concept* (VSC) scale; verbal self-concept about mathematics, an example of one item is, 'I have no problems learning mathematics.' Means and standard deviations were presented for both scales.

In choosing a statistical test the first consideration is,

What is the general research design, how many groups (measures) are involved?

The study is designed to investigate differences in self-concept in mathematics (MSC) vs verbal self-concept (VSC) so there are two measures for the same individuals MSC scores and VSC scores. Beginning in the left column of the decision chart under the heading **design** and moving down this column we need to decide whether this is a one-sample, two-sample or multiple-sample design. In its simplest form, this is a two-sample design, that is two sets of scores, MSC measures and VSC measures, for the same individuals. We also need to consider under the **design** heading, the nature of the research question;

Is the research question concerned with association, prediction or comparison/ differences between groups (or samples of scores)?

This part of the study was concerned with testing whether there were any *differences* between MSC and VSC measures *within subjects*. It is an example of a two-sample comparison, that is a comparison of two sets of scores for the same individuals. The response variables are the scale scores for MSC and VSC. Having identified the appropriate location in the design column '2 sample', we then move along the row until we intersect an appropriate column describing the type of data distribution for the response variable, i.e., binomial rank or normal distribution.

In this example the response variables are MSC and VSC scale scores, the authors' report means and standard deviations for these scores, and, in the absence of any other information about score distributions, the reader is invited to make the assumption of continuous response measures which are normally distributed.

The choice of statistical test has now been narrowed down to a statistical procedure

---

to test for differences with two groups of scores (maths and verbal self-concept). The only remaining consideration is,

Are the measures (groups of scores) independent or related?

Considering all the criteria presented in the decision chart, the final choice of statistical test is between the independent *t*-test or the related (paired) *t*-test. As there are two sets of measures for the same subjects, this is a within subjects design, and therefore a related *t*-test is an appropriate statistical test to see whether there is any difference between mean MSC and VSC scores. Before using this test a number of other assumptions specific to the *t*-test need to be checked (see, Chapter 8). A point which may cause some confusion is how any gender differences are related to observed within subject differences in measures of maths and verbal self-concept. The authors simply completed the within subjects analysis separately for boys and girls.

Skaalvik and Rankin (1994) reported that, 'Paired *t*-tests showed that boys in sixth grade had significantly higher mathematics than verbal self-concept [MSC vs VSC] ($t = 3.60$, $p < 0.001$). In comparison, girls in the sixth grade had significantly higher verbal than mathematics self-concept ($t = -3.91$, $p < 0.001$)', (p. 424).

Using Confidence Intervals for Significance Testing

In a typical between-subjects design to see whether there is any difference in mean test anxiety scores between boys and girls, the null and alternative hypotheses might be:

H_0: $\mu_1 = \mu_2$
H_1: $\mu_1 \neq \mu_2$

If the 95 per cent confidence interval for the difference in means, $\mu_1 - \mu_2$, *does not* include zero, then we reject the null hypothesis and conclude that there is a significant difference between boys and girls. As Gardner and Altman (1990) state,

> The excessive use of hypothesis testing at the expense of more informative approaches to data interpretation is an unsatisfactory way of assessing and presenting statistical findings ... We prefer the use of confidence intervals, which present the results directly on the scale of data measurement pp. 15–16.

Gardner and Altman's book, *Statistics with Confidence*, although written with medical researchers in mind, has much to offer the social science researcher. The authors present in a very readable fashion worked examples for calculating confidence intervals with parametric and nonparametric data.

Significance Tests – Some Caveats:

- Remember that a 5 per cent significance level is a statement about conditional probability. It means that given the null hypothesis is true, then significant results (& consequent rejection of H_0) would occur only 20 times out of every 100 tests of a true null hypothesis – that is the results would be unlikely.

- Report both confidence intervals, and *p*-values.
- Beware of outliers (a few outliers can produce significant results).
- Lack of statistical significance may be important – do not ignore it.
- When interpreting treatment effectiveness research you should report the attained statistical power of your test (applicable for parametric procedures).
- There should be a probability model for the data if formal statistical inference is used.
- Statistical inference as referred to in this chapter should not be used when data is collected haphazardly or is biased.
- Generally avoid fishing expeditions that is do not go searching for statistical significance. Decide on your hypotheses at the design stage. Set up a level of significance in advance, such as $p \leqslant 0.05$, but use this as a guide to satisfactory evidence (i.e., can I reject the null hypothesis) rather than an absolute decision rule for the outcome of a statistical test. Only when many studies and statistical tests have been completed on independent samples is there really sufficient evidence in favour of a decision (This is the specialist topic of meta-analysis, the synthesis of results of many tests of significance).
- Once data has been collected it is easy to conduct many statistical tests without thinking about underlying assumptions and in particular your (one) sample. Suppose you choose alpha, your cut-off significance level at $p \leqslant 0.05$. Even if there was in reality no difference between two treatment groups, a hypothesis test based on formal statistical inference will give a difference by chance, 5 per cent of the time. If you were to conduct 5 *t*-tests on your sample and in reality there were no differences between treatments, you will detect a significant difference (spurious treatment effect) with probability about 0.23 $(1 - (0.95)^5)$ or you would have a 23 per cent chance of detecting a difference somewhere. If you conduct 10 statistical tests then you will have about a 40 per cent chance of detecting a significant difference even if one does not exist.

  Additional hypotheses may be explored but multiple significance tests should generally be avoided or adjusted for. If we deem it necessary to consider several comparisons then we should reduce the significance level for each comparison to make the overall experiment error level equal to 5 per cent. For example, if we want alpha to be 5 per cent and we make five comparisons, the *p* value for each test should be 0.01 (0.05/5). So $p \leqslant 0.01$ is the cut-off point for attainment of statistical significance at the 5 per cent level. There are special procedures for *post hoc* *t*-tests following a significant *F*-test (see Chapter 8).
- Do not confuse statistical significance with educational or clinical significance.

5.4 Statistical Power

Whenever we conduct a statistical test of a null hypothesis we run the risk of making either a Type I error, α, (probability of attaining statistical significance falsely), or a Type II error, β, (the probability of not finding a population difference when one exists). For an explanation of Type I and Type II errors see Chapter 4. In this section we will consider how to influence, indirectly, the probability of making a Type II error and in so doing control the statistical power of a test. The **power** of a statistical test, $1 - \beta$, is the probability that statistical significance will be attained (we reject a null hypothesis) given there is a significant difference or relationship to detect (that is H_0 is false). Put simply, statistical power is the ability to detect a relationship or a real difference should one exist.

Sensitivity and Precision

When planning a study we usually refer to the sensitivity of an experimental design or the precision of a survey design. Sensitivity refers to the likelihood that a real treatment effect, if present, will be detected. We usually refer to a significant difference or significant treatment effect meaning the experimental design is sufficiently sensitive to detect a statistically significant and meaningful difference between treatments. In survey design precision refers to the probable accuracy of a sample estimate. The precision of a sample estimator, (a method for estimating the population parameter from the sample data, for example, a sample mean) is influenced by the sample size and the variability in the population.

Attainment of statistical significance, effect size or treatment effect (that is the magnitude of any detectable difference) and statistical power are closely related. Generally larger treatment effects are easier to detect than smaller treatment effects, other things being equal. Statistical power analysis is an important part of research planning. The relationship between the chosen significance level alpha (usually $p \leqslant 0.05$ or $p \leqslant 0.001$), the effect size, statistical power and sample size is complex, but essential to understand, if an efficient study is to be planned. It is important to consider the statistical power of any inferential tests prior to collecting data because if the power is too low then the researcher has limited options namely:

- increase the sample size to attain adequate statistical power;
- increase alpha the probability of making a Type I error, that is the level of significance for the test (this has the effect of reducing β because α and β are inversely related);
- or in the most drastic scenario abandon the study or completely revise the design (for example, change from an independent to a repeated measures design)

What influences the sensitivity of a design and our ability to detect a significant difference?

There are four interrelated features of a study design that can influence the detection of significant differences, hence the statistical power of a test: **sample size**; the **population variability** on the measures of interest; **alpha Type I error rate**; and the **effect size** (magnitude of difference or relationship) that we are trying to detect.

Sample size and statistical power

The effect of sample size is related to both variability of measures and statistical power (the probability of detecting a difference should one exist). These effects can be illustrated by considering the standard error of the mean (SEM). From the Central Limit Theorem, the population variance of a sampling distribution of means is normally distributed with mean μ, and a variance of σ^2/n (standard deviation is $\sigma/\sqrt{n}$ – usually called the standard error, in this example it is the SEM). When computing many test statistics the denominator is usually a standard error, for example, in computing the t-statistic (independent) it is evaluated as a ratio of the difference between two sample means divided by the standard error of the difference between the sample means.

You can think about the standard error of the difference between two means as representing, under the null hypothesis, the variability expected in the differences between the means of pairs of samples drawn from a single population. If a t-test is performed and the calculated t-statistic or more correctly the obtained t-ratio is sufficiently large when looked up in a table of t-values (with appropriate df), then statistical significance is attained (at a specified α). The two sample means are said to be significantly different. The importance of sample size is most noticeable if we think about the denominator in the t-ratio, the standard error of the difference between two means. As the sample size, n, increases, then the value of the standard error decreases. This is easily shown if you consider the SEM of a single mean, i.e. $\sigma/\sqrt{n}$. If you divide by a larger number, the SEM is reduced. The same principle applies to the standard error of the difference between two means as evaluated in the t-ratio. The standard error of the difference forms the denominator in the t-ratio and hence a smaller value increases the size of t. Larger t-values increase the chance of attaining statistical significance for a given magnitude of effect (effect size). Larger sample sizes yield larger degrees of freedom which are associated with smaller critical test statistic values for attaining a specified level of statistical significance. For example, a critical t-value with 10 df, α two-tailed test and $p \leq 0.05$ is 2.228, and if df increases to 25, all other attributes remaining the same, then the critical t-value is only 2.060.

Variability of population measures and statistical power

The more homogeneous groups are (less variability), the easier it is to detect differences (relationships). Even when random samples are used, if the measure of interest is heterogeneous with respect to the population, then real treatment effects will be more difficult to detect than would be the case if measures were homogeneous.

The researcher has direct control over the sample size and can therefore increase the statistical power of a design by increasing the sample size. A researcher can do little directly about the population variability, denoted by sigma squared σ^2, and hence the standard error, $\sigma/\sqrt{n}$. When population variability is large statistical power is reduced. You should note that by increasing the sample size this has the effect of reducing the standard error and hence increasing statistical power.

Alpha Type I error rate and statistical power

Generally in experimental and survey designs we try to minimize α, that is the problem of finding a difference that does not actually exist in the population. However, the alpha Type I error rate is inversely related to beta Type II error rate, the problem of not finding a difference that does exist in the population. As we increase alpha, at the same time we reduce beta and hence increase statistical power $(1 - \beta)$. The larger the chosen α or significance level, for example, $p \leq 0.10$ rather than the conventional $p \leq 0.05$, then the smaller is the critical t-ratio required for statistical significance and hence the easier it is to attain significant difference. Also, the direction of any differences tested, such as a one-tailed or a two-tailed test influences the attainment of statistical significance. For a chosen alpha, a one-tailed test (one-direction test, such as H_1: either $\mu_1 > \mu_2$ or $\mu_1 < \mu_2$) will be significant at a smaller critical t-ratio value than a comparable two-sided test.

Effect size and statistical power

The effect size for a given difference between sample means can be defined as the ratio of the size of difference between sample means divided by the population standard deviation. In notational form this is:

$$ES = \frac{\mu_1 - \mu_2}{\sigma} \qquad \textbf{Effect size} - 5.1$$

When calculating an effect size from sample data sample means replace μ_1 and μ_2 and the pooled standard deviation replaces the population standard deviation. The pooled standard deviation for two samples is evaluated as:

$$S_p = \sqrt{\frac{(n_1 - 1)S_1^2 + (n_2 - 1)S_2^2}{(n_1 - 1) + (n_2 - 1)}} \qquad \textbf{Pooled standard deviation} - 5.2$$

where S_1^2 and S_2^2 are the sample variances, and n_1 and n_2 are the respective sample sizes. For worked examples and what to do when sample sizes are substantively different see Lipsey (1990).

As the population effect size increases, the t-ratio increases as does the likelihood of attaining statistical significance. Put simply, the power of a statistical test is related to the effect size, the larger the effect the more probable is statistical significance and the greater is the statistical power.

To summarize, the following design attributes increase statistical power:

- larger sample sizes;
- homogeneous populations (low variability in population measures of interest);
- larger alpha Type I errors (problem of finding a difference that does not actually exist in the population);
- larger effect sizes.

Estimating Sample Size and/or Power for a Design

To compute a sample size for an investigation using charts that depict statistical power for various values of effect size, alpha, and sample size, the general procedure is to enter the power charts with any of the three parameters, say effect size, alpha and power, and the fourth parameter the corresponding sample size, can be determined. Alternatively, you could enter the power charts with a sample size and determine the statistical power of a test. The reader is referred to Lipsey (1990) for power charts and illustrated examples of how to use them.

In this section, rather than refer to charts and tables, three SAS programmes are presented for sample size and power estimation calculations. These SAS programmes use the SAS functions PROBIT and PROBNORM to generate appropriate values and thereby avoid the necessity to use tables and charts. The programmes are suitable for four common study designs: binomial data two independent groups; binomial data (paired groups cross-over design); normally distributed data independent groups design; and normally distributed data paired groups cross-over design (or simply paired/related groups). These programmes are presented in Appendix A3.

For all three programmes either sample size or power can be estimated provided three other parameters are entered. For example, to calculate sample size for a normally distributed response variable in an independent groups design the following three parameters would need to be specified (in the programme): Power (power), Type I error (alpha), difference between the two means that is to be detected (diff), pooled within group standard deviation (sd), and −9 for the fourth parameter, sample size. When −9 is entered this missing parameter is estimated by the programme. If we wanted to estimate power for a given sample size, then −9 would be entered for power and the given sample size would be substituted for the −9 in the above example. There can only be one missing parameter for each sample size or power calculation.

Example 5.2:   Estimating Sample Size for Difference in Proportions (Independent)

A review of the reading recovery (RR) programme literature suggests that between 5–7 per cent of children who enter RR programmes are not significantly helped (Clay, 1990). The RR programme is an intervention programme designed for children who show difficulties in reading and writing. Pupils are screened on six subtests, and those that score in the bottom 20 per cent of their class are considered to be 'poor' readers and eligible for entry into a RR programme. Programme success is defined as the percentage of children who after 20 weeks individualized RR intervention are reading at 'average' levels for their class or school.

A study is planned to compare poor readers' response to a reading programme intervention in terms of 'success' or 'failure'. A group of poor readers is to be randomly allocated to one of two intervention programmes. One group will receive a 'usual' remedial help reading programme (comparison group) and the other group will receive the RR programme. The anticipated percentage of children in the comparison

---

group who are expected to fail is 12 per cent and this is compared to an expected 6 per cent of failures in the RR programme.

> *How many children will be required in each group (comparison group and RR group) to detect a significant difference in the proportions of 'failure' of 0.06 (0.12–0.06) with a two-sided test, a Type I error (alpha) of 0.05 per cent and 80 per cent power?*

Two-proportions independent-groups design

To estimate the number of children in each group, the SAS programme POWER1 is used. The SAS programme calculates sample size and power for the difference between two proportions with independent groups (see Appendix A3, Figure 2). The required power is 0.80, alpha is 0.05, pie1 is the smaller proportion, 0.06 (RR proportion) and pie2 is the larger proportion 0.12 (usual remedial programme), the parameter to be estimated is sample size and this is entered as −9. The output from this programme is shown in Figure 5.2. From this it can be seen that 354 children per group would be required.

	Comparison of Two Proportions (independent groups)			
	Finding number of subjects (n)			
				Calculated value
Power	alpha	pie1	pie2	of N (per group)
0.8	0.05	0.06	0.12	354

Figure 5.2: Output from SAS programme POWER1

The programme POWER1 allows a number of 'what . . . if' power and sample size calculations to be performed. For example, an investigator may ask what would be the required sample size if the anticipated percentage of failures in the remedial teaching group increased from 12 per cent to 25 per cent. Intuitively a larger effect size, (that is magnitude of difference) would suggest a smaller sample size is required. The following two lines of 'data' are entered in the programme POWER1:

```
0.80 0.05 0.06 0.12 -9
0.80 0.05 0.06 0.25 -9
```

Notice the first line of data input is the same as the previous example but in the second line of data 0.25 represents the increased failure rate of 25 per cent. The output for these sample size estimates is shown in Figure 5.3.

	Comparison of Two Proportions (independent groups)			
	Finding number of subjects (n)			
				Calculated value
Power	alpha	pie1	pie2	of N (per group)
0.8	0.05	0.06	0.12	354
0.8	0.05	0.06	0.25	54

Figure 5.3: Sample size estimates for two different proportions

From Figure 5.3 it is evident that to detect a larger difference in proportions requires a considerably smaller sample size, given the same alpha and power.

The number of subjects in a design is related to the level of measurement and summary statistics being used. In general, when data can be appropriately summarized by means, (rather than binomial, percentage of 'failures' and 'successes') then smaller samples are required.

Proportions in a Two-group Two-period Cross-over Design (Related Measures)

In a two-group two-period cross-over design subjects receive both interventions, for example, A and B in a randomized order. This is an appropriate design when the intervention in the first period does not effect the intervention in the second period. In many educational interventions a carry-over effect, learning, is precisely what is intended and a cross-over design would therefore be unsuitable. However, in some psychological experiments and clinical settings the cross-over design is desirable because it eliminates subject variability and has the practical advantage of needing fewer subjects than a comparable independent groups design. Paired difference between treatments for each subject are calculated and the comparison of interest is either the average difference (the mean of the difference scores for normal data) or a count of those subjects who have a 'difference' and those who have 'no-difference' between treatments (for count data).

Example 5.3: Estimating Sample Size for Difference in Proportions with a Two-group Two-period Cross-over Design (Related Measures)

Johnston, Rugg and Scott (1987) have demonstrated that poor readers tend to rely on phonological decoding when processing unfamiliar written words. Phonological decoding of unfamiliar written words is when a reader uses letter–sound mappings in order to create a familiar phonological representation (word sound) which is recognizable.

A PhD researcher based part of her thesis on this work and in planning the study she decided to use a two-group two-period cross-over design. One of the experimental tasks is to ask a sample of 9-year-old poor readers to sort written sentences presented to them as either correct or incorrect (meaningless). Treatment A will include twenty sentences in which 10 have a word replaced by a homophone, for example, 'She *blue* up the balloon', blue is the homophone. Treatment B will include twenty sentences in which 10 have a word replaced by non-homophonic non-word, for example, 'He tain the ball', *tain* is the non-word. Homophones and non-words will be equivalent in visual similarity and pronounceability, and sentence length will be held constant across both sets of sentences. The number of correct sentences will be counted after presentation of each treatment. The cross-over design is illustrated in Figure 5.4.

Treatment sequence	Difference between treatment sequence		No difference between treatment sequence
	n correct on A $> n$ correct on B	n correct on B $> n$ correct on A	n correct on A $= n$ correct on B
A–B	n_{11}	n_{12}	n_{13}
B–A	n_{21}	n_{22}	n_{23}

Figure 5.4: How to determine estimates of pie1 and pie2 for a 2 x 2 cross-over design

From Figure 5.4 estimates of pie1 and pie2 can be derived as follows:

$\text{pie}1 = n_{11}/(n_{11} + n_{12})$ and $\text{pie}2 = n_{21}/(n_{21} + n_{22})$

where n is the number of cases in that cell. Subjects with no difference between treatments are excluded from subsequent sample size calculations.

Once pie1 and pie2 have been estimated, the sample size analysis proceeds as in the comparison of independent proportions using the SAS programme POWER1 (see Appendix A3, Figure 2). However, the estimated sample size will have to be increased by a small factor, perhaps 5 per cent, to allow for those subjects who show no difference (cells n_{13} and n_{23}). Unfortunately, there is no rule of thumb inflation factor and either previous studies should be consulted or a range of possible factors should be tried.

> *What sample size would be required to detect a significant difference in proportions between treatment A ($P = n_{11}/(n_{11} + n_{12})$) and treatment B ($P = n_{21}/(n_{21} + n_{22})$), given 80 per cent power and 5 per cent alpha?*

Typically estimates of pie1 and pie2 are unknown in 2×2 cross-over designs. The researcher often has to complete a pilot study to determine these estimates for use in subsequent power analysis calculations. In a small pilot study with 12 children in each treatment sequence the following values were determined:

$n_{11} = 8$ $n_{12} = 3$ $n_{13} = 1$
$n_{21} = 4$ $n_{22} = 8$ $n_{23} = 0$
then $\text{pie}1 = n_{11}/(n_{11} + n_{12}) = 0.727$ and $\text{pie}2 = n_{21}/(n_{21} + n_{22}) = 0.333$.

When these values are entered into the SAS programme POWER1 the number of subjects required per treatment sequence group is 22. If this value is inflated by 5 per cent, i.e., 1 additional subject, then in total 46 subjects would be required.

Example 5.4: Estimating Power for Difference in Means (Independent Groups)

In the evaluation of a classroom management programme for use in teacher education, Martin and Norwich (1991), report a significant difference, $p < 0.01$ between a treatment group and a control group of teachers with respect to effective classroom management. The treatment group, $n = 12$, mean score on a effective classroom management question was 1.25 (sd = 0.45) and the control group, $n = 12$, comparable mean score was 1.92 (sd = 1.17). The control group consisted of teachers who had not received training with the classroom management programme but were similar in other respects with the treatment group in terms of sex, location of school, class taught, and length of teaching experience. While acknowledging a number of evaluation design limitations, the authors claim that the study showed how research-based concepts and principles of classroom management are amenable to translation into practice via a well planned inservice programme.

What is the power of the significant difference in means between the intervention and control groups reported by the authors?

Difference between Two Means, Independent Groups

To estimate the statistical power of the reported difference in means the SAS programme POWER2 is used, power and sample size for comparison of two means with independent groups (see Appendix A3, Figure 3). From the author's paper, the reported alpha is 0.01, the difference in means is 0.67 (1.92–1.25), the pooled standard deviation is 0.88. (using equation 5.2), and the sample size in each group is 12. The power is estimated to be 24 per cent. The SAS output is shown in Figure 5.5. If sample sizes are unequal the harmonic mean, n', of n_1 and n_2 should be used. This is evaluated as $2(n_1 n_2)/(n_1 + n_2)$. Alternatively, two power estimates can be determined, one for each n.

	Comparison of Two Means (unpaired data)			
	Finding the power			
alpha	diff	sd	n	Calculated value of power
0.01	0.67	0.88	12	0.24

Figure 5.5: Output from SAS programme POWER2: Estimated power for difference between means (independent groups)

We can use the same SAS programme to determine the required sample size to achieve 80 per cent power, other parameters remaining the same. The number of subjects required in each group is 41 (see Figure 5.6)

	Comparison of Two Means (unpaired data)			
	Finding number of subjects (n) per group			
power	alpha	diff	sd	calculated value of n per group
0.8	0.01	0.67	0.88	41

Figure 5.6: Output from SAS programme POWER2: Estimated sample size for power set to 80 per cent

Example 5.5: Estimating Sample Size for Difference in Means (Related Groups)

In a paper by Hart, Wearing, and Conn (1995) which reported on the evaluation studies that were conducted as part of a programme on a Whole School Approach to

Discipline and Student Welfare (WSADSW–Statewide Australian Programme), changes in teachers' stress, discipline skills and aspects of school organizational climate were analyzed. Data abstracted from the paper include:

Variable	n	r^*	Before WSADSW		After WSADSW		p-values paired
			$M^\dagger$	SD	M	SD	t-test
Teachers' Psychological Distress	828	.59	10.3	4.08	9.7	4.04	$< .001$
Student Misbehaviour	812	.37	24.7	19.55	23.9	17.29	$> .10$

r^* is a Pearson correlation coefficient; † M represents the mean.

A five-point rating scale, the General Strain Index, was used to assess teachers' psychological distress. Student Misbehaviour was measured using a single self-report scale. Teachers' rated on a 100-point scale their perceptions, related to one class, of the amount of time they spent dealing with student misbehaviour in that class.

> *What is the power of these t-tests used to detect the change in teachers psychological distress following the programme? What minimum sample size would be required to detect a change of 0.8 (24.7–23.9) in teachers' perceptions of student misbehaviour, assuming 80 per cent power, and 5 per cent alpha (two-sided test)?*

Differences between Two Means, Related Samples (Groups)

To answer these questions the SAS programme POWER3 is used (see Appendix A3, Figure 4). Five parameters are required, power, alpha level, difference to be detected, standard deviation of the difference scores and sample size.

The first question relates to determination of power (set to −9 in the programme) given an alpha of .001, a difference in means of 0.6 (10.3–9.7), and a sample size of 828. The missing and problematic parameter is the standard deviation of the difference scores, $\sigma_{x_1-x_2}$. This is generally not available. Not all is lost, however, provided we make an assumption of homogeneity of variance (here similar variance in pre- and post-intervention measures, $\sigma_{x_1}^2 = \sigma_{x_2}^2 = \sigma^2$), then the standard deviation of the difference scores can be estimated if we have a measure of the correlation (or an estimate of this) between the related measures (pre- and post-intervention scores).

Using the **variance sum law**, the variance of the difference of two variables is equal to the sum of the two variances minus twice the correlation between the two variables times the product of the two standard deviations.

In notational form this is $\sigma_{x_1-x_2}^2 = \sigma_{x_1}^2 + \sigma_{x_2}^2 - 2\rho\sigma_{x_1}\sigma_{x_2}$

Assuming homogeneity of variance, then by rearrangement,

$$\sigma_{x_1-x_2}^2 = 2\sigma^2 - 2\rho\sigma^2$$

$$\sigma_{x_1-x_2}^2 = 2\sigma^2(1-\rho)$$

$$\sigma_{x_1-x_2} = \sigma\sqrt{2(1-\rho)} \qquad \textbf{Standard deviation difference scores – 5.3}$$

where ρ is the correlation between the two related measures. We also require an estimate of the pooled standard deviation. For related measures the sample size in the two groups is equal and therefore a simplified version of equation 5.2 (pooled standard deviation for independent samples) is:

$$pooled\ \sigma = \sqrt{(\sigma_1^2 + \sigma_2^2)/2}$$ **Pooled standard deviation – 5.4**

The pooled standard deviation is 4.06 $((4.08^2 + 4.04^2)/2)^{0.5}$. Note, a value raised to the power 0.5 is equivalent to the square root of that value, for example, $4^{0.5} = 2$. Using equation 5.1 to evaluate the standard deviation of the difference between pre- and post-intervention measures of the teachers' psychological distress variable,

$$\sigma_{x_1 - x_2} = 4.06 \times (2 \times (1 - .59))^{0.5} = 3.676.$$

To answer the first question, the values to enter into the SAS programme are, power = −9, alpha = 0.001, diff = 0.6, sd = 3.676 and n = 828; to answer the second question the values to enter into the programme are, power = 0.80, alpha = 0.05, diff = 0.8 sd = 20.715 and n = −9. Relevant sections of the SAS programme POWER3 are shown in Figure 5.7 and the SAS output from this programme is shown in Figure 5.8.

```
data a;
   input power alpha diff sd n;
   cards;
-9    0.001  0.6   3.676  828
0.80  0.05   0.8   20.715  -9
;
```

Figure 5.7: SAS code for POWER3 programme to determine power and sample size for the related groups design (Example 5.5)

Comparison of Two Means (paired data)
Finding the power

alpha	diff	sd	n	calculated value of power
.001	0.6	3.676	828	0.92

Comparison of Two Means (paired data)
Finding number of subjects (n)

power	alpha	diff	sd	calculated value of n
0.8	0.05	0.8	20.715	5263

Figure 5.8: Estimated power for difference between means (related measures), output from SAS programme POWER3

Notice in Figure 5.7, in the first line of data input power is set to −9. This is evaluated as 92 per cent power and is shown in Figure 5.8. In the second line of data input in Figure 5.7 sample size is set to −9. This is evaluated as a required sample size of 5263, and shown in Figure 5.8.

In reporting the results the authors comment, 'The paired sample t-tests suggested that the WSADSW programme was effective in bringing about an improvement in teacher stress, discipline policies . . . but that it made no difference to the mean levels of student misbehaviour' (p. 34). From Figure 5.8 it is evident that the obtained power for the teachers' psychological distress variable exceeds the 80 per cent level. The researchers therefore have a 90 per cent chance of detecting a difference as small as the one reported. To detect a difference of 0.8 in teachers' perceptions of student misbehaviour with 80 per cent power and an alpha of 0.05, a sample size of 5263 would be required. It is not surprising that the authors report there is no significant change at the 0.10 level on this variable.

We should pause for a moment to reflect on the finding of this power analysis. *Why should we require such a large sample size?* On reading the full article you might notice that the variance on the student misbehaviour variable is more than 4 times larger than the variance on any of the other measures reported by the authors. Recall from section 5.4 that the more homogeneous the groups are (less variability), the easier it is to detect differences. With such large variability in this measure, to detect a relatively small difference a large sample is required.

Considering interpretation of these findings, there certainly appears to be some change in teachers' perceptions about student misbehaviour before and after the intervention because the correlation between pre- and post-intervention measures is low ($r = .37$) The t-test only provides information about overall means and not about change in perceptions for individual teachers. It is possible that teachers' scores had changed in different directions, some improved and some reduced and the effect of these changes might cancel out – resulting in no overall average change. Perhaps supplementary analyses are required to detect individual changes, these may be more informative than the average effects.

5.5   Checking for Normality

Parametric statistical procedures are based on the assumption of underlying normality in the population from which a sample is selected. Whereas many univariate test statistics such as t- and F-tests are said to be robust (not drastically affected by moderate departures from underlying assumptions of normality and homogeneity of variance) Boneau (1960) and more recently Bradley (1984) have questioned this assumption of robustness. Monte Carlo studies (repeated sampling and testing from a distribution with known properties) have found that non-normality has only minor consequences in the majority of research applications (Hopkins and Weeks, 1990). As a consequence of the general robustness of t- and F-tests, many researchers do not report information about the shape of a distribution. This is despite the fact that many distributions are novel measures for which underlying population distributions are not well known. Newell and Hancock (1984) point to the dangers of erroneous statistical inferences when only means and standard deviations of distributions are reported and **skewness and kurtosis** is ignored especially when either n is small or alpha is extremely small, and data is skewed.

Checking for outliers and normality should therefore be an important preliminary to many inferential statistical procedures. The simplest way to check for departures from underlying normality in the population is to plot the distribution of sample scores. Outliers can be identified and the general shape of a distribution indicates whether it is skewed and whether it has positive or negative kurtosis (see Chapter 3 section, Describing Distributions).

As well as plotting the distribution of sample scores the values of skewness and kurtosis can be determined routinely in many statistical packages. These values can be used inferentially to test whether the distribution departs significantly from normality.

In SAS the basic assumption of underlying normality can be checked using the **univariate** procedure with the options **plot** and **normal**. The relevant SAS code which produced Figures 5.9, 5.10 and 5.11 is:

```
proc univariate plot normal;
   var corrd corre vocab;
run;
```

The first line of code has the procedure statement followed by the two options 'plot' and 'normal'. In the second line of code the three variables 'corrd', 'corre' and 'vocab' are specified.

Examining Data Distributions

Example 5.6:   Distributions of Three Reading Scores

A PhD student collected data on a number of reading measures including two syntactic awareness measures: a measure of syntactic awareness in a difficult reading passage; a measure of syntactic awareness in an easy reading passage, and as a third variable a measure of pupils' vocabulary. Both syntactic awareness variables were measured as percentage correct scores and the vocabulary score was a raw score with maximum possible score of 25. The data distributions and moments of all three variables are shown in Figures 5.9, 5.10 and 5.11. Non-relevant sections of SAS output have been deleted for clarity of presentation.

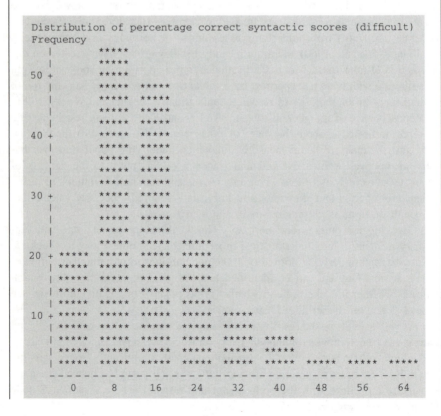

```
                          CORRD Midpoint
Variable=CORRD
                            Moments
      N                 161          Sum Wgts      161
      Mean           14.96894        Sum          2410
      Std Dev        11.38224        Variance      129.5553
      Skewness        1.547577       Kurtosis        3.151665
      W:Normal        0.874266       Pr<W            0.0001
      50% Med        12
      Mode            3

Variable=CORRD
Stem  Leaf                                                    #    Boxplot
   6  4                                                       1       *
   5  5                                                       1       0
   5  02                                                      2       0
   4  9                                                       1       0
   4  3                                                       1       0
   3  56678                                                   5       |
   3  000011                                                  6       |
   2  5567788                                                 7       |
   2  00012222333333444                                      17    +------+
   1  5555567777889999999999                                 23    |  +  |
   1  00000011111111222222223333333333344444                 38    *------*
   0  5555666666677777777778888889999999                     34    +------+
   0  0011122233333333333444444                              25       |
      ----+----+----+----+----+----+----+----+---
Multiply Stem Leaf by 10**+1
```

```
                        Normal Probability Plot
   62.5 +                                                             *
        |                                                           *
        |                                                        **
        |                                                     *
        |                                                 *     ++++
        |                                              ***+++++
   32.5 +                                            **+++
        |                                        ++**+
        |                                      ++****
        |                                   ++****
        |                               +******
        |                         *******
    2.5 +*  *  *  ***********++
        +----+----+----+----+----+----+----+----+----+----+
             -2        -1         0        +1        +2
```

Figure 5.9: Percentage correct score of syntactic awareness (difficult reading passage) with a positive skew

The variable 'corrd', percentage correct in difficult reading passage, has a typical positive skew with the tail of the distribution extended to the right (hence +ve), and the majority of values to the left (see the histogram and stem and leaf plots). Also notice the positive kurtosis (too few values under one tail of the distribution) and the relative positioning of the mean, median and mode, i.e., mode < median < mean (see Chapter 3, Describing Distributions).

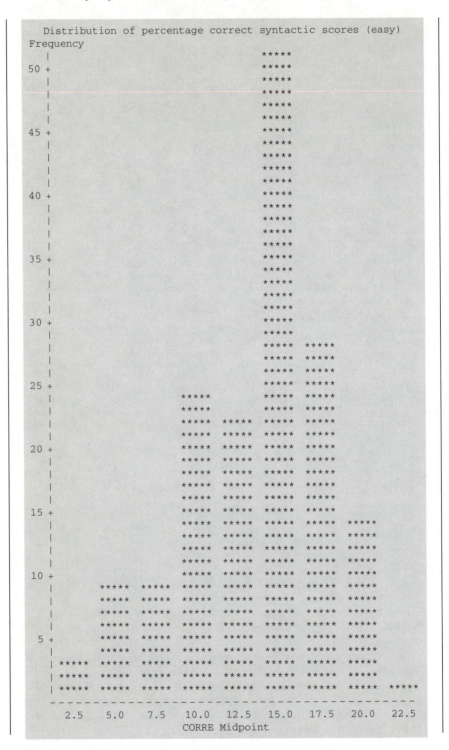

Distribution of percentage correct syntactic scores (easy)

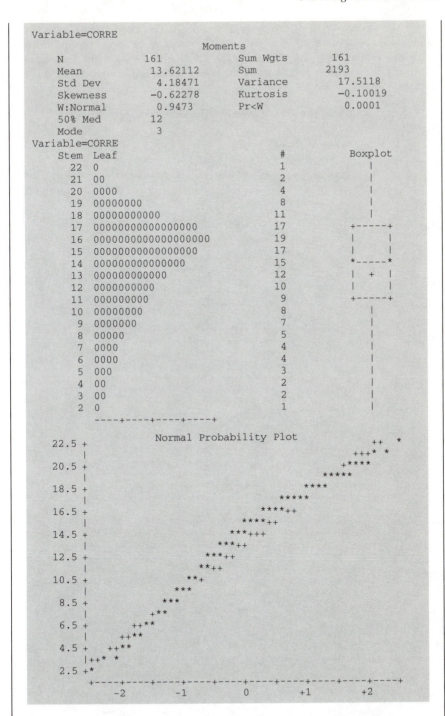

```
Variable=CORRE
                              Moments
    N                 161         Sum Wgts        161
    Mean          13.62112        Sum            2193
    Std Dev        4.18471        Variance     17.5118
    Skewness      -0.62278        Kurtosis     -0.10019
    W:Normal       0.9473         Pr<W          0.0001
    50% Med        12
    Mode            3
Variable=CORRE
    Stem Leaf                              #        Boxplot
      22 0                                 1          |
      21 00                                2          |
      20 0000                              4          |
      19 00000000                          8          |
      18 00000000000                      11          |
      17 00000000000000000                17       +-----+
      16 0000000000000000000              19       |     |
      15 00000000000000000                17       |     |
      14 000000000000000                  15       *-----*
      13 000000000000                     12       |  +  |
      12 0000000000                       10       |     |
      11 000000000                         9       +-----+
      10 00000000                          8          |
       9 0000000                           7          |
       8 00000                             5          |
       7 0000                              4          |
       6 0000                              4          |
       5 000                               3          |
       4 00                                2          |
       3 00                                2          |
       2 0                                 1          |
         ----+----+----+----+
                     Normal Probability Plot
   22.5 +                                        ++   *
        |                                      +++* *
   20.5 +                                    +****
        |                                  *****
   18.5 +                               ****
        |                             *****
   16.5 +                          ****++
        |                        ****++
   14.5 +                      ***+++
        |                    ***++
   12.5 +                  ***++
        |                **++
   10.5 +              **+
        |            ***
    8.5 +          ***
        |        +**
    6.5 +      ++**
        |    ++**
    4.5 +  ++**
        |++* *
    2.5 +*
        +----+----+----+----+----+----+----+----+----+
            -2        -1         0        +1        +2
```

Figure 5.10: *Percentage correct score of syntactic awareness (easy reading passage) with a negative skew*

The variable 'corre' is negatively skewed, the tail is extended to the left (-ve), and the majority of values are to the right. In contrast to the variable 'corrd' it has negative kurtosis (light tail), that is, too few values under the right tail of the distribution and the relative positioning of the mean, median and mode is reversed i.e., mode > median > mean.

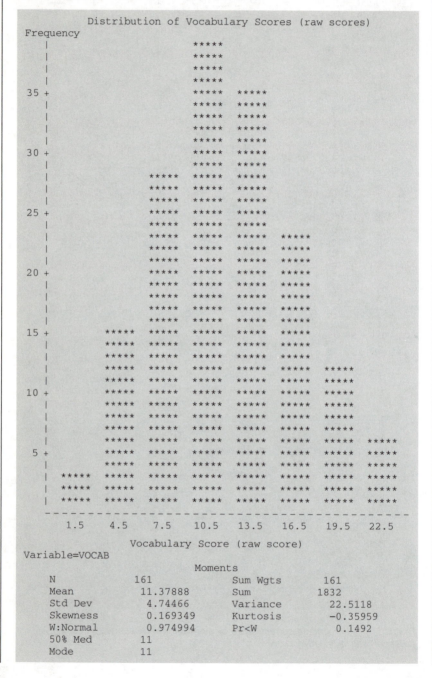

```
                    Distribution of Vocabulary Scores (raw scores)
     Frequency
         |                                    *****
         |                                    *****
         |                                    *****
         |                                    *****
     35 +                                    *****   *****
         |                                    *****   *****
         |                                    *****   *****
         |                                    *****   *****
         |                                    *****   *****
     30 +                                    *****   *****
         |                                    *****   *****
         |                            *****   *****   *****
         |                            *****   *****   *****
         |                            *****   *****   *****
     25 +                            *****   *****   *****
         |                            *****   *****   *****
         |                            *****   *****   *****   *****
         |                            *****   *****   *****   *****
         |                            *****   *****   *****   *****
     20 +                            *****   *****   *****   *****
         |                            *****   *****   *****   *****
         |                            *****   *****   *****   *****
         |                            *****   *****   *****   *****
         |                            *****   *****   *****   *****
     15 +                    *****   *****   *****   *****   *****
         |                    *****   *****   *****   *****   *****
         |                    *****   *****   *****   *****   *****
         |                    *****   *****   *****   *****   *****   *****
         |                    *****   *****   *****   *****   *****   *****
     10 +                    *****   *****   *****   *****   *****   *****
         |                    *****   *****   *****   *****   *****   *****
         |                    *****   *****   *****   *****   *****   *****
         |                    *****   *****   *****   *****   *****   *****
         |                    *****   *****   *****   *****   *****   *****   *****
      5 +                    *****   *****   *****   *****   *****   *****   *****
         |                    *****   *****   *****   *****   *****   *****   *****
         |            *****   *****   *****   *****   *****   *****   *****   *****
         |            *****   *****   *****   *****   *****   *****   *****   *****
         |            *****   *****   *****   *****   *****   *****   *****   *****
         ------------------------------------------------------------------------
              1.5     4.5     7.5    10.5    13.5    16.5    19.5    22.5
                          Vocabulary Score (raw score)
```

Variable=VOCAB

Moments

N	161	Sum Wgts	161
Mean	11.37888	Sum	1832
Std Dev	4.74466	Variance	22.5118
Skewness	0.169349	Kurtosis	-0.35959
W:Normal	0.974994	Pr<W	0.1492
50% Med	11		
Mode	11		

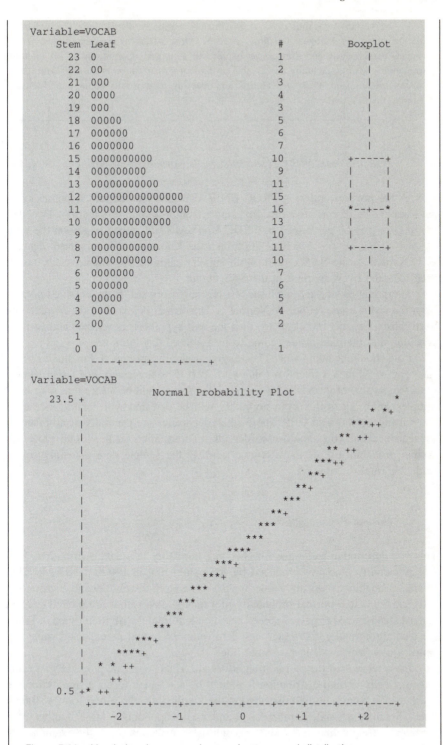

```
Variable=VOCAB
   Stem  Leaf                                  #          Boxplot
    23  0                                       1           |
    22  00                                      2           |
    21  000                                     3           |
    20  0000                                    4           |
    19  000                                     3           |
    18  00000                                   5           |
    17  000000                                  6           |
    16  0000000                                 7           |
    15  0000000000                             10         +-----+
    14  000000000                               9         |     |
    13  00000000000                            11         |     |
    12  000000000000000                        15         |     |
    11  0000000000000000                       16         *--+--*
    10  0000000000000                          13         |     |
     9  0000000000                             10         |     |
     8  00000000000                            11         +-----+
     7  0000000000                             10           |
     6  0000000                                 7           |
     5  000000                                  6           |
     4  00000                                   5           |
     3  0000                                    4           |
     2  00                                      2           |
     1                                                      |
     0  0                                       1           |
        ----+----+----+----+
```

```
Variable=VOCAB
                          Normal Probability Plot
    23.5 +                                                        *
         |                                                   *  * +
         |                                                 ***+++
         |                                               **  ++
         |                                             **  ++
         |                                           ***++
         |                                         **+
         |                                       **+
         |                                     ***
         |                                   **+
         |                                 ***
         |                               ***
         |                             ****
         |                           ***+
         |                         ***+
         |                       ***
         |                     ***
         |                   ***
         |                 ***
         |               ***+
         |             ****+
         |       *  *  ++
         |           ++
    0.5 +*  ++
         +----+----+----+----+----+----+----+----+----+----+
             -2        -1         0        +1        +2
```

Figure 5.11: Vocabulary (raw scores) approximate normal distribution

> The variable vocabulary is approximately normally distributed. The values of skewness and kurtosis are close to zero. (Most statistical packages adjust the values of skewness and kurtosis to be zero in a normal distribution to aid interpretation – kurtosis actually has a value of 3 when a distribution is normal), and the mean, median and mode are almost identical (as they would be in a perfectly normal distribution).

Interpretation of the Test Statistics W:Normal (or D:Normal)

In SAS the **normal** option in PROC UNIVARIATE tests the null hypothesis that the sample data represents a random sample from a normal distribution. Two statistical tests may be performed by PROC UNIVARIATE depending upon the sample size. If the sample size is > 2000 then the Kolmogorov test is used, denoted as D:Normal in the SAS output. With smaller samples the Shapiro-Wilk test is used, denoted by W:Normal in the SAS output.

Interpretation of the hypothesis test is straightforward. If the obtained p-value from the test statistic (either W:Normal or D:Normal) is *less* than the p-value you have chosen (usually 0.05 or 0.15) then the null hypothesis is rejected and you can conclude that the data do not come from a normal distribution.

Care should be taken when choosing your significance level. For small sample sizes say < 30 then a liberal p-value such as 0.15 is suggested. For larger sample sizes the p-value of 0.05 is more appropriate. You should be aware that with large samples small departures from normality will be detected with significance even when using a p-value of 0.05. These small departures are generally of no practical consequence but you should consider other information such as data plots and normal probability plots to determine whether the sample data plausibly comes from a normal distribution.

Normal Probability Plot

This is a descriptive technique for checking normality in a data distribution. Normal probability plots are produced by the option plot in PROC UNIVARIATE. Normal probability plots are shown for the three score distributions in Figures 5.9, 5.10 and 5.11. In a normal probability plot ranked data values are plotted (y axis) against standardized expected values based on a normal distribution (x axis). When the data are normally distributed any data value will equal its expected value and hence a plot will result in a straight line.

Interpretation of the plot is straightforward. Data points are plotted by an * and a theoretically normal distribution is plotted by a + which forms a straightline. So if the data is from a normal distribution the * will cover the + and form a straight line. Therefore a small number of + and a correspondingly large number of * forming a straight line will indicate a normal distribution. See, for example, the normal probability plot for the variable VOCAB in Figure 5.11. The approximate normal distribution of this variable can be checked by examining the distribution (histogram), stem and leaf, and box and whisker plots.

Departure from normality is evident when a number of + are visible and the data values indicated by an * deviate from a straight line, see Figures 5.9 and 5.10. Notice in both the variables CORRD and CORRE the * do not cover most of the + signs and the data values (*) deviate from a straight line. We could reasonably conclude that the data for the percentage correct scores do not come from a normal distribution. The pattern of the deviation of data points (*) provides a clue as to the shape of the underlying distribution. The variable CORRE in Figure 5.10 has a negative or left skew and the data points (*) form a curve from bottom left to top right rising steeply at first and then flattening off. The variable CORRD in Figure 5.9 has a distinct right or positive skew, the data points (*) form a curve from bottom left to top right but rising slowly and then steeply so that high ranked scores correspond to larger than expected (the straight line) standardized scores.

To see whether the normal probability plot is reasonable, (i.e., no gross errors) you should check that when the standardized expected value on the x axis equals zero, the corresponding ranked value on the y axis should be an approximate estimate of the median. For example, in Figure 5.10 the standardized score of zero corresponds to a score on the variable CORRE of about 14, the value of the median.

What can be Done when Data is not Normal?

If you face the problem of non normal data there are four possible strategies.

1 Check that there are no extreme outliers indicated by individual data points in a normal probability plot that depart significantly from both the straight line and other data points. If outliers are extreme remove them and check again for normality.

2 Consider using distribution free **nonparametric** statistical procedures.

3 Consider transforming your data.

4 Consider alternative non normal continuous distributions (these are beyond the scope of this text and you should consult a statistician for help).

Strategy 1) may improve a distribution and should always be considered. It is an essential part of IDA. However, you should consider the implications of removing outliers in your results section and in any interpretation. Strategy 2) is useful when data can be ranked. Examples of nonparametric statistical procedures are given in later chapters. Strategy 3) is helpful on occasions if data is skewed. Data transformations will minimize the effect of outliers but extreme observations should be dealt with as in strategy 1). Transformations should also not be applied directly to the data when there are a large number of zeros in the data. A constant such as 0.5 should be added to all data values prior to transformation (this is because values of zero cannot be multiplied and therefore do not work well in transformations, for example, logarithms are only defined for non-zero positive numbers). Strategy 4) is beyond the scope of this book. See also the end of Chapter 8 for further discussion.

Data Transformations

The benefits from normative data transformations for extreme skewness or kurtosis are worth considering but transformations should not be used on a routine basis because statistical procedures such as F and t-tests are generally robust and inter-pretation of transformed values can be problematic. Transformations should there-fore be the exception rather than the rule and are generally performed with the intention of: i) making skewed distributions more symmetric and closer to a normal distribution ii) to obtain homogeneity of variance in 'scores', and iii) to achieve a more meaningful scale of measurement. This does not always work and trans-formed data should be checked using normal probability plots to see whether there is any improvement in normality.

What Transformations to Use

Positively skewed or when the standard deviation is proportional to the mean

There are two possible transformations for positively skewed data, the square root transformation for moderate +ve skewness and the logarithmic transformation for data with a severe positive skew. Both transformations 'pull-in' the right tail of a distribution. Skewness is affected by outliers so check these first.

The logarithmic transformation generally uses $\log_{10}$ (log to the base 10). $\log_{10}(10) = 1$, means the power to which 10 must be raised to give 1. Similarly, $\log_{10}(1000) = 3$. When there are a number of zeros in the data set a constant of 0.5 is added to each data value. The transformation then becomes $\log_{10}(x_i + 0.5)$ where x_i = original data value. In SAS code this would be placed in a DATA step as NEWX= LOG10(OLDX + 0.5);. If there were negative values in the data then the largest negative value should be treated as an absolute value, $(|a|)$, and + 0.5 should be added to $|a|$ to make it positive, i.e., $\log_{10}(x_i + (|a| + 0.5))$ where x_i = original data value. Log to the base$_e$ ($e = 2.7182\ldots$) can be used rather than $\log_{10}$ as this has the same transformation effect. Switching from one base to another only changes the scale, not the shape of a distribution. Figure 5.12 shows a histogram and normal probability plot for the log transformed variable CORRD – percentage correct in difficult reading passage. The relevant SAS code that produced this output is:

```
data a;
     infile 'a:amanda.dat' lrecl= 72;
     input id 1-3 corre 57-58 vocab 67-69 corrd 70-72;
newlog=log10(corrd+0.5);
label corrd = 'Percentage Correct Syntactic Score (difficult)';

proc print;
  var corrd newlog; run;

proc chart;
   vbar newlog;
title1 'Distribution of Log Percentage Correct Syntactic Scores (DIFFICULT)';
run;
```

```
proc univariate plot normal;
  var newlog;
run;
```

Only the first few cases are shown from the PROC print output:

OBS	CORRD	NEWLOG
1	4	0.65321
2	12	1.09691
3	13	1.13033
4	19	1.29003
5	14	1.16137
6	19	1.29003

Distribution of Log Percentage Correct Syntactic Scores (difficult)

```
Frequency
60 +                                      *****
   |                                      *****
   |                                      *****
   |                                      *****
   |                                      *****
50 +                                      *****
   |                                      *****
   |                                      *****
   |                                      *****
   |                                      *****
40 +                                      *****
   |                                      *****
   |                               *****  *****
   |                               *****  *****
   |                               *****  *****  *****
30 +                               *****  *****  *****
   |                               *****  *****  *****
   |                               *****  *****  *****
   |                               *****  *****  *****
   |                        *****  *****  *****  *****
20 +                        *****  *****  *****  *****
   |                        *****  *****  *****  *****
   |                        *****  *****  *****  *****
   |                        *****  *****  *****  *****
   |                        *****  *****  *****  *****
10 +                        *****  *****  *****  *****
   |                        *****  *****  *****  *****
   |                 *****  *****  *****  *****  *****  *****
   |                 *****  *****  *****  *****  *****  *****
   | *****           *****  *****  *****  *****  *****  *****
   ------------------------------------------------------------
     -0.3    0.0    0.3    0.6    0.9    1.2    1.5    1.8
                     NEWLOG Midpoint
```

Skewness	-0.8778	Kurtosis	1.579415
W:Normal	0.951765	Pr<W	0.0001
Mean	1.06502		
50% Med	1.09691	90%	1.4843

153

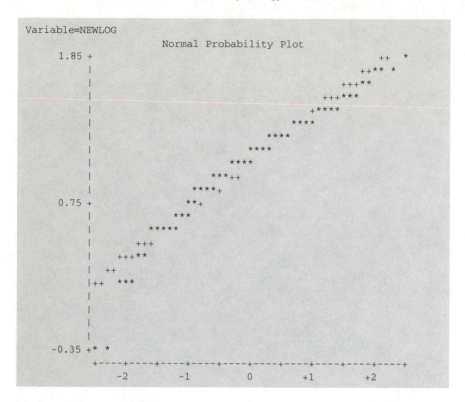

Figure 5.12: Histogram and normal probability plot for log transformed variable 'CORRD' – percentage correct difficult reading passage

Notice the distribution for the log transformed data in Figure 5.12 has considerably improved the shape of the original distribution shown in Figure 5.9. Examining the transformed data, however, shows that it still departs significantly from normality, $Pr < W$ 0.0001. An alternative transformation suitable for data which is in the form of percentages or proportions is the **arcsine** transformation.

Count data, especially proportions or percentages with skewed distributions

When the variance is a direct function of the mean ($\sigma^2 = P(1 - P)$) for example with proportions and percentages, the arcsine transformation should be considered. Generally, percentage scores tend to cluster around the high or the low end of a range, rather than the middle. The effect of the arcsine transformation is to move high scores towards the centre of the distribution. A modified arcsine transformation:

$$2 \text{ ARCSINE } \sqrt{x\%/100}$$

has the effect of moving both high and low percentage scores towards the middle of a distribution.

The original distribution for the variable CORRD – percentage correct score of syntactic awareness (difficult reading passage) in Figure 5.9 had a positive skew. The variable CORRE – percentage correct score of syntactic awareness (easy reading passage) shown in Figure 5.10 had a negative skew. Both of these variables were transformed using the modified arcsine transformation using the following SAS code:

```
data a;
     infile 'a:amanda.dat' lrecl= 72;
     input id 1-3 corre 57-58 vocab 67-69 corrd 70-72;
label corrd = '% CORRECT SYNTACTIC SCORE (difficult)'
      vocab = 'VOCABULARY SCORE (RAW SCORE)'
      corre = '% CORRECT SYNTACTIC SCORE (easy)'
      newd  = 'ARCSINE % CORRECT (difficult)'
      newe  = 'ARCSINE % CORRECT (easy)';
data a; set a;
newd=round(2*(arsin(sqrt(corrd/100))),.001);
newe=round(2*(arsin(sqrt(corre/100))),.001);
```

Shown in Figures 5.13 and 5.14 are histograms and normal probability plots for the two transformed variables NEWD arcsine transformed percentage correct difficult reading passage (original +ve skew), and NEWE arcsine transformed percentage correct easy reading passage (original -ve skew).

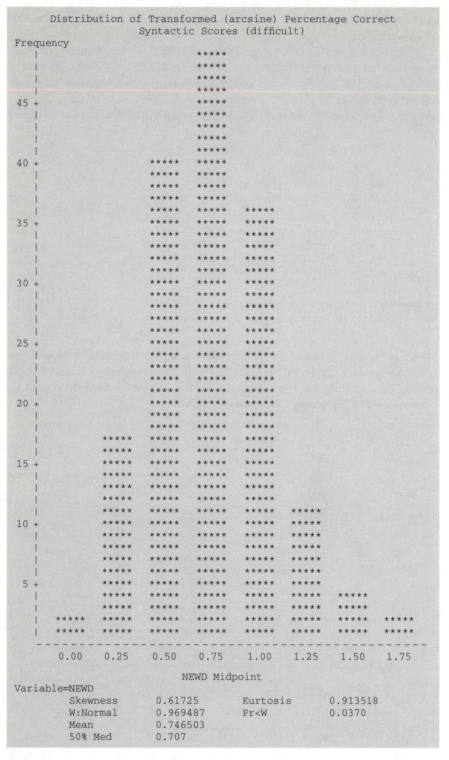

```
         Distribution of Transformed (arcsine) Percentage Correct
                      Syntactic Scores (difficult)
    Frequency
        |                              *****
        |                              *****
        |                              *****
        |                              *****
     45 +                              *****
        |                              *****
        |                              *****
        |                              *****
        |                              *****
     40 +                       *****  *****
        |                       *****  *****
        |                       *****  *****
        |                       *****  *****
        |                       *****  *****  *****
     35 +                       *****  *****  *****
        |                       *****  *****  *****
        |                       *****  *****  *****
        |                       *****  *****  *****
        |                       *****  *****  *****
     30 +                       *****  *****  *****
        |                       *****  *****  *****
        |                       *****  *****  *****
        |                       *****  *****  *****
        |                       *****  *****  *****
     25 +                       *****  *****  *****
        |                       *****  *****  *****
        |                       *****  *****  *****
        |                       *****  *****  *****
        |                       *****  *****  *****
     20 +                       *****  *****  *****
        |                       *****  *****  *****
        |                       *****  *****  *****
        |                *****  *****  *****  *****
        |                *****  *****  *****  *****
     15 +                *****  *****  *****  *****
        |                *****  *****  *****  *****
        |                *****  *****  *****  *****
        |                *****  *****  *****  *****
        |                *****  *****  *****  *****  *****
     10 +                *****  *****  *****  *****  *****
        |                *****  *****  *****  *****  *****
        |                *****  *****  *****  *****  *****
        |                *****  *****  *****  *****  *****
        |                *****  *****  *****  *****  *****
      5 +                *****  *****  *****  *****  *****
        |                *****  *****  *****  *****  *****  *****
        |                *****  *****  *****  *****  *****  *****
        |         *****  *****  *****  *****  *****  *****  *****  *****
        |         *****  *****  *****  *****  *****  *****  *****  *****
        -----------------------------------------------------------------
            0.00   0.25   0.50   0.75   1.00   1.25   1.50   1.75

                              NEWD Midpoint
    Variable=NEWD
              Skewness      0.61725      Kurtosis      0.913518
              W:Normal      0.969487     Pr<W          0.0370
              Mean          0.746503
              50% Med       0.707
```

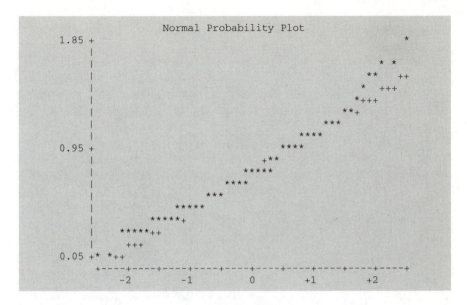

Figure 5.13: Histogram and normal probability plot for arcsine transformed variable 'CORRD' – percentage correct difficult reading passage

It is evident from Figures 5.13 and 5.14 that the modified arcsine transformations have improved both original distributions. There are however particular problems of interpretion with this transformation and in certain circumstances (when the null hypothesis is false) statistical power is reduced (see Chapter 8 section 8.11 for further discussion).

Negatively skewed distributions or when the variance is proportional to the mean

With count data the variance is often proportional to the mean rather than the standard deviation and this often results in a negatively skewed distribution. A modified square root transformation should be considered for negatively skewed distributions. When values are small, i.e., less than 5, then it is suggested that 0.5 is added to all values prior to transformation of the data. The form of the transformation is:

$$\sqrt{(J - x_i)} \qquad \textbf{Modified square root transformation – 5.5}$$

where x_i is the original score and J is a constant from which each score is subtracted so that the smallest score is 0.5. J is the largest score + 0.5. In SAS code this would be newx = sqrt(j-oldx).

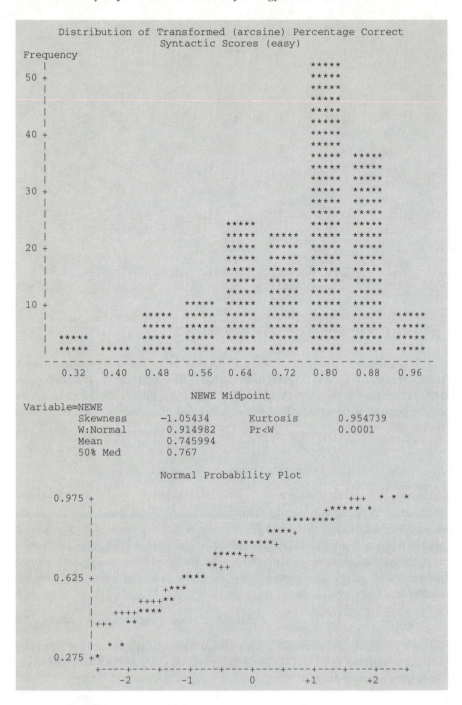

Figure 5.14: Histogram and normal probability plot for arcsine transformed variable
'CORRE' – percentage correct easy reading passage

Interpretation of Transformed Scores

Interpretation of transformed scores is sometimes difficult. For example, if a log transformation is used then a mean log score of 1.065, see Figure 5.12, is difficult to comprehend. This mean log score should be back-transformed (antilog taken) into the original metric. The antilogarithm (base 10) of the value 1.065 is 11.61. This is now comparable with the original mean of 14.96. The antilogarithm of the mean of the log scores is known as the geometric mean (see Chapter 3, section 3.4). The antilogarithm of the natural log (log to base e) would give the same result. The geometric mean is not equivalent to the metric mean and therefore it is not appropriate to transform the 95 per cent confidence intervals back to the original metric values. This is a drawback of transforming data. It is suggested that when reporting geometric means for transformed data the medians of the original data distributions are also reported. Transformations can also be used to stabilize variances prior to t- or F-tests of means. If variances of different groups are heterogeneous, transforming the distributions can improve the homogeneity of variances and hence make use of a t- or F-test more justified as well as making the analysis more exact. These are called variance stabilizing transformations. In this chapter only an overview of some of the more common data transformations has been presented. The reader is referred to Mosteller and Tukey (1977) for a more detailed account.

Summary

This chapter has presented the issues to consider when choosing a statistical test for the most common research situations in education and psychology. These considerations can be viewed as an extension of IDA prior to inferential analysis. Appraisal of the research design and likely data structure as well as choice of statistical test(s) and consideration of statistical power should be born in mind when planning a study or when evaluating a reported study. The point of determining statistical power for a given research plan is that should power be deemed insufficient, that is generally $< 80\%$, then the research plan can be revised prior to implementation.

After IDA, data will have been screened and out of range, missing values and outliers will have been detected and dealt with. A plausible underlying data distribution will also have been identified, such as binomial/categorical, ordered data or normal data. The next step will be to check skewness and kurtosis either inferentially or by using a normal probability plot. The later approach has the advantage of highlighting any outliers.

A preliminary choice of a statistical test can then proceed based on the research design, specific research questions addressed and the type of data distribution and inference for the variables of interest. The statistical decision chart, Figure 5.1, can be used at this point. Consideration should also be given to the statistical power of any proposed inferential analyses as well as any advantages or disadvantages of transforming any non normal data distributions. The final choice of statistical test will rest upon consideration of test specific assumptions, such as homogeneity of variance for a *t*-test. These specific assumptions can be checked in the relevant chapter that deals with the particular statistical test under consideration.

Chapter 6

Inferences Involving Binomial and Nominal Count Data

One-Sample Tests (two measures)

Two-Sample Tests

Introduction

Many research studies in the social sciences use observations or measures that are
in the form of count data. Whenever data is obtained from a population which can
be thought of as discrete in nature, then any statistical inferences we make using
data such as frequency counts, percentages or proportions are, in fact, inferences
that involve count data. For example, if we were interested in a possible difference
between the proportions (or percentages) of male and female students studying
Advanced Level (A-level) science subjects, then the parameters about which we
would make inferences are the population proportions and data sampled from the
population would be in the form of counts or frequencies.

Count data can be **binary** when only two mutually exclusive categories exist,
for example, gender. Count data may also be: **nominal**, when counts can be classified into more than two mutually exclusive groups and there is no order implied in
the groupings (mode of transport to work; walk, public transport, bicycle, own car);
ordered category, when frequency counts are arranged into ordered categories
(social class group – I to V where I refers to the most affluent group); or **individual
ranked** when each subject or object is assigned a numerical value designating its
rank position relative to all other objects (position of school in Local Education

Authority school league tables). In this chapter we examine the use of statistical inferences involving binary and nominal count data.

A number of inferential statistical techniques have been developed for analyzing count data. These nonparametric techniques do not require the data to be drawn from a normally distributed population (the underlying distribution may be binomial, multinomial, product multinomial or simply unknown) and therefore do not require interpretation based on the normal distribution. However, some statistical tests used with count data do approximate a normal distribution when sample sizes are large, such as binomial and χ^2 distributions.

The examples used to illustrate the use and interpretation of inferential statistical tests, in this and in subsequent chapters, are drawn from research questions and analyses that have appeared in sections of research reports, journal articles and students' theses. My intention in this and the following chapters is to explain why and how statistical tests should be used and to illustrate their application in a variety of research contexts. In Chapter 5, a number of considerations important when choosing a statistical test were outlined, namely research questions and design, data distribution, type of inference and specific test assumptions. These considerations are used to organize in a logical way the presentation of statistical tests in this and in subsequent chapters.

Each statistical procedure is introduced by beginning with a real research problem and concentrating on the reasons why a particular test is appropriate. This helps to clarify the relationship between statistical theory and statistical practice. Brevity of reporting of statistical analyses in many research journals means that much statistical theory and many assumptions are taken as understood. For the new researcher this can be frustrating. In the examples of the use of statistical tests drawn from the literature, I have filled in details about the inferential process used in a statistical analysis, that is the parameters estimated and the hypotheses tested and how these relate to underlying statistical theory, necessary test assumptions, and where appropriate I have commented on the original author(s) interpretation.

To move the reader from understanding why a test is used to consideration of how a statistical test works, simplified worked examples are presented. Formulae are explanatory and kept to a minimum. These worked examples, intended to help understanding, are for the most part based on sections of real data but necessarily simplified. Interpretation of the analysis is related to both statistical theory, such as one-sided or two-sided tests, alpha, statistical power, sample size and to the purpose behind the study such as original research question(s). The examples address the usual kinds of problems that a researcher will face when analyzing real data, for example, unequal groups sizes, missing or out of range values, outlier observations and skewed distributions. Emphasis is given to computer analysis of real data. Computer programmes for statistical analysis are presented alongside related computer output and interpretation of the analysis. Where relevant procedures for checking any specific test assumptions are also shown and the pragmatic consequences of particular violations, some of which are more serious than others, are discussed.

In summary, each statistical procedure is introduced and discussed using the following subheadings:

- when to use the test;
- statistical inference (and null hypothesis);
- test assumptions;
- example from the literature;
- worked example (simplified data);
- interpretation (using statistical tables);
- computer analysis (real data);
- interpretation of computer output.

We begin this chapter with tests appropriate for one-group (sample) designs using binary or nominal data. These tests are appropriate when the research question is concerned with either association between two variables (or correlation), or differences between proportions, or percentages. We then consider tests for two-group (sample) designs, both related and independent groups with binary and nominal data. Research questions may again relate to association or to differences and comparisons between the two groups. Finally, multiple group designs are considered for binary and nominal data. These tests are appropriate when interest focuses on differences or association between three or more groups which may be either related or independent.

6.1 Chi-square Tests for Contingency Tables

In this section both the **One-sample Chi-square test of independence** and the **Two-sample Chi-square test of homogeneity** are considered together because of their similarity in both computation and interpretation.

When to Use

The Chi-square test (χ^2 is pronounced ky similar to by) is an approximate test of significance for association between two categorical variables when data is in the form of frequency counts and interest focuses on how many subjects fall into different categories. The precise hypothesis tested depends upon the sampling design used. Observed frequencies in a 2×2 table (the first '2' indicates the number of rows in the table and the second '2' refers to the number of columns) may arise from a number of different research designs and this often causes confusion. Two common sampling designs are the χ^2 test of independence with random row and column marginal totals and the χ^2 test of homogeneity of proportions with either fixed row or fixed column marginal totals.

One-sample χ^2 test of independence with random row and column marginal totals

In this design a random sample is drawn from a single population of subjects but with two measures for each subject, that is the row and column binary variables. The total sample size, n, is **fixed** but the frequencies in both row and column marginal totals are random and not known or fixed in advance. The random marginal frequencies depend upon (contingent upon, hence the term contingency table) how each subject is classified on both binary variables. That is, each subject would be allocated to one of the four cells in the 2×2 table.

For example, a researcher investigating the carers' role in supporting relatives with dementia may be specifically interested in the relationship between length of experience as carers (column variable) and dominant feelings about their roles as carers (row variable). A single random sample of 100 carers was selected from a population of carers who have relatives suffering from dementia. The carers were asked two questions: how long have they been looking after their relatives? (responses classified into greater than or equal to five years or less than five years), and what were their dominant feelings about their carer role? (responses were classified into predominantly anger or guilt). The research hypothesis was that feelings about the carer role was related to the length of experience as a carer. The null hypothesis is that the row and column variables are independent, that is the expected proportions (counts) in each cell of the contingency table would be equal and would not differ from the observed counts. In more general terms this would be stated as there is no relationship between time as a carer and dominant feelings about the carers' role.

Two-sample χ^2 test of homogeneity of proportions with fixed column (or row) marginal totals

This design is used to compare the distribution of proportions in two independent populations. In a 2×2 contingency table each variable is treated as binary. For example, the column variable in a 2×2 table may represent two independent populations, males and females, and the row variable (response variable) may represent examination performance classified as pass or fail. The researcher may want to investigate whether the proportion of candidates passing is related to gender. For example, an independent random sample of fifty males, and a separate random sample of fifty females would be selected. The column total for males and females in this example is **fixed** by the researcher. Each male and female would be classified into a pass or fail category, the row marginal totals are **random** (not fixed by the researcher) and subject to sampling error. If the proportion of candidates who pass is represented by P, then the proportion of fails would be $1 - P$ (the variable is binary). Usually a count of the number of passes is given as a percentage, and a comparison is made between the percentage of males and females who pass. The null hypothesis would be the population proportion (or percentage) of males and females who pass is equal, or put another way there is no difference between males and females in the percentage who pass the exam. A more general form of this null hypothesis is that there is no relationship between gender and examination performance.

Statistical Inference and Null Hypothesis

Statistical inferences are about counts or relative frequencies with respect to defined characteristics in two populations. The number of observations that fall into a particular category in one group are compared with the proportion of observations that fall into the same category from the other group. Groups may refer to two independent measurements from one population (sample) of subjects, or to two independent populations from which two samples have been randomly selected. For example, in a study of the impact of an MEd in-service programme, one measure of interest might be confidence following completion of the in-service degree programme (professional confidence increased/not increased) another measure could be gender (male/female). The one-sample χ^2 test of independence would be used with this design to detect any association between confidence and gender.

Groups may also refer to two independent populations, for, example in a study of parents of children who have special educational needs two populations of parents (two independent samples) may be investigated; parents who were contacted via voluntary organisations, and parents who were contacted by the psychological services. With this sampling design a two-sample χ^2 test of homogeneity of proportions would be appropriate.

Whereas the precise form of the research hypothesis differs depending upon the sampling design, fortunately, the null hypothesis is the same for both the χ^2 tests of independence and homogeneity. For the one-sample χ^2 test of independence (random row and column marginal totals) the parameters being estimated are the proportions of each of the four outcomes (frequency distributions in each cell of the 2×2 table) in the population from which the sample was drawn. The research hypothesis is that the row and column variables interact, that is they are not independent, and the observed proportions in the four cells will therefore differ depending upon the particular row and column classification. Similarly, for the two-sample χ^2 test of homogeneity of proportions (fixed column or row marginal totals) the parameters being estimated are the proportions in the four outcomes in the population which the sample proportions are intended to estimate. The research hypothesis is that the distribution of proportions (for one categorical variable) is different in the two populations (the other categorical variable with fixed marginal totals). A more general way of stating this research hypothesis is to say that there is a relationship between the two categorical variables. The null hypothesis for both one-sample and two-sample χ^2 tests is that there is no interaction (relationship) between column and row variables. If the null hypothesis were true, the four cell proportions would be equal, and there would be no significant differences between observed cell frequencies and expected cell frequencies (under the null hypothesis of no interaction).

The χ^2 distribution is completely determined by a single parameter, the degrees of freedom (df). Whenever we evaluate the χ^2 statistic we need to consider the appropriate df. Degrees of freedom are determined by the number of rows and columns in a contingency table specifically, df = (number of rows − 1) × (number of columns − 1) and is hence always 1 in a 2 × 2 table. The χ^2 test and associated df provides a probability for the difference between observed and expected frequencies. When the observed and expected frequencies are identical the χ^2 statistic will be zero. Any deviation from this will always be positive, the larger the χ^2 value, the greater the statistical significance (departure from the null hypothesis).

Test Assumptions

The Chi-square test is widely used but is also one of the most misused statistical procedures. Basic assumptions of both χ^2 tests of independence and homogeneity for 2 × 2 tables are:

1   Observations are representative of the populations of interest.
2   Data is in the form of observed frequency counts.
3   Observations should be independent, that is, the probability of an observation falling in any particular row of a contingency table does not depend on which column it is in (and vice versa).
4   Observations should fall in only one cell of a contingency table.
5   The χ^2 test should not be used when any expected cell frequencies (see later for computational procedure) are *small* because the probability distribution of χ^2 gives a poor approximation to the sampling distribution of the χ^2 statistic. There has been considerable debate in the literature about what constitutes small expected frequencies. In a seminal paper on the use and misuse of the Chi-square test, Lewis and Burke (1949) claimed that small expected frequencies were the most common weakness in the use of Chi-square tests (p. 460). They suggested expected values of 5 as the absolute lowest limit. More recently Camilli and Hopkins (1978) suggest that provided the total sample size is ≥ 20, then expected frequencies in one or two cells can be as low as 1 or 2. Delucchi (1983), in reviewing the literature, concluded that the Chi-square test was a robust procedure and expected cell frequencies of < 5 did not substantively effect the Type I error rate. The general view would seem to be that small expected frequencies are acceptable in at least one or two cells provided the overall sample size ≥ 20.

   Many statistical texts suggest using Yate's (1934) correction for continuity (add 0.5 to observed cell frequencies) with small sample sizes in 2 × 2 tables. The variables in a contingency table are discrete but χ^2 is a continuous distribution, therefore adding 0.5 to each observed cell frequency is believed to improve the Chi-square approximation. Use of this correction is also contested in the statistical literature (not on theoretical grounds but based on its application). On balance it is suggested that Yate's correction should not be used because it results in unnecessary loss of power and conservative probability estimates. With small sample sizes, Fisher's exact test (Fisher, 1935) should be used (see section 6.3).

Examples from the Literature

One sample χ^2 test of independence

Cope *et al.* (1992) invited students who had completed a part-time in-service MEd programme to complete a questionnaire relating to their experience of the course and the impact it was perceived to have had on them. One of the questions asked related to the professional significance of the programme. The investigators commented that one of the most frequently reported categories of effect was an increased understanding of educational issues. Data as presented in the original paper is shown in Figure 6.1.

	Understanding of Educational Issues		
	An increase reported	No increase reported	
Gender:			Total
Male	21	27	48
Female	10	69	*49
Total	31	96	127

Figure 6.1: Number of former students reporting increased understanding of educational issues as an effect of the MEd programme
*see Comment on the Analysis below

The investigators reported that there were some interesting gender differences in the teachers' responses. Males reported an increased understanding of educational issues more frequently than did females, $\chi_1^2 = 14.00$, p < 0.001. (χ_1^2 means a Chi-square with 1df).

In this study the investigators used a χ^2 test of independence with a fixed total sample size of 127 but random observed row and column marginal totals. Each subject was categorized on two variables, reported understanding of educational issues (increased/not increased) and gender (male/female). The distribution of frequencies in each of the four cells was recorded in a 2×2 contingency table, see Figure 6.1. The research question addressed was whether, after the MEd programme, there was any association between increased understanding of educational issues and gender? Put another way this alternative hypothesis could be stated as: There is a statistical relationship between increased understanding of educational issues and gender following completion of an in-service MEd programme.

It would follow that if understanding and gender are related, then the row and column proportions would not be independent. That is the probability that a member of the population reported increased understanding and the probability that the person is a male would not be independent.

The null hypothesis tested by the investigators was that of no interaction between the row and column variables, namely increased understanding and gender. If the null hypothesis were true, the row and column variables would be independent (no interaction) and there would be no significant differences between observed cell frequencies and expected cell frequencies.

Comment on the Analysis

The three measurement assumptions are clearly met, namely, data is in the form of observed frequency counts; observations are assumed to be independent (the probability of reporting does not depend on gender); and each observation falls into only one cell of the contingency table. The sampling assumption, namely respondents are representative of part-time MEd students, in the absence of any data to suggest otherwise can also be taken as reasonable. An analysis of non-response by gender would strengthen the independence of observations assumption. (Close scrutiny of the published data shows that the total of males and females does not add up to 127. The sum of females should be 79 and not 49. As a check in a Chi-square analysis the sum of the cell frequency counts should equal the total sample size, that is no observation is double counted or missed out.)

Two-sample χ^2 test of homogeneity of proportions

In a study of parents of children with special educational needs by Riddell, Brown and Duffield (1994), parents of twenty-two children attending private schools and the parents of 131 children attending state schools were sampled. The investigators examined, as part of the overall purpose of the study, whether there was any association between sampling method of contacting parents to elicit study information (via voluntary organizations or psychological services) and type of school attended (state or private). Data as presented by the investigators is shown in Figure 6.2.

	Voluntary Organizations	Psychological Services	Random Row Total
Private	21	1	22
State	62	69	131
Fixed Column Total	83	70	153

Figure 6.2: Method of contacting parents by type of school child attended

The authors used a χ^2 test of homogeneity of proportions with fixed column marginal totals, 83 parents contacted via voluntary organizations and 70 parents contacted via psychological services. The column variable in the 2×2 table represents two independent populations of parents. The authors suggest that the achieved samples from these two populations are likely to be unrepresentative of parents (non-random samples). Each parent contacted was classified on a response variable into state or private according to the type of school his or her child attended. The row marginal totals were therefore random and subject to sampling error.

The research question addressed by the investigators was whether there was a statistical relationship between method of contacting parents and type of school the child attended. This research question could be rephrased as: 'Of the parents whose children attend private school, how does the proportion (or per cent) of parents contacted by voluntary organizations compare with the proportion of parents contacted by the psychological services?'

The null hypothesis would be that the population proportions (or percentages) of parents contacted via voluntary organizations and psychological services whose children attend private schools are equal. A more general form of this null hypothesis is that there is no relationship (statistical interaction) between the row and column variables – that is method of contact and type of school attended.

From the observed frequencies, 4.55 per cent ($1/22 \times 100$) of parents whose children attended private schools were contacted by psychological services and 95.45 per cent ($21/22 \times 100$) of these parents were contacted by voluntary organizations. It is evident from these results that there is no need for a statistical test of any significant interaction between method of contact and type of school, however, the investigators reported a Chi-square value of $\chi_1^2 = 15.693$, $p < 0.001$, and went on to conclude that there was, not unexpectedly, an association between method of contact and type of school attended by the child.

Comment on the Analysis

All assumptions appear to be met with the possible exception that the samples may not have been representative of the two populations of parents. This is a good example where it is difficult to define target populations. Sampling is always a critical aspect of a study design if inferential statistical procedures are to be used and the authors rightly draw the readers attention to this aspect of the study.

Worked Example

The χ^2 statistic for a contingency table is a kind of standardized measure of the overall difference between the entire set of observed and expected cell counts. The χ^2 test compares the observed frequency counts (we already know these) in each of the cells in the contingency table with the expected frequency counts for each of the cells (we have to estimate expected frequencies). The expected cell counts are estimated under the assumption that the null hypothesis is true, that is there is no association between the row and column variables.

The expected count for any cell in a 2×2 table is estimated by the **joint probability** of the appropriate row i and column j in the 2×2 table. For example, the probability, say, of increased understanding *and* being a male is equal to the probability of increased understanding multiplied by the probability of being a male, derived from the multiplication rule for independent events (P(U and M) = P(U)P(M)). This joint probability is the product of the marginal probabilities for the appropriate row i and column j in a contingency table.

These marginal probabilities are not themselves observable but can be estimated by the row and column sample proportions, that is row proportion = (row total)/sample total, and column proportion = (column total)/sample total.

In a 2 × 2 table, each categorical variable is binary and the mean (expected) count for a binary variable $B(n,\pi)$, is np for sample data, where p is the joint probability $r_i c_j$ for a particular cell frequency and n is the sample total. The **expected frequency count** is therefore:

$$np = nr_i c_j = \text{sample}_{total} \times (\text{row}_{total}/\text{sample}_{total}) \times (\text{col}_{total}/\text{sample}_{total})$$

Expected count $= (\text{row}_{total} \times \text{col}_{total})/\text{sample}_{total}$

The χ^2 value is calculated for each cell in a contingency table. It is calculated as the difference between each observed and corresponding expected count squared (this squared difference makes all values positive or zero) and then divided by the expected count (this standardizes all values). Each cell's contribution to χ^2 is then added to provide an overall χ^2 statistic for the contingency table. The degrees of freedom are calculated as (rows − 1 × columns − 1) which is 1 in a 2 × 2 table. The χ^2 statistic in notational form is:

$$\chi^2 = \sum \frac{(O - E)^2}{E} \qquad \qquad \textbf{Chi-square – 6.1}$$

where O is the observed cell frequency and E is the expected cell frequency.

Data from the first example (Figure 6.1) on the effect of the MEd programme on teachers' understanding of educational issues is used to illustrate calculation of the overall χ^2 statistic. For clarity of presentation each cell in the table is labelled A to D. (The number of females has been changed to seventy-nine, as there was an error in the original paper. See earlier comment, p. 169.)

Understanding of Educational Issues

	An increase reported	No increase reported	Total
Gender:			
Male	21 (A)	27 (B)	48
Female	10 (C)	69 (D)	79
Total	31	96	127

Computational steps:

1 Calculate **expected** values for each cell A to D
   Cell A: Expected = (48 × 31)/127 = 11.717
   Cell B: Expected = (48 × 96)/127 = 36.283
   Cell C: Expected = (79 × 31)/127 = 19.283
   Cell D: Expected = (79 × 96)/127 = 59.717

2 Calculate the value of χ^2 for each cell A to D. Use formulae 6.1
   Cell A: $\chi^2 = (21 - 11.717)^2/11.717 = 7.355$

$$\text{Cell B: } \chi^2 = (27 - 36.283)^2/36.283 = 2.375$$
$$\text{Cell C: } \chi^2 = (10 - 19.283)^2/19.283 = 4.469$$
$$\text{Cell D: } \chi^2 = (69 - 59.717)^2/59.717 = 1.443$$

3   Sum all the χ^2 values
$$= 7.355 + 2.375 + 4.469 + 1.443$$
$$\text{Total } \chi^2 = 15.64, \text{ df} = 1$$

The investigators reported a χ^2 value of 14.00, df = 1. The difference between the reported value in the original paper and the calculated value in the worked example is attributable to the investigators' use of a continuity adjusted χ^2 (which was not reported in the original paper). This adjustment was unnecessary, the sample size was > 20 and none of the expected cell frequencies were < 5. The tendency for the continuity adjusted χ^2 to provide conservative probabilities is evident here because the adjusted χ^2 is less than the unadjusted statistic, $\chi_{1\,adj}^2 = 14 < \chi_1^2$ 15.64 (χ_1^2 refers to χ^2 with 1 df). In this particular instance, the different values of the adjusted and unadjusted χ^2 statistics do not affect the interpretation.

Interpretation

To evaluate the statistical significance of the estimated χ^2 statistic you need to calculate the appropriate degrees of freedom for the contingency table, here df = 1, and refer to a table of critical χ^2 values (see Table 2, Appendix A4). An alpha level is first selected, usually $p \leq 0.05$ or $p \leq 0.001$, although depending upon the statistical table there may be other alpha values to choose from. If we select alpha as $p < 0.001$, the last column in Table 2 of Appendix A4, we then move down this column until we intersect with the appropriate row for degrees of freedom.

In this example the critical χ^2 value is 10.828, rounded to 10.83, the intersection of last column and first row in Table 1. Since the calculated value is greater than the value from the statistical tables (what would be expected under the null hypothesis of no interaction between row and column variables) then we can reject the null hypothesis and conclude that the two variables, increased understanding of educational issues, and gender are related. Generally, it is good practice to inspect and report on the differences in observed and expected frequencies, that is to consider how the null hypothesis is untrue. Descriptive percentages are helpful in doing this. For example, the results of the analysis could be presented as follows:

Understanding of Educational Issues

| | An increase reported | | No increase reported | |
	Observed	Expected	Observed	Expected
Gender:				
Male	21	12	27	36
Female	10	19	69	60
Total		31		96

Notice as a check, observed and expected totals are equal. Proportionately more males 43.8 per cent ($21/48 \times 100$) than females 12.7 per cent ($10/79 \times 100$) reported an increase in understanding of educational issues following the in-service MEd course.

Computer Analysis

Data from the example of the χ^2 test of independence (see Figure 6.1) is illustrated. When data is in the form of frequency counts a simple way to enter and analyze this data in SAS is to use the frequencies procedure PROC FREQ with the **weight** statement. For example, if we want to analyze data from the study about teachers' understanding of educational issues following their MEd course (see Figure 6.1), this data can be entered into a SAS programme using the following lines of code:

```
data chi;
    input row col celln @@;
    cards;

1 1 21 1 2 27 2 1 10 2 2 69
;
```

The first three values in the data lines, 1 1 21 refer to row 1 (row variable on the input line), col 1 (col variable on the input line) cell frequency value 21 (celln variable on the input line). The double trailing at sign, @@, is used because the input data line, 1 1 21 1 2 27 2 1 10 2 2 69, contains data values for more than one variable and more than one observation. In this example, there are three variables (row, col, celln) and four observations (the frequency count for each cell). The **weight** statement when used with PROC FREQ specifies the variable that contains the cell frequencies. The SAS code is:

```
proc freq data=chi;
    weight celln;
    table row*col / nopercent chisq;
title 'Chi square test for gender (row var) and understanding(col var)';
run;
```

The complete programme is shown in Figure 5, Appendix A3.

Interpretation of Computer Output

Output from the Chi-square programme for the teachers' data is shown in Figure 6.3. For clarity of presentation only the relevant sections of output are illustrated.

```
Chi square test for gender (row var) and understanding(col var)

                          Table of row by col

          Row         Col
          Frequency |
          Row Pct   |
          Col Pct   |           1 |           2 |      Total
          - - - - - +- - - - - - - - +- - - - - - - - +
                1 |          21 |          27 |        48
                  |       43.75 |       56.25 |
                  |       67.74 |       28.12 |
          - - - - - +- - - - - - - - +- - - - - - - - +
                2 |          10 |          69 |        79
                  |       12.66 |       87.34 |
                  |       32.26 |       71.88 |
          - - - - - +- - - - - - - - +- - - - - - - - +
          Total              31            96          127

                    Statistics for table of row by col

Statistic                       DF              Value             Prob
_____

Chi-Square                      1              15.643            0.000
Phi Coefficient                                0.351
Cramer's V                                     0.351
Sample Size = 127
```

Figure 6.3: Output for Chi-square analysis

The computed χ^2 value is the same as the value in the worked example. Notice an actual probability is given rather than p at a pre-specified value (i.e., $p \leqslant 0.05$ or $p \leqslant 0.01$). Clearly the actual value is statistically significant at the 1 per cent ($p \leqslant 0.001$) level. Each cell in the contingency table contains a cell frequency count and row and column per cents.

Phi Coefficient and Cramer's Phi

The χ^2 procedure is sensitive to sample size and is nearly always significant with large samples. The χ^2 test assesses the statistical significance of an association and not the strength of the association. Correlational type statistics are therefore required to determine the strength of any statistically significant association detected by the χ^2 statistic. Two of the most useful measures of association provided in the SAS output are i) Φ, (Phi Coefficient) and ii) Cramer's V (sometimes called Cramer's Phi Coefficient). Phi should only be used as a measure of the strength of association when both variables are binary (scored as 0,1; present, absent; +, −, etc.) and can be used when data is in the form of a 2×2 contingency table. There is a direct relationship between χ^2 and Φ given by the formulae:

$$\Phi = \sqrt{\frac{\chi^2}{n}}$$ **Phi – 6.2**

where n is the total sample size and χ^2 is the statistic from the same contingency table.

The value of Phi for the data shown in Figure 6.1 is 0.351 $(15.643/127)^{0.5}$. Phi has a lower limit of 0, no strength of association (variables are not related) and an upper limit of 1, maximum strength of association (variables are perfectly correlated). When a contingency table has more than four cells Cramer's V should be used to measure the strength of association. Similar to Phi the range of this statistic varies between 0 and 1. Cramer's V is calculated using the following formulae:

$$V = \sqrt{\frac{\chi^2}{n(j-1)}}$$ **Cramer's V – 6.3**

where χ^2 is the value for the entire contingency table, n is the total sample size and j is the smaller of the number of rows or number of columns in the contingency table.

The value of Cramer's V for the data shown in Figure 6.1 is 0.35, $(15.643/127 \times (2-1))^{0.5}$, the same value as Phi. For discussion of the use of measures of association in conjunction with the Chi-square statistic, see Delucchi (1983).

When a significant association between two variables is detected, it is sensible to consider whether a third variable might explain this association. If this variable is in the data set, a three-way frequency table could be produced stratifying on the third variable. For example, if the variable 'teaching experience' (number of years as a classroom teacher) was measured in the study by Cope, et al., (1992) this might have some explanatory power for the apparent relationship between gender and increased understanding. If a study used several different Chi-square tests, it would be advisable to adjust the probability level associated with each statistical test (make it more conservative) to take account of a significant result occurring simply by chance.

6.2   Binomial Test

When to Use

The Binomial test is not widely used by educational researchers but is suitable when a single random sample is selected from a binary population and each sampled observation can be classified into one of two mutually exclusive categories. The sample proportion of observations in one of the two categories is used to estimate the population proportion in the same category. As this is a one-sample test, both proportions (or percentages) must equal one (or 100 per cent).

The test is particularly useful when it is believed that the population proportion falling into one of the two categories is 0.5. This is, in effect, a hypothesis of no difference in the proportion of responses in the two categories, that is $P_1 = P_2 = 0.5$, which would equal the population proportion. If P_1 equals the proportion of observations in one category then $1 - P_1$ (sometimes called Q) is the proportion of observations in the other category.

Often research designs involve comparison between matched groups on a binary variable of interest. For example, following the introduction of student loans, an investigator may be interested in whether students incur serious financial debts during their time at college. The binary variable would be, in serious debt/not in serious debt. A random sample of fourteen males might be matched with a random sample of fourteen females, same age, same college and the proportion of males in debt compared with the proportion of females who were in debt. The achieved sample might be:

	In serious debt at college	Total
Male	10	14
Female	6	14
100 per cent	16	28

The null hypothesis is that the population proportions are equal, that is there is no difference between the probability of males and the probability of females who incur serious debt problems during college. If the null hypothesis were true we would expect to find in the sample of 16 students who were in debt, eight males and eight females.

The binomial test is also useful for analyzing responses to multiple choice questions. Given ten true/false multiple choice questions, a teacher may want to know how many correct answers would be expected if a candidate were guessing at random. (Caution is required because candidates often do not guess at random; they may use partial knowledge.)

Statistical Inference and Null Hypothesis

The parameters estimated are population proportions. The null hypothesis is often H_0: π (population proportion) $= 0.5$. If the proportion of responses in category 1 is P and the proportion in category 2 is Q, then there are three alternative hypotheses: i) H_1: $P > Q$, ii) H_1: $P < Q$ iii) H_1: $P \neq Q$. A one-tailed test is used when we predict in advance which of the two categories should contain the smaller number of counts (i and ii above). If the alternative hypothesis is simply that the counts in the two categories will differ (iii above) then a two-sided test should be used. The sampling distribution used is the binomial distribution, in this example $B(n,\pi)$ would be Binomial $(16,0.5)$ see Chapter 4, section 4.4 for details.

Test Assumptions

The test assumptions are those of the binomial distribution which are as follows:

1 Observations are sampled at random from a binary population.
2 Each observation is independent (does not effect the value of any other observations sampled)

3   The probability of any sample observation being classified into one of the two categories is fixed for the population.

4   With small sample sizes such as $n \leq 25$, the exact binomial probability can be evaluated. With larger sample sizes, especially when P is close to 0.5, the binomial approximation to the normal distribution with a continuity correction (because the normal distribution is continuous but the binomial distribution is discrete) can be used. In this case the normal variate Z is used to evaluate the probability of the observed outcome.

Example from the Literature

Blasingame and McManis (1977), in a study of retarded adults, investigated developmental aspects of cognition, specifically transitivity of inequality ($A > B$, $B > C$, therefore $A > C$), classification (subjects had to select a geometric figure to complete a missing cell in a 2×2 matrix) and relative thinking (measured by the right–left test, Elkind, 1961). Sequentiality of development among the three tasks was evaluated by cross classification of subjects on pairs of tasks according to performance (achieve/not achieve). The number of subjects performing discrepantly in each direction on two tasks (achieve one task but not the other) was evaluated for statistical significance using the binomial test. The authors give the following results:

Discrepant Performance between relative thinking and transivity tasks	Number of retarded adults
transitivity *achieved* but relative thinking *not achieved*	4
transitivity *not achieved* but relative thinking *achieved*	13
100 per cent	17

The null hypothesis is that there should be no difference between the proportion (number) of subjects who can achieve transitivity but not relative thinking, and the proportion of subjects who do not achieve transitivity but do achieve relative thinking. Put another way, we could say that the number of subjects performing discrepantly in each direction on two tasks should not differ significantly from a chance distribution. A one-sided (directional) test would be appropriate here if the authors were, in advance, looking for discrepancies in a given direction.

Worked Example

Data from the study by Blasingame and McManis (1977) is used to illustrate computational details for the binomial test when $\pi = 0.5$, (sample proportion $P = Q = 0.5$) and $n < 25$. The exact probability of obtaining values as extreme or more extreme than the observed values is evaluated using the binomial equation, see equation 4.1 Binomial Probability in Chapter 4.

$$p = {}^nC_r \times p^r \times (1 - p)^{n-r}$$ **Binomial probability**

The probability of obtaining 4 or fewer discrepant performance ratings is given by the sum of the 5 probabilities:

p 0 discrepant observations = $17!/(0! \times 17!) \times 0.5^0 \times 0.5^{17} = 0.0000076$
p 1 discrepant observations = $17!/(1! \times 16!) \times 0.5^1 \times 0.5^{16} = 0.0001297$
p 2 discrepant observations = $17!/(2! \times 15!) \times 0.5^2 \times 0.5^{15} = 0.0010376$
p 3 discrepant observations = $17!/(3! \times 14!) \times 0.5^3 \times 0.5^{14} = 0.0051880$
p 4 discrepant observations = $17!/(4! \times 13!) \times 0.5^4 \times 0.5^{13} = 0.0181579$

which equals 0.0245 allowing for rounding error. To avoid tedious calculations binomial tables can be referred to or the SAS function PROBBNML can be used (see computer analysis).

Interpretation

The null hypothesis of no difference in proportions is rejected at the 5 per cent level. In the original paper the authors reported that there was a significant difference in performance between relative thinking and transitivity, $p = 0.025$. The authors interpreted these findings as indicating a sequential development of relative thinking and transitivity, in that order. (In a situation where a two-sided test would be appropriate, then the calculated probability, using the above procedure, would simply be multiplied by two.)

Computer Analysis

Binomial calculations can be accomplished with ease using the PROBBNML function in SAS. Functions are a valuable feature of SAS because they allow a variable to be defined which is equal to a kind of built-in expression in the SAS language. There are nearly 150 different functions which fall into different types, for example, probability, arithmetic, quantile, trigonometric, random numbers and others. The reader should refer to the SAS Institute Inc. (1993b) *SAS Language Guide Version 6*, for details.

The following SAS code will produce the exact probability for the specified binomial distribution in the SAS log file:

```
data a;
 p=probbnml (0.5,17,4);
 put p=;
```

The function is used here in a data step, data a: defines a temporary data set in SAS given the arbitrary name of 'a'. p is the name of a variable which takes on the value of the SAS function PROBBNML with three defined parameters, 0.5, 17 and 4. The first parameter represents the population probability of success, the second parameter is the total number of trials (sample size), and the third parameter is the number of successes (the smaller frequency count in the two categories). The **put** statement tells SAS to write the variable P (evaluation of the binomial function) to the LOG File.

Interpretation of Computer Output

The three lines of SAS code produce the following SAS output in the LOG File:

```
data a;
  p=probbnml(0.5,17,4);
    put p=;
  run;

P=0.024520874
Note: The data set WORK.A has 1 observation and 1 variable.
Note: The DATA statement used 22.57 seconds.
```

The returned probability value of 0.025 is the probability that an observation from a binomial distribution, with probability of success 0.5, and number of trials 17, has 4 or fewer successes.

Worked Example (n > 25)

Data from the study of upper limb injuries and handedness plasticity (Dellatolas, *et al.*, 1993) (used to illustrate Fisher's exact probability test, in section 6.3) is used here to investigate whether, for left-handed males, there is any difference between the probability of young ($\leqslant$ 6-years-old) and the probability of older ($>$ 6-years-old) subjects incurring upper limb injuries. The sample data is:

Age when injured	Left-handed males with upper limb injuries
$\leqslant$ 6 yrs	7
$>$ 6 yrs	59
100%	66

The null hypothesis is that there is no difference in the probability of upper limb injury between the two age categories: H_0:π (population proportion for $>$ 6-years-old) = 0.5 and, H_1: $P \neq Q$. A two-tailed test is required.

For the binomial test when $\pi = 0.5$, (sample proportion $P = Q = 0.5$) and $n > 25$, the following formula can be used to evaluate the binomial approximation to the normal distribution (with continuity correction)

$$Z = \frac{(X +/- 0.5) - nP}{nPQ^{0.5}}$$

**Binomial approximation
to normal distribution
with continuity correction** – 6.4

where X is the smaller of the two frequency counts (one for each category), n is the total sample size, and P is 0.5.

The correction for continuity is +/− 0.5 depending upon the expected value for X which is evaluated as nP or simply half of the sample size. If X is $< nP$ we add 0.5 to X and if X is $> nP$ we subtract 0.5 from X. In this example, X is $< nP$ ($7 < 33$) and we therefore *add* 0.5 to X when evaluating formulae 6.4:

$$Z = \frac{(7 + 0.5) - (66 \times 0.5)}{(66 \times 0.5 \times 0.5)^{0.5}}$$

$$Z = -6.2777$$

Interpretation

This Z-value of −6.2777 is so extreme that it is not even tabulated in the table of Z-values, (see Table 1, Appendix A4). We can say from this table that the one-tailed probability associated with this Z-value is p $<$ 0.0000 (probability associated with the most extreme tabulated Z-value of 4.0). Since our alternative hypothesis was simply that the two frequencies would differ, a two-sided test is appropriate. For a two-sided test the probability is doubled, here the value of P remains as $p <$ 0.0000. The null hypothesis of no difference in the probability of upper limb injury between the two age categories is therefore rejected. Proportionately, significantly more injuries were incurred among left-handed males when they were $>$ 6-years-old than when they were $\leq$ 6-years-old.

Computer Analysis

The exact probability can be evaluated using the PROBBNML function. The appropriate SAS code is,

```
data a;
 p=probbnml (0.5,66,7);
    put p=;
```

The probability is given in the Log File for example,

```
P=1.718532E - 10
Note: The data set WORK.A has 1 observations and 1 variables.
Note: The DATA statement used 39.1 seconds.

Note: E - 10 means move the decimal point 10 places to the left.
```

Interpretation of Computer Output

When $P = Q = 0.5$ the normal approximation with correction for continuity provides a good approximation as can be seen if the obtained Z-value of −6.27766 is evaluated using the PROBNORM function in SAS. This function returns the one-tailed probability that a Z-value is less than or equal to the value entered. For example, in the following SAS code a Z-value of -6.27766 is entered,

```
data a;
  p=probnorm (-6.27766);
    put p=;
```

and a probability of $p = 1.718532E - 10$ is returned in the Log File. This value ($p = 1.718532E - 10$) is the same as the exact probability that was returned by the binomial probability function.

6.3   Fisher's Exact Test

When to Use the Test

Fisher's exact test is used to test the significance of any association or difference between two independent samples. The test determines whether two independent groups differ significantly in the proportions of observations that are classified by a dependent binary variable. Suppose that in total twelve male subjects who had sustained upper limb injuries were sampled. One group was a random sample of six males from a population who had sustained their injuries before school age (injured when $\leq$ 6-years-old). The second independent sample of six males was selected from a population who had sustained their injuries when older (injured when $>$ 6-years-old). The dependent variable was handedness (left or right). Investigators may want to know whether there is any association between age when the injury occurred and handedness.

Fisher's exact test is a useful alternative to the $r \times 2$ sample χ^2 test of association when total sample sizes are small, $n < 20$ or when expected frequencies in any of the four cells of the contingency table are less than 5. The test provides an exact probability for observing a particular frequency distribution in a 2×2 table.

Statistical Inference and Null Hypothesis

Inferences made in the Fisher's exact test are about population proportions. Stated in general terms the null hypothesis is that the proportions in the two independent samples are not related (statistically independent) to the dependent binary variable. In the example of upper limb injuries and handedness the null hypothesis would be that age when the injury occurred is independent of handedness.

Test Assumptions

Data should be discrete (counts) and may be nominal or ordinal provided members of each independent sample can be classified into one of two mutually exclusive groups. The test should be used when the underlying distribution is **hypergeometric**. This implies that both row and column marginals are fixed. For example, assume that in total ten male subjects with upper limb injuries are *randomly assigned* to two groups (A and B). Each subject is then classified as right- or left-handed, and the following 2 × 2 table is obtained:

Ten subjects with upper limb injuries
randomly assigned to two groups

	Left-handed	Right-handed	
Group A	2	3	5 (Fixed row total)
Group B	4	1	5 (Fixed row total)
(Fixed column totals)	6	4	

Provided there is no association between handedness and group membership then each group can be treated as a random sample from the population with upper limb injuries described by the column marginal totals (6,4). This population is described by the fixed column marginal totals (6,4). Whereas a different randomization is likely to have produced different cell frequencies, the column marginal totals would remain as before (6,4), provided there was no difference between Group A and Group B. In this case both marginal totals are fixed and the distribution of cell frequency counts is described by the hypergeometric distribution. Inferences are made with respect to the target population of subjects (males with upper limb injuries).

Two alternative sampling strategies that can give rise to a 2 × 2 contingency table are simple random sampling and stratified random sampling. If ten male subjects with upper limb injuries were sampled at random from the population (simple random sampling), and each subject was asked two questions: Are you left- or right-handed? Did your injury occur ⩽ 6-years-old or > 6-years-old ? The only fixed marginal total is the overall total, and the row and column marginal totals will be random. The following data may be obtained:

Ten subjects with upper limb injuries
selected at random

	Left-handed	Right-handed
⩽ 6-years-old	3	3
> 6-years-old	1	3

10 (Fixed total)

In this design, inferences can be drawn with respect to the target population of males with upper limb injuries. The null hypothesis would be no association between the row and column variables and the distribution of frequencies is described by the **multinomial** distribution.

The third sampling design is **stratified random sampling**. If two groups of 5

male subjects are sampled at random from each of two populations, male subjects
with upper limb injuries that occurred when they were ≤ 6-years-old and a similar
group but with injuries occurring when subjects were > 6-years-old, and these
subjects were asked, 'Are you right- or left-handed?' The following contingency
table may be obtained:

Random sample of five subjects with upper limb injuries
selected from two populations

	≤ 6-years-old	> 6-years-old
Left-handed	1	0
Right-handed	4	5
(Fixed column totals)	5	5

In this table, the column marginal totals are fixed, the row marginals are random
and the underlying frequency distribution is described by the **product multinomial**
distribution. The null hypothesis in this design is that the proportions of left-handers
(or we could say right-handers) is the same in both age cohort populations (≤ 6
years, and > 6 years). Inferences are made with respect to the target populations
and the notion of independence does not make sense in this sampling design.

What should be done if we have a small overall sample or small expected cell
values in a 2 × 2 table, or we want to consider a question about statistical
*independence between row and column variables **but** have used the wrong*
sampling design?

We can still use Fisher's exact test, but any inferences are made conditional
on the *observed* marginal totals.

Example from the Literature

In a study of handedness plasticity, part of which was designed to investigate
handedness (left or right) and upper limb injury, Dellatolas *et al.* (1993) surveyed
9591 men aged 17–27 who were conscripted into the French army. Of this sample
577 reported that they had previously sustained an upper limb injury, 25 were ≤
6-years-old when the injury occurred and 552 sustained their injuries when they
were > 6-years-old. One question addressed by the investigators was whether there
was any difference between two age groups in the proportions of left-handed males
who had sustained upper limb injuries. Data was set out in a 2 × 2 contingency
table as follows:

577 subjects with upper limb injuries
Age when injury occurred

Handedness:	≤ 6-years-old	> 6-years-old	(Random row totals)
Left-handed	7	59	66
Right-handed	18	493	511
(Fixed column totals)	25	552	577

If the two age groups are treated as separate populations, and the achieved samples are treated as random samples from these populations, then the appropriate underlying distribution is product multinomial and inferences are made with respect to the populations, conditional on the observed marginal totals. A two-tailed test is appropriate given the exploratory nature of the study. The investigators reported that among the 577 injured men, the proportion of left-handers was significantly higher when the age the accident occurred was $\leq$ 6 years (28 per cent) [$7/25 \times 100$] than when it occurred later (10.7 per cent) [$59/552 \times 100$], Fisher's exact test: $p < 0.02$.

Worked Example

Assume the following data table was obtained when a random sample of males with upper limb injuries was selected.

Handedness:	Age when injury occurred		(Random row totals)
	$\leq$ 6-years-old	> 6-years-old	
Left-handed	3(A)	1(B)	4(A + B)
Right-handed	3(C)	3(D)	6(C + D)
(Random column totals)	6(A + C)	4(B + D)	10 (TOTAL *N* FIXED)

Figure 6.4: *Ten subjects with upper limb injuries selected at random*

Cells in the table are labelled A to D and marginal totals are (A + B), (C + D), (A + C) and (B + D).

In this example the overall total, *N*, is fixed and the row and column marginal totals are random. Whereas the sampling design suggests that the multinomial distribution is appropriate, if we make the assumption that inferences are conditional on the **observed** marginal totals, then the hypergeometric distribution can be used. The exact probability, under the null hypothesis (assuming random assignment), of observing this frequency distribution in the four cells, or a more extreme distribution, can be evaluated using the following equation:

$$P = \frac{(A + B)! \times (C + D)! \times (A + C)! \times (B + D)!}{N! \times A! \times B! \times C! \times D!}$$

Probability of observed frequency distribution for Fisher's test – 6.5

where *N* is the overall total, 10, and A to D are the cell frequencies and marginal totals as illustrated in Figure 6.4.

Using data presented in Figure 6.4, the null hypothesis is that the proportions of left-handed males with upper limb injuries is the same in both age cohorts ($\leq$ 6 years, and > 6 years), that is H_0: $P_1 = P_2$ where P_1 is the probability that a male from the age cohort $\leq$ 6 years will be left-handed (cell *A*) and P_2 is the probability that a male from the age cohort > 6 years will be left-handed (cell *B*).

There are three possible alternative hypotheses: H_1: $P_1 > P_2$, H_1: $P_1 < P_2$ and H_1: $P_1 \neq P_2$. In most situations the two-tailed test is the appropriate test. In this example a two-tailed alternative hypothesis is considered; Does the younger age cohort (≤ 6 years) have a significantly larger or smaller proportion of left-handed subjects with upper limb injury? Fishers's exact test determines the probability under the null hypothesis of obtaining the observed frequencies, or more extreme distributions of cell frequencies, with the same (fixed) marginal totals.

1   The first step is to identify all possible frequency distributions with the same fixed marginal totals as the observed frequency counts ($A + B = 4$; $C + D = 6$; $A + C = 6$; and $B + D = 4$). The number of possible tables is equal to the smallest marginal frequency plus 1 if none of the cells are 0. In this example there are 5 possible tables ($4 + 1$). These are numbered (i) to (v) according to the frequency of cell A:

Table (i)				Table (ii)				Table (iii)		
0	4	| 4		1	3	| 4		2	2	| 4
6	0	| 6		5	1	| 6		4	2	| 6
6	4	| 10		6	4	| 10		6	4	| 10

Table (iv)				Table (v)		
3	1	| 4		4	0	| 4
3	3	| 6		2	4	| 6
6	4	| 10		6	4	| 10

2   Select an appropriate alpha level, for example, 0.05 (two-tailed).
3   The probability of each possible frequency distribution, with the same fixed marginal totals is then evaluated using equation 6.5.

As a check, the total probability of $p(i)$ to $p(v)$ should sum to 1.
$p(i)$ $= (4! \times 6! \times 6! \times 4!)/ (10! \times 0! \times 4! \times 6! \times 0!) = 0.0048$
$p(ii)$ $= (4! \times 6! \times 6! \times 4!)/ (10! \times 1! \times 3! \times 5! \times 1!) = 0.1143$
$p(iii)$ $= (4! \times 6! \times 6! \times 4!)/ (10! \times 2! \times 2! \times 4! \times 2!) = 0.4286$
$p(iv)$ $= (4! \times 6! \times 6! \times 4!)/ (10! \times 3! \times 1! \times 3! \times 3!) = 0.3810$
$p(v)$ $= (4! \times 6! \times 6! \times 4!)/ (10! \times 4! \times 0! \times 2! \times 4!) = 0.0714$
Total $= p(i) + p(ii) + p(iii) + p(iv) + p(v)$ $= 1.0001$

4   For a two-tailed test, the probability is the sum of the probabilities of all tables with a probability less than or equal to the probability of the observed table. That is ($p(i)$ 0.0048 + $p(ii)$ 0.1143 + $p(iv)$ 0.3810 + $p(v)$ 0.0714) p = 0.5715.

For one-tailed tests the right tail probability is the sum of the probabilities of all tables more extreme and including the probability of the observed table (when tables are arranged in order of magnitude from cell A minimum frequency to cell A maximum frequency). The right-tail probability is therefore ($p(iv)$ 0.3810 + $p(v)$ 0.0714) = 0.4524. The left-tail probability is the sum of the probabilities of all tables less extreme and including the probability of the observed table, that is (p(iv) 0.3810 + p(iii) 0.4286 + p(ii) 0.1143 + p(i) 0.0048) = 0.929.

Interpretation

The obtained p value of 0.5715 (two-tailed) is clearly not significant at the 5 per cent level.

Computer Analysis

The calculation of exact probabilities for each contingency table is tedious and time consuming. PROC FREQ in SAS produces both one-tailed and two-tailed probabilities for Fisher's exact test. Data from the worked example using the following lines of SAS code is shown:

```
data fisher;
    input row $ col $ count @@;
    cards;
1 1 3 1 2 1 2 1 3 2 2 3
;
```

To analyze this data PROC FREQ is used with the **weight** statement (this specifies the variable that contains the cell frequencies). The appropriate SAS code is:

```
proc freq data=fisher;
    weight count;
    table row*col / nopercent chisq;
title "Fisher's exact test";
run;
```

The complete programme is shown in Figure 6, Appendix A3.

Interpretation of Computer Output

Computer output for the 2 × 2 contingency table relating to Fisher's exact test for the group and handedness data (data used in the worked example) is shown in Figure 6.5. For clarity of presentation only the relevant sections of output are illustrated.

The probabilities shown in Figure 6.5 are the same as those calculated in the worked example. The null hypothesis cannot be rejected, and we conclude there is no difference between the two age groups in the proportions of left-handed subjects with upper limb injury. In other words the observed frequency distribution could have arisen by chance.

```
                          Table of row by col

       Row                    Col

       Frequency        |
       Row Pct          |
       Col Pct          | 1            | 2            |      Total
       -----------------+--------------+--------------+
       1                |       3      |      1       |       4
                        |    75.00     |    25.00     |
                        |    50.00     |    25.00     |
       -----------------+--------------+--------------+
       2                |       3      |      3       |       6
                        |    50.00     |    50.00     |
                        |    50.00     |    75.00     |
       -----------------+--------------+--------------+
       Total                   6              4               10

                Statistics for table of row by col

Statistic                             DF        Value          Prob
--------------------------------------------------------------------
Chi-Square                             1        0.625          0.429
Continuity Adj. Chi-Square             1        0.017          0.895
Fisher's Exact Test (Left)                                     0.929
                    (Right)                                    0.452
                    (2-Tail)                                   0.571
Sample Size = 10
WARNING: 100% of the cells have expected counts less than 5. Chi-
         Square may not be a valid test.
```

Figure 6.5: Output for Fisher's exact test

6.4 Proportions Test (or difference in percentages)

When to Use

When an investigator is interested in a simple difference in proportions between two independent groups, rather than a relationship (when χ^2 would be used), the proportions test is appropriate. This test procedure is used to compare the proportions of two independent groups (such as boys and girls) with respect to a nominal variable of interest, for example, blue eyes/brown eyes; IQ $\geq$ 100/ < 100; pass/fail. The groups are the result of two independent random samples from specified populations and the sample sizes do not have to be equal. The test procedure illustrated here is based on the confidence interval of the difference between two population proportions which is estimated using the difference between the observed proportions in the two random samples. The test is also applicable to comparison of the difference between two percentages.

Statistical Inference and Null Hypothesis

Statistical inferences for this procedure relate to population proportions, the null hypothesis is that these are equal. The test is based on a normal approximation to the binomial distribution, the normal variate Z is used to evaluate a confidence interval for the difference, D, between population proportions. To calculate the significance of this difference, D, the standard error (standard deviation) of the observed difference is calculated and an appropriate confidence interval for the difference, based on this observed standard error, is evaluated. The unknown difference between population proportions, D, is estimated using the observed difference in sample proportions, $P_1 - P_2$. If the confidence interval excludes 0 we can be confident that the groups are significantly different.

Technically, the null hypothesis is tested using a pooled estimate of the standard error of the difference in proportions because the null hypothesis actually states that the population proportions are equal, $\pi_1 = \pi_2$. When a pooled estimate is used, the total population proportion is estimated using the information contained in the two samples. In fact a weighted mean proportion is used (the overall proportion of successes in the two samples). This is the procedure most often presented in introductory statistical texts. For reasons already mentioned, it is this author's belief that whenever possible it is preferable to give a confidence interval for any difference accordingly, the test procedure presented here is to evaluate a confidence interval for the difference in proportions. This leads to a test of essentially the same null hypothesis of no difference between proportions but additionally provides a zone of confidence for any population difference in proportions. The reader should note that the main difference between the confidence interval approach and a direct test of the null hypothesis is the procedure used for estimating the standard error.

Test Assumptions

- Observations are sampled at random from a specified binary population. The population can be treated as binary with respect to a continuous variable provided that values for the statistical variable can be assigned to two mutually exclusive categories.
- Each observation is independent (does not effect the value of any other observations sampled).
- This test is based on a normal approximation to the binomial distribution (normal variate Z is used). The test procedure should not therefore be used when sample sizes are small, say < 25, or when the proportions are outside the range 0.1 to 0.9.

Examples from the Literature

In a study of social–cognitive modes of play Roopnarine *et al.* (1992) observed playmate selection in different classroom structures (same age/ mixed age classrooms). The study included analysis of the proportions of child-initiated play activities with same sex peers in same age and mixed-age classrooms. The investigators performed tests of differences between the proportions of initiated play activities in the two different classroom organizations (two independent samples of observations). The null hypothesis here is that the proportions of initiated play activities with same sex peers would be equal in same age and mixed-age classrooms. The alternative two-tailed hypothesis was that the proportions would be different in the two types of classroom organization. The investigators reported two Z-scores of 2.29, $p < 0.05$ (boys) and 2.22, $p < 0.05$ (girls) and concluded that both 4-year-old-boys and 4-year-old-girls in same age classrooms were more likely to initiate play with same sex peers than were their age equivalent counterparts in mixed-age classrooms.

In a second example where percentage differences rather than proportions were analysed MacKay and Boyle (1994) report on an investigation of primary headteachers' expectations of their local education authorities educational psychologists. Specifically the investigators looked at the importance placed by headteachers on provision of advice on materials for pupils with learning difficulties.

The following three questions were included in a questionnaire survey of primary school headteachers (with 96 per cent return rate). Respondents' replies as reported by the investigators are shown:

To what extent do you feel that the Psychologist should be involved in the following areas?

	n = (100%)	Very much/ much involved		in between		Little/ not involved	
		%	n	%	n	%	n
Q1 Advice on materials (for pupils with learning difficulties)	110	87.3	96	11.8	13	0.9	1
Q2 INSET for school staff (in-service education and training)	108	66.7	72	26.9	29	6.4	7
Q3 Primary/secondary school liaison	109	65.1	71	26.6	29	8.3	9

The investigators reported that provision of advice was judged to be of significantly greater importance than either INSET or primary–secondary school liaison ($p < 0.05$).

Worked Example

Data from the study of headteachers' perceptions will be used to illustrate application of the proportions test for detecting the significance of any difference between percentages. As the investigators indicate that the response rate is 96 per cent, it is reasonable to assume that the achieved sample is representative of headteachers in the LEA(s) concerned. We also need to assume that the sample is random and that responses to the three questions are independent, that is, a headteacher's response to the third question is not influenced by his or her response to the first or second questions. The samples of responses are sufficiently large for the normal approximation to apply. The investigators do not state precisely the comparisons made, but it is reasonable to assume that the proportion of respondents endorsing the category very much/much involved in Q 1 is compared with proportions of responses in the same categories in Q 2 and 3. Thus two null hypotheses are tested at the 5 per cent level:

H_0: Q1 $\pi_{\text{very much/much}}$ = Q2 $\pi_{\text{very much/much}}$
H_0: Q1 $\pi_{\text{very much/much}}$ = Q3 $\pi_{\text{very much/much}}$

It is also assumed that the alternative hypotheses are two-tailed tests.

The sample standard deviation of the difference in proportions, S_D, that is the **standard error of the difference in proportions** is used to estimate the unknown population parameter, the standard deviation (or standard error) of the difference in proportions, σ_D. That is S_D (from sample) estimates σ_D in the population. The computational formula for S_D is:

$$S_D = \sqrt{\frac{P_1(1-P_1)}{n_1} + \frac{P_2(1-P_2)}{n_2}}$$

Standard error of difference in proportions – 6.6

where P_1 and P_2 are the observed sample proportions for the two independent samples of size n_1 and n_2. The sample proportion is the number of counts in the relevant category divided by the sample size.

Confidence Intervals

Consider the first hypothesis, the difference in the proportions of respondents who endorsed the category very much/much to the two questions. Advice on materials (observed proportion $P_1 = 96/110$), and INSET for school staff (observed proportion $P_2 = 72/108$).

The 95 per cent CI for the population difference in the two proportions $(\pi_1 - \pi_2)$ is:

$$(P_1 - P_2) - (Z^* \times S_D) \text{ to } (P_1 - P_2) + (Z^* \times S_D)$$

where Z^* is the upper value from a standard normal distribution for the selected $100(1 - \alpha/2)$. For example, for a 95 per cent CI $Z^* = 1.96$. Unlike the t-distribution this standard normal critical value does not depend on the sample size.

In this example the standard error of the observed difference is:

$$\sigma_D = \sqrt{\frac{(0.873)\,(0.127)}{110} + \frac{(0.667)\,(0.333)}{108}}$$

$$= 0.055$$

The 95 per cent CI is

$(P_1 - P_2) - (Z^* \times S_D)$ to $(P_1 - P_2) + (Z^* \times S_D)$

$(0.873 - 0.667) - (1.96 \times 0.055)$ to $(0.873 - 0.667) + (1.96 \times 0.055)$

$= (0.10 \text{ to } 0.31).$

Interpretation

The 95 per cent CI does not include the value zero and we can therefore conclude with 95 per cent certainty that the population proportions are significantly different, $p < 0.05$. As the investigators concluded, advice on materials for children with learning difficulties was judged by primary school headteachers to be of greater importance than in-service training for school staff.

Computer Analysis

Once again this analysis is accomplished with ease with a few lines of SAS code. A complete SAS programme for the proportions test is shown in Figure 7, Appendix A3. In this programme 5 data values n_1, n_2, x_1, x_2, and the required CI need to be entered. For this example the 5 data values are:

```
data a;          **  Enter 5 data values on following 5 lines    **;
n1=110;          **  n1 is sample size for sample 1              **;
n2=108;          **  n2 is sample size for sample 2              **;
x1=96;           **  x1 is relevant count for sample 1           **;
x2=72;           **  x2 is relevant count for sample 2           **;
CI=95;           **  Required confidence interval e.g. 95, 90    **;
```

Output from the procedure PROC PRINT, which simply prints the values of the variables is

```
OBS  N1    N2    X1  X2  CI  P1       P2        ALPHA  SEDIFF    Y
1    110   108   96  72  95  0.87273  0.66667   0.05   0.055384  1.95996

LOWERCI  UPPERCI
0.10     0.31
```

From this output the computed 95 per cent CI, 0.10 to 0.31, is the same as the interval values calculated in the preceding section. Computer output for a test of the second null hypothesis, that of no difference in the proportion of respondents between Q1 and Q3 who endorse the category very much/much, is shown below:

OBS	N1	N2	X1	X2	P1	P2	CI	ALPHA	SEDIFF	Y
1	110	109	96	71	0.87273	0.65138	95	0.05	0.055616	1.95996

LOWERCI	UPPERCI
0.11	0.33

Interpretation of Computer Output

Interpretation is straightforward, in neither comparison does the 95 per cent confidence interval include the value zero. We can therefore conclude with 95 per cent certainty that the population proportions of affirmative responses to the two questions, Q1 and Q2 and to the questions Q1 and Q3 (two comparisons) are significantly different, $p < 0.05$. The estimate of the *difference* in the percentage of respondents who endorse the statement that they 'very much or much' believe that the educational psychologist *should* be involved in providing advice on materials compared with those who endorse the statement 'should be involved with in-service work' is 20.6 per cent ($0.873 - 0.667 \times 100$). The 95 per cent confidence interval ranges from 10 per cent to 31 per cent, and the standard error of the difference is 5.5 per cent.

It is good practice to note both the confidence interval and the p value (and any test statistic values) when reporting results.

6.5 Sign Test (Matched pairs)

When to Use

One of the simplest and most useful distribution-free tests is the sign test. As its name implies the sign test makes use of the counts of the direction of any differences between two measures, that is whether a difference between two measures is + or −. It does not use the difference of the actual score values (if they are available). The sign test is useful when quantitative measures are not possible, but when it is possible to determine for each pair of observations which is the largest in some meaningful sense.

There are a number of different forms of the sign test, all based on frequency counts and the binomial sampling distribution. Perhaps the most common use of the test is the sign test for paired differences (or matched pairs). In this form it is a two-sample repeated measures test and is used to determine the significance of any change (or difference) between two related measures. Other forms of the sign test are: one-sample location problems, test for trends in location, sign test for correlation and sign test for association. For discussion of these other applications see Sachdeva (1975).

Statistical Inference and Null Hypothesis

Inferences for the matched pairs sign test relate to the population median, η, (Greek letter eta) of the differences. The null hypothesis is that the median of the differences is 0 (similar to the paired t-test when the mean of the differences is 0). When the probability of a $+$ is 0.5 by chance, there will be an equal number of $+$ and $-$ differences above and below the median and therefore the median difference is 0. In notational form H_0: $\eta = 0$. The alternative hypothesis may be one-tailed, i.e., H_1: $\eta > 0$ (median difference is positive, more $+$ than $-$ signs), or H_1: $\eta < 0$ (median difference is negative, more $-$ than $+$ signs). A two-tailed alternative hypothesis would be H_1: $\eta \neq 0$ (median is $\neq 0$, different number of $+$ and $-$ signs).

Test Assumptions

The sign test (matched pairs) is applicable when:

- The response variable analyzed has a continuous (or at least a theoretical continuous) distribution.
- Data is in the form of frequency counts of $+$ and $-$ differences.
- Each pair of observations is independent of other observations.

Examples from the Literature

In a study by Gardiner (1989) of priming effect on a word fragment completion task, twenty-four undergraduate students were presented with a list of word fragments which they had to complete. A priming effect is the facilitatory effect of prior experience on performance of a cognitive task. In this example, students were first presented with a set of twelve target words in a reading passage and were subsequently presented with word fragments for the same set of twelve words. The number of fragment words completed were counted. A new set of twelve fragment words were also presented, these had not been previously presented in a reading passage. This was a matched pairs design, that is each student attempted to complete two sets of fragment words, twelve that had previously been read in passage and twelve that had not. If the student completed more word fragments for the set of twelve words previously presented in the reading passage, (compared with the twelve words that had not been presented) this constituted a priming effect.

For the twenty-four students, seventeen showed a priming effect and three had tied scores, that is completed equal numbers of word fragments for both sets. The investigator concluded that there was a significant priming effect for items that had been read previously, $p < 0.001$, by the sign test.

In a numerical example of the sign test given by Sachdeva (1975), twelve randomly selected pairs of students (each pair matched on age, sex and IQ) were randomly assigned to two different conditions. The obtained data are:

Pair No.	1	2	3	4	5	6	7	8	9	10	11	12
Condition I	17	18	26	24	26	14	17	29	36	25	44	30
Condition II	22	32	25	22	27	21	14	41	37	24	43	31
Sign for difference	$-$	$-$	$+$	$+$	$-$	$-$	$+$	$-$	$-$	$+$	$+$	$-$

The investigator wanted to find out whether there was any difference between the two experimental conditions in the average performance of students.

The sign test was used and alpha was set to 5 per cent, with a two-tailed test. The null hypothesis of no difference in the average performance of students under the two experimental conditions was not rejected, and the investigator concluded that the average performance of students under the two conditions was the same.

Worked Examples

Data from the study by Gardiner (1989) on the influence of priming on implicit memory is used to illustrate the paired difference sign test. The sign test determines the probability associated with an observed number of +'s and −'s when in this case the probability of a + or a − is 0.5. The test statistic is the count of the number of pairs with a difference in the desired direction. Pairs with a zero difference are not included in the analysis and n, the number of pairs, is reduced accordingly.

Gardiner reported that 17/21 students showed a basic priming effect, that is seventeen subjects completed more word fragments for the set of twelve words previously presented in the reading passage, compared with the twelve new words not previously presented (here 17 +'s). Three subjects had tied scores, that is, completed an equal number of word fragments for both sets of twelve words. Under the null hypothesis of an equal number of +'s and −'s, the null hypothesis is rejected if too few differences of one sign occur. The probability of obtaining the observed distribution of 17/21 +'s, or a more extreme distribution (fewer differences for the sign with the smallest count) is evaluated using the binomial equation (see Chapter 4, section 4.1). The binomial equation with probability 0.5, sample size twenty-one and number of successes set to four or fewer evaluates whether four or fewer subjects would be expected to occur by chance (four is the smaller observed frequency, twenty-one less seventeen). The probabilities associated with obtaining counts of 4, 3, 2, 1, and 0 are:

$$p_4 = 2.85 - 3; \ p_3 = 6.34 - 4; \ p_2 = 1.00 - 4; \ p_1 = 1.00 - 5; \ p_0 = 4.77 - 7.$$

Note, 2.85 −3 is equal to 0.00285. The probability of obtaining 4 or fewer is the sum of these five probabilities which is 0.0036.

Interpretation

Gardiner (1989) did not state in his paper whether a one- or a two-tailed test was used or the alpha level selected (see earlier comment about brevity of statistical test details when results are presented in periodicals). A cautious approach would be to use a two-tailed test with alpha set to 5 per cent. When a two-tailed test is used the probability associated with the smallest observed frequency is doubled. The p-value for the two-tailed sign test is thus 0.0072. The null hypothesis is therefore rejected, and we conclude that there is a statistically significant priming effect.

Computer Analysis

Calculation of binomial probabilities using the binomial equation is tedious and either tables of binomial probabilities for p = 0.5 can be consulted or the probabilities can be determined using the SAS binomial function PROBBNML. Appropriate lines of SAS code are:

```
   data a;
 p4=probbnml(0.5,21,4);
   put p4=;
 run;
```

The PROBBNML function is used as part of a SAS data step, here the first line of code specifies the data set a (this is just a convenient name). The PUT statement tells SAS to write the variable p4, evaluation of the binomial function, to the LOG File. See earlier section 6.2 for details of the PROBBNML function. The following value is returned in the SAS LOG file, p4 = 0.00359869

Worked Example

The numerical example of the sign test given by Sachdeva (1975) for twelve randomly selected pairs of students is used to illustrate an extraordinary simple computational procedure for evaluating the sign test which is based on the sample size only. For the twelve matched pairs of students the signs of the differences are:

Sign for difference   − − + + − − + − − + + −

A simple formulae for making tests of significance at the 5 per cent level for a two-tailed alternative hypothesis is,

$$(s_+ - f)^2 \geq 4n$$

where n is the number of matched pairs (ties, if present, would not be included and n reduced accordingly), s_+ is the number of designated + signs (count of observations > median) and f is the count of − signs. If the square of the difference between the number of + and − signs is ≥ four times the sample size then the null hypothesis of no difference is rejected.

Interpretation

In this example, $s_+ = 5$; $f = 7$; and $n = 12$. Since $(s_+ - f)^2 = (5 - 7)^2 = 4$, which is < 48, (4 × 12) the null hypothesis is not rejected and it is concluded that the average performance of students under the two conditions is not significantly different. If an investigator wanted to use alternative alpha levels the following comparable formula could be used:

Alternative hypothesis	Alpha	Formula
two-tailed	1%	$(s - f)^2 \geq 6.7n$
one-tailed	5%	$(s - f)^2 \geq 2.7n$
one-tailed	1%	$(s - f)^2 \geq 5.4n$

This simple test is particularly useful for detecting significant change in pre-test/post-test designs.

6.6 $r \times k$ Chi-square Test

When to Use

This test is an extension of either the $r \times 2$ Sample χ^2 test of homogeneity when there are more than two independent groups (samples), or the one sample χ^2 test of independence when there are more than two categories in the row or column variables. In the homogeneity design k independent random samples are drawn (the columns' variable) from each of k populations and the distribution of proportions in the r (row variable) categories are compared hence the term $r \times k$ Chi-square. An alternative model is the test of independence when a single random sample is drawn from a single population of subjects with two categorical measures for each subject, that is the row and column variables. For the homogeneity design an investigator would be interested in the effect of the column variable on the response or row variable. For the independent design an investigator would be interested in testing whether the two categorical variables are independent.

Statistical Inference and Null Hypothesis

For the homogeneity design the general form of the null hypothesis is that the k independent samples come from one single population (or identical populations). This may be stated as the proportions of subjects in each category of the row variable (measured variable) is the same in each of the k independent groups (samples) of the column variable. The parameters being estimated are the proportions in each cell of the contingency table which the observed sample proportions are intended to estimate. The column variable describes from which population an observation comes, and the row variable is a categorical response (measured) variable.

The research hypothesis is that the distribution of proportions for one categorical variable, the row variable, is different in the k populations (the other categorical column variable). A more general way of stating this research hypothesis is to say that the proportions differ across the two groups. To test the null hypothesis we compare observed cell counts with the expected cell counts under the assumption that there is no difference in proportions.

For the χ^2 test of independence the null hypothesis is that the two categorical variables are independent. The alternative hypothesis is that there is a relationship between the row and column variables. No matter which sampling design is used, it is essential that each subject appears in only one cell (is counted once) in the contingency table.

Test Assumptions

In general these are the same as for the two sample χ^2 test (see section 6.1) except that at least one of the categorical variables has three or more categories.

Example from the Literature

In a study which investigated aspects of maternal employment and child health care, Dowswell and Hewison (1995) examined the relationship between maternal employment, full-time, part-time or at home, and educational achievements, no examinations, CSEs or O-levels. In this study a sample of mothers was selected from a target population consisting of white families where the youngest child was attending school. The statistical analysis used by the investigators was a Chi-square test of independence, since a single sample of mothers was selected.

If, however, we were to assume that samples were selected from three in-dependent populations based on maternal employment categories this sampling design would require an $r \times k \; \chi^2$ test of homogeneity (3-sample design). Whichever sampling design is used, computational details are the same only the nature of the inferences differ. Data was set out in a contingency table as follows:

	Maternal employment		
Mothers' educational achievements	At home $n = 41$	Part-time $n = 65$	Full-time $n = 30$
No examinations	19	32	10
CSEs	9	10	5
O-levels or above	13	23	15

In this example the column variable represents the three populations of maternal employment (full-time, part-time or at home) and the row variable (examination achievement) is the categorical response variable. A research question that could have been considered by the investigators was whether the distribution of responses for the variable examination achievement was the same in the three populations. A homogeneity χ^2 test is appropriate.

The null hypothesis tested with this sampling design is that the proportions of subjects in each category of the row variable, examination achievement, is the same in each of the three independent samples (column variable).

We can conclude that there is no significant difference in examination achievements between the three populations, of maternal employment, $\chi_4^2 = 3.515$, (with 4df). This is not significant at the 5 per cent level.

Worked Example

Computation of an $r \times k$ χ^2 statistic follows the same procedure as that presented earlier in this chapter when discussing the two-sample χ^2 test (section 6.1). The procedure is outlined only briefly here. χ^2 is calculated as the difference between each observed and corresponding expected cell count squared and then divided by the expected count $(O - E)^2/E$). The total χ^2 value for the contingency table is the sum of the χ^2 values calculated for each cell in the contingency table. The degrees of freedom are calculated as (rows $-$ 1 $\times$ columns $-$ 1).

Interpretation

A non-significant χ^2 value would indicate either no significant difference between the k populations with respect to the categorical response variable (homogeneity test) or no significant association between the two categorical variables (test of independence).

Computer Analysis

Data from the study on maternal employment is used to illustrate an $r \times k$ Chi-square analysis. The following lines of SAS code show how the data is entered and how the procedure PROC FREQ is used:

```
data chi;
    input row col celln @@;
    cards;                                /* Data entered on next line*/
1 1 19 1 2 32 1 3 10 2 1 9 2 2 10 2 3 5 3 1 13 3 2 23 3 3 15
;
proc freq data=chi;
    weight celln;
    table row*col / chisq expected ;
title 'Chi square test';
run;
```

The option **expected** is used to obtain the expected frequencies for each cell in the contingency table. Output from this SAS programme is shown in Figure 6.6:

```
                         Table of row by column

   Row                   column

   Frequency         |
   Row Pct           |
   Col Pct           |      1  |       2  |       3  |    Total
   ---------------+---------+----------+----------+
              1  |     19  |      32  |      10  |      61
                 |   31.15 |   52.46  |   16.39  |
                 |   46.34 |   49.23  |   33.33  |
   ---------------+---------+----------+----------+
              2  |      9  |      10  |       5  |      24
                 |   37.50 |   41.67  |   20.83  |
                 |   21.95 |   15.38  |   16.67  |
   ---------------+---------+----------+----------+
              3  |     13  |      23  |      15  |      51
                 |   25.49 |   45.10  |   29.41  |
                 |   31.71 |   35.38  |   50.00  |
   ---------------+---------+----------+----------+
   Total               41        65        30        136

                  Statistics for table of row by col
   Statistic                   DF            Value              Prob
   -----------------------------------------------------------------
   Chi-Square                   4            3.515              0.476
   Sample Size = 136
```

Figure 6.6: SAS output for r × k Chi-square analysis

Interpretation of Computer Output

The results of the analysis in Figure 6.6 show no difference in educational achievement between the three populations: mothers working full-time; part-time; or at home, $\chi_4^2 = 3.514$ is not significant. The interpretation is the same as that given in the example from the literature section. An overall significant χ^2 value for a $r \times k$ table would show that there are significant none chance deviations somewhere in the table. An investigator is usually interested in which cells the important discrepancies appear. The *expected* option in the tables statement of PROC FREQ produces expected cell frequencies under the null hypothesis of homogeneity of proportions (or independence). The cells with the largest discrepancy between observed and expected values can easily be identified.

6.7 Cochran's Q Test

When to Use

This procedure is appropriate when a research design involves subjects each performing under different treatment conditions (repeated measures) for which the response (outcome) variable is binary (scored 1, 0). The response variable is designated arbitrarily 1 for success and 0 for failure. The repeated measures may be two or more observations on the same subjects over a series of independent trials (treatment conditions) or it may involve matched subjects. Cochran's Q test is appropriate for detecting whether the proportions of successes are constant over trials (treatment groups).

For example, a research student wanted to assess the effectiveness of vocabulary acquisition among primary school pupils under three teaching approaches (treatments): storytelling with pictures, storytelling alone and silent reading. Thirty target word meanings of equal difficulty were selected (factors considered included context, word length, word type classification), and ten words were used in each of the three treatment conditions. For each treatment condition, if a subject scored better than chance on the ten target words the subject was assigned a score of 1, success. If the subject did not score better than chance, the treatment response was assigned a score of 0. Data for this design can be arranged in a contingency table where columns represent treatments or measurement occasions and subjects form the rows of the table, for example:

	Treatments (measurement occasions)			
Subjects	Storytelling + pictures	Storytelling alone	Silent reading	Row totals
1	1	0	1	
2	1	0	0	
3	0	1	0	
4	1	0	0	
.			.	
.			.	
.			.	
Column Totals				Grand total N

The purpose of the test is to determine whether related sets of binary observations differ. When the related measures correspond to a series of observations on the same subjects under different treatment conditions the Q statistic provides a test of whether the treatments differ significantly.

Statistical Inference and Null Hypothesis

The null hypothesis is that the population parameter for the probability of a success under each treatment condition is the same. That is the treatments are equally effective and any variation in the column totals is simply due to sampling variation. The alternative hypothesis is that the treatments do not have the same effect.

Test Assumptions

Cochran's Q test may be used when the following assumptions are met:

1 The response variable is binary and observations are related, same subjects observed under different treatment conditions (measurement occasions), or matched subjects.

2   The sampling distribution of the Q statistic approximates to a χ^2 distribution with degrees of freedom as the number of columns $- 1$. Under the null hypothesis the probability associated with the value of Q as large as the observed value is determined by reference to the χ^2 distribution. However, this approximation is only valid when the product of the number of subjects (rows) and treatments (columns) is ≥ 24. When the product of rows and columns is < 24 tables of exact distributions should be consulted, see Patil (1975).

3   Population covariances for all pairs of treatments are the same. Heterogeneity of variances and covariances is common in studies involving binary repeated measures. Interactions between subjects and treatment conditions would indicate heterogeneity of covariance. Severe heterogeneity introduces a positive bias to the Type I error rate and if this is suspected, Q should be corrected. (See Myers, *et al.*, 1982). In most cases the procedure described by Myers *et al.* should be followed:

   a   Evaluate the Q statistic against a conservative criterion, $(c - 1) \times \chi_1^2$ (χ_1^2 means Chi-square with 1 df and c is number of columns). For example, with alpha of 5 per cent and with four columns in a contingency table, we would evaluate Q against the conservative critical value of $3 \times \chi_1^2 = 11.52$ (3×3.84). If the test statistic Q exceeds the critical value of 11.52 we would reject the null hypothesis.

   b   If the first conservative test is not significant (this allows for covariance) at the same alpha level compare the test statistic Q with a χ_{c-1}^2 (df is $c - 1$). If this liberal criterion is not significant, do not reject the null hypothesis and stop at this point.

   c   If the first test against the conservative critical value is not significant but the second test against the more liberal critical value is, consider computing an adjusted Q (see Myers, 1975) and test this against χ^2 with $(c - 1)$ df.

Example from the Literature

In a comparative study of four diagnostic systems (majority opinion of medical specialists, and three computer-based diagnostic systems) Gustafson *et al.* (1973) tested the null hypothesis that all four diagnostic methods were equally effective. Each diagnosis for eleven hypothyroid patients was coded as correct, 1, or incorrect, 0.

Alpha was set to 5 per cent and the null hypothesis was that all four methods were equally effective in diagnosing hypothyroid patients. The alternative hypothesis was that the four methods differ in their ability to produce a correct diagnosis. There were 44 (11×4) cells in the original contingency table but this was reduced to 28 (7×4) because 4 subjects had either all 1's or 0's. These rows of

1's or 0's do not contribute to the value of Q (Q would be the same if all eleven subjects were included in the calculation). As the obtained number of cells, 28, exceeds 24 the χ^2 approximation is valid. The obtained test statistic Q was 7.70, which is not significant at the 5 per cent level, $\chi^2_{c-1} = \chi^2_3 = 7.81$. As Q has an approximate χ^2 distribution with $c - 1$ df, A Q (or χ^2) value ≥ 7.81 is required to reject the null hypothesis. The investigators were able to conclude that there was no significant difference in the diagnostic performance of the four methods.

Worked Example

Returning to the example of the vocabulary acquisition experiment which was part of a student's dissertation study, the complete data set for eleven pupils is presented in Figure 6.7.

	Treatments (Measurement occasions)				
Subjects	Storytelling + pictures	Storytelling alone	Silent reading	Row totals R	R²
1	1	0	1	2	4
2	1	1	0	2	4
3	0	1	0	1	1
4	1	0	0	1	1
5	1	1	0	2	4
6	1	1	1	3	9
7	1	1	1	3	9
8	0	0	0	0	0
9	1	0	1	2	4
10	1	0	1	2	4
11	0	0	1	1	1
(C)olumn Totals	8	5	6	$\Sigma C = \Sigma R = N = 19$ $\Sigma (R^2) = 41$	
(C)olumn Total²	64	25	36	$\Sigma (C^2) = 125$	

Figure 6.7: Contingency table for vocabulary acquisition experiment

For completeness *all* subjects are shown in the computation of Q. If subjects 6 and 7, (all 1's) and subject 8 (all 0's) were excluded from the computation, we would obtain the same value of Q that we obtain with all subjects included in the analysis.

The null hypothesis is that there is no difference in vocabulary acquisition under the different teaching approaches. Alpha is set to 5 per cent and the number of cells is 33 (11×3). After adjusting for the 3 rows with all 0's or all 1's (subjects 6, 7, and 8) the number of cells reduces to 24 (8×3) which is the minimum number for use of the χ^2 approximation.

The computational steps are as follows:

Step1   Compute the column and row totals and the square of the column and row totals.

Step2   Sum the column totals which should equal the sum of the row totals, here, $\Sigma C = \Sigma R = N = 19$. N is the grand total.

Step3   Sum the squares of the column and row totals here, $\Sigma(C^2) = 125$ and $\Sigma(R^2) = 41$

Step4   The test statistic Q is evaluated as:

$$Q = \frac{J - 1(J(\Sigma C^2) - N^2)}{JN - \Sigma R^2} \qquad \qquad \textbf{Cochran's } Q - 6.7$$

where J is the number of treatments (columns), R^2 is the row total squared for each row, C^2 is the column total squared for each column, and N^2 is the grand total squared. Here Q is:

$$Q = \frac{3 - 1((3(125)) - (19)^2)}{3(19) - 41} = 28/16 = 1.75$$

Interpretation

With alpha set to 5 per cent the obtained Q of 1.75 is first evaluated against the **conservative critical value** of $(c - 1)\chi_1^2$, that is $2 \times \chi_1^2$ or $2 \times 3.84 = 7.68$. This conservative estimate adjusts for heterogeneity in the covariances and the resultant inflated Type I error rate. The observed value of Q, 1.75, fails to exceed this conservative critical value (not significant at 5 per cent level) and Q is therefore tested against the more liberal critical value. This liberal critical value is equivalent to χ^2 with $(c - 1)$ df. Here we see the obtained value of Q, $1.75 < 5.99$ (χ_2^2), the Q statistic fails to reach the liberal critical value and is not significant at the 5 per cent level.

We do not reject the null hypothesis, the probabilities of 1's (successes) are not different under the three teaching approaches, and we conclude that vocabulary acquisition is similar under the three approaches, storytelling enhanced by pictures, storytelling alone and silent reading. The reader should carefully consider the design of this experiment particularly threats to internal validity (are the three stories comparable, are the target words comparable-what would be the advantages/disadvantages of a between subjects design?)

Computer Analysis

A SAS programme for calculating Cochran's Q and evaluating the significance of the Q statistic at the conservative and liberal critical values is presented in Figure 8, Appendix A3. To use this programme two sections need to be edited: the number of variables, that is treatment occasions (repeated measurements), t1 t2 t3 ... tn and the actual lines of data, one subject per line. Three subjects are not included in the data input because they have either all 0's or all 1's. The total number of lines of data input (subjects) is therefore eight. With a larger data set a separate data file could be read using the INFILE statement rather than entering data in the SAS programme with the CARDS statement. Illustrated in Figure 6.8 is the data entry section of this SAS programme using the vocabulary acquisition data.

```
******************************************************************************;
**  Filename:  COCHRAN.JOB                                               **;
**                                                                       **;
**  Purpose:  Cochran's Q test                                           **;
**                                                                       **;
**            Tests whether there is a difference between two or         **;
**            more treatments in a repeated measures design when         **;
**            the response variable is binary, 1 (success) 0             **;
**            (fail)                                                      **;
**                                                                       **;
**  Created:  16 April 1995                                              **;
**                                                                       **;
**  Input file:   NONE (Data entered in programme)                       **;
**  Output file:  NONE (see notes)                                       **;
**                                                                       **;
**  Notes:  The number of treatment groups (repeated measures)           **;
**          is entered sequentially (separated by a space)               **;
**          after the input statement e.g. t1 t2 t3 . . . tn             **;
**          Data is entered after the cards statement,                   **;
**          one subject per row, each value (either 1 or 0)              **:
**          separated by a space.                                        **:
**          Subjects (lines of data) with all 1's or 0's                 **;
**          should be excluded (not entered in the data step)            **;
******************************************************************************;
data a;
                  ** On next line enter vars t1 t2 etc after      **;
                  ** input statement                              **;
                  ** see notes above                              **;
   input t1 t2 t3;
   cards;         /* Enter data on following lines one subject    */
                  /* per line                                     */
                  /* see notes above                              */
1 0 1
1 1 0
0 1 0
1 0 0
1 1 0
1 0 1
1 0 1
0 0 1
;
                  ** Do not edit beyond this line                 **;
```

Figure 6.8: Data entry section of SAS programme for computing Cochran's Q

The statement data a; is the beginning of the data step. Following the input statement are the variables t1 t2 and t3. These need to be numbered consecutively and separated by a space. They correspond to the treatment periods (measurement occasions) in the repeated measures design. The cards statement indicates that data lines follow. The SAS system recognizes the end of the data when the first line after the last data line contains a single semicolon.

Output from this analysis is shown in Figure 6.9.

```
                    Cochran Q Test Results
Cochran Q test value =1.75
p-value with liberal df:
df = 2
Not significant at 5% level (p-value =0.417)
p-value with conservative critical value:
Not significant at 5% level
```

Figure 6.9: *SAS output from Cochran's Q analysis for vocabulary data*

Interpretation of computer output

The value of the Q test statistic is the same as that calculated in the previous worked example. Interpretation is also the same. The SAS programme prints out the significance levels for both liberal and conservative tests, the p-value is given for the liberal degrees of freedom. The programme automatically tests alpha at 1 per cent and alpha at 5 per cent and prints a p value for either 1 per cent or if this is not significant the p value for the 5 per cent level. A warning is printed if the number of cells is less than 24.

6.8 Summary

In this chapter the use of tests has been discussed where data has been discrete and observations have been classified in contingency tables. The role of scores has been to label and classify data. Whereas these procedures are suitable for many occasions they do not make use of as much of the information contained in data as is sometimes possible. There are other nonparametric techniques which make use of the scores attributed to observations. Numerical scores, may not be from an underlying normal distribution but may lend themseles to rank ordering. Rank order statistics, which use more information contained in the data and are generally more powerful than nominal tests, may be used with numerical scores that assign each observation to a relative position in the score distribution. These rank order procedures are introduced in the next chapter.

Chapter 7

Inferences Involving Rank Data

Introduction

Educational researchers may be less familiar with nonparametric methods and in particular rank test procedures than with parametric methods. Use of nonparametric rank procedures is more common among research psychologists. In this chapter, six nonparametric or **distribution free** statistics that make use of rank scores are introduced: Spearman's correlation, Run's test, Wilcoxon M-W test, Signed ranks test, Kruskal Wallis ANOVA and Friedman's ANOVA. The term distribution free is strictly not accurate. Whereas parametric statistical procedures are dependent upon distributional theory, they make certain specific assumptions about patterns of variability in the population (referred to as statistical test assumptions). Nonparametric tests do not rely on population distributional assumptions. Nonparametric procedures are not entirely distributional free. Whilst not making use of distribution theory in the same way that parametric procedures do, (mathematical descriptions of patterns of variation are used to make inferences about population parameters or constants based on sample data) they nevertheless definitely do make use of the distribution of sample observations. In this sense they are not distribution free.

Nonparametric statistical tests are generally less powerful than parametric tests and are also less likely to mislead investigators because they are not dependent upon certain restrictive measurement and distributional assumptions. Nonparametric procedures are also well suited to small sample sizes, and rank tests are particularly helpful when outliers are present in a data set since ranks of raw scores are not affected by extreme values. Data may naturally form ranks, or ranks may be assigned on the basis of measurement (or combinations of different measures) or subjective judgment.

Many introductory statistical textbooks relegate nonparametric procedures to the later chapters and promulgate the view that they should be used when assumptions of normality and **homogeneity of variance** (equal population variances) are not met. Whereas nonparametric tests are useful for solving certain statistical difficulties (small sample sizes, unrealistic measurement and distributional assumptions), they are not a panacea for all problems. They are subject to assumptions of independence of observations (groups are comprised of random samples and successive observations within samples are independent) and are also sensitive to unequal variances especially in combination with unequal sample sizes. As Zimmerman and Zumbo (1993) point out, psychologists (and probably educational researchers) are not yet fully appreciative of this. Therefore, general advice is that nonparametric procedures are sometimes an effective way of dealing with non-normal or unknown distributions but are not always the answer to unequal variances. What can be done when assumptions of homogeneity of variance are violated? *What* is referred to in the statistical literature as the **Behrens-Fisher problem**. Strategies are discussed in Chapter 8, but essentially the answer involves using a modified test procedure with estimated degrees of freedom.

7.1 Correlation an overview

In psychological and educational research many questions are concerned with the extent of covariation between two variables. In a review of two journals, the *British Educational Research Journal* (BERJ) and the *British Journal of Educational Psychology* (BJEP), looking at two consecutive volumes over the same time period, the following was observed. In the BERJ authors from 32 per cent (25) of the papers used some statistical analyses, in total 12 per cent (9) used correlations; whereas in the BJEP authors from 84 per cent (61) of the papers reported statistical findings and in total 51 per cent (37) used correlations. **Correlational analysis**, a statistical technique for examining the extent of the relationship between two variables, is a technique with which researchers should certainly be familiar.

Correlations coefficients, r, computed from sample data provide an index of the strength of the relationship between two variables e.g., r_{xy} is the sample correlation between the variables X and Y. Data usually consists of a random sample of subjects each of whom has two scores, one for each of the variables measured. When introducing the idea of correlation it is helpful to make two distinctions:

1. We need to be clear about when a correlation from sample data is used as a *descriptive* statistic and when it is used to make *inferences* about true relationships in the population (whether there is a true linear relationship between two variables or indeed any relationship). A population correlation is denoted by the Greek letter rho (ρ).

2. We should distinguish between **correlation** and **association**. When observations on each variable can be ordered relative to all other observations on the same variable, (for example, higher scores represent more of an attribute – continuous or rank scores,) then we can speak of correlation. When observations are discrete counts and it is not meaningful to arrange these counts in individual ranks or ordered categories then we use the term association rather than correlation.

A correlation between two variables does not imply causality, however an underlying causal relationship may exist. In Chapter 3, Initial Data Analysis, we described ways of plotting data when examining the distribution of variables. A useful way to explore bivariate (two-variable) relationships is to plot two variables at a time on a scatterplot (one variable on the Y axis and the other on the X axis). The scatter of points depicted enables interpretation of the relationship between the variables, for example, see Figure 7.1.

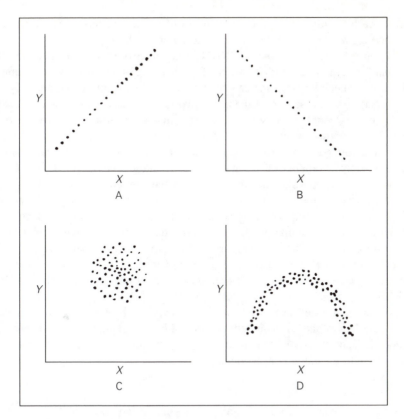

Figure 7.1:   Interpreting scatterplots for two variables

In these plots we are looking for a linear relationship between the two variables which is summarized by the spread and scatter of points. If one variable is linearly related to the other, then as one variable changes, the other will change in proportion and the points will tend to fall on a straight line. The size of a Pearson correlation coefficient indicates the degree to which the points in a scatter diagram tend to fall along a straight line (summarizes the linear relationship). The value of the Pearson correlation coefficient, can range between -1 to $+1$, in both cases this would indicate a perfect linear relationship. The Pearson correlation is used when the underlying data distribution is normal (see Chapter 8).

  Diagram A indicates a near perfect positive correlation, as X increases Y increases proportionately, r (the correlation) would be close to $+1$; Diagram B shows a near perfect negative correlation as X increases Y decreases proportionately, r would be close to -1; Diagram C shows no correlation, r would be 0 and Diagram D shows dependence but no linear correlation, Pearson correlation r should not be used to summarize this relationship. There are, of course, non-linear relationships that may exist between two variables and other correlation type statistics are then appropriate for summarizing this relationship (e.g., the eta statistic is the correlation coefficient which describes a curvilinear relationship).

If you have access to SAS/INSIGHT, an interactive tool for data exploration and analysis, graphical representation of bivariate relationships for any number of variables taken two at a time can be shown using the menu driven analysis and data display features (see exploring data in two dimensions SAS/INSIGHT User's Guide). In this chapter we will consider **Spearman's rank order correlation**, which is appropriate when variables are measured at an ordinal level, or when data is transformed to an ordinal scale, this would include percentages. It is one of a number of alternative distribution-free correlation-type statistics. Other non-parametric coefficients include: the **point biserial correlation** (when both variables are discrete true dichotomies); **biserial correlation** (when variables have been dichotomized from an underlying continuous distribution) and **Kendall's Tau coefficient** (an alternative to Spearman's rank correlation which is actually a measure of concordance – similarity of two rank orders rather than a correlation). For discussion and illustrated examples of these alternative correlation statistics see Siegel and Castellan, (1988); Hays, (1981); and Guilford and Fruchter (1973).

We are concerned in this and in the subsequent chapter with the inferential use of correlations and consequently, we should bear in mind how sample data was generated, especially possible bias and range restrictions which can attenuate correlations (reduce sample correlations).

7.2   Spearman's rho (rank order correlation coefficient)

When to Use

Spearman's rank order correlation should be used when:

- the relationship between two variables is not linear, (this can be checked by plotting the two variables);
- when measurement and distributional assumptions are not met (the variables are not interval or ratio measures and observations do not come from a bivariate normal distribution);
- when sample sizes are too small to establish an underlying distribution, or
- when the data naturally occur in the form of ranks.

Spearman's rank order correlation is equivalent to the Pearson Product Moment correlation (a parametric correlation procedure) performed on the ranks of the scores rather than on the raw scores themselves. The rank order correlation procedure is probably used less often than it should be. In the review of the BERJ and the BJEP periodicals mentioned earlier only two papers used rank order correlations (Spearman's correlation coefficient). It is generally not good practice to go fishing for significant correlations among researchers should note, a large number of variables.

Statistical Inference and Null Hypothesis

Provided the pairs of sample observations are drawn at random from a population of interest, Spearman's rho, ρ_s (population rank order correlation), can be used to assess the likelihood that two variables are associated in the population. The null hypothesis is, H_0: there is no association between the two variables and the alternative hypothesis, H_1: is that there is an association. This is a two-tailed alternative hypothesis. If we had specified the nature of the relationship, i.e., positive or negative association, this would be a one-tailed alternative hypothesis. In some introductory statistical texts, the null hypothesis is specified as H_0: $\rho_s = 0$. Unlike the case with a parametric correlation, this does not necessarily imply that the variables are independent. Only when values are normally distributed does a correlation of 0 mean that variables are independent of one another.

The exact sampling distribution for Spearman's rho for sample sizes $1 \leq n \leq$ 10 has been evaluated and is available in statistical tables, see for example, Kendall, (1948); Documenta Geigy (1970); Zar (1972). There is no generally accepted procedure for calculating confidence intervals for r_s (sample rank order correlation) when sample sizes are small, $n < 10$.

When sample sizes are large, here, $n \geq 10$ r_s approximates to that of Pearson's product moment correlation r (Kendall, 1948). Confidence intervals can therefore be constructed by using a transformation of r_s to z (Fisher's z transform), which is approximately normally distributed. Siegel and Castellan (1988) suggest sample size should be > 20 for the sampling distribution of r_s to approximate to r. Use of confidence intervals for r_s when sample sizes are < 20 are therefore of dubious value, recall as well that r_s is most likely to be used with small samples. If a 95 per cent confidence interval is calculated, we would interpret it in the usual way, that is, we would be 95 per cent certain that the obtained interval includes the true population value ρ_s. The confidence interval also enables a test of the null hypothesis. If the obtained confidence interval excludes zero, we can conclude that there is a significant correlation between the two variables. The computational procedure for estimating confidence intervals for r_s is identical to the procedure for estimating the confidence interval for r and this is illustrated in Chapter 8.

Test Assumptions

Spearman's rank order correlation is used when:

- observations do not come from a bivariate normal distribution;
- observations are ranked (given rank values);
- observations are ranked in two ordered series (one for each variable).

If observations represent a random sample from a specified population then r_s can be used to test whether there is a significant relationship between two variables in the population.

Example from the Literature

In a study designed to investigate implementation of an integrated science curriculum, Onocha and Okpala (1990) examined classroom interaction patterns of student and practising teachers. They used a questionnaire to assess teachers' reception of the science curriculum and an observation schedule to identify teachers' classroom interaction patterns. Fifty-six student teachers and forty-two practising teachers participated in the study.

The authors do not specifically say anything about the distribution of scores for the reception questionnaire but it can be assumed to be a continuous measure because a **Cronbach alpha** (measure of internal consistency) was reported. The observation schedule used by the investigators enabled teachers to be placed into one of seven behaviour categories. Again nothing was reported about the specific measurement assumptions underpinning the behaviour schedule but in the analysis it appears to have been treated as an ordinal scale.

Considering the two different categories of teachers, the authors reported a significant relationship between student-teachers' classroom interaction patterns and their reception of the science curriculum, $r_s = 0.87$, $p < 0.05$ and, rather confusingly, reported that; 'the magnitude of correlation between practising teachers' interaction patterns and their reception of the science curriculum was low and not statistically significant ($r_s = 0.21$, $p < 0.05$)' (p. 26). The authors presumably meant $r_s = 0.21$, $p > 0.05$. It is preferable to quote the actual p value as this avoids mistakes and misunderstandings.

In the above situation it is reasonable to assume that a two-tailed test was being used. The null hypothesis was that there was no association between reception of the science curriculum materials and teacher classroom interaction patterns. Here we have pairs of sample observations, two measures per teacher (interaction patterns and reception) and two distinct samples, student and practising teachers. Assuming the samples were random and representative of defined populations of student and practising teachers, the conclusions drawn from this analysis are that among student teachers there is a strong and statistically significant relationship between their reception of the curriculum and classroom interactions. However, this relationship is weak and statistically not significant (at the 5 per cent level) among practising teachers.

Worked Example

Data abstracted from a study on school funding for non-statemented special education needs is used to illustrate computation of Spearman's rank order correlation. Marsh (1995) gives for each of ten schools the percentage of pupils with free school meal entitlements (%FSME) and the aggregated percentage cognitive abilities test (%CAT) score for pupils who scored within the bottom 21 per cent on the CAT. This data is shown in Table 7.1.

Table 7.1: FSME and CAT measures for ten schools

School	%FSME	%CAT
A	24.0	24.1
B	24.3	21.8
C	15.3	23.3
D	40.8	36.4
E	10.7	8.4
F	6.3	13.1
G	23.1	35.1
H	45.0	36.0
I	12.9	17.7
J	13.9	18.5

In the population is there a correlation, at the school level, between the socio-economic indicator FSME and performance on the CAT?

The first step in answering this question is to plot the data to identify the nature of the relationship between the two variables. In this case both variables have been standardized, they are percentages and are therefore ranked. The data from Table 7.1 on %FSME and %CAT scores are plotted in Figure 7.2.

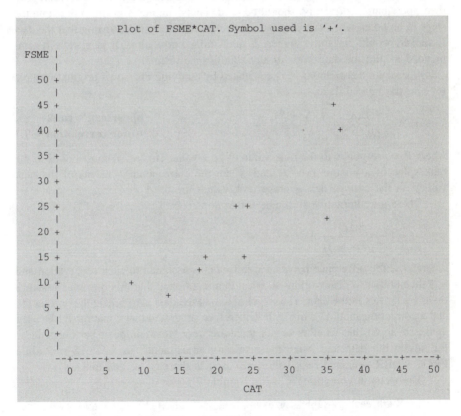

Figure 7.2: Scatterplot of %FSME and %CAT scores for ten schools

The SAS code that produced this plot is given below:

```
    data a;
    infile 'a:nonpara.dat';
    input school $ fsme cat;
proc plot;
    plot fsme*cat ='+' /vaxis=0 to 50 by 5 haxis=0 to 50 by 5;
title 'FSME vs CAT';
run;
```

Looking at the plot there is a suggestion that the data are related in a positive way, that is as FSME scores increase so do CAT scores. It is not absolutely clear that the relationship is linear although this is plausible. One school with the scores 23.1 and 35.1 seems as though it may be an outlier, but with so few points plotted, it is difficult to discern whether this point is apart from the main cluster of points and the upward trend. Interpreting such plots is as much an art as a science and it is difficult to be definitive with so few points plotted.

Given that there is a question about the linearity, there are only ten data points, there may be an outlier and most importantly the data are ranked (percentages), then Spearman's correlation should be used. This example is given to illustrate the steps to be taken when carrying out a correlational analysis. Knowing that the data is ranked would certainly suggest a rank order correlation. It is always recommended to plot the data prior to any significance testing.

Spearman's correlation r_s is calculated by applying Pearson's original formula for r to the ranked data:

$$r_s = \frac{\Sigma(R_i - \bar{R})(S_i - \bar{S})}{(\Sigma(R_i - \bar{R})^2 \Sigma(S_i - \bar{S})^2)^{0.5}}$$

Spearman's rank order correlation – 7.1

where R_i corresponds to the rank value of an x value (x_i) and S_i corresponds to the rank value of a y value (y_i). $\bar{R}$ and $\bar{S}$ are the corresponding means of the rank values. In the case of ties, average rank values are used.

There are alternative formulae for example:

$$r_s = 1 - \frac{6\Sigma D^2}{n(n^2 - 1)}$$

where D is the difference between x and y ranks assigned to each observation and n is the number of observations. It is seldom mentioned that this formulae assumes there are no ties in the data. The effect of ties in the data is to inflate the correlation and a correction should be made. It is therefore suggested that equation 7.1 be used as this is applicable whether or not there are ties. Most computer packages allow for ties in the data and make the necessary adjustments. In the SAS procedure PROC CORR averaged rank values are used in the case of tied ranks.

The steps in computing r_s using formula 7.1 are:

1   Rank each variable, for example, FSME and CAT separately (two series of rank scores), assign a rank of 1 to the smallest value.

2 For each subject compute $(R_i - \bar{R})$, $(R_i - \bar{R})^2$, and $(S_i - \bar{S})$, $(S_i - \bar{S})^2$ ... These computations are shown in Table 7.2.

Table 7.2: *Original and rank scores for ten schools*

SCHOOL per cent	%FSME	Rank	$(R_i - \bar{R})$	$(R_i - \bar{R})^2$	%CAT	Rank	$(S_i - \bar{S})$	$(S_i - \bar{S})^2$
A	24.0	7	1.5	2.25	24.1	7	1.5	2.25
B	24.3	8	2.5	6.25	21.8	5	-0.5	0.25
C	15.3	5	-0.5	0.25	23.3	6	0.5	0.25
D	40.8	9	3.5	12.25	36.4	10	4.5	20.25
E	10.7	2	-3.5	12.25	8.4	1	-4.5	20.25
F	6.3	1	-4.5	20.25	13.1	2	-3.5	12.25
G	23.1	6	0.5	0.25	35.1	8	2.5	6.25
H	45.0	10	4.5	20.25	36.0	9	3.5	12.25
I	12.9	3	-2.5	6.25	17.7	3	-2.5	6.25
J	13.9	4	-1.5	2.25	18.5	4	-1.5	2.25
		$\bar{R} = 5.5$		$\Sigma = 82.5$		$\bar{S} = 5.5$		$\Sigma = 82.5$

3 The denominator for equation 7.1 is given by $(82.5^2)^{0.5} = 82.5$ and the numerator, $\Sigma(R_i - \bar{R})(S_i - \bar{S})$, (the products summed) is given by:

SCHOOL	$\Sigma(R_i - \bar{R})(S_i - \bar{S})$
A	2.25
B	-1.25
C	-0.25
D	15.75
E	15.75
F	15.75
G	1.25
H	15.75
I	6.25
J	2.25
	$\Sigma = 73.5$

4 Using formula 7.1, $r_s = 73.5/82.5 = 0.89$.

If there are tied ranks, the rank value given to each member of the tied group is the average of the ranks which would have been assigned if there were no ties. For example, if schools E and F both had FSME scores of 10.7, the rank value assigned to each would be 1.5 (the average of the 1st and 2nd ranks ie $(1 + 2)/2$).

Interpretation

If the ten schools represent a random sample from a population of schools in an education authority, the null hypothesis of no relationship between FSE and CAT scores in the population can be tested. Looking at the scatterplot shown in Figure 7.2 a one-tailed alternative hypothesis would seem reasonable. That is FSE and CAT scores are positively related. The probability associated with the observed r_s 0.89 is obtained by treating the value, $((n - 2)^{0.5} \times r_s) / (1 - r_s^2)^{0.5}$ as coming from a t distribution with $n - 2$ df where r_s is the evaluated Spearman's correlation and n is the number of observations. Here $t = 5.520$ (2.5173/0.4560) with 8 degrees of freedom. Looking at Table 3 in Appendix A4, the observed value of t (5.520) is larger than the critical value of 5.041 which is in the row with 8df. The associated one-tailed probability is $p < 0.0005$. We can reject the null hypothesis of no relationship and conclude that the alternative hypothesis of a positive relationship between FSME and CAT scores is tenable.

Computer Analysis

The SAS procedure PROC CORR with the option SPEARMAN computes Spearman's rank order correlation. The relevant SAS code is:

```
    data a;
    infile 'a:nonpara.dat';
    input school $ fsme cat;
proc corr spearman;
var fsme cat;
 run;
```

The first three lines of SAS code relate to the data step and the second three lines are the procedure step.

The first line specifies the temporary data set as a. The external data file nonpara.dat is then read from the directory a: with the INFILE statement. In the third line of code the INPUT statement specifies the three variables, the first variable 'school' is designated as a character variable because of the following $ sign. The variables to be correlated are specified in the VAR statement. The correlation procedure PROC CORR with the option SPEARMAN produces the following output:

```
                        Correlation Analysis

                 2 VAR Variables: FSME CAT

                      Simple Statistics
```

Variable	N	Mean	Std Dev	Median	Minimum	Maximum
FSME	10	21.6300	12.7326	19.2000	6.3000	45.0000
CAT	10	23.4400	9.7484	22.5500	8.4000	36.4000

```
Spearman Correlation Coefficients / Prob > |R| under Ho: Rho=0 / N = 10

                          FSME              CAT

            FSME       1.00000           0.89091
                       0.0               0.0005

            CAT        0.89091           1.00000
                       0.0005            0.0
```

Interpretation of Computer Output

The first two sections of the output contain summary statistics for the sample data. The next section of the output contains a matrix of rows and columns with the variables forming the column and row headings. Each cell in the matrix contains two numbers, the first number is the correlation r_s and the second number is the associated p-value. In the second cell along in the first row, the correlation, r_s, between the variables FSME and CAT is 0.890. This is significant at the 1 per cent level, the actual probability is $p = 0.0005$. Notice that a variable that is correlated with itself is always one.

The null hypothesis tested is that the population correlation, Rho is zero. This is what the heading on the output refers to, |R| under H_0: Rho = 0. This is an approximate one-tailed test, the probability printed in the SAS output is the one-tailed p-value associated with the observed correlation in a predicted direction, in this example positive. If a two-tailed test is required, the p-value should be doubled (no assumption would be made about the direction of the relationship). In this example the correlation for a two-tailed test would have an associated probability of 0.001, that is it would be significant at the 1 per cent level.

The significant p-value means that the null hypothesis can be rejected, we conclude there is strong evidence that the true population correlation is non-zero. The upward trend in the scatterplot reflects this.

7.3   One-sample Runs Test for Randomness

When to Use

This test is used whenever we want to conclude that a **series** (or **run**) of binary events is random. The inference underlying this test is that the order (sequence) of observations obtained is based on the sample being random. Many statistical procedures are based on the assumption of random sampling. The runs test enables a test of this assumption if randomness of the sample is suspect. The test can be used as part of initial data analysis. For example, in a regression analysis it is often necessary to examine the distribution of residuals (the difference between an observed value of the response variable and the value fitted by the regression model). Residuals are either positive or negative and the signs of the residuals are lined up in the sequence in which they occur. A run is a sequence of identical events (here + or −) that is preceded or followed by a different event or no event at all (beginning and end of a sequence). A lack of randomness in the pattern of residuals is shown by either too few or too many runs and this would indicate that one or more of the assumptions underlying the regression analysis has been violated. The runs test uses information about the order of events unlike nominal test procedures such as the Chi-square test which use information about the frequency of events.

Statistical Inference and Null Hypothesis

The inference on which the test is based is that the total number of runs in a sample of observations provides an indication of the randomness of the sample. The null hypothesis is that the pattern of events is determined by a random process. There are two one-sided alternative hypotheses, the pattern is not random because there are either too few or too many runs to be attributed to chance. A two-sided alternative hypothesis is that the pattern of runs is not random. The test statistic is U, the number of runs. The exact sampling distribution of U is known. For samples where the frequency of events in either of the binary categories is > 20 a large sample approximation to the sampling distribution of U can be used. For example, assume the total number of $+$ and $-$ signs is 44, of which the first 21 are $+$ and the remaining 23 are $-$. The number of runs equals 2 and the frequency in both binary categories is > 20. In this example the large sample approximation could be used.

Test Assumptions

This is a simple one-sample test with few assumptions, namely:

- Observations can be classified as binary (data may be dichotomized – above or below a median value).
- Observations are recorded in the sequence (order) of their occurrence.

Example from the Literature

An example of use of the runs test can be found in a paper by Cliffe (1992) who investigated symptom-validity and testing of feigned sensory or memory deficits. Symptom validity testing has been used to detect feigning in patients claiming sensory and memory deficits. Such patients typically give fewer correct responses on forced choice testing than would be expected by chance (non-random). In an experiment in which six subjects were asked to feign blindness (the task was to identify which of two numbers , 0 or 1 was presented on a display monitor), it was hypothesized that subjects would simply decide which stimulus, 0 or 1 to nominate prior to each forced choice.

To test the hypothesis it was necessary to identify non-randomness in the sequence of observed responses to a series of trials. The investigator reported 148 runs in 240 trials (the number of observations in each binary category was not reported) and concluded that this number exceeded the number expected for a random sequence, $p < 0.00046$ (two-tailed). The null hypothesis of random choice of digits (1 or 0) was rejected. The investigator reported that in subsequent interviews subjects confirmed this strategy.

Worked Example

Small sample

In a study of teachers' classroom interactions a research student video-recorded fifteen science lessons taught by two teachers. Each lesson was subsequently coded and classified as either teacher interaction predominantly with boys (B) or teacher interaction predominantly with girls (G). As the lessons were recorded during different times of the day and week and considering the possibility of the teachers awareness of being observed influencing their behaviour (this might change over the study period) the researcher wanted to test the randomness of the fifteen observed lessons. The sequence of lessons were coded as:

LESSON	1	2	3	4	5	6	7	8	9	10	11	12	13	14	15
CODE	B	B	G	B	B	G	B	B	B	G	G	G	G	B	B

there are 9Bs 6Gs and 7 runs (runs are indicated by underlining). These data meet the assumptions underlying the one-sample runs test, each event belongs to a dichotomy (B/G), and the events are recorded in the sequence of their occurrence.

The research hypothesis is to determine, prior to further analysis, whether the pattern of teachers' interactions is a non-random process (two-tailed test). The selected alpha is $p = 0.05$ and the number of predominant interactions with boys is 9 (n_1) and the number of interactions with girls is 6 (n_2). The exact sampling distribution of U (number of runs) is used because the number in both of the categories n_1, n_2 is < 20.

Table 4 in Appendix A4 gives the critical values for U when n_1, or $n_2 \leq 20$. We enter Table 4 with n_1 equals 9 and n_2 equals 6 and find that the critical values are 4 and 13. (It makes no difference if you enter the tables with the values n_1 equals 6 and n_2 equals 9.)

Interpretation

Table 4 in Appendix A4 shows that for values of n_1, equals 9 and n_2 equals 6, a random sample would contain, 95 times out of 100, between 4 and 13 runs. The observed number of runs, 7, is within this region, and we do not reject the null hypothesis of non-randomness. The researcher is able to conclude that the sequence of teacher interactions observed over the 15 science lessons is random.

If the researcher had decided in advance that departure form randomness would be in a direction such that too many runs would be observed (for example, the teacher may have been conscious of being observed and may therefore make an extra effort to interact with girls rather than boys), then only the larger of the two values in the body of the table should be used (13). If the observed number of runs is greater than this critical value, we reject the null hypothesis and conclude that the alternative directional hypothesis is tenable.

With a one-tailed test alpha would be 0.025 rather than 0.05 (for the two-tailed test). Since the observed value is less than the upper critical value ($7 < 13$) we would not reject the null hypothesis of non-randomness and could not conclude that there were too many runs.

Worked Example

Large Sample Approximation

Consider the data from the previous example but assume that an additional twenty science lessons were observed. The complete data set is now:

Lesson	1	2	3	4	5	6	7	8	9	10	11	12	13	14	15
Code	B	B	G	B	B	G	B	B	B	G	G	G	G	B	B

Lesson	16	17	18	19	20	21	22	23	24	25	26	27	28	29	30
Code	G	G	B	G	G	B	B	B	G	B	B	B	B	G	G

Lesson	31	32	33	34	35
Code	B	B	B	B	G

There are 21 Bs, 14Gs and 16 runs, as $n_1 > 20$ the large sample approximation can be used. The researcher chooses a two-sample test and an alpha of 0.05. The null hypothesis is tested using the normal approximation for the sampling distribution of U. When either n_1 or $n_2 \geq 20$ the probability associated with an observed U is evaluated using formula 7.2 which gives a normal Z deviate:

$$Z = \frac{[U + (j - (2n_1n_2/N))] - 1}{\sqrt{[(2n_1n_2\,(2n_1n_2 - N))\,/\,(N^2(N - 1))]}}$$

Normal approximation for the sampling distribution of U – 7.2

where N is the total sample size, U is the number of runs, n_1 and n_2 are the frequencies for the two categories of the response variable and j is an adjustment for continuity where it is 0.5 if $U < 2n_1n_2/(N + 1)$ or -0.5 if $U > 2n_1n_2/(N + 1)$. The calculated value of Z is -0.465 ($-1.3/2.7941$).

Interpretation

Since Z is not greater than the two-tailed critical value, $+/-1.96$, the null hypothesis of randomness cannot be rejected at the 5 per cent level. The associated probability of obtaining a Z value of -0.465 when the null hypothesis is true is $p = 0.638$. As the normal distribution is symmetrical, a Z value of -0.465 has the same associated probability as a Z value of $+0.465$. From Table 1 of Appendix A4 which indicates the proportion of the total area under the normal curve which is beyond a +ve **Z**

score, the associated p-value for a Z of 0.465 for a two-tailed test is 0.638 (the tabled p-value is doubled, 0.319 × 2, for a two-tailed test).

Computer Analysis

Evaluation of equation 7.2 can be easily accomplished using the SAS programme, Runs.job. This is shown in Figure 9, Appendix A3. The following data values would be entered into this programme: $N = 35$, $U = 16$, $n_1 = 21$, $n_2 = 14$. The relevant section of SAS code is:

```
data a;       ** Enter, after the cards statement, the values for  *;
              ** N, U, CAT1, CAT2, in this order. Each value should*;
              ** be separated by a space. In this example N=35,    *;
              ** U=16, CAT1=21, and CAT2=14                        *;
   input n u cat1 cat2;
   cards;
   35 16 21 14
   ;
```

Interpretation of Computer Output

The SAS programme Runs. produced the following output:

OBS	Z	One-tailed test p-value	Two-tailed test p=value
1	0.46526	0.3209	0.6418

The associated probability of obtaining a |Z| value (absolute Z value) of 0.46526 when the null hypothesis is true is $p = 0.6418$ (the *p*-value is doubled, 0.3209 × 2, for a two-tailed test). The null hypothesis of randomness cannot be rejected at the 5 per cent level and the researcher can therefore conclude that the sequence of classroom observations is random.

7.4 Wilcoxon Mann-Whitney Test (also called Wilcoxon's rank sum test)

When to Use

This is a test of the difference between two independent random samples which is used to determine whether two samples could have reasonably come from the same population. The Wilcoxon M-W test is sensitive to differences in the location of the central tendency of distributions. If two distributions have similar shape and dispersion it is effectively a test of the difference in medians between the two groups. It is often described as a nonparametric analogue to the independent *t*-test but unlike the *t*-test it does not test specifically for differences between means.

When assumptions of an underlying normal distribution are not satisfied, or data are already in the form of ranks, the Wilcoxon M-W test is a useful and powerful alternative to the independent *t*-test. As it is based on rank scores, in practice, the procedure can be used with ordinal, interval and ratio levels of measurement. The test is particularly useful when distributions are heavy tailed, that is the distribution contains many values that are distant from the mean (see kurtosis in Chapter 3, section 3.4). The test is more powerful than the *t*-test for heavy tailed distributions, for both relatively small sample sizes and in the **asymptotic** limit (large sample sizes).

The two samples (groups) need not be the same size and the test has an exact sampling distribution for the test statistic S_R (sum of rank scores) which rapidly approaches the normal distribution as sample sizes increase (i.e., when there are about twenty scores in the larger of the two samples). Many statistical texts provide tables of critical values of S_R for different combinations of sample sizes (for the two groups being compared). However, a normal approximation based on the standard error of the test statistic S_R is adequate for most occasions and with smaller samples, < 20 in any of the groups, a **continuity correction** can be applied to the calculated Z score. A few tied scores will have little effect on the test statistic but if there are a number of tied scores, and in particular if sample sizes are small, then the variance of the test statistic S_R should be *corrected for ties*.

The Wilcoxon M-W test is also useful for *post hoc* analysis following a nonparametric one-way analysis of variance although there are more sophisticated *post hoc* procedures (see Keselman and Rogan, 1977; Marascuilo and Dagenais, 1982). A statistically equivalent test to the Wilcoxon Mann-Whitney procedure is the Mann-Whitney *U* test. This is illustrated in many introductory statistical textbooks. There is a perfect linear relationship between the two test statistics,

$$S_R = \frac{n_1(n_1 + 2n_2 + 1)}{2} - U,$$ where U is the Mann-Whitney U test statistic.

Statistical Inference and Null Hypothesis

The null hypothesis tested is that the two random samples are from one population, that is there is no difference in the rank order values found in the two data distributions being compared. Rejection of the null hypothesis is usually interpreted as meaning that the two distributions represent two different populations which have different distributions. When the shape and dispersion of the two distributions is similar it is a test of difference in population medians. The alternative hypothesis may be directional (a one-tailed test), for example, the majority of larger rank scores are found in one sample and this sample would have a larger mean rank score, or nondirectional, for example, this simply states that the two sample distributions of rank scores are different. The test statistic, S_R, is the rank sum for the sample (group) which has the smallest sample size. With small sample sizes,

< 10, this test statistic, S_R, has an exact sampling distribution, however S_R rapidly approaches a normal distribution as the sample size of one or both of the groups increases – for sample sizes ≥ 20.

The Wilcoxon M-W test is based on the idea that if there are two populations and not one (i.e., H_0 is false) the rank order scores in one sample will generally be larger than the rank scores in the other sample. This difference, that is higher ranking scores found mostly in one sample, could be detected by ranking all scores irrespective of what group they belong to and then summing the rank scores according to group membership. If H_0 is true, we would expect the rank scores to be similarly represented in both samples (groups) and the average ranks in each of the two groups to be about equal. We would not reject the null hypothesis and conclude that there is no difference in the two distributions being compared. If the two samples were different, that is having come from two distinct populations, then we would expect higher (or lower) rank sum totals (allowing for differences in sample size) in one of the samples. The sampling distribution of the rank sum S_R is known and hence the probability associated with extreme values of the test statistic. Given regard to the sample sizes of the two groups, and whether a one-tailed or two-tailed test is used, the probability associated with an observed value of S_R can be determined.

Test Assumptions

The test assumptions are as follows:

- Observations are compared which have been selected at random from an underlying theoretically continuous distribution, but measurement is at least at the ordinal level (ranks).
- Observations are from two independent samples.
- The two distributions compared should have similar variances.
- Tied scores (after ranking) are given the average of the ranks they would have had if no ties had occurred. A small number of ties have little effect on the test statistic S_R, however when the proportion of ties is large and, in particular when sample sizes are small, the test statistic S_R tends to be conservative (p-values are inflated) and a correction for ties should be applied. The effect of tied values is to reduce the standard error of the test statistic S_R leading to an overall increase in the value of Z.
- With small sample sizes, $n < 20$, a correction for continuity should be used, most statistical analysis programmes automatically apply a continuity correction.

Example from the Literature

Given that ranking methods are particularly useful in many educational settings, where measurement can only reasonably be made at the ordinal level, it is surprising that the Wilcoxon M-W test or the comparable Mann Whitney U test are not more widely used by educational researchers.

In a study on the place of alcohol education and its (implied) effectiveness Regis, Bish and Balding (1994) compared the alcohol consumption (units of alcohol) of 10-year-old self-declared drinkers for a number of independent groups of pupils. Four comparisons amongst independent groups were made of which two are illustrated: i) comparison of alcohol consumption among pupils where alcohol education was delivered through science vs. pupils where it was not delivered through science and ii) comparison of alcohol consumption among pupils where alcohol education was delivered through personal and social education (PSE) vs. pupils where it was not delivered through PSE.

Data for these comparisons amongst girls is shown below:

Comparison group (10-year-old girls)	Alcohol education delivered Mean Rank Score	Alcohol education not delivered Mean Rank Score	p-value
Science	298.74	253.77	0.0009
PSE	281.84	260.51	0.2237

The investigators reported that Mann Whitney U tests were used (directly comparable with Wilcoxon M-W test) as the statistical test for detecting differences between groups. They go on to say that a nonparametric test was used because it made fewest assumptions about the underlying population distribution and the nature of the variables.

Given the non-normal distribution of the data reported by the investigators (skewed distribution of alcohol consumption attributable to outlier observations) and the comparisons among independent groups then the nonparametric equivalent to a t-test, either a Wilcoxon M-W test or Mann Whitney U test, is appropriate provided the distributions to be compared have similar dispersion. The investigators do not provide any information about the dispersion of observations in the data set.

The null hypothesis tested by the investigators was that the distribution of units of alcohol consumed by 10-year-old girls was the same amongst two groups of pupils; one group where alcohol education was delivered in science vs. the other group where alcohol education was not delivered in science lessons. A similar null hypothesis was tested comparing pupils where alcohol education was delivered through PSE or not. Although not specifically stated by the investigators, the alternative hypotheses appear to be non-directional and therefore a two-tailed test is appropriate.

Each case was assigned a rank with the ranking done from the lowest upwards so that the direction of difference can be determined by inspection of the mean ranks. The investigators concluded that there was a significant difference in alcohol consumption where it was delivered through science, the higher mean rank score indicates that consumption is higher where alcohol education is delivered in science, $U = 320695$, $p < 0.0009$.

Worked Example

Based on an investigation by Kyriacou (1992) into active learning in secondary school mathematics, a research student designed her dissertation study to address, amongst other issues, the following research question, 'Is there any difference in the percentage of active learning activities as a percentage of all mathematics learning activities for upper school classes and lower school classes?'

Data from this study is used to illustrate computational details of the Wilcoxon M-W test. The investigator identified, based on classroom observation, interviews with teachers, and exploratory group discussions, seven types of learning activity in mathematics classes, four of which were regarded as active and three as traditional learning. The second phase of the study sought the views of mathematics teachers regarding the extent to which any of the four types of active learning occurred in mathematics lessons in their school. Two independent samples of teachers were approached, lower school maths teachers (first second and third years) and upper school maths teachers (fourth and fifth year groups). Each teacher was asked to rate, on a scale of 1 to 100, an indication of the expected frequency of the activity in 100 randomly selected mathematics lessons in their school (either upper or lower school as appropriate). This was recorded as the percentage of lessons that could be described as active learning. The obtained results of the survey are shown in Table 7.3.

Table 7.3: Results of a survey of learning activities in upper and lower school mathematics lessons

Maths teachers:	per cent maths lessons active learning											
Lower school	($n_1 = 10$)	30	51	48	28	26	42	44	66	68	21	
Upper school	($n_2 = 12$)	30	31	54	32	34	38	40	52	65	30	40	39

The Wilcoxon M-W test is appropriate because the null hypothesis to be tested is:

H_0: There is no difference in the distribution of active learning activities, as a percentage of the total types of learning activities in maths lessons, for upper-and lower-school teachers.

The data meets the necessary requirements for this test: two independent random samples (need not be of the same size), ordinal measurement, (ranked as percentages), and similar shaped distributions, although the dispersion of scores is less among upper-school teachers (see Figure 7.3).

225

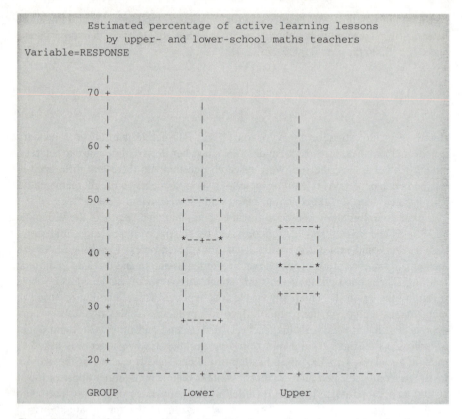

```
                    Estimated percentage of active learning lessons
                         by upper- and lower-school maths teachers
        Variable=RESPONSE

                   |
             70 +
                   |
                   |                   |
                   |                   |                   |
             60 +                      |                   |
                   |                   |                   |
                   |                   |                   |
                   |                   |                   |
             50 +           +------+    |                   |
                   |         |      |   |                   |
                   |         |      |   |          +------+
                   |         *--+--*    |          |      |
             40 +            |      |   |          |  +   |
                   |         |      |   |          *------*
                   |         |      |   |          |      |
                   |         |      |   |          +------+
             30 +            |      |   |          |
                   |         +------+   |
                   |                    |
                   |                    |
             20 +                       |
                   - - - - - - - - - + - - - - - - - - - + - - - - - - -

        GROUP               Lower              Upper
```

Figure 7.3: Plot of upper- and lower-school teachers estimated percentage of active learning maths lessons

The alternative hypothesis is non-directional (two-tailed, alpha set to 5 per cent) and simply states that the distribution of scores in the two groups is different. This is equivalent to saying the median scores are different, we can see from the box and whisker plots that the median scores for the two groups are not the same but it is not possible to judge from the plots whether this difference is statistically significant. The Wilcoxon M-W test is therefore performed.

The computational steps are:

1 Combine the two samples and rank the entire data set, assign the rank 1 to the lowest score. In the case of two or more raw score values being equal assign the average rank to each.

2 Sum the rank scores for each group separately.

3 Select the test statistic S_R which is the sum of the ranks for the smallest group (n). The twenty-two observations, ranked from smallest to largest are shown (lower school teachers are underlined):

Observation	21	26	28	30	30	30	31	32	34	38	39
Rank	1	2	3	5	5	5	7	8	9	10	11

Observation	40	40	42	44	48	51	52	54	65	66	68
Rank	12.5	12.5	14	15	16	17	18	19	20	21	22

The test statistic S (Sum of the rank scores) for the smallest group ($n = 10$) is 116. This approximates to the following sampling distribution:

$$Z = \frac{Observed\ (S_R) - Expected\ (S_R)}{SE\ of\ (S_R)} \text{ where SE is the standard error}$$

The observed S_R is 116, and the expected Sum $S_R = n_s \frac{(N+1)}{2}$ where n_s is the number in the smaller group and N is the total sample size ($n_1 + n_2$). Expected or mean S_R is 115 (10×11.5).

The standard error of S_R is $\sqrt{\dfrac{n_1 n_2}{N(N-1)} \left[\dfrac{(N^3 - N)}{12} - \sum_{j=1}^{h} \dfrac{t_j^3 - t_j}{12} \right]}$

where t is the number of ties in the jth group and h is the number of groupings of different tied scores. In this example $\sum_{j=1}^{h} \dfrac{t_j^3 - t_j}{12}$ is evaluated as:

tied score	n of ties	$\dfrac{t_j^3 - t_j}{12}$	Total
30	3	$\dfrac{(3^3 - 3)}{12}$	$= 2$
40	$2 \times$	$\dfrac{(2^3 - 2)}{12}$	$= 0.5$

Summed over all tied scores $= 2.5$
The standard error of S_R is therefore:

$$\sqrt{\frac{120}{22(21)} \times (885.5 - 2.5)} = 15.144$$

4 The test statistic Z, adjusted for continuity (observed score $- 0.5$) and corrected for ties in the data is:

$$Z = \frac{(116 - 0.5) - 115}{15.144} = 0.0330$$

Many statistical textbooks give special tables for the test statistic S_R with upper and lower critical values for different combinations of sample sizes. In some of these tables the p-values associated with sample sizes of 20 or more are actually large sample approximations. With very small sample sizes of $n \leq 5$ the exact sampling should be used, for explanation of the use of these tables and illustrated worked examples, see Conover (1980) and Siegel and Castallan (1988). The normal approximation of S_R with continuity correction is adequate for most occasions.

Interpretation

The obtained Z-value of 0.0330 has an associated p-value of 0.4880, the nearest value in the Table of Z-scores in Appendix A4. This is the probability beyond a Z-value of 0.0330, for a two-tailed test this is doubled. The p-value is therefore 0.976. This is clearly not significant and the null hypothesis is therefore not rejected at the 5 per cent level. We conclude that teachers' estimates of active learning in maths lessons do not differ among lower and upper school maths teachers.

Rejection of the null hypothesis is usually interpreted as a difference in the central tendency of the two distributions. However, caution is required with this interpretation because the null hypothesis may be rejected when the means of the two samples are very similar (not so in this example). This is because the Wilcoxon M-W test is sensitive to differences in variance in the two samples (the Behrens Fisher problem). Under the null hypothesis, the Wilcoxon M-W test assumes that the two samples come from a single population with an underlying continuous distribution even though measurement is only at the ordinal level. If we assume that the two distributions are the same we are also assuming that the variances are the same. If they are not, the means may still be similar but clearly the distributions are not identical.

Computer Analysis

The SAS procedure PROC NPAR1WAY with the option WILCOXON performs a Wilcoxon M-W test on the ranks of scores when there are two independent groups (data is classified by a variable into two levels). The following SAS code illustrates use of the procedure PROC NPAR1WAY:

```
data a;
    input group response @@;
    cards;
1 30 1 51 1 48 1 28 1 26 1 42 1 44 1 66 1 68 1 21
2 30 2 31 2 54 2 32 2 34 2 38 2 40 2 52 2 65 2 30 2 40 2 39
;
proc nparlway data=a wilcoxon;
    class group;
    var response;
run;
```

The data step begins in the first line where the internal SAS data set is designated a. On the second line two variables are specified, 'group' and 'response', the double trailing at sign, @@, indicates that each input line contains several observations, for example, the first observation belongs to group 1 and has a value of 30, the second observation also belongs to group 1 and has a value of 51. Data values are input after the cards statement, note the semicolon on a separate line by itself (the programme will fail if the semicolon is not on a line of its own). The CLASS statement identifies the variable that classifies the observations into two groups, here it is the variable group. The VAR statement identifies the response or outcome variable to use for the group comparison, here the variable is called response. This section of SAS code produces the output shown in Figure 7.4.

```
               N P A R 1 W A Y  P R O C E D U R E

        Wilcoxon Scores (Rank Sums) for Variable RESPONSE
                    Classified by Variable GROUP

                  Sum of      Expected      Std Dev        Mean
   GROUP     N    scores      under H0      under H0       score

     1      10    116.0        115.0       15.1443273    11.6000000
     2      12    137.0        138.0       15.1443273    11.4166667

               Average Scores were used for Ties
         Wilcoxon 2-Sample Test (Normal Approximation)
                (with Continuity Correction of .5)

    S= 116.000        Z= 0.033016     Prob > |Z| = 0.9737

    T-Test approx. Significance = 0.9740

    Kruskal-Wallis Test (Chi-Square Approximation)
    CHISQ= 0.00436    DF= 1         Prob > CHISQ= 0.9474
```

Figure 7.4: *Output for Wilcoxon M-W test using PROC NPAR1WAY*

Interpretation of Computer Output

The heading summarizes the name of the test performed, Wilcoxon Scores (Rank Sums) test, the response variable analyzed, and the CLASS variable used to define the groups for the analysis. In this example, the class variable is called GROUP, and the levels of GROUP are 1 (lower school) and 2 (upper school). The number of observations in each group are indicated by N and the sum of the rank scores for each group is printed. The rank sum that belongs to the smaller N, here 116, is the test statistic S_R and this is printed separately on the following line. The expected Wilcoxon rank sums (under the null hypothesis) are printed along with their associated standard errors labelled 'Std Dev under H0'. Should the sample sizes for the two groups be equal then the expected values of S_R would also be equal. The average ranks sum for each group is also output. This gives a useful indication of which group has the largest proportion of higher ranking scores. In this example both groups are similar.

The test statistic, the evaluated normal approximation, Z, and associated probability, Prob > |Z| labelled in the output S and not S_R, are all output on the same line. In this example a p-value of 0.9737 is printed, this is a two-tailed value, twice the probability associated with a Z-score of 0.0330 (nearest tabled value for one-tailed is 0.4880). As the two-tailed *p*-value is larger than the 5 per cent significance level, $0.9737 > 0.05$, we can conclude that the two distributions are not significantly different and that the average of teachers' estimates of active learning in maths for lower and upper school maths teachers are not significantly different. As this is a two-tailed test, a Z-value of ≥ 1.96 would be required for the results to be statistically significant at the 5 per cent level.

7.5 Wilcoxon Signed Ranks test (for related data)

When to Use

This is a test of the difference between pairs of related observations or matched pairs of subjects, and is the nonparametric equivalent of the related *t*-test. The Wilcoxon **signed ranks test** should be considered when researchers are interested in comparing two related samples on some rankable measure and when the shape of the population is unknown or assumptions underlying use of the related *t*-test are not met, typically distribution of the measures in the population are non normal or measurements are not on an interval or ratio scale (see Chapter 8 for details of *t*-test assumptions).

The Wilcoxon Signed Ranks test is a more powerful version of the sign test because the procedure uses information about both the *direction* and *magnitude* of differences within pairs. When we can determine the magnitude of a difference, observations can be ranked. Parametric tests are often held to be more powerful than nonparametric counterparts but this is only true when underlying normal theory assumptions are met. It is seldom acknowledged that nonparametric tests may be as powerful or more powerful than parametric counterparts under certain circumstances, for example, 'heavy-tailed' distributions, log-normal distributions and exponential distributions, in these situations the Wilcoxon Signed Ranks test is more powerful than the related t-test, with a truncated normal distribution the Wilcoxon Signed Ranks test and related *t*-test are equal in terms of statistical power (Blair and Higgins, 1985).

The logic underpinning this test is elegantly simple. The aim of the test is to find out about the distribution of the difference scores, that is the difference for each pair of observations. We can think of, for example, a pre-post-test study design where each individual has a before (pre) and after (post) intervention score. The distribution of difference scores, pre-post-, would be asymmetrical about zero, that is predominantly negative if the majority of subjects showed an improvement in scores after the intervention. If there were an equal number of positive and negative differences, such as only chance differences, and these differences were roughly equal magnitude, this would suggest no significant difference between pre- and post-intervention samples of scores.

The null hypothesis tested is that the median of the population differences is zero and that the distribution of differences is symmetrical about zero. It is based on the assumption that the amount of positive and negative difference which occurs by chance should be approximately equal in each direction. A non-directional alternative hypothesis (two-sided) would be that the median of the population of differences is non-zero and a directional alternative hypothesis would be that the median of the population of differences is either greater or less than zero. The test statistic, T, is the rank sum totals for selected pairs of observations. The absolute values of difference scores are first ranked then the sign of the difference score is assigned (positive and negative). The signed ranked differences are then summed separately (positive differences and negative differences), the smaller of the two sums of the absolute values of the signed rank differences (the +/− signs are again ignored) is the test statistic T. A sufficiently small value of T provides evidence for rejection of the null hypothesis. The exact sampling distribution for T with sample sizes ≤ 15 is determined and tabulated, for larger sample sizes there is a normal approximation.

Test Assumptions

These are:

- Data consists of pairs of observations which have been selected at random and each pair is independent of other pairs.
- The differences between pairs of observations are also independent.
- The original measures in the two samples are rankable (in practice may be ratio, interval or ordinal).
- The differences between the two measures are rankable.
- Pairs of observations may be two measurements taken on the same subject or two subjects that are matched (paired) with respect to one or more important variables.

Example from the Literature

Teachers are frequently cited as the reason pupils dislike school. In a study involving 101 pupils from three schools, Boser and Poppen (1978) examined the qualities of teachers that are generally liked and disliked by pupils. Pupils were asked to describe, using seven descriptive categories, a teacher with whom they had poor relationships, 'difficult getting on with' and a teacher with whom they had good relationships, 'get along with well'.

One quality identified in the research literature that is associated with good teacher–pupil relationships is the teacher role of 'sharing' that is when a teacher shares personal ideas, opinions, or feelings about things. The investigators wanted to determine whether there was a difference in sharing behaviour between best relationships and poorest relationship situations. Sharing behaviour was scored on an ordinal scale 1–5 where 1 means always behaves like this and 5 means never behaves like this.

The null hypothesis tested was that teachers sharing behaviour is the same in poorest and best relationship situations. The alternative hypothesis was non-directional (two-tailed). In this situation the Wilcoxon signed ranks test was used rather than a related *t*-test because measures were ordinal. The investigators did not specify in advance an alpha level but reported that sharing behaviour was significantly different at the 0.0001 level on a two-tailed test. The mean score for sharing in best relationship situation was 2.198 compared with 3.830 in poorest relationship situation, a low mean denotes a high frequency of behaviour.

Worked Example

A student's PhD study was concerned with teacher–pupil communication skills and part of the empirical investigation was based on Boser and Poppen's (1978) study on student–teacher relations. In a pilot study with ten pupils the researcher investigated pupils' experiences of good and poor relationships with teachers. A videotape was produced and shown to pupils to demonstrate five types of teacher behaviours, one of which was sharing as originally described in Boser and Poppen's study. Students were asked to indicate, on a 5-point scale, how often a particular teacher with whom they had a poor relationship had behaved in a manner similar to that demonstrated on the videotape (example of sharing behaviour). Pupils also rated a teacher with whom they had good relationships in a similar manner. In this study, a score of 5 indicates that the teacher always behaves like this (reversed scoring to original Boser and Poppen study). Current teachers were excluded from consideration. In this example, data or teachers sharing behaviour is used, see Table 7.4:

Table 7.4: Teachers sharing behaviour in best and poorest relationship situations

Subject	Best	Poorest	Idifferencel*	Rank difference
1	4	2	2	+5
2	3	1	2	+5
3	5	3	2	+5
4	2	2	0	–
5	3	1	2	+5
6	5	1	4	+8
7	1	1	0	–
8	4	3	1	+1.5
9	3	4	1	−1.5
10	4	2	2	+5

* Difference is (best–poor)
Observed test statistics $T^+ = 34.5$; $T^- = 1.5$

The null hypothesis tested by the researcher was that teachers sharing behaviour is the same in poorest and best relationship situations. The alternative hypothesis was non-directional (two-tailed) and the selected alpha was 5 per cent.

The computational steps are:

1   For each pair of observations determine the absolute difference score |d|.
2   Rank these absolute differences (ignore sign of difference) and give the rank of 1 to the smallest score. Should the absolute difference, |d| be zero that is no difference between the original pair of observations, do not rank this difference score (drop it from the analysis) and reduce the sample size accordingly. Should two or more difference scores be tied, the rank assigned to each member of the tied group is the average of the ranks which would have been assigned were the differences not equal.
3   Assign each ranked difference score either +ve or −ve indicating the sign of the difference it represents.
4   The test statistic T is either i) for small samples, $n \le 15$, the smaller sum of the rank signed differences regardless of whether it is + or − (that is compute the sum of the positive ranked differences and the sum of the negative ranked differences and choose the smaller of the two sums), or ii) with a large sample approximation, T^+, the sum of the positive ranked differences.

In this example there are only 8 subjects for analysis (two have zero differences and are thus eliminated) and therefore the test statistic, T, is 1.5 because this is the smaller of the two rank totals in Table 7.4. This test statistic is compared with tabled critical values (see Table 5, Appendix A4). Should n be > 25 then the following large sample approximation should be used:

$$Z = \frac{T - \left[\dfrac{N(N+1)}{4} \right]}{\sqrt{\dfrac{N(N+1)(2N+1)}{24}}}$$

Z-score approximation for sampling distribution of T, Wilcoxon Signed Ranks test − 7.3

The large sample test is a good approximation even with samples as small as 10.

Interpretation

Small sample test

If for a chosen number of observation pairs and a chosen alpha level the observed test statistic, T (rank sum total), is larger than the tabled critical value then statistical significance has *not* been attained at the selected alpha level. In this example $1.5 < 4$ (critical value from Table 5, Appendix A4 with $n = 8$, two-tailed test and alpha = 0.05) the result is therefore significant at the 5 per cent level. The null hypothesis can be rejected and we conclude that teachers' sharing behaviour is not the same in poorest and best relationship situations. Higher scores (more frequent sharing behaviour) were found predominantly in the best relationship situations. The exact sampling distribution is tabled in some statistical texts in which case T^+ should be used, see for example Siegel and Castallan, (1988). Table 5 in Appendix A4 provides small sample critical values for selected significance levels.

Computer Analysis

The Wilcoxon signed ranks test is automatically performed by the procedure PROC UNIVARIATE in SAS when the response variable analyzed is a difference score. SAS code for data entry and analysis, using the same data as in the worked example, is shown in Figure 7.5.

```
data a;
  input best poor @@;
    diff=best-poor;
cards;
4 2 3 1 5 3 2 2 3 1 5 1 1 1 4 3 3 4 4 2
;

proc univariate data=a;
  var diff;
title 'Difference between best and poor relationships two-tailed test';
run;
```

Figure 7.5: SAS code for computation of the Wilcoxon Signed Rank statistic

Output from this SAS programme is shown in Figure 7.6:

```
    Difference between best and poor relationships two-tailed test
                      Univariate Procedure
Variable=DIFF

                              Moments
            N              10          Sum Wgts     10
            Mean           1.4         Sum          14
            Std Dev        1.429841    Variance     2.044444
            Skewness       -0.03421    Kurtosis     0.215703
            USS            38          CSS          18.4
            CV             102.1315    Std Mean     0.452155
            T:Mean=0       3.096281    Pr> |T|      0.0128
            Num ^=0        8           Num > 0      7
            M(Sign)        3           Pr>= |M|     0.0703
            Sgn Rank       16.5        Pr>= |S|     0.0234
```

Figure 7.6: Output from PROC Univariate for paired difference best–poor relationship

Interpretation of Computer Output

SAS automatically performs a two-way test if a variable representing the difference between the two repeated observations is analyzed as the response variable, here difference=best–poor. In Figure 7.6 the row labelled Sgn Rank gives the value of the expected signed rank statistic, here 16.5. This Wilcoxon Signed Rank statistic is equivalent to the observed – expected value of T^+ which is the numerator of equation 7.3. The associated probability, $Pr \geq |S|$, is also output in this example p = 0.0234. Since this p-value is less than 0.05, for a two-tailed test, we can conclude that there is a difference between teachers sharing behaviour in best and poorest relationship situations. If the p-value associated with the Wilcoxon Signed Rank test had been larger than 0.05, we could not reject the null hypothesis and would have concluded that the median of the population differences was not significantly different from zero.

Large sample procedure approximate test

With an effective sample size of 8 you would not normally use the large sample approximation but it is used here to illustrate the procedure.

Similar to the Wilcoxon M-W test procedure with large sample approximation, Z is given by the general formulae, (observed–expected)/standard error where observed test statistic is T^+, (sum of the positive ranked differences), the expected value is $= (n(n + 1))/4$, and the standard error is $\sqrt{\dfrac{N(N + 1)(2N + 1)}{24}}$.

Here $Z = (34.5 - 18)/7.141 = 2.311$. The associated p-value is 0.021 (see Table of Z scores in Appendix A4). This gives substantively the same answer as the small sample test.

SAS does not automatically output the observed test statistic T^+ or its standard error when the Wilcoxon signed ranks test is performed with PROC UNIVARIATE. The SAS programme Wilcoxsr, see Figure 10, Appendix A3, outputs the rank scores, the sum, T^+, standard error, expected T and a Z score with associated probability (2-tailed). Output from this SAS programme using data from the worked example is shown:

```
                    Wilcoxon signed ranks test

         first      second     absolute                        ranked
OBS      value      value      difference    difference      differences

 1         4          2           2             2               5.0
 2         3          1           2             2               5.0
 3         5          3           2             2               5.0
 4         3          1           2             2               5.0
 5         5          1           4             4               8.0
 6         4          3           1             1               1.5
 7         3          4           1            -1               1.5
 8         4          2           2             2               5.0

                       Summary Statistics

               observed                                       p-value
Number of       value       expected                         (2-tailed
subjects         (T)         value         SE      z score     test)
   8            34.5          18        7.14143   2.31046     0.0208
```

This SAS programme is useful even for small samples (the z-value would not be used) because it enables T^+ and T^- to be easily computed from the column of ranked differences in the output. The difference column gives the sign + or − associated with an observation, so that the two rank sums can be evaluated, that is the sum of the + rank differences and the sum of the − rank differences.

Comment on Use of the Wilcoxon Signed Ranks Test

The assumption of rankability of the differences is frequently not met with operational measures. Kornbrot (1990) discusses this point in some detail with particular reference to operational measures of times, rates and counts. These are common operational measures in psychology and education for example, time as an index of information processing, and counts are often used to determine errors on tasks. Kornbrot presents a practical alternative statistical test to the Wilcoxon Signed Ranks test called the **rank difference** test. This procedure is applicable when operational measures do not meet the assumptions underlying use of the Wilcoxon Signed Ranks test, in particular if there is doubt about rankability of the difference scores. Both exact sampling distributions and large sample approximations for the sample statistic *D* are given in Kornbrot's paper.

7.6 Kruskal-Wallis One-way ANOVA

When to Use

A common research problem is to decide whether or not sample differences in central tendency reflect true differences in parent populations (Walsh and Toothaker, 1974). The Kruskal-Wallis test is often the chosen procedure to test two or more (k-sample case) independent groups for location equality when assumptions of a one-way ANOVA (analysis of variance) are suspect (non-normality and heterogeneity of variance, see Chapter 8 for details) or when the observations are naturally in the form of ranks. The rationale underpinning this procedure is that if all scores are considered initially as one group, assigned a rank value, and the rank values are then reallocated into the independent (or treatment) groups, then under the null hypothesis of chance the sum of the ranks in each group will be about the same, apart from sampling variation.

Researchers use this test as they would a one-way ANOVA to determine whether two or more groups have similar score distributions, Ciechalski (1988) suggests that the Kruskal-Wallis test is not a substitute for a parametric procedure, but an additional decision tool.

This procedure is also useful for analyzing count data in contingency tables when the response variable is categorical *and* ordered. Traditionally this type of data is analyzed by a Chi-square procedure, however, provided there is an underlying continuity to the response variable, the Kruskal-Wallis test is a more powerful alternative than an r × k Chi-square test.

Statistical Inference and Null Hypothesis

The Kruskal-Wallis test statistic, *H*, is sensitive to location shifts and under the null hypothesis (equal populations) is asymptotically (large sample) distributed as Chi-square with k − 1 degrees of freedom. The null hypothesis is that the independent samples come from the same population or from populations which have the same median. The non-directional alternative hypothesis is that at least one sample has a different median to the others. A large value of the test statistic leads to rejection of the null hypothesis.

Test Assumptions

The test assumptions are as follows:

- Data consists of observations which have been selected at random from an infinitely large population.
- The population(s) have an underlying continuous distribution but the response variable is a rank measurement.
- It is preferable that there are at least 4–5 subjects in each sample (independent group) because of the use of the Chi-square approximation for the *H*-test statistic. It is not necessary to have a balanced design (equal numbers in each independent group).

With heterogeneity of variance, different variances for the independent samples, it is possible with this test procedure to reject the null hypothesis (equality of medians), when **means** are in fact equal. A significant test statistic value, *H*, is therefore no assurance of differences in treatment means.

Example from the Literature

Elliott and Hewison (1994) investigated type of reading help given by different (independent) groups of parents. In their study there were four groups of parents/other family members: 24 middle-class families; 26 working-class families, 17 families who had been involved in a Paired Reading Project; and 24 families of Asian origin. Four response variables were analyzed separately, rapid corrections (maintaining flow in reading), Semantic-based corrections; phonic-based corrections; and anomalies (deliberate non-correction or missed correction). Kruskal-Wallis non-parametric analysis of variance was performed on each response variable separately. The authors reported differences between groups for all four response variables: rapid correction ($H = 32.34$, p < 0.00001); semantic-based corrections ($H = 30.33$, p < 0.00001); phonic corrections ($H = 11.39$, p < 0.009); and anomalies/non-corrections ($H = 20.10$, p < 0.0002). *Post hoc* tests were not reported.

Worked Example

Small sample Kruskal-Wallis test procedure

Data shown in Table 7.5 is similar to that obtained by Elliott and Hewison (1994), who investigated types of reading help given by different groups of parents. In their study there were four groups of parents, but the data presented in Table 7.5 refers to only three groups, middle-class, working-class and Asian families, and one ordinal response variable, number of rapid reading corrections.

Table 7.5: Rapid correction reading correction scores for three groups of families

Subjects	Middle-class value	rank	Working-class value	rank	Asian value	rank
1	22	10.5	31	15	13	2
2	26	12	30	14	16	3
3	27	13	21	8	21	8
4	22	10.5	17	4.5	17	4.5
5	18	6	21	8	12	1
Sum of ranks		52		49.5		18.5
Mean of ranks ($\bar{R}$)		10.4		9.9		3.7

The null hypothesis is that there is no difference among the three groups of middle-class, working-class and Asian families in the way that they correct reading errors using rapid correction. The alternative hypothesis is that the three groups differ in the way they use the rapid correction strategy to correct childrens' reading errors. Alpha is set to 5 per cent.

The computational steps are:

- Combine all scores into one group and assign a rank to each score representing its position in the single series.
- Each ranked value is then reassigned to its respective group (in this example middle-class, working-class or Asian) and the sum of rank values and the mean is calculated for each group. In this example sample numbers in each group are equal but this is not necessary.

The Kruskal-Wallis test statistic, H, is then calculated using the following formula:

$$H = \left[\frac{12}{N(N+1)} \sum_{j=1}^{k} n_j \bar{R}_j^2 \right] - 3(N+1)$$

Kruskal-Wallis
H-test statistic – 7.4

where k refers to the number of groups (independent samples), n_j is the number of observations in the jth group, N is the total number of observations in the combined sample, and $\bar{R}_j$ is the mean of the ranks in the jth group,

$$H = \left[\frac{12}{15(15+1)} [5(10.4)^2 + 5(9.9)^2 + 5(3.7)^2] \right] - 3(15+1)$$

$$H = 0.05 \ (1099.3) - 48 = 6.965$$

As in the Wilcoxon signed ranks test, the variance of the sampling distribution of the test statistic is influenced by ties among the scores regardless of to which group the tied scores belong. The correction for ties is given by:

$$1 - \frac{\sum\limits_{i=1}^{g}(t_i^3 - t_i)}{N^3 - N}$$ **Correction for ties in K-W *H*-statistic – 7.5**

where g = the number of groups of different tied values, t_i is the number of tied ranks in each of the groups of tied values and N is the total number of observations in the combined sample. The Kruskal-Wallis H statistic is then divided by this correction factor.

$$\text{Correction factor is } 1 - \frac{(2^3 - 2) + (3^3 - 3) + (2^3 - 2)}{15^3 - 15}$$
$$= 1 - (36/3360) = 0.989$$

The value of H corrected for ties is therefore $6.965/0.989 = 7.04$

Interpretation

When any of the independent groups has fewer than five observations we can describe this as a **small sample** design. In this situation we use the exact sampling distribution of the test statistic H. This is shown in Table 6, Appendix A4 (for three independent groups only). The rejection region for the H-test statistic is $H >$ tabled critical value, which is based on the sample size in each of three groups and on the chosen alpha level.

In this example we have selected alpha of 0.05. The critical value given in Table 6, Appendix A4 for alpha = 0.05 and $n_1 = n_2 = n_3 = 5$ is 5.78. The rejection region for the test includes all values of $H > 5.78$. Since the observed H is greater than the critical value, $7.04 > 5.78$, the probability of obtaining an H-value as large as 7.04, when the null hypothesis is true, is equal to or less than $p = 0.05$. We reject the null hypothesis at the 5 per cent level and conclude there is sufficient evidence of a difference(s) among the three groups of middle-class, working-class and Asian families in the way they correct reading errors.

When H is found to be statistically significant it indicates that the k-samples do not come from the same population, that is at least one of the samples has a different median to at least one of the others. The H-statistic is not informative about which or how many of the samples are significantly different from each other. When the number of comparisons are small the Wilcoxon Mann-Whitney test may be used for *post hoc* analysis following a significant Kruskal-Wallis H test. A more detailed procedure which makes use of the normal approximations is described by Siegel and Castellan (1988), and Keselman and Rogan (1977) discuss the relative merits of K-W *post hoc* procedure (similar to the multiple comparison procedures described by Siegel and Castallan but based on the Chi-square distribution) and the Tukey test under varying conditions.

Computer analysis

To perform a Kruskal-Wallis test in SAS, PROC NPAR1WAY is used with the option wilcoxon. Using this nonparametric ANOVA test on the reading correction data shown in Table 7.5 the following SAS code would be used:

```
data a;
  input group response @@ ;
  cards;
1 22 1 26 1 27 1 22 1 18
2 31 2 30 2 21 2 17 2 21
3 13 3 16 3 21 3 17 3 12
;
**** kruskal-wallis test ****;
proc nparlway data=a wilcoxon;
  class group;
  var response;
title 'Kruskal-Wallis test - worked example';
run;
```

Data is entered after the cards statement. The group value followed by the response value is input for each subject. The option wilcoxon performs a Kruskal-Wallis test when there are more than two groups. The class statement denotes the variable that divides the observations into independent groups, here there are three groups and each group, for convenience, is given a numeric value of 1, 2, or 3 (these are only nominal categories, the class variable does not imply any order). Output from this programme is shown in Figure 7.7.

```
            Kruskal-Wallis test - worked example
                N P A R 1 W A Y   P r o c e d u r e
        Wilcoxon Scores (Rank Sums) for Variable response
                  Classified by Variable group

                 Sum of      Expected      Std Dev       Mean
 GROUP    N      Scores      Under H0      Under H0      Score
   1      5    52.0000000      40.0       8.12110713   10.4000000
   2      5    49.5000000      40.0       8.12110713    9.9000000
   3      5    18.5000000      40.0       8.12110713    3.7000000
              Average Scores were used for Ties

           Kruskal-Wallis Test (Chi-square Approximation)
             CHISQ= 7.0404  DF= 2  Prob > CHISQ= 0.0296
```

Figure 7.7: Output from PROC NPAR1WAY for reading correction data

Interpretation of Computer Output

Unlike the worked example, where the exact sampling distribution of H was used, SAS output automatically provides a Chi-square approximation. The computed value of H (corrected for ties) in the worked example is the same as the Chi-square value shown in this output. The only difference is in the interpretation of the test statistic. In the worked example the significance of H was evaluated using the exact sampling distribution and tabled critical values (Table 6, Appendix A4). The SAS output refers to the Chi-square approximation, (primarily intended for large samples studies) which is based on $k - 1$ degrees of freedom (k is the number of independent samples or groups). The rejection region for the Kruskal-Wallis test includes all values of Chi-square larger than $\chi^2_{(2)}$ (means Chi-square with 2 df) with p = 0.05, that is 5.99147. Since the calculated value, 7.0404 exceeds the critical value (falls in the rejection region) we know that the observed value has an associated probability under the null hypothesis that lies between p = 0.05 and p = 0.02, (see Table 2, Appendix A4) which may be expressed as $0.05 > p > 0.02$. In fact the SAS output shows that the associated probability is 0.0296. This probability is small, less than 5 per cent so we can reject the null-hypothesis of no difference and we arrive at the same conclusion as in the worked example. If an investigator was concerned about using the Chi-square approximation with small samples, less than 5 observations in any of the groups, H can be evaluated using the exact sampling distribution (Table 6, Appendix A4). For discussion on the adequacy of this Chi-square approximation for small samples the reader is referred to Gabriel and Lachenbruch (1969).

Pairwise Multiple-comparisons for post-hoc Analysis

When an obtained H-statistic is significant, an investigator may wish to determine which of the groups differ. A *post hoc* pairwise multiple-comparison procedure and computational formula is described by Siegel and Castellan (1988), the SAS programme Krusk-W1 (see Figure 11, Appendix A3) performs this procedure for all pairwise comparisons in a design. An investigator should note that to control for experiment-wise error, that is, to adjust for many non-independent pairwise comparisons, the initial alpha level should be set to a liberal level (possibly 10 per cent). For a two-tailed test the effective pairwise alpha level will be the original alpha level used for the Kruskal-Wallis test divided by the number of possible comparisons, c, multiplied by two ($\alpha/(c \times 2)$). The number of comparisons is given by ($k(k - 1)/2$) where k refers to the number of groups. So, if an initial alpha of 10 per cent was selected with 3 groups, the effective alpha level for the pairwise comparisons would be $0.1/6 = 0.0167$. Output from the SAS programme Krusk-W1 using data from Table 7.5 is shown in Figure 7.8.

		No. of	NO. of	Abs. diff				sig. at
First group	Second group	subjects (gp 1)	subjects (gp 2)	in mean ranks	SE of diff.	critical Z value	Adjusted alpha	adjusted alpha
1	2	5	5	0.5	2.82843	2.12805	0.016667	no
1	3	5	5	6.7	2.82843	2.12805	0.016667	yes
2	3	5	5	6.2	2.82843	2.12805	0.016667	yes

Significance is based on an initial alpha of 0.1 (two-tailed test) but adjusted for the number of pairwise comparisons tests

Figure 7.8: Post hoc pairwise multiple comparisons for reading corrected data in Table 7.5

Interpretation

Looking at these pairwise comparisons, Group 3, Asian, is significantly different from the other two groups, but there is no significant difference between Group 1 (middle-class) and Group 2 (working-class).

Large sample Chi-square approximation for Kruskal-Wallis test

When the number of observations in the independent groups exceeds 5 then the test statistic H is approximated by the Chi-square distribution with $k - 1$ degrees of freedom (k is the number of independent samples or groups). SAS output would be interpreted as in the previous example.

Use of Kruskal-Wallis Test with Data from $r \times k$ Contingency Tables

Marascuilo and Dagenais (1982) describe the use of the Kruskal-Wallis H-test with ordered categorical data that is typically presented in the form of a contingency table. Data collected by these authors, originally as part of an evaluation study, is presented in Table 7.6 in the form of a contingency table.

Table 7.6: *Frequency distribution of responses to a question about perceived success of an integration programme for six ethnic groups**

Response categories to question:		Type of Student					
		Isolates			Integrates		
		Asian	Black	White	Asian	Black	White
Definitely YES	(1)	0	5	1	2	6	10
YES	(2)	11	32	20	14	7	76
Too soon to tell	(3)	3	5	10	3	5	15
NO	(4)	1	4	3	2	0	4
Definitely NO	(5)	1	0	3	1	1	1
Total		16	46	37	22	19	106

* Data originally collected as part of an evaluation study described in Dagenais and Marascuilo (1981)

Educational researchers typically collect questionnaire data in which respondents are asked to answer a question or state an opinion and to give their response on an ordered response scale. For example, data shown in Table 7.6 is in response to the question:

Has the integration of Berkeley's schools been successful?
The ordered response scale is:
Definitely Not   No   Too soon to tell   Yes   Definitely yes

These are mutually exclusive categories which *can* be treated as **ordered categories**. Typically this kind of data would be analyzed using an r × k Chi-square analysis. The majority of two-dimensional contingency tables that appear in educational journals are analyzed by the traditional Chi-square procedure. Researchers, therefore, generally fail to use the inherent information contained in an ordered response variable.

If the response variable is a qualitative (categorical) variable which has a theoretically underlying continuum, the original nominal categories can be replaced by rank values 1, 2, 3 . . . N and a more powerful Kruskal-Wallis test could be applied. Looking at the data in Table 7.6, the number of subjects with each response in each group is given in each of the cells of the table, for example, 11 subjects belonging to the group Isolates/Asian gave the response YES. If we now create a response score for each subject, based on the frequency in a cell, for example, for the Isolates/Asian group with the response YES, 11 response scores of 2 (YES) would be created. These response scores can then be ranked and the Kruskal-Wallis test applied. This procedure is performed by the SAS programme, Krusk-W2 (see Figure 12, Appendix A3). Output from the SAS programme Krusk-W2, using data from Table 7.6, is shown in Figure 7.9.

```
                    N P A R 1 W A Y   P r o c e d u r e

        Wilcoxon Scores (Rank Sums) for Variable Response
                    Classified by Variable Group

                   Sum of       Expected      Std Dev        Mean
   GROUP    N      Scores       Under H0       Under H0       Score
     1      16    1712.0000     1976.0000     233.387792   107.000000
     2      46    6000.5000     5681.0000     369.018501   130.445652
     3      37    3560.0000     4569.5000     338.320436    96.216216
     4      22    2623.0000     2717.0000     270.078228   119.227273
     5      19    2618.5000     2346.5000     252.664342   137.815789
     6     106   13867.0000    13091.0000     468.674341   130.820755
                Average Scores were used for Ties

        Kruskal-Wallis Test (Chi-Square Approximation)
           CHISQ= 12.110  DF= 5  Prob > CHISQ= 0.0333
```

Figure 7.9: Kruskal-Wallis test using frequency data presented in Table 7.6 (data in the form of an r x k contingency table)

Interpretation of Computer Output

The Kruskal-Wallis test statistic is 12.110 (Chi-square approximation) and since χ^2_5 with alpha equal to 5% = 11.07, it can be concluded that the six distributions are not identical.

7.7 Friedman's ANOVA by Ranks (for related data)

When to Use

The Friedman's ANOVA by ranks is the last statistical procedure to be presented in this chapter. It should be considered when an investigator is interested in testing difference among related groups (repeated measurements) and when measures are naturally ranked or can be rank ordered. The test can be considered as an extension of the Wilcoxon signed ranks test, for more than two conditions. It is particularly suited for within-subject experimental designs in psychology and education. Often a response variable is a score representing, for example, the number of correct items, the number of errors, or the number of tasks completed.

The procedure is most practical when there are at least five subjects and a minimum of four conditions (repeated measures). With fewer subjects or treatments the exact sampling distribution of the test statistic, χ^2_{Fr}, should be consulted (see tables in Siegel and Castallan, 1988). With more than three treatment groups and more subjects, χ^2_{Fr} approximates to the Chi-square distribution. The test procedure is based on the idea that under the null-hypothesis of no difference between conditions, we would expect the rank values to be distributed randomly within each condition. We would also expect the rank sum and mean rank in each condition to be similar.

The repeated measures design is intended to eliminate intra-subject variability (subject-to-subject variability) and thereby make comparisons among conditions more sensitive to treatment effects. If the rank sums for the various conditions are unequal, this suggests that the scores in each condition are drawn from different populations. The Friedman's rank test is particularly sensitive to population differences in central tendency and is generally considered to be more powerful than Cochran's Q test.

Test Assumptions

The test assumptions are:

- Data consists of more than two related samples.
- The response variable is measured at least at an ordinal level.
- The response variable has an underlying continuous distribution.

Statistical Inference and Null Hypothesis

The null-hypothesis tested is that the repeated measures (conditions) have been sampled from a single population (or k-populations with the same medians), the alternative hypothesis is that at least one of the conditions has a different median to the others. In this situation the rank sum and the mean rank for each condition would vary.

Example from the Literature

In a study to test the hypothesis that measured level of success in the coordination of spatial perspectives is related to the mode of response employed in their representation, Robinson and Robinson (1983) tested twelve infants and twenty-four junior school children (ages 5–6 years, 8–9 years and 10–11 years) on a repeated measures representation task. Each child was presented with four tasks (modes of response representation): matching; drawing; verbal; and making. In the matching condition a child had to select an appropriate card from a set of eight picture cards. Each card depicted a particular view and one matched the view of a model placed in front of the child. In the drawing condition a child was asked to draw a particular view (that matched the model), in the verbal condition the child was asked to describe a view and in the making condition the child was invited to construct the particular view from cut-out and coloured shaped cards. Binary scoring was used for each test (three tests for each condition), a value of 1 was awarded for a correct response and 0 for an incorrect response.

The investigators reported the average test scores for infants in each condition: Matching 2.25; Drawing 0.42; Verbal 0.91; and Making 0.67. For infants, matching seemed the easiest. To elucidate the descriptive findings the investigators carried out a Friedman's ANOVA on the rank score of performance across the four conditions (repeated measurement factor). A significant difference among the four presentation modes was reported. In this example the outcome variable is a count of correct responses which can be ranked and the within-subjects factor is the four repeated measurements corresponding to the experimental conditions of matching, drawing, verbal and making. The investigators wanted to know whether the apparent differences in average performance across the four tasks were large enough to indicate a statistically significant difference in central tendency between the four modes of presentation (no specific alpha level was mentioned). The keen reader should look carefully at the reported significance levels in this paper.

Worked Example

In a replication of Robinson and Robinson's study (1983) a PhD research student wanted to know whether there was a difference in successful task performance among four presentation conditions: matching, drawing, verbal and making (repeated measures). Data from a pilot study with 6 subjects aged 7 years is shown in Table 7.7.

Table 7.7: Task success (number correct) for four representation conditions

Subject	Matching Score	Matching Rank	Drawing Score	Drawing Rank	Verbal Score	Verbal Rank	Making Score	Making Rank
1	5	3.5	1	2	0	1	5	3.5
2	5	4	3	3	2	2	1	1
3	3	3	2	2	4	4	0	1
4	5	4	1	1	2	2	4	3
5	5	4	0	1	3	3	1	2
6	4	4	2	2	0	1	3	3
Σ Ranks (R)		22.5		11		13		13.5
Σ Ranks squared (R)^2		506.25		121		169		182.25

In the pilot study each task had five conditions so the maximum possible score was 5, a score of 1 was awarded for a correct response and 0 for an incorrect response. The underlying rationale for the analysis is simply whether the number of correct responses is higher or lower in comparing one condition with another. The least number of correct responses receives a rank of 1 and the condition with the highest number of correct responses receives a rank of 4 (ranked across the four conditions). Ties are assigned average rank values (see section 7.4, Wilcoxon Mann-Whitney test for an explanation of average ranks). Alpha was once again set to 5 per cent.

The null-hypothesis tested was that different modes of representation of spatial perspectives do not effect measured levels of success on the tasks. The researcher should note that what is actually tested by Friedman's ANOVA procedure is that the distribution of responses in each of the repeated measurement occasions come from the same population, that is they have the same population median. The alternative hypothesis is that at least one pair of repeated measurements (conditions) has a different central tendency (median).

Computational steps:

1 For each subject the response variable (number correct) is ranked across the four conditions. The smallest score is given a rank of 1.

2 The rank sum (R) and the rank sum squared (R^2) for each condition are evaluated.

3 Using the data presented in Table 7.7 the Friedman's Test statistic, χ^2_{Fr} is calculated as follows:

$$\chi^2_{Fr} = \frac{12\sum_{j=1}^{k} R_j^2 - 3N^2k(k+1)^2}{Nk(k+1) + \dfrac{\left(Nk - \sum_{i=1}^{N}\sum_{j=1}^{g_i} t_{i,j}^3\right)}{(k-1)}}$$

Friedman's Chi-square adjusted for ties – 7.6

where: N = number of subjects (or sets of matched subjects);

k = number of conditions (repeated measures);

R_j = rank sum of the conditions (i.e., sum of the rank for each repeated measure);

g_i = number of different rank values for the ith subject;

t_{ij} = number of observations of the jth rank value in the ith subject.

Consider, for example, the first subject in Table 7.7. There are 3 different rank values, that is $g_i = 3$, these rank values are 3.5 (two observations), 2 (one observation) and 1 (one observation), therefore;

$$\sum_{j=1}^{g_i} t_{i,j}^3 = 2^3 + 1^3 + 1^3 = 10$$

If there are no tied values in the ranked data then, $\sum\limits_{i=1}^{N}\sum\limits_{j=1}^{g_i} t_{i.j}^3 = Nk$ and therefore the denominator for χ_{Fr}^2 becomes $Nk(k + 1)$.

For all 6 subjects in Table 7.7 $\sum\limits_{i=1}^{N}\sum\limits_{j=1}^{g_i} t_{i.j}^3 = 8 + 1 + 1 + 1 \ldots$ (*total* 1's $= 22$) $= 30$, the numerator is given by: $12(22.5^2 + 11^2 + 13^2 + 13.5^2) - 3 \times 36 \times 4 \times (4 + 1)^2 = 942$. The denominator is given by: $6 \times 4(5) + (24 - 30)/3 = 118$ so, χ_{Fr}^2 942/118 $= 7.983$. This is evaluated using χ^2 distribution with k $-$ 1 degrees of freedom. The table of critical values of χ^2 is shown in Table 2, Appendix A4. In this example, 7.983 with 3 df and alpha set to 5 per cent is greater than the tabled critical value (7.82).

Interpretation

Given the significant χ_{Fr}^2 test statistic, the null-hypothesis of different modes of representation of spatial perspectives having similar levels of success on the representation tasks can be rejected, and we can conclude that the average ranks (medians) for the four conditions differ significantly. Task performance would seem to depend upon the nature of the task (matching, drawing, verbal and making) and looking at Table 7.7 the highest mean rank was for the matching condition (higher rank score equates with a greater number of correct responses). This finding is consistent with Robinson and Robinson's (1983) study.

Computer Analysis

Friedman's ANOVA by ranks can be performed in SAS using PROC FREQ. The following SAS code, using data from Table 7.7, illustrates how to perform this analysis.

```
data a;
  input subject cond $ rank @@;
  cards;
1 1 3.5 1 2 2 1 3 1 1 4 3.5
2 1 4   2 2 3 2 3 2 2 4 1
3 1 3   3 2 2 3 3 4 3 4 1
4 1 4   4 2 1 4 3 2 4 4 3
5 1 4   5 2 1 5 3 3 5 4 2
6 1 4   6 2 2 6 3 1 6 4 3
;
proc freq;
  tables subject*cond*rank / noprint cmh;
run;
title 'Friedmans ANOVA by ranks test - worked example';
run;
```

SAS can handle repeated measurement designs using ordinal data with PROC CATMOD, or with PROC FREQ, the later approach is by far the simplest. The tables statement in PROC FREQ identifies the variables to be used in the contingency table analysis. When a statement is of the form A*B*C (A, B and C representing different variables) the last variable, here C, forms the columns of a contingency table; values of the next to last variable form the rows, and the first variable is used as a stratifying factor, a separate contingency table being produced for each level of stratification.

In a repeated measures design, if a subject is placed as the first variable in the tables statement, it is used as a stratifying factor and a separate contingency table is produced for each subject. In this example, if the option NOPRINT is not used (it suppresses printing of the contingency tables) six separate contingency tables would be produced, one for each subject in the design, each table would have as the columns, rank scores and for the rows, the four conditions, mat, draw, verb and make. In the situation where there is one subject per contingency table the Cochran-Mantel-Haenszel Chi-square statistic (CMH statistic) is identical to the Friedman's Chi-square, χ^2_{Fr}. The CHM statistic can only be interpreted in this way if the column variable is ordinal. The null-hypothesis tested in this case is that the mean score (median) of the row variables (repeated measures) are equal.

Interpretation of Computer Output

Output from PROC FREQ for the repeated measures analysis of spatial perspectives and different modes of representation is shown in Figure 7.10.

```
              Summary Statistics for COND by Rank
                    Controlling for Subject
         Cochran-Mantel-Haenszel Statistics (Based on Table Scores)

  Statistic      Alternative Hypothesis      DF      Value      Prob
  ---------------------------------------------------------------------

      1          Nonzero Correlation          1      1.144      0.285
      2          Row Mean Scores Differ       3      7.983      0.046
      3          General Association         12     13.100      0.362

  Total Sample Size = 24
```

Figure 7.10: CMH statistic from PROC FREQ based on data shown in Table 7.7

In this example, the ANOVA CMH statistic is equivalent to Friedman's Chi-square with $k - 1$, i.e., 3 degrees of freedom. The appropriate statistic and alternative hypothesis for the repeated measures design is statistic 2 in the output, the row means (medians) differ. Looking at the CMH test statistic this is 7.983, identical to the value in the worked example, adjusted for ties. This Chi-square statistic is evaluated with 3 df. The associated probability of obtaining a test statistic as large as this is given in the third column of the output and is 0.046. SAS outputs the actual probability rather than a set probability level. We can conclude that there is a significant difference, at the 5 per cent level, among the four experimental conditions.

Sometimes it is inconvenient to consult a Chi-square table for critical values, on these occasions the SAS function, PROBCHI can be used instead. For example, to determine the probability associated with a Chi-square value of 7.983 with 3 df the following SAS code can be entered:

```
   data a;
p=1-probchi(7.983,3);
put p=;
run;
```

The probability value returned in the SAS LOG is:

```
P=0.0463643541
NOTE: The data set WORK.A has 1 observations and 1 variables.
```

Pairwise Multiple-comparisons for post hoc Analysis

Similar to the Kruskal-Wallis test when an obtained *H* statistic is significant, an investigator may wish to determine which of the conditions (repeated measures) differ when the Friedman test statistic is found to be statistically significant. A *post hoc* pairwise multiple-comparison procedure, adjusting for the number of pairwise comparisons should be used. Computational details and worked examples are described by Siegel and Castellan (1988). The SAS programme Friedx automatically performs multiple comparison tests for all possible pairwise comparisons and adjusts for experimentwise error (see Figure 13, Appendix A3). The initial alpha level should be set to a liberal level; output from this programme using the data from Table 7.7 is shown in Figure 7.11.

```
           Friedmans ANOVA by ranks test – worked example
            post hoc multiple comparison tests between the groups

    Significance is based on an initial alpha of 0.1 (two-tailed test)
        but adjusted for the number of pairwise comparisons tests

                    Abs. diff                                  sig. at
    First    Second  in mean   SE of    critical   Adjusted   adjusted
    group    group    ranks    diff.    Z value     alpha      alpha
      1        2       11.5    4.47214   2.39398    .0083333     yes
      1        3        9.5    4.47214   2.39398    .0083333     no
      1        4        9.0    4.47214   2.39398    .0083333     no
      2        3        2.0    4.47214   2.39398    .0083333     no
      2        4        2.5    4.47214   2.39398    .0083333     no
      3        4        0.5    4.47214   2.39398    .0083333     no
```

Figure 7.11: Post hoc multiple comparisons for Friedman's ANOVA by ranks using data from Table 7.7 (four repeated measures)

Interpretation

Looking at these pairwise comparisons, groups 1 and 2 are the only conditions that are significantly different, the initial alpha level was set to 10 per cent in this analysis and the pairwise comparisons should also be evaluated at this alpha level.

Summary

In this chapter six nonparametric tests based on rank data have been illustrated. These nonparametric procedures are probably not used in educational research as often as they should be. They are generally thought to be less powerful than their parametric analogues although it is not widely known that under certain circumstances nonparametric statistical tests can be as powerful or more powerful than their parametric counterparts. For this reason alone researchers should be familiar with these procedures.

A well known problem with many parametric tests is that the assumption of independence of sample observations should be met. Violation of this assumption strongly influences statistical tests. It is generally less well known that certain nonparametric tests are also subject to this assumption and are influenced by dependence among initial scores. Any dependence amongst scores also results in dependence amongst ranks (Zimmerman, 1993).

The general principle to follow when choosing a nonparametric rank test is the same as that outlined in Chapter 1, use your judgment and common sense, consider what is operationally measured or observed, and wherever possible keep the analysis simple, do not rely on sophisticated techniques which are likely to be based on assumptions which are questionable. The next chapter introduces parametric procedures which are based on more restrictive assumptions but in certain circumstances are also more powerful than binary and rank order statistical tests. They should be viewed not as alternatives to the tests in this chapter but as complementary statistical procedures.

Chapter 8

Inferences Involving Continuous Data

Introduction

In this chapter parametric statistical procedures are introduced. These include linear regression, correlation and tests for differences in location in two-sample and multiple sample designs. Parametric statistical techniques require that a number of assumptions about the nature of the population from which data were drawn be met and in this sense are more restrictive than non-parametric procedures. For example, for statistical inferences to be valid, variables should be continuous (variables measured on interval or ratio scales) and data should be drawn at random from a population with an underlying normal distribution. Parametric tests are based on an underlying normal probability distribution of a statistical variable (see Chapter 4, section 4.6). For example, an important property of sample means is that they tend to be normally distributed even when individual scores may not be (based on the central limit theorem). This enables parametric techniques to be used in many situations. Also, parametric procedures are reasonably robust, that is tolerant of moderate violations of assumptions, although, as we shall see in later sections, violation of particular assumptions, especially when in combination, are critical and can invalidate inferences drawn.

There is much misunderstanding about what is meant by **assumptions of normality**. It is often believed, for example, that to use parametric tests such as the paired *t*-test (for 'before' and 'after' designs) or linear regression, the response variables should be **normally distributed**. This not true. It is only necessary that, in the case of the paired *t*-test, the difference scores are normally distributed, and in the case of linear regression it is the residuals (difference between observed and predicted scores, i.e., errors) after fitting the explanatory variable that should be normally distributed. The assumption of normality refers to the population of interest and not just the sample of scores. Therefore, in the above examples what is meant is that the difference scores and the residuals **in the population of interest** are normally distributed. The assumptions of normality are usually based either on faith or as Siegel and Castallan (1988) put it, 'rest on conjecture and hope' (p. 35). Generally, when results are reported in journals the normality assumptions (and other assumptions, such as independence of observations, homogeneity of variance) are simply assumed to hold and are seldom tested and reported. When space is at a premium, brief details about the validity of underlying assumptions would greatly enhance the trustworthiness of conclusions.

In this chapter, the general format of previous chapters is followed but the section on test assumptions is extended to include details of how to check assumptions. An overview of the general ideas and statistical models underlying regression and analysis of variance (ANOVA) is presented before each of these procedures is illustrated. Discussion about what can be done when various parametric assumptions are not met is presented at the end of this chapter.

8.1 Introduction to Regression and Correlation

In educational research regression analysis is one of the most widely used statistical procedures. It should be considered when interest is centred on the **dependence** of a response variable on an explanatory variable(s). For example, a primary school headteacher may want to know whether a class teacher's estimate of a pupil's maths ability will predict that pupil's maths score on a standardized test of maths ability. Regression analysis can be used to: **Describe the relationship** between the response variable (score on a standardized maths test in the above example) and an explanatory variable (teacher's estimate of pupil ability in the above example) and **Predict the values of a response variable** from explanatory (independent) variables. When there is a linear relationship between response and explanatory variables and when there is only one explanatory variable and one response variable we refer to this as a **simple linear regression**. When there is one response variable but more than one explanatory variable this is referred to as a **multiple regression analysis**. We use the term **multivariate regression** when we have more than one response variable and any number of explanatory variables.

Correlation analysis is when a measure of the linear relationship between two or more random variables is estimated. The parametric correlation statistic is the Pearson product moment correlation. This is a quantitative index of the strength of the linear relationship between two variables. If a researcher wants to determine the strength of relationship between two variables then correlation analysis is appropriate, however, if interest is centred on how well a least squares model fits the data or on prediction of one variable given values on another variable(s) then regression is the appropriate analytic technique.

In simple linear regression analysis, a random sample of observations is selected from a defined population of interest, and data consists of quantitative (continuous) measurements on a response variable and usually qualitative measures on an explanatory variable (sometimes called independent variable). Often in educational research regression analysis is used with survey data as opposed to data generated from experimental designs. Regression is sometimes seen as being a completely different analytic technique and unrelated to that of analysis of variance, this is possibly because these techniques arose in different research traditions. In fact both techniques are based on the General Linear Model (GLM). In its simplest form the GLM says that a response variable is related to an independent variable(s) by a weighting factor and that the response variable is given by the sum of all weighted independent variables. The term **general linear model** means a general statistical model that is linear in its parameters. That is the parameters, one for each independent variable, are summed. Regression and analysis of variance are simply different variants of the same General Linear Model and different disciplines have traditionally favoured certain research approaches and analytic techniques.

Educational research, for example, has a strong survey tradition and has relied more heavily on correlation and regression techniques. In the language of regression, the response variable is related to the weighted sum of independent variables. The weighting factor is called a regression weight (coefficient) and the influence of a weighted explanatory variable on the response variable is referred to as a regression effect or simply in terms of whether a regression coefficient is statistically significant.

In contrast, psychology has a strong experimental tradition and associated with this are ANOVA techniques. In the language of analysis of variance, the independent variable is a categorical variable, and we are interested in treatment effects and tests of significance. The weighted independent variables which depend upon treatment combinations represent treatment effects.

Random error, generally defined as the difference between observed scores and those predicted from a statistical model in the regression framework, is estimated by the difference between observed scores and those predicted from the fitted regression line, whereas in an ANOVA statistical model error is estimated as the difference between observed scores and cell means (treatment combination means). It is important to consider regression and analysis of variance in the context of general linear models because they are treated in a uniform way in many propriety statistical computer packages. When using propriety statistical analysis programmes such as SPSS or SAS interpretation of statistical output is much easier to understand if terms such as **model sums of squares, error sums of squares, mean square error, r-square, parameter estimates** and **regression weights** are seen to be derived from a unified **general linear model**.

When an investigator is interested in predicting the value of a response variable (either mean predicted values for subgroups or individual predicted values) given the value of another explanatory variable and has a random sample of pairs of observations (X,Y) which have continuous measurements, and when it is reasonable to assume a linear relationship between X and Y, then simple linear regression should be considered as a possible analytic approach. There are additional assumptions which would need to be met before a regression analysis could be properly used to make inferences about the dependence of one variable on another and these are discussed in section 8.2.

The Simple Linear Regression Model

Regression analysis may be used to investigate the straight line (linear) relationship in a population between a random response variable, Y, and an independent explanatory variable, X. This linear relationship can be expressed as a regression equation which takes the general form

$$y = \beta_0 + \beta_1 x + \varepsilon \qquad \textbf{Simple linear regression equation} - 8.1$$

This equation says that the observed value of the response variable, y, varies as a linear function of the explanatory variable x and a random error term, ε, (the Greek letter epsilon). The term linear function refers to the additive sum of the two parameters in the model, β_0 (Greek letter beta$_0$), the intercept and β_1 (Greek letter beta$_1$) the population regression weight for the value of the explanatory variable x. The model can be thought of as consisting of two components, the deterministic part of the model, $\beta_0 + \beta_1 x$, which describes the straight-line relationship, and a random component, ε. The observed response variable, y, can be predicted from a weighted value of the explanatory variable, x which is the **explained** straight-line part of the model and an **unexplained** error component, ε, which allows for random variation of the y values about their mean. This error component accounts for random fluctuations of the y variable values and possibly other important variables not included in the statistical model.

The Linear Regression Line

A simple estimated linear regression line with Y as the predicted response variable and X as the explanatory variable is described as the **regression of Y on X**. (The regression of X on Y would give a different regression line.) We can think of the regression line in the population being described by two parameters: β_0, the intercept which is the point at which the regression line cuts the Y axis, that is the value of the variable Y when the value of variable X is zero, and β_1 the regression coefficient (weight) which represents the slope of the regression line, that is the increase or decrease in the variable Y corresponding to a unit change in the value of variable X. A third parameter, σ, the standard deviation of the response variable Y about the regression line is frequently estimated in regression analysis as this provides an indication of extent of the linear relationship between the response and explanatory variable.

As in previous statistical procedures, we use sample estimates of these population parameters namely, b_0 is the sample statistic which estimates β_0 the unknown population intercept and b_1 is the sample regression statistic which is used to estimate β_1 the unknown population regression parameter. The sample standard deviation of Y about the regression line, S, (which is equivalent to the mean square error, that is sums of squares for error/df error) is used to estimate the unknown population standard deviation of Y about the regression line, σ (sigma). The population regression model and corresponding estimated (sample) regression equation are:

$$y = \beta_0 + \beta_1 x_1 + \varepsilon \quad \text{Population model}$$
$$\hat{Y} = b_0 + b_1 x_1 \quad \text{Estimated equation}$$

where the population regression model specifies an observed value of y for a particular value of x_1, the explanatory variable. Sample statistics are used to estimate the corresponding population parameters. In the estimated sample regression equation $\hat{Y}$ denotes the predicted (estimated) value of the response variable y given the value of the explanatory variable x_1.

The procedure used to find the best fitted regression line, or least squares line is called the **method of least squares**. The principle of least squares involves determination of the regression statistics b_0 and b_1 such that errors of estimation are minimized. An error of estimation is the difference between the observed value of y and the corresponding predicted value, $\hat{Y}$ obtained from the regression model. That is $\varepsilon = \hat{Y} - (b_0 + b_1 x_1)$. The error estimates in a sample are called **residuals**.

Why is the least squares method used?

An error of estimation (prediction) for a linear regression model may be either positive or negative and if these errors were summed they should equal zero because the effects of opposing signs will cancel each error. If however the sums of squared errors is evaluated this will give a positive number. The optimal situation is when there is minimal error of prediction and the sums of squared errors is minimized. A mathematical procedure called differentiation allows values of the regression statistics b_0 and b_1 to be chosen which will minimize the sums of squared errors of estimation.

Estimation and Prediction

Using a regression model, a researcher may want to estimate the intercept and slope parameters and thereby describe the nature of the dependence between response and explanatory variables. Once values have been estimated for the parameters they can be used to predict the unknown value of a response variable from the known value of an explanatory variable. However, it is recommended that values of an explanatory variable which are beyond the sample range of the explanatory variable should not be used to predict the value of the response variable Y. This is because the errors of prediction are likely to be inflated.

Tests of Significance and Confidence Intervals

To test whether the linear regression model is useful for prediction we need to test whether the explanatory variable X does in fact explain variation in the response variable Y. If X contributes no information to the prediction of Y, the true slope of the population regression line would be zero. In a test of significance of a predictor (explanatory) variable the null hypothesis would be, H_0: $\beta_1 = 0$. The alternative hypothesis, that is X and Y are linearly related, is H_1: $\beta_1 \neq 0$, and X makes a significant contribution to the prediction of Y. To test this null hypothesis we evaluate the ratio of b_1/standard error of b_1, and compare this with the sampling distribution of the t-statistic with $n - 2$ degrees of freedom. To use the sampling distribution of the regression test statistic, b_1, certain assumptions about the random error term in the regression model must be met, these are discussed under test assumptions. It has already been stated in previous chapters that whenever possible confidence intervals should be used in conjunction with tests of significance. A confidence interval for the population regression slope is estimated from sample data using the following formula:

$$b - [t_{1-\alpha/2} \text{ SE}(b_1)] \quad \text{to} \quad b + [t_{1-\alpha/2} \text{ SE}(b_1)]$$

Confidence interval for the regression slope – 8.2

with df $= n - 2$.

If a 95 per cent confidence interval was required then $t_{1-\alpha/2}$ would equal $t_{0.025}$. The confidence interval for the intercept of the regression line is similar to formula 8.2 except that $\text{SE}(b_1)$ is changed to $\text{SE}(b_0)$, the standard error of the intercept.

Multiple Regression

A simple linear regression model can be easily extended to accommodate two or more explanatory variables. Practical applications of regression analysis often require two or more predictor variables. The general notation for a multiple regression model is

$$y = \beta_0 + \beta_1 x_1 + \beta_2 x_2 + \ldots + \beta_k x_k + \varepsilon$$

The intercept, β_0, sometimes called the constant term, is the value of the response variable y when all the explanatory variables are zero. The regression statistics, $b_1, b_2 \ldots b_k$ as in simple linear regression estimate the unknown parameters β_1, $\beta_2 \ldots \beta_k$.

Steps in Regression Analysis

There are seven steps in a typical regression analysis; the first two can be regarded as part of initial data analysis:

1 Check the reasons for fitting a regression model – is it a description of a linear relationship, estimation of parameters and significance of explanatory variables or the prediction of an individual or mean response value?

2 Examine the means and standard deviations of the response and explanatory variable(s) and explore the main features of the data using scatterplots of response variable against each explanatory variable (and plots of pairs of explanatory variables in multiple regression) to see whether there appears to be any relationship between the variables and to check for linearity (see test assumptions in section 8.2).

3 An initial regression model based on background information or theoretical considerations is then fitted to the data and a regression line is estimated. Consider what sources of information, in the model, contribute to the total variation in the response variable, i.e., consider overall model fit – Are the explanatory variables related in any way to the response variable? What proportion of the total variation in the response variable is explained by the independent variables in the model?

4 Consider the parameter estimates – especially their standard errors and significance tests and confidence intervals for the intercept and slope. Do not report these at this stage because the next step is to check the regression assumptions and to evaluate the fitted regression model. (N.B. In regression analysis assumptions are checked after the initial model has been fitted because the regression residuals are used.)

5 Regression assumptions are checked by looking at the residuals from the fitted model. This is called **regression diagnostics**, that is residual plots are scrutinized (residuals are plotted against case-numbers and against explanatory variables), and standard errors of fitted coefficients and residuals are examined.

6 Alternative regression models are built if necessary (independent variables added or dropped, polynomial terms fitted, for example, $\beta_1 x_1^2$ rather than $\beta_1 x_1$, outlier observations are identified) and further regression diagnostics are performed to evaluate the adequacy of the model and the overall model fit (look at adjusted R^2). Polynomial model, refers to higher powers of x, denoted by the degree of polynomial e.g. x^2 is quadratic and x^3 is cubic.

7 A parsimonious regression model is selected, the three parameters, β_0, β_1, and σ are estimated, and tests of significance and confidence intervals for the intercept and slope are performed. Caution is required with interpretation of the statistical significance of individual explanatory variables in a multiple regression model when the explanatory variables are orthogonal (not correlated). Tests of statistical significance can be misleading.

8.2 Linear Regression Analysis

When to Use

To use linear regression, measures for the response variable should be continuous (at least theoretically) and there should be observations on at least a pair of variables, a response variable Y and an explanatory variable X. For every value of Y there should be a corresponding value of X. It is also assumed that the relationship between Y and X is linear. The size of the correlation, r, between two variables provides an indication of linearity.

Regression analysis is often used by researchers in an exploratory way to discover relationships between variables, to generate new ideas and concepts, to find important variables and to identify unusual cases (outliers) in a data set. It can of course be used in a more formal way to predict certain response values from carefully chosen explanatory variables but by far the greatest number of applications of regression analysis in education and psychology are what may be termed exploratory. Exploratory analysis should not mean 'blind analysis' and all regression models should be guided by either theoretical or empirical considerations and common sense. For example, an educational researcher may want to know whether individual level variables, (for example, IQ, gender, pre-school experience) and/or school level variables (for example, class in school, measure of school resources, teacher experience) can explain pupil achievement. A research psychologist may be interested in the relationship between recent life events (stressors) and work performance. In a more formal way data from personality appraisals can be used to predict vocational success and may be used, amongst other criteria, in personnel selection and guidance (Bernadin and Bownas, 1985). If y, the observed value of a response variable, is an outcome or effect, and x_1, x_2, are particular values of explanatory variables (or causes), then just because a regression model containing y and x_1, x_2 fit the data this does not mean that x_1, x_2 are the only cause or explanation of y. There may be other important explanatory variables not in the model. Emphasis in regression analysis should therefore be on model comparison and choice of the most appropriate regression model. A decision on the most appropriate model will be based on statistical results, theoretical and empirical considerations and common sense. It is possible to have a well fitted (statistically) regression model which is nonsense. All to common bad practice includes the fitting of a regression model to sparse data (too few data points) and interpretation of parameter estimates based on values of explanatory variables which are beyond the range of explanatory variables in the sample data. We should also not assume that there is only one 'correct' statistical model. For discussion of model uncertainty and statistical inference see Chatfield (1995).

Statistical Inference and Null Hypothesis

Researchers are often interested in determining whether there is a relationship between a response and explanatory variable. In effect this is a test of the hypothesis to determine the predictive ability of the regression model. To determine the utility of the model we test whether the regression slope is zero. The null hypothesis is, H_0: $\beta_1 = 0$, and the alternative hypothesis is that the explanatory variable makes a significant contribution to the prediction of the response variable Y, namely H_1: $\beta_1 \neq 0$. Inferences are based on the sampling distribution of the regression statistic b_1 which is used to estimate the population regression parameter β_1. The t-distribution with $n - 2$ degrees of freedom is used to evaluate the test statistic b_1.

A second hypothesis is sometimes tested, whether the intercept is zero, but this is generally of less interest. The null hypothesis and alternative hypotheses are in this case, H_0: $\beta_0 = 0$ and H_1: $\beta_0 \neq 0$. When there is more than one independent variable, the overall model fit is evaluated with the F statistic. The null hypothesis tested involves all regression parameters except the intercept. For example if there were three explanatory variables in the model then the null hypothesis would be: H_0: $\beta_1 = \beta_2 = \beta_3 = 0$. The alternative hypothesis would be that at least one of the parameters is zero. The F statistic is evaluated as the ratio of the mean square for model to mean square for error (see worked example).

Test Assumptions for Regression Analysis

Inferences based on hypothesis tests for the regression slope, intercept, and overall model fit require the following assumptions to be met: (The reader should also look up the assumptions required for the Pearson correlation, r, with particular reference to the distinction between descriptive and inferential use of regression and correlation statistics.)

- Data should consist of measures on at least a pair of variables, a response variable Y and an explanatory variable X. Measurement of the response variable should be at least theoretically continuous. (It is possible for example to use scores on a rating scale; 0, 1, 2, 3 ... n), and in multiple regression one or more of the explanatory variables may be binary (in regression these are called **dummy variables**, for example, the binary variable sex may be coded 0 = male, 1 = female).
- The relationship between response and explanatory variables should be approximately linear. *(Verify by plotting the response variable against each independent variable in the model. Strong correlation is indicated by an obvious straight line trend in the scatter of points. To check for correlations between independent variables in multiple regression plot pairs of independent variables. The computed correlation also indicates the strength of any linear relationship – see section 8.3.)*
- The error term in the regression model, ε, should have a normal probability distribution. The residuals in a regression analysis represent the sample estimates of the error terms. These should have a mean of zero and constant variance (this is called homoscedasticity). Note that neither the response variable or the explanatory variables are required to have a normal

distribution, it is the fitted residuals that should be normal. *(Verify the normality assumption by doing a normal probability plot of residuals. The distribution of residuals only provides an indication of the underlying error distribution in the population and may be unreliable with small sample sizes. Interpret the normal probability plot in the same way as described in Chapter 5 section 5.5 'Checking for Normality'.*

Verify the assumption of constant variance by plotting residuals against predicted values. A random scatter of points about the mean of zero indicates constant variance and satisfies this assumption. A funnel shaped pattern indicates nonconstant variance. Outlier observations are easily spotted on this plot.)

- The error terms (residuals) associated with pairs of *Y* and *X* variables should be independent. *(Verify by checking that each pair of measurements comes from a different independent subject, i.e., no repeated measures on the same subject.*

If data is collected over time there may be a time series (trend) in the data (data points close in time may be more highly correlated and certainly not independent). Verify by plotting residuals against case number (ID).)

- The model should be adequate and correctly specified. This is strictly not an assumption but part of the diagnostic procedure for checking model fit. *(Verify model fit and the possible requirement for more terms in the model, such as a quadratic term (the value of an independent variable squared) or more variables by using an* **overlay plot** *of predicted values vs. values of the independent variable (this gives the linear fitted regression line) and overlaying this with a plot of observed values of the response variable against the independent variable. This overlay gives an indication of the scatter of data points about the fitted regression line. Look for a nonrandom scatter, that is any discernible pattern especially curvature. This indicates that the model is not well fitted. A more sophisticated regression plot can be output from the SAS procedure PROC GPLOT (see Figure 8.7).*

Once a suspect model has been identified using an overlay plot, an indication of the lack of model fit and possible extent of departure from linearity is given by a plot of residuals against each of the independent variables. Any discernible pattern, other than a random scatter of points indicates that the model is not well fitted. Influential data points can easily be identified. You should consider whether you have chosen the most parsimonious model. For example, can any further variables be removed? Do other or additional variables need to be added? How robust is the fitted model? Is the model fit dependent upon a few influential data points?)

The general idea when examining residuals is to look for any systematic trends or patterns in the plots. These usually indicate departure from linearity and model fit. All the assumptions are important but some are more so than others. Experience enables the researcher to judge how far assumptions can be relaxed before inferences are invalidated – this is as much an art as a science. Lack of normality of the residuals, for example, is not critical because the sampling distribution of the regression test statistics are stable for minor departures from normality and therefore do not seriously affect regression estimates. However, standard errors may be inflated. Similarly, lack of constant variance of errors is unlikely to seriously distort the regression coefficients but the associated p-values would need to be interpreted with caution. The most serious violation is a significant departure from linearity. In this situation transformation of the data or an alternative analytic approach should be considered. The literature is rather sparse on what to do in these circumstances. However, an excellent book which is very readable is *Alternative Methods of Regression* by Birkes and Dodge (1993). Another text which has good advice about robust regression analysis is Tiku, Tan and Balakrishnan (1986).

The important principle to bear in mind is to distinguish between minor departures from model assumptions and major violations or combinations of departures such as non-linearity and non-constant variance.

Example from the Literature

In a study of factors that improve teacher competence, Raudenbush *et al.* (1993) investigated a number of regression models one of which looked at key predictors of instructional quality. This response variable, was measured as a 12-item student rating scale of teachers classroom behaviour (for example, frequency that teachers explained objectives of a new lesson, tested new knowledge, provided feedback on test performance, etc.). The mean of the 12-item scale was used as the response score. The explanatory variables included internal in-service-training (provided by the principal or by another teacher in the school), measured as a count of sessions, and pre-service education, a dummy variable, coded as less than bachelor's degree versus bachelor's degree or more.

Results of this regression analysis are shown in Table 8.1.

Table 8.1: Results of regression analysis

Predictors	Regression coefficient	SE	t
Intercept	−1.76	0.97	−1.81
Pre-service Education	2.36	1.41	2.06
In-service Training (Internal)	1.28	0.43	2.99

The investigators (Raudenbush *et al.*, 1993) reported that, 'The model was remarkably parsimonious, including just two predictors: preservice training, $b = 2.36$, $t = 2.06$, and internal supervision [in-service training], $b = 1.28$, $t = 2.99$' (p. 292). p-values were not reported in the table or the text but with a sample size of

2111 students and 103 classrooms, any absolute t values greater than 1.96 would indicate statistical significance at the 5 per cent level. As a quick estimate with large sample sizes, if the regression coefficient is more than twice the size of its standard error then it is statistically significant at the 5 per cent level. In this example in-service training is significant and pre-service education might be although the reported t-value of 2.06 is not consistent with the ratio of 2.36/1.41 (1.67), which is how t is evaluated (see worked example).

The authors concluded that there is strong evidence that teacher supervision (internal in-service training) improves teachers' instructional quality ($b_1 = 1.28$, $SEb_1 = 0.43$). The authors went on to show that there was no support for the proposition that INSET by inspectors or other staff outside of the school would be helpful in improving instructional quality. The subjects in this study were teachers and pupils from small rural primary schools in Thailand.

In the particular analysis described here the null hypothesis tested is 'no linear relationship between instructional quality and internal in-service training', that is H_0: β_1 (internal in-service training) $= 0$. The alternative hypothesis is that internal in-service training makes a significant contribution to the prediction of teachers instructional competence. Assumptions for linear regression were checked and some variables including number of sessions of internal in-service training were transformed to a logarithmic metric because they had positively skewed distributions (as would be expected with a count variable). Linear relations between log-transformed variables and a response variable imply a diminishing effect of the predictor as it increases. In this example, it would mean that when internal in-service training was low, the effect on instructional quality would be significant and positive but with an increase in exposure to internal in-service training the beneficial effects would be reduced.

In another study which examined the influence of state-level centralization on innovation in post-secondary education the authors Hearn and Griswold (1994) provide a good description of model building and variable selection for a multivariate regression and describe how checks were made for model fit. Their regression model was developed from a general theoretical model but was also influenced by empirical analyses which revealed significant relationships between candidate independent variables. They reported that initial exploratory analyses, 'eliminated several other potentially influential independent variables . . . on the basis of a lack of theoretical rationale and promise, a lack of statistical strength, measurement problems, multicollinearity with other factors already in the model, or some combination of these' (p. 170). Multicollinearity means highly correlated explanatory variables, the consequence being that information specified in the model is redundant. The authors went on to warn that, 'In regressions with only fifty cases and as many as thirteen potential independent variables, there are dangers of instability in regression coefficients' (p. 170). To check for this the authors examined the behaviour of suspicious coefficients under different model specifications and adjusted R^2 was used rather than R^2 to make comparisons of the fit of different regression models.

Worked Example

The following data, abstracted from part of a study on referential communication skills by the author and colleagues, is used to illustrate computational details for simple linear regression. The two variables shown in Table 8.2 represent pupils' standardized maths attainment score (age adjusted), and teacher estimated score of pupils' general maths ability based on a rating scale of 1 (well below average) to 10 (well above average). A simple linear regression model is fitted to these data with standardized maths score (SMATHS) as the response variable, and teacher estimate of maths ability (MATHS) as the explanatory variable.

Table 8.2: *Teachers' estimate of maths ability (MATHS) and standardized maths attainment score (SMATHS) for ten pupils*

Pupil (ID)	MATHS (X)	SMATHS (Y)
17	5	110
18	10	133
19	5	109
20	3	114
24	8	128
27	5	109
28	8	119
29	5	119
60	1	95
61	6	118

When an investigator wants to i) find a regression relationship between a response variable, Y, and an explanatory variable, X, or ii) find the effect of different values of x_i; on the response variable y, there are three computational steps involved. These are:

1   Compute the sums of squares for X (denoted SS_{XX}) and for Y (denoted SS_{YY}) and the cross product sums of squares for XY (denoted SS_{XY}).
2   Estimate the parameters β_0, β_1 and σ.
3   Write out the least squares regression line substituting parameter estimates for β_0 and β_1.

Regression analysis would be inappropriate when there are only ten cases and is performed here for illustrative purposes only. Most statistical analysis programmes handle the tedious calculations for regression and correlation and the researcher would seldom have need to compute sums of squares and regression weights from raw data. However, it is important that you understand how these quantities are derived because sums of squares and mean squares appear in the regression and ANOVA output of many propriety statistical packages.

Significance tests and confidence intervals for the slope of the line as well as confidence intervals for the mean value of the response variable, $\bar{y}$, for a given value of x_i, and a prediction interval can be calculated once the regression model has been determined.

1 Computation of Sums of Squares and Cross Product Sums of Squares

The total corrected sums of squares for Y is given by:

$$SS_{YY} = \Sigma Y^2 - \frac{(\Sigma Y)^2}{n} \qquad \textbf{Total corrected Sums of Squares for } Y - 8.3$$

The **corrected sums of squares** is the same as the sum of squared deviations about the mean (recall the idea of least squares regression to sum the squared deviations about the regression line, which goes through the mean of Y).

A correction term, $\frac{(\Sigma Y)^2}{n}$, is subtracted from the total sums of squares to give the corrected total sums of squares. This is done to correct for the fact that the original values of the variable Y were not expressed as deviations from the mean of Y. To calculate the corrected sums of squares the following values are required: ΣY^2 and ΣY. The terms ΣX^2 and ΣX will also be required for computing the corrected sums of squares for X (SS_{XX}), and ΣXY will be needed to compute the corrected sums of squares for cross products XY (SS_{XY}). These values are most easily computed if a table is set out as follows:

Y	Y²	VARIABLES X	X²	XY
110	12100	5	25	550
133	17689	10	100	1330
109	11881	5	25	545
114	12996	3	9	342
128	16384	8	64	1024
109	11881	5	25	545
119	14161	8	64	952
119	14161	5	25	595
95	9025	1	1	95
118	13924	6	36	708
$\bar{y}$ = 115.4	ΣY^2 = 134202	$\bar{x}$ = 5.6	ΣX^2 = 374	ΣXY = 6686
ΣY = 1154		ΣX = 56		
n = 10				

The corrected sums of squares for Y is therefore:

$$134202 - \frac{(1154)^2}{10} = 1030.4$$

The corrected sums of squares for X, is calculated in a similar way, substituting values of X for Y and is 60.4.

The corrected sums of squares for the cross product XY, denoted SS_{XY}, is calculated as follows:

$$SS_{XY} = \Sigma XY - \frac{\Sigma X \ \Sigma Y}{n}$$ **Sums of squares for cross product XY – 8.4**

which is $6686 - \dfrac{56 \times 1154}{10} = 223.6$

2   Parameter Estimates

The regression statistic, b_1, which estimates the regression slope parameter is given by:

$\dfrac{SS_{XY}}{SS_{XX}}$ which is $\dfrac{223.6}{60.4} = 3.702$ **Estimate of regression slope parameter – 8.5**

The regression statistic, b_0, which estimates the regression intercept parameter is given by:

$b_0 = \bar{y} - b_1\bar{x}$ which is $115.4 - (3.702 \times 5.6) = 94.669$

Estimate of intercept parameter – 8.6

The variation of the response variable, Y, about the fitted regression line is called the sums of squared residuals and is crucial in interpreting model fit. The square root of this value divided by the appropriate degrees of freedom is the standard deviation of the residuals and provides an indication of how well the regression line fits the sample data. This statistic, which estimates σ, the population standard deviation of error about the regression line, is called the **root mean square error** (RMSE) in SAS statistical output. It is evaluated as:

$$RMSE = \sqrt{\frac{SS_e}{df_e}}$$

where $SS_e = SS_{YY} - b_1 SS_{XY}$
$= 1030.4 - (3.701987 \times 223.6)$
$= 202.636$ (it is important not to round the value of b_1 as this will lead to large errors in the estimate)

The degrees of freedom for the error component are estimated as n, the number of data points, less the number of estimated parameters in the model, that is $n-$(the number of b parameters). In a simple linear regression model with one explanatory variable there are two b parameters, b_0 (intercept) and b_1 (slope). With ten cases the appropriate degrees of freedom, in this example are 8. The value of RMSE is therefore $(202.636/8)^{0.5} = 5.0328$.

3 Regression Model

The least squares regression line can therefore be written as: Predicted value of SMATHS = 94.7 + 3.7(MATHS)

Interpretation

We should first note that the slope parameter is positive, this means that an increase in teachers' estimated maths ability (MATHS) is associated with an increase in the pupils' maths attainment score on a standardized test (SMATHS). Since the slope represents the change in standardized maths score per unit change in teachers' estimate, we can say that for every 1-mark increase in the teachers' estimate of a pupil's ability we can estimate an increase in standardized maths attainment score of 3.7. On the teachers' rating scale there was no value of zero (it was assumed that none of the pupils would have zero ability), therefore an X value of zero is not meaningful and interpretation of the Y intercept has little practical value.

Once the least squares regression line has been determined (provided the assumptions are valid) it is possible to predict the standardized maths score of a pupil who the teacher estimates as having a maths ability rating score of 7 as follows: Predicted standardized maths score = 94.7 + 3.7(7) = 120.6.

Significance Tests and Confidence Intervals

Significance test for overall model fit

For a simple linear regression model with one explanatory variable and ten cases, the sources of variation (sums of squares, SS) and degrees of freedom can be partitioned as follows:

$y =$	β_0	$+$	$\beta_1 x_1$	$+$	ε
SS_Y		SS_{model}			SS_e
Total		Model sums of squares			Error sums of squares
$df = n - 1$		df for model = (number of parameters in model -1)			$df = n -$ (number of b parameters)
9		$(2 - 1) = 1$			8

Mean square model = SS_{model}/df_{model} Means square error = SS_e/df_{error}

The model sums of squares, SS_{model} is evaluated by subtraction of the error sums of squares from the total corrected sums of squares. That is $SS_{model} = (SS_{YY} - SS_e)$ = (1030.4 − 202.636) = 827.764.

The MS_{model} term is then evaluated as = 827.764/1 = 827.764 (associated df = 1). The MS_{error} term is 202.636/8 = 25.329 (associated df = 8).

If the model makes a significant contribution to the prediction of the response variable then SS_{model} should be greater than SS_e. This is, in fact, equivalent to the alternative hypothesis when expressed in terms of the mean squares, H_1: $MS_{model} > MS_{error} > 1$.

The null hypothesis tested is, H_0: $MS_{model} = MS_{error} = 1$. The test statistic used is F. This null hypothesis is a test of the strength of the linear relationship between the explanatory variable(s) and the response variable. An F statistic close to 1 would indicate that the null hypothesis of no linear relationship is true. As the F statistic increases in size this provides evidence for the alternative hypothesis that there is a linear relationship between the response and explanatory variables, i.e., rejection of the null hypothesis. In this example, F = MS_{model}/MS_{error} = 827.764/ 25.329 = 32.680 with 1 and 8 df.

Interpretation

To evaluate the statistical significance of the obtained F-statistic we refer to Table 7, Appendix A4, Critical values of the F-distribution. If we select a 5 per cent significance level (there is one table for each level of significance) and want to look up the critical F-value using this table we need to know the two degrees of freedom which are associated with our observed F-statistic. In this example the values with which we enter the table are 1 (numerator) and 8 (denominator). In Table 7, the numerator df are shown along the top row and the denominator df are shown down the left column. We therefore locate 1 on the top row and follow the column down until we intersect with 8 for the denominator df. The critical value of F entered in the table is 5.32. Since the obtained value of F is larger than the tabled critical value, 32.68 > 5.32, we can reject the null hypothesis and conclude that the independent variables, just one in this case, makes a significant contribution to the prediction of the response variable.

The statistic RMSE is an estimate of the variation of the response variable about the population regression line. It is sometimes referred to as the residual standard deviation of Y about the regression line. The sum of squared residuals, SS_{res} (which is given in SAS output for PROC REG if the residual option is specified), if divided by n − 2 and then square rooted, is equivalent to RMSE. The residual standard deviation of residuals is calculated as:

$$\sqrt{\frac{SS_{res}}{n-2}} = \sqrt{\frac{\Sigma(Y - \hat{Y})^2}{n-2}} \qquad \textbf{Standard deviation of residuals} - 8.7$$

The sampling distribution of RMSE (equivalent to the sampling distribution of the standard deviation of the residuals) is normal and we would therefore expect that most of the observed values of y would be within +/− 1.96 × RMSE = (1.96 × 5.0328) = 9.864 of the least squares predicted values of Y. This provides another indication of the extent of model fit. Once the overall significance of the least squares regression line has been established, we can then examine in more detail the parameter estimates.

Statistical test for a regression slope

After a suitable regression model has been fitted to the data and a least squares prediction equation determined, a significance test for the regression slope can be performed. When there is only one explanatory variable in the model there will be only one slope parameter to estimate and hence only one significance test for the slope. In a multiple regression, however, there will be a parameter estimate and a significance test for each explanatory variable in the regression model.

The test of the significance of the slope provides information on the utility of the regression model, that is whether the linear regression model explains variation in the response variable. The null hypothesis tested is as shown in an earlier section, H_0: $\beta_1 = 0$. The alternative hypothesis is that the variables X and Y are linearly related, H_1: $\beta_1 \neq 0$. This means that the variable X makes a significant contribution to the prediction of the variable Y. The null hypothesis is tested by computing the ratio of the parameter estimate to its standard error (b_1/standard error of b_1) and comparing this with the sampling distribution of the t-statistic with $n - 2$ degrees of freedom.

The standard error of b_1, denoted as SE_{b_1}, is:

$$SE_{b_1} = \frac{RMSE}{\sqrt{SS_X}} = 5.0328/\sqrt{60.4} = 0.6476 \qquad \textbf{Standard error of slope parameter} - 8.8$$

In this example the significance of the slope is evaluated as:

$t = 3.702/0.6476 = 5.716$, with $n - 2$ df.

Interpretation

With a significance level of 5 per cent, a two-tailed test, and df = 8 (10 − 2), the critical t-value shown in Table 3, Appendix A4 is 2.306. Since the calculated value falls beyond this critical value, $5.716 > 2.306$, we can reject the null hypothesis and conclude that a simple linear model describes the predictive relationship between the variables MATHS and SMATHS. With a two-parameter regression model, intercept and one explanatory variable, the null hypothesis, H_0: $\beta_1 = 0$ and test statistic value, $t = 5.716$ are equivalent to the null hypothesis of model fit given by the F-statistic, because $F = t^2$. The t-value is equal to $32.680^{0.5} = 5.717$ which is the value obtained earlier (allowing for rounding errors).

Use of the t-statistic for testing model fit when there is one explanatory variable is preferable to the F-statistic because it allows for one-sided alternative hypotheses to be tested, namely H_1: $\beta_1 > 0$ or H_1: $\beta_1 < 0$, where t has $n - 2$ df. The rejection region for the two-sided test is the absolute value of $t > t_{1-\alpha/2}$, where $t_{1-\alpha/2}$ is the t-value such that $\alpha/2 = p(t > t_{1-\alpha/2})$. For a one sided test, $t > t_{1-\alpha}$ where $t_{1-\alpha}$ is the t-value such that $\alpha = p(t > t_{1-\alpha})$.

Confidence interval for the regression slope

Whenever possible we should calculate a confidence interval as well as a p-value for a test of significance. Confidence intervals for a regression slope, similar to the tests of significance, are based on the sampling distribution of t (the slope estimate b_1 is approximately normally distributed). The 95 per cent confidence interval for the population value of the regression slope is evaluated using equation 8.2. For a 95 per cent CI around the slope relating teachers' estimate of maths ability to pupils' maths attainment, with the values alpha = 0.05, df = $n - 2$ (= 8), b_1 = 3.7019, SE_{b_1} = 0.6475 and $t_{1-\alpha/2} = t_{0.025}$ = 2.306, when we substitute these into equation 8.2 we obtain:

3.7019 − (2.306 × 0.6475) to 3.7019 + (2.306 × 0.6475)
The 95 per cent confidence interval estimates are 2.2087 to 5.1950.

Interpretation

The confidence interval does not include zero and all the values are positive so it is reasonable to conclude that we would be 95 per cent confident of finding a positive relationship in the population between teacher estimated maths ability and pupils' maths attainment on the standardized test. (This conclusion would be reasonable if we had obtained these results with a larger sample.) We would expect the mean standardized test score to increase with every unit increase in teachers' estimated ability scores, this increase may range from 2.209 to 5.200 with the average unit increase being 3.70. However, this is a rather large confidence interval width and is likely to be attributable to the small sample size ($n = 10$). With a larger sample the confidence interval width is likely to be reduced.

Confidence Interval Limits for the Predicted Mean Response

The 95 per cent CI limits for the predicted mean response with a fixed value for the explanatory variable, in this example, 8, is given by:

$$\hat{Y} - [t_{1-\alpha/2} \; SE \; \hat{Y}] \text{ to } \hat{Y} + [t_{1-\alpha/2} \; SE \; \hat{Y}] \qquad \textbf{CI for mean response} - 8.9$$

where $\hat{Y}$, the predicted mean value obtained from the regression equation when $x_i = 8$ is:

$$\hat{Y} = b_0 + b_1 x_1$$
$$\hat{Y} = 94.669 + 3.702 \times 8$$
$$\hat{Y} = 124.285 \text{ and,}$$

$$SE_{\hat{y}} = RMSE \times \sqrt{\frac{1}{n} + \frac{(x_i - \bar{x})^2}{SS_X}}$$

$$SE_{\hat{y}} = 5.0328 \times \sqrt{\frac{1}{10} + \frac{(8 - 5.6)^2}{60.4}} = 5.0328 \times 0.4420$$

$$= 2.2245$$

The 95 per cent CI is therefore 124.285 − [2.306 × 2.2245] to 124.285 + [2.306 − 2.2245] = 119.155 to 129.415

When this calculation is made for all of the observed values of x_i in the sample, these confidence intervals can be plotted (see the output from PROC GPLOT in Figure 8.7b).

Interpretation

We can predict that the population mean for the response variable, SMATHS, will lie within the range 119 to 129 given a value of 8 for the explanatory variable. Note that the population mean is a fixed parameter and it is the sample estimates which will vary from sample to sample. Any inference based on results would only be valid for the target population from which the sample was selected. The large width of the confidence interval here is probably attributable to the small sample size.

Confidence Intervals for an Individual Response Score (Prediction Interval)

A computational procedure similar to that in the previous worked example is followed when a prediction interval is estimated. A 95 per cent CI for the prediction interval is given by,

$$\hat{Y} - [t_{1-\alpha/2}S_{pred}] \text{ to } \hat{Y} + [t_{1-\alpha/2}S_{pred}] \qquad \textbf{CI for individual response} - 8.10$$

where $\hat{Y}$, the predicted value obtained from the regression equation when $x_i = 8$ is the same as in the previous example (124.285), S_{pred} is the estimated standard deviation of individual values of y when x is the specified value x_i, and,

$$S_{pred} = RMSE \times \sqrt{1 + \frac{1}{n} + \frac{(x_i - \bar{x})^2}{SS_X}}$$

$$S_{pred} = 5.0328 \times \sqrt{1 + \frac{1}{10} + \frac{(8 - 5.6)^2}{60.4}} = 5.0328 \times 1.0933$$

$$= 5.5024$$

The 95 per cent CI is therefore 124.285 − [2.306 × 5.5024] to 124.285 + [2.306 × 5.5024] = 111.596 to 136.974.

Interpretation

We would be 95 per cent confident that a pupil with a teacher estimated maths ability score of 8 would have a standardized maths attainment score within the interval 112 to 137. Notice that the interval width for prediction of an individual score is larger than the width when predicting a mean score. These prediction intervals can be plotted for each case in the data set, and if they are compared with a similar plot for the mean response, it will be seen that the confidence intervals for the individual predictions are much wider (see Figure 8.7c). The confidence interval does not include zero which indicates that a teacher's estimate of a pupil's maths ability is a significant predictor of that pupil's attainment on a standardized maths test.

Computer Analysis

Whereas the worked examples demonstrate the general principles of regression analysis, it is clear that such computations are both time consuming and tedious to perform. In most research situations the researcher will use a propriety statistical package to perform these analyses. The same data and the same regression model is now analysed using the **least squares regression procedure** in SAS called PROC REG. In this section the appropriate SAS code is described and related to the tests for regression assumptions. In the next section interpretation of the output is discussed.

The procedure PROC REG is a general purpose interactive procedure in SAS that fits linear regression models by least squares. PROC REG can also produce scatter plots of variables, diagnostic plots and regression and diagnostic statistics. The parameter estimates in the linear model are adjusted to optimize the model fit.

Assuming that the data has been input screened and edited and an initial regression model formulated which is based on theoretical/empirical considerations, an extension of IDA means standard deviations and corrected sums of squares should be calculated for all variables in the candidate model. The following SAS code produces these statistics for the two variables SMATHS and MATHS.

```
proc means maxdec=3 fw=10 n nmiss min max range mean std stderr
          uss css t prt;
  var maths smaths;
run;
```

The SAS output is shown:

Variable Label	N	Nmiss	Minimum	Maximum	Range
MATHS	10	0	1.000	10.000	9.000
SMATHS	10	0	95.000	133.000	38.000

Variable Label	Mean	Std Dev	Std Error
MATHS	5.600	2.591	0.819
SMATHS	115.400	10.700	3.384

Variable Label	USS	CSS	T	Prob>|T|
MATHS	374.000	60.400	6.836	0.0001
SMATHS	134202.000	1030.400	34.105	0.0001

Notice under the heading CSS that the corrected sums of squares for both the response variable SMATHS and the explanatory variable MATHS correspond with the values for the sums of squares for Y and X computed in step 1 of the worked example (see pp. 265–6).

An important regression assumption to check is whether there is a linear trend between the independent and response variable. A separate plot of the response variable SMATHS against the explanatory variable MATHS could be performed but this output can also be produced by PROC REG which is more convenient and has the advantage of allowing an **overlay plot** to be produced. The overlay plot which is a plot of response against explanatory variable – with a plot of predicted scores against the explanatory variable overlayed – gives a visual indication of model fit by showing the extent to which the observed scores are scattered about the fitted regression line (indicated by the plot of predicted values).

The SAS code that generates the regression output and the overlay plot is:

```
proc reg;
  model smaths=maths /p r clm cli;
  output out=outreg p=p r=r;
  id id;
run;
 proc plot data=outreg vpercent=75 hpercent=75;
  plot smaths*maths='#' p*maths='*' / overlay;
titlel 'Plot of Observed response var vs Independent var (#) and';
title2 'Predicted values vs Independent var (*)';
run;
```

The first line of code, PROC REG, is the beginning of the regression procedure. The next line contains the **model** statement which is required to fit a regression line. Here the model statement tells SAS to fit a linear regression model with the response variable SMATHS and one explanatory variable MATHS. The options after the forward slash tell SAS to i) calculate predicted values (p) for the specified model. (This option is unnecessary if any of the options R, CLI or CLM are specified. It is only entered in the code here to explain its function); ii) produce residuals (r) and the standard errors of the predicted and residual values; iii) calculate and print the 95 per cent lower- and upper-confidence interval limits for the mean value of the response variable for each observation (CLM); iv) calculate and print the 95 per cent lower- and upper-confidence interval limits for a predicted score (CLI). The OUTPUT statement produces an SAS output data set called 'outreg' containing the predicted scores, residuals and a number of statistics.

The procedure PROC PLOT uses the data set created by the regression procedure to produce two diagnostic plots (VPERCENT and HPERCENT simply reduces the size of the plot to 75 per cent of the page length). The first plot is response against explanatory variable and is indicated in the plot by the symbol #. The second plot which overlays the first, hence the different plotting symbol*, shows the predicted values against the explanatory variable. This is the fitted linear regression line. SAS output for the overlay plot is shown in Figure 8.1.

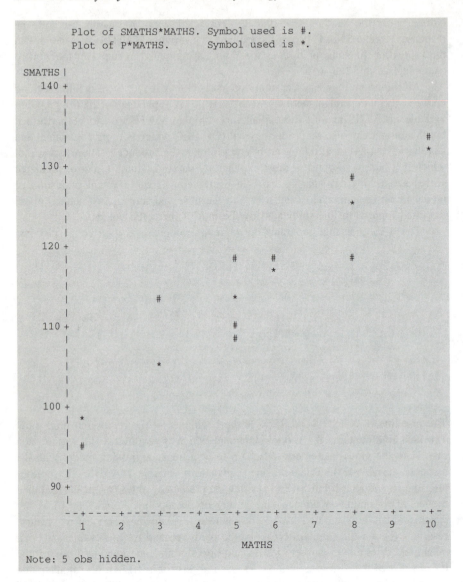

```
        Plot of SMATHS*MATHS.  Symbol used is #.
        Plot of P*MATHS.       Symbol used is *.

SMATHS |
   140 +
       |
       |
       |
       |                                                               #
       |                                                               *
   130 +
       |                                                     #
       |
       |                                                     *
       |
       |
   120 +
       |                        #       #              #
       |                                *
       |
       |             #              *
       |
   110 +                               #
       |                               #
       |
       |        *
       |
       |
   100 +
       | *
       |
       | #
       |
       |
    90 +
       |
     --+----+----+----+----+----+----+----+----+----+----+-
        1    2    3    4    5    6    7    8    9    10

                              MATHS
Note: 5 obs hidden.
```

Figure 8.1:   Overlay plot of response vs. explanatory and predicted vs. explanatory variables

The normality assumption is checked by examining a normal probability plot of the residuals from the fitted model. This is produced by the following SAS code:

```
proc univariate data=outreg plot;
   var r; ** r represents the residuals from PROC REG **;
run;
```

The SAS plot of the residuals is shown in Figure 8.2.

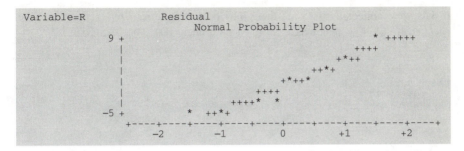

Figure 8.2: *Normal probability plot of residuals*

The assumption of constant variance of errors is checked by plotting residuals against predicted values. The SAS code that produces the plot in Figure 8.3 is

```
proc plot;
  plot r*p='*' / vref=0;
title 'Plot of Residuals vs Predicted';
run;
```

The option/VREF places a reference line on the plot at zero.

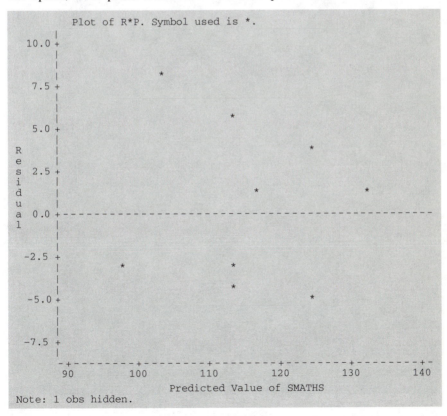

Figure 8.3: *Plot of residuals vs. predicted values for data in Table 8.2*

If data were collected over time there may be a time series (trend), this would be checked by plotting residuals against case number (ID). The SAS code is

```
proc plot;
   plot r*id='*' / vref=0;
   title 'Plot of Residuals vs Case Number (id)';
run;
```

The SAS output is shown in Figure 8.4.

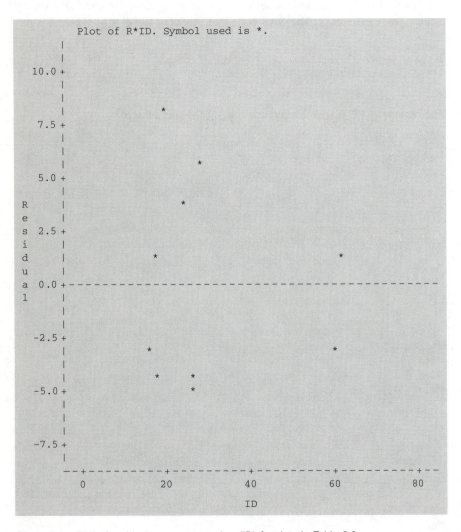

Figure 8.4: *Plot of residuals vs. case number (ID) for data in Table 8.2*

A check on the adequacy of model fit can be seen visually by plotting the residuals against each independent variable. Output for this plot is shown in Figure 8.5.

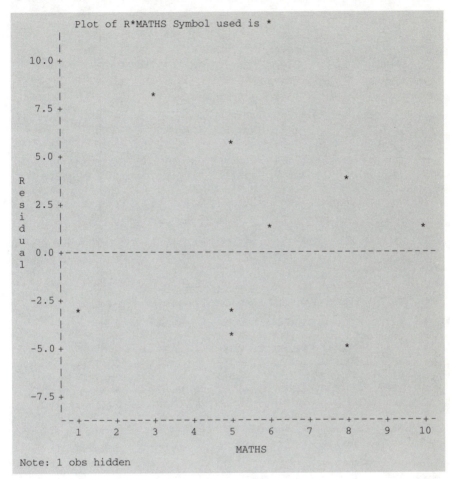

Figure 8.5: *Plot of residual vs. maths score (explanatory variable)*

The regression output produced by PROC REG for the maths data presented in Table 8.2 is shown in Figure 8.6.

```
Model: MODEL1
Dependent Variable: SMATHS
                          Analysis of Variance

Source        DF    Sum of Squares    Mean Square    F Value    Prob>F

Model          1        827.76424       827.76424     32.680     0.0004
Error          8        202.63576        25.32947
C Total        9       1030.40000
```

```
      Root MSE            5.03284        R-square        0.8033
      Dep Mean          115.40000        Adj R-sq        0.7788
      CV                  4.36121

                         Parameter Estimates

                    Parameter     Standard      T for H0:
Variable     DF     Estimate        Error     Parameter=0     Prob>|T|

INTERCEP      1    94.668874      3.96032096      23.904        0.0001
MATHS         1     3.701987      0.64758172       5.717        0.0004
```

Obs	ID	Dep Var SMATHS	Predict Value	Std Err Predict	Lower 95% Mean	Upper 95% Mean	Lower 95% Predict
1	17	110.0	113.2	1.638	109.4	117.0	101.0
2	18	133.0	131.7	3.264	124.2	139.2	117.9
3	19	109.0	113.2	1.638	109.4	117.0	101.0
4	20	114.0	105.8	2.317	100.4	111.1	92.9984
5	24	128.0	124.3	2.225	119.2	129.4	111.6
6	27	109.0	113.2	1.638	109.4	117.0	101.0
7	28	119.0	124.3	2.225	119.2	129.4	111.6
8	29	119.0	113.2	1.638	109.4	117.0	101.0
9	60	95.0000	98.3709	3.377	90.5826	106.2	84.3941
10	61	118.0	116.9	1.612	113.2	120.6	104.7

Obs	ID	Upper 95% Predict	Residual	Std Err Residual	Student Residual	-2-1-0 1 2
1	17	125.4	-3.1788	4.759	-0.668	| *| |
2	18	145.5	1.3113	3.831	0.342	| | |
3	19	125.4	-4.1788	4.759	-0.878	| *| |
4	20	118.6	8.2252	4.468	1.841	| |*** |
5	24	137.0	3.7152	4.515	0.823	| |* |
6	27	125.4	-4.1788	4.759	-0.878	| *| |
7	28	137.0	-5.2848	4.515	-1.171	| **| |
8	29	125.4	5.8212	4.759	1.223	| |** |
9	60	112.3	-3.3709	3.731	-0.903	| *| |
10	61	129.1	1.1192	4.768	0.235	| | |

Obs	ID	Cook's D
1	17	0.026
2	18	0.043
3	19	0.046
4	20	0.456
5	24	0.082
6	27	0.046
7	28	0.166
8	29	0.089
9	60	0.334
10	61	0.003

```
Sum of Residuals                       0
Sum of Squared Residuals        202.6358
Predicted Resid SS (Press)      316.4016
```

Figure 8.6: Regression output for data shown in Table 8.2

A refinement on the regression plot which shows the fitted regression line (see predicted vs. explanatory variable in Figure 8.1) can be produced by using PROC GPLOT. This produces a least squares fitted line and prints this on the plot. This output would be suitable for inclusion in a report or research paper. SAS code to produce the fitted regression line as well as plots of the 95 per cent confidence intervals for a mean response and a 95 per cent prediction interval (individual response), is shown in Figure 14, Appendix A3. The output for these three plots is shown in Figures 8.7a–c. The 95 per cent confidence interval for the mean standardized maths score for the mean teachers' score is narrower than the comparable 95 per cent confidence interval for individual observations (compare Figures 8.7b and 8.7c).

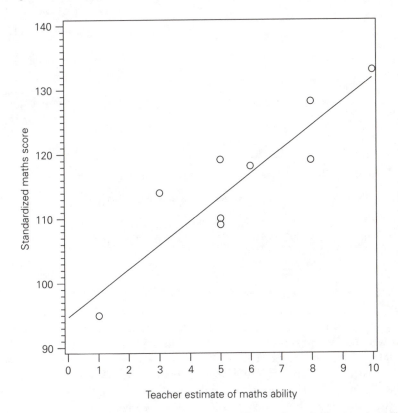

Figure 8.7a: *Fitted least squares regression line for prediction of standardized maths ability score from teacher estimate of maths ability*

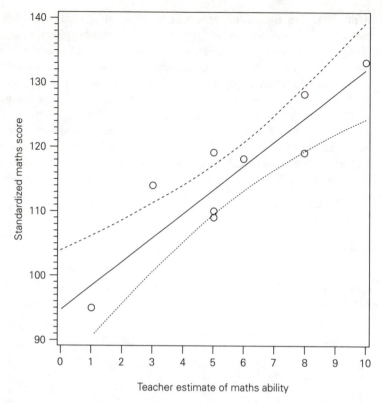

Figure 8.7b: Fitted least squares regression line for prediction of standardized maths ability score from teacher estimate of maths ability with 95 per cent confidence level for mean predicted values

Interpretation of Computer Output

The overlay plot shown in Figure 8.1 indicates that the model fits the data reasonably well, the data points are scattered randomly about the regression line and there are no obvious outliers. Look for plotted points, #, being some distance from the main cluster of other points, or for points that are distant from the fitted regression line (plotted by *). The normal probability plot (see Figure 8.2) indicates that the residuals are reasonably normal (see Chapter 5 for interpretation of normal probability plots).

The plot of residuals against predicted values shown in Figure 8.3 would ideally have a random scatter of points around the reference line (mean of zero). There is a suggestion of non-constant variance in this plot because of the funnel shape indicating that the variance reduces as the response values increase. With so few data points such an interpretation of this actual plot would not be sensible.

The plot of residuals vs. case ID in this example has no meaning because the data were collected at the same point in time. The adequacy of model fit is shown

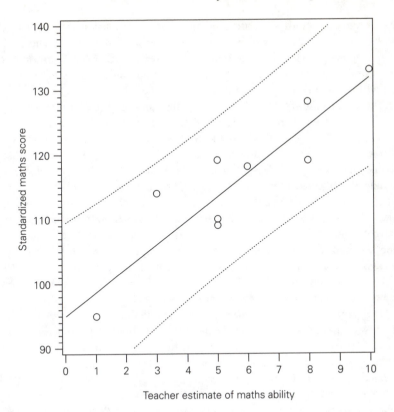

Figure 8.7c: Fitted least squares regression line for prediction of standardized maths ability score from teacher estimate of maths ability with 95 per cent confidence level for individual predicted values

in Figure 8.5 where residuals are plotted against the explanatory variable. Again the suggestion of a pattern to the data, a funnel shape, narrowing as MATHS score increases, is indicative of a non-linear relationship, i.e., lack of model fit. It will be clear by now that interpretation of residual diagnostic plots is somewhat subjective and if you have any doubts about the model fit then try different variables or combinations of variables and consider deleting outlier data points. The next section of output provides results of statistical tests of model fit and parameter estimates.

The first section of SAS printout shown in Figure 8.6 is an ANOVA table for regression which provides information on sources of variation in the response variable and overall model fit. The first line of output identifies a model label which, by default, is assigned MODEL1. Following this the response variable, SMATHS is labelled. The sources of variation in the response variable are partitioned into **model** variation accounted for by the linear regression, and **error** variation that is all other sources of variation in the response variable. The corrected total sums of squares, printed as C total in the output, is the total variation in the response variable (the sum of model and error). Associated degrees of freedom and sums of squares for these sources of variance are printed in the output. These values are the same as the values computed in the worked example. The TOTAL_{df} is given by $n - 1$ where n is the number of cases, MODEL_{df} is equivalent to the number of explanatory variables, one degree of freedom is assigned to the intercept, and ERROR_{df} is given by n (number of b parameters).

The **mean square** (MS) values are the sums of squares divided by their appropriate degrees of freedom. The F-test, which is a test of overall model fit, is the $\text{MS}_{model}/\text{MS}_{error}$, again this is the same F-value as that obtained in the worked example. Here the small p-value associated with the F-statistic indicates that it is probable that $\text{MS}_{model} > \text{MS}_{error}$, that is the null hypothesis is rejected and we conclude that the least squares regression line explains a significant proportion of the variation in the response variable. An estimate of the proportion of this explained variation is given by the **coefficient of determination** labelled R-square in the SAS output. More precisely, this statistic provides a measure of the variation in the response variable about its mean that is explained by the linear regression line. It is evaluated as $1 - (\text{SS}_{error}/\text{SS}_{total})$ which in this example is $1 - 0.1967 = 0.803$. We can say that about 80 per cent of the sample SMATHS scores are explained by the least squares regression model.

The coefficient of determination is equivalent to the Pearson correlation squared (r^2) between the explanatory and independent variable and is sometimes called r squared. In a multiple regression the statistic R^2 is called the squared multiple correlation and it represents the proportion of variation in the response variable explained by the linear combination of explanatory variables. The Multiple Correlation R is the correlation between the observed and predicted scores on the response variable. An r^2 (Pearson correlation squared) or R^2 of zero would indicate no linear relationship and a value of 1 would suggest a perfect linear relationship. In the SAS output a value for an **Adjusted R-square** is printed. This is evaluated as $1 - \text{MS}_{error}/\text{MS}_{total}$ which in this example is $1 - 0.2212 = 0.7787$. This value is less than the unadjusted R^2 because it accounts for both sample size, and in multiple regression the number of explanatory variables in the model. Too much importance should not be attributed to the interpretation of R^2 without considering the substantive meaning of the regression model. That is, does the model make sense and are there any redundant variables? It is recommended that the adjusted R^2 be used when comparing multiple regression models because it adjusts for the number of parameters in the regression model (independent variables).

Also contained in the ANOVA table is the **Root MSE** value, the square root of the mean square error which can be interpreted as the variation of the response variable about the fitted regression line in the population (an estimate of the parameter σ). The response variable mean is printed as well as the coefficient of variation, **CV** which is a unitless measure of variation evaluated as (RMSE/ mean of the response variable) $\times$ 100.

The next section of output contains the parameter estimates. In Figure 8.6 there are two parameter estimates, the **intercept** and MATHS. Point estimates for the parameters and associated standard errors are also printed, these values correspond with the values in the worked example (see formulas 8.5 and 8.6). Interpretation of these parameter estimates is also the same. The *t*-test for the hypothesis of zero regression slope is printed. The *t*-value, evaluated as the ratio of the parameter estimate to its standard error is 5.717, which has an associated p-value of 0.0004. This indicates that the variable MATHS makes a significant contribution to the prediction of the response variable SMATHS. If the parameter estimate is more than twice its standard error this suggests that the explanatory variable is significant at the 5 per cent level.

The last section of output in Figure 8.6 contains a printout of predicted values and residuals scores for the fitted model as well as statistics for regression diagnostics. These latter diagnostic statistics are not particularly informative. Student Residuals, evaluated as residual/$SE_{residual}$, are printed and shown in a schematic plot. They are interpreted as a *t*-like statistic. Two diagnostic statistics are also printed, Cook's D a kind of influence statistic and a Press statistic. The former indicates what effect a particular observation has on the regression when an observation is deleted. Look at the change in the predicted value. The Press statistic (the sum of the squared press residuals) is interpreted in a similar way. For both statistics, the smaller they are the better. Finally, the sum of squared residuals is printed; notice this is the same as the error sums of squares in the ANOVA part of the output.

8.3 Pearson's Correlation *r*

When to Use

The Pearson product moment correlation, *r*, may be used as a sample estimate of the population correlation, ρ (rho). It is a dimensionless index of the linear relationship between two random variables, a value of zero means that there is no linear relationship between the variables and a score of one indicates a perfect linear relationship. If a correlation is negative it means that high values on one variable are associated with low values on the other variable. Values of *r* may vary between −1 and +1 irrespective of the dimensions of measurement of two variables (assuming they approximate at least an interval level of measurement). Thus the correlation between age, measured in months, and a teacher's estimate of maths ability, measured on a 10-point scale, would be unaffected by the units of measurement (but may well be affected by the different measurement ranges of each variable – p. 285). A partial correlation is an index of the relationship between two variables while partialling out the effect (holding constant) of a third variable.

The Pearson correlation, *r*, should be considered as a descriptive statistic when a researcher wants to quantify the extent of linear relationship between variables. A parametric correlation would be appropriate whenever quantitative measures are taken simultaneously on two or more variables, the relationship between the two variables is linear and both variables are normally distributed. Correlations should always be examined prior to more sophisticated multivariate analyses such as factor analysis or principal component analysis. The extent of a linear relationship between two variables may be difficult to judge from a scatterplot and a correlation coefficient provides a more succinct summary. However, it would be unwise to attempt to calculate a correlation when a scatterplot depicted a clear non-linear relationship. When a researcher is interested in both the extent and the significance of a correlation then r is used in an inferential way as an estimate of the population correlation, ρ (rho).

Statistical Inference and Null Hypothesis

As well as estimating the size of the population correlation we may want to test whether it is statistically significant. In testing this hypothesis the same logic is followed as that described in Chapter 7 when testing the significance of a nonparametric correlation. The null hypothesis is H_0: $\rho = 0$, that is, the variable X is not linearly related to the variable Y. The alternative hypothesis is H_1: $\rho \neq 0$. The null hypothesis is a test of whether any apparent relationship between the variables X and Y could have arisen by chance. The sampling distribution of r is not normal when the population correlation deviates from zero and when sample sizes are small ($n < 30$). For tests of significance r is transformed to another statistic called Fisher's z (which is not the same as the Z deviate for a normal distribution).

Assumptions

In some statistical texts for social scientists it is asserted that to use the Pearson correlation both variables should have a normal distribution, yet in other texts it says that the distributions of both variables should be symmetrical and unimodal but not necessarily normal. These ideas cause great confusion to researchers and need to be clarified. If the correlation statistic is to be used for descriptive purposes only, then normality assumptions about the form of the data distributions are not necessary. The only assumptions required are that

- quantitative measures (interval or ratio level of measurement) are taken simultaneously on two or more random variables;
- paired measurements for each subject are independent.

The results obtained would describe the extent to which a linear relationship *would apply* to the sample data.

This same idea applies to the descriptive use of regression statistics. Should the researcher wish to make any inference about the extent of a population linear relationship between two variables or in a regression context to make a prediction which went beyond the sample data, the following assumptions should be met:

- Two random variables should be linearly related, but perfect linearity is not required as long as there is an obvious linear trend indicated by an elliptical scatter of points without any obvious curvature (look at the scatterplot).
- The underlying probability distribution should be bivariate normal, that is the distribution of the variable X and the distribution of the variable Y should be normal *and* the joint distribution of these variables should be normal (for all values of x_i, the conditional distribution of y_i is normal and vice versa). This particular assumption is required for hypothesis tests of statistical relationships to be valid.

Cautionary comments about use of r

These are not strictly assumptions but are typical research situations when Pearson's r either should be interpreted with great caution, or should not be used at all.

- When the variances of the two measures are very different, often associated with different ranges or possibly a restricted range for one variable, then the sample correlation is affected. For example, if one variable was to suffer from range restriction, (part of the score range not used or not appropriate) then this would tend to *attenuate* (lower) the correlation between the two variables. The reader is referred to an informative chapter on reliability and validity (Bartram, 1990) for discussion of this problem.
- When outliers are present, r should be interpreted with caution.
- When the relative precision of measurement scales/instruments differ. Measurement error will reduce the size of a correlation and r should therefore be interpreted with caution.
- When observations are taken from a heterogeneous group, for example, different subgroups in the sample such as age groups, then r should be interpreted with caution.
- When data is sparse (too few measures available), r should not be used. With too few values it is not possible to tell whether the bivariate relationship is linear. The Pearson correlation r is most appropriate for larger samples, $(n > 30)$.
- The correlation r should not be used when the values on one of the variables are fixed in advance.

Example from the Literature

In an empirical study to examine the relationships between adolescent attitudes towards Christianity, interest in science and other socio-demographic factors,

Fulljames, Gibson and Francis (1991) used an attitude questionnaire to survey 729 secondary school pupils. Attitude towards Christianity was measured by a 24-item scale with known reliability and validity indices, index of interest in science was measured by a four-item scale, and pupils' mothers' and fathers' church attendance were each measured on a five-point scale from 'never' to 'weekly'.

The authors reported that the first stage of the analysis involved assessing the psychometric [measurement] properties of the indices, (reliability coefficients and Cronbach alphas were reported but data distributions were not), the second stage of analysis involved inspection of bivariate relationships (correlations). Part of the correlation matrix of the variables reported by the authors is shown in Table 8.3:

Table 8.3: Correlation matrix of the variables in Fulljames' et al., *study of adolescent attitudes*

	Attitude towards Christianity	Fathers' church attendance	Interest in science
Attitude towards Christianity	–	+0.4573 p = 0.001	–0.0926 p = 0.010
Father's church attendance	–	–	–0.0179 p = ns
Interest in science	–	–	–

The authors reported that there were significant relationships between attitude towards Christianity and interest in science, and between Fathers' church attendance and their sons' or daughters' attitude towards Christianity. The authors went on to caution that whereas a simple bivariate correlation coefficient is able to demonstrate where significant covariation exists between variables, it is not able to detect whether this covariance is the artefact of other significant relationships. It is therefore wise to delay interpretation of bivariate relationships between variables until the complex patterns of inter-relationships between all the variables have been ordered into some sequence according to hypothesized relationships.

In this study the correlation analysis was used in both a descriptive and inferential way. The pattern of relationships between variables was scrutinized prior to a third phase of the analysis which involved causal modelling of the data using path analysis. As results of statistical significance tests were reported the data was clearly used in an inferential way. Although no mention was made about whether the data met the assumptions required for correlational analysis, as in most papers, the reader has to assume, in the absence of any specific information, that the variables are linearly related and have an underlying bivariate normal distribution.

The null hypotheses tested were of the type, 'there is no linear relationship between attitude towards Christianity and attitude towards science' or put simply these two attitudes are independent. The authors concluded, following a path analysis of the data, (causal modelling of relationships between variables) that whereas there was a significant negative correlation between Christianity and attitude towards science, interest in science did not influence attitude towards Christianity – a good example of the need for caution when interpreting the meaning of significant correlations.

Prior to drawing conclusions from these findings and correlational data in general, the reader might want to consider answers to questions such as: What is the shape of the data distributions? What evidence is presented related to underlying assumptions required for correlational analysis? Are the samples random, and if yes, what is the population? Is a hypothesis test really needed? What guidance does the author give on the substantive meaning of the size and significance of the correlations?

Worked Example

Correlation and regression are closely related techniques and therefore data from the worked example in section 8.2 (shown in Table 8.2) is used to show how the Pearson correlation r is computed from raw data. To illustrate computation of a partial correlation, another variable, a Raven score, is added. This is a standardized (age adjusted) measure of reasoning ability and is often used as an indication of intelligence (IQ). The data is shown in Table 8.4.

Table 8.4:   Teacher estimate of pupil maths ability (MATHS), standardized maths attainment (SMATHS) and Raven score (RAVEN) for ten pupils

ID	MATHS	SMATHS	RAVEN
17	5	110	1
18	10	133	1
19	5	109	2
20	3	114	1
24	8	128	1
27	5	109	1
28	8	119	2
29	5	119	1
60	1	95	7
61	6	118	1

Two research questions are considered: i) Is SMATHS linearly related to MATHS? and ii) Is RAVEN score linearly related to MATHS? To obtain a visual impression of the strength of any linear relationships between these variables two scatterplots are produced: a plot of MATHS vs SMATHS (plot symbol *) and a plot of MATHS vs RAVEN scores (plot symbol #), see Figure 8.8.

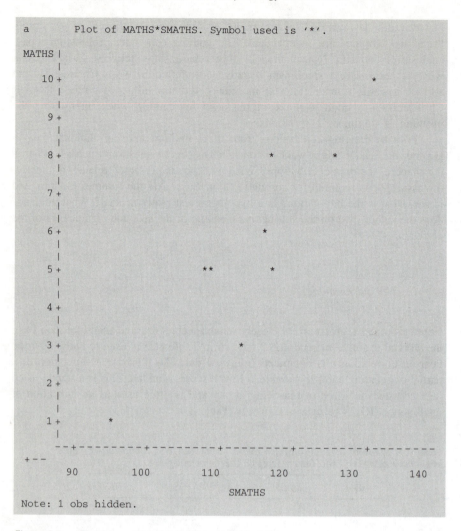

Figure 8.8a: Bivariate scatterplot for data in Table 8.2

To obtain a quantitative index of the strength of a relationship, the Pearson *r* statistic would be calculated. The correlation between two variables, *X* and *Y* is denoted r_{XY}. An equation for computing *r* which is an analogue of the correlation formula for Spearman's correlation shown in Chapter 7 is,

$$r_{xy} = \frac{\Sigma(x_i - \bar{x})(y_i - \bar{y})}{\sqrt{\Sigma(x_i - \bar{x})^2 \, \Sigma(y_i - \bar{y})^2}}$$

where *X* and *Y* are two random quantitative variables. This formula is equivalent to the cross product sums of squares (SS_{XY}) divided by the square root of the sums of squares for X (SS_{XX}) multiplied by the sums of squares for Y (SS_{YY}). This can be written as,

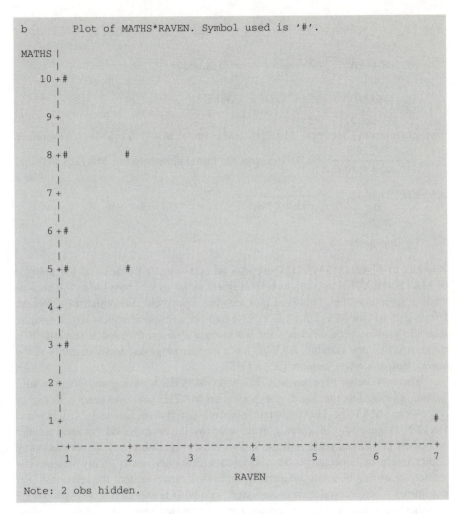

b   Plot of MATHS*RAVEN. Symbol used is '#'.

Figure 8.8b: *Bivariate scatterplot for data in Table 8.2*

$$r_{xy} = \frac{SS_{XY}}{\sqrt{SS_{XX}SS_{YY}}} = \frac{\Sigma XY - \dfrac{\Sigma X\ \Sigma Y}{n}}{\sqrt{\Sigma X^2 - \dfrac{(\Sigma X)^2}{n}\ \Sigma Y^2 - \dfrac{(\Sigma Y)^2}{n}}}$$

Pearson correlation *r* – 8.11

which is computationally an easier formula to use with a pocket calculator.

Using the data in Table 8.4, for the variables MATHS and SMATHS, SS_{XY} = 223.6, SS_{YY} (MATHS) = 60.4 and SS_{XX} (SMATHS) = 1030.4. (These correspond with the values calculated in the previous regression example). Using the general formula for calculating sums of squares, for the two variables MATHS and RAVEN,

$$SS_{XY} = \left(75 - \frac{56 \times 18}{10}\right) = -25.8,$$

$$SS_{XX}(RAVEN) = \left(64 - \frac{324}{10}\right) = 31.6, \text{ and}$$

$$SS_{YY}(MATHS) = \left(374 - \frac{3136}{10}\right) = 60.4$$

The correlation between MATHS (M) and SMATHS (SM) is therefore $r_{m \cdot sm} = \dfrac{223.6}{\sqrt{60.4 \times 1030.4}} = 0.8963$, and the correlation between MATHS (M) and RAVEN (R) is $r_{m \cdot sm} = \dfrac{-25.8}{\sqrt{31.6 \times 60.4}} = -0.5906$

Interpretation

The plot of MATHS*SMATHS suggests an approximate linear trend but the plot of MATHS*RAVEN appears to be non-linear as far as it is possible to tell with as small a sample as this. This later plot also has a very obvious outlier observation. If this pattern (for MATHS vs RAVEN) had been obtained with a larger sample, it would provide good evidence for *not* using a Pearson correlation statistic. It is noticeable that one variable, RAVEN has a smaller range and less variability in the scores than the other variable (SMATHS).

The correlation between MATHS and SMATHS is strong and positive suggesting a linear relationship, higher scores on MATHS are associated with higher scores on SMATHS. The moderate negative correlation between MATHS and RAVEN is generally in keeping with what would be expected because smaller values on the Raven scale indicate higher reasoning ability and higher reasoning ability might be expected to be associated with higher maths ability scores. The scatterplot of this bivariate relationship indicates, however, that the relationship is not linear. When a correlation is consistent with what is expected it is easy to forget that there may not be a linear relationship between the two variables (the obvious benefit of examining scatterplots is demonstrated here). When a large correlation is found between two variables ($r_{m.sm} = 0.89$) it is tempting to attribute a cause and effect relationship. This is incorrect. The only valid conclusions to be drawn from these descriptive correlations is that there is a linear trend between MATHS and SMATHS but not between MATHS and RAVEN. It is important to stress that these interpretations are only illustrative, with a sample size of 10 a Pearson correlation would not be generally appropriate.

Significance of Correlation r

Once a correlation has been computed the researcher may want to know how likely is this obtained correlation, that is, is this a chance occurrence or does it represent a significant population correlation?

As with previous tests of significance the sampling distribution of the test statistic is used to determine whether the observed statistic is likely to have occurred by chance. Unfortunately, the sampling distribution of r is not normal in form when sample sizes are small ($n < 30$) and when the population correlation deviates from zero. To overcome this problem r is transformed, and the probability of this estimator is based on the sampling distribution of the t-statistic. The significance of an obtained Pearson correlation is therefore evaluated using the t-distribution with $n - 2$ degrees of freedom and is given by the following equation:

$$t = \sqrt{n - 1}\frac{r}{\sqrt{(1 - r^2)}} \qquad \textbf{Significance of } \boldsymbol{r} - \textbf{8.12}$$

The null hypothesis tested is that the two variables are independent, that is there is no linear relationship between them, $H_0: \rho = 0$, and the rejection region (for the null hypothesis) is $/t/$ (the absolute value of t) $> t_{1-\alpha/2}$. The alternative hypothesis is, $H_1: \rho \neq 0$, and the rejection region (one sided-tests) is $t < -t_{1-\alpha}$ or $t > t_{1-\alpha}$.

To answer the question, *Is there a significant correlation, at the 5 per cent level, between MATHS and RAVEN scores?* t would be calculated as follows:

$$t = \sqrt{10 - 2}\frac{-0.5906}{\sqrt{(1 - (-0.5906)^2)}}$$

$$= 2.8284 \times -0.7319$$

$$t = -2.070 \text{ with 8df}$$

Interpretation

The critical t-value from Table 3, Appendix A4 is 2.306. The test statistic does not exceed this critical value, ($2.070 < 2.306$), and the null hypothesis is therefore not rejected. We would conclude that the correlation is not significant at the 5 per cent level.

Confidence Intervals for Correlation r

A 95 per cent confidence interval for the population correlation allows the accuracy, hence trustworthiness of any statistical inferences to be estimated. The confidence interval is based on a transformation of the statistic r to a statistic called Fisher's z. This is not the same as the Z-deviate from a normal distribution (sometimes called a Z-score). To interpret the confidence interval the Fisher's z-score has to be transformed back to the correlation metric. Fisher's z is evaluated as,

$$z = 0.5 \log_e\left(\frac{1 + r}{1 - r}\right), \qquad \text{the SE of } z \text{ is } \frac{1}{\sqrt{n - 3}}$$

(SE is standard error)

The 95 per cent CI for the bivariate correlation between SMATHS and MATHS ($r = 0.896$) is

$$z - 1.96 \times \frac{1}{\sqrt{n-3}} \quad \text{to} \quad z + 1.96 \times \frac{1}{\sqrt{n-3}} \qquad \textbf{95 per cent} \\ \textbf{CI for r} - 8.13$$

Fisher's z is $z = 0.5 \log_e\left(\dfrac{1.896}{0.104}\right) = 0.5 \times 2.9031 = 1.452$

and the 95 per cent CI is

$$1.452 - 1.96 \times \frac{1}{\sqrt{7}} \quad \text{to} \quad 1.452 + 1.96 \times \frac{1}{\sqrt{7}}$$
$$= 0.7112 \text{ to } 2.1928$$

These values now have to be transformed back to the original metric.

$$\frac{e^{2 \times 0.7112} - 1}{e^{2 \times 0.7112} + 1} \quad \text{to} \quad \frac{e^{2 \times 2.1928} - 1}{e^{2 \times 2.1928} + 1}$$

$$= 3.1471/5.1471 \quad \text{to} \quad 79.2864/81.2864$$
95 per cent CI $= 0.6114 \quad \text{to} \quad 0.9754$

Interpretation

We can conclude that we are 95 per cent certain that the population correlation is positive and is in the interval 0.61 to 0.98. This confidence interval does not include zero which indicates that the correlation is statistically significant at the 5 per cent level.

Computer Analysis

The SAS procedure PROC CORR with the option Pearson computes Pearson correlations. Sums of squares and cross product sums of squares can also be requested using the option CSSP. The relevant SAS code is:

```
proc corr data=a pearson csscp ;
   var maths smaths raven;
run;
```

The variables to be included in the correlation analysis are specified with the VAR statement. Output from this procedure is shown in Figure 8.9.

Correlation Analysis

3 VAR Variables: MATHS SMATHS RAVEN

Corrected Sum-of-Squares and Crossproducts

	MATHS	SMATHS	RAVEN
MATHS	60.400000	223.600000	-25.800000
SMATHS	223.600000	1030.400000	-125.200000
RAVEN	-25.800000	-125.200000	31.600000

Simple Statistics

Variable	N	Mean	Std Dev	Sum	Minimum	Maximum
MATHS	10	5.6000	2.5906	56.0000	1.0000	10.0000
SMATHS	10	115.4000	10.6999	1154	95.0000	133.0000
RAVEN	10	1.8000	1.8738	18.0000	1.0000	7.0000

Pearson Correlation Coefficients / Prob > |R| under Ho: Rho=0 / N = 10

	MATHS	SMATHS	RAVEN
MATHS	1.00000	0.89629	-0.59055
	0.0	0.0004	0.0723
SMATHS	0.89629	1.00000	-0.69384
	0.0004	0.0	0.0260
RAVEN	-0.59055	-0.69384	1.00000
	0.0723	0.0260	0.0

Figure 8.9: SAS output for bivariate correlations between the variables MATHS, SMATHS and RAVEN

Interpretation

The second line of output shown in Figure 8.9 contains the names of the variables included in the correlation analysis. This list of variables is followed by a table of the corrected sums of squares and cross products for the variables. The names of the variables form the rows and columns of this table. For example, the sums of squares for the variable RAVEN is found in the body of the table where the third row and third column intersect, the value here is 31.6. The cross product sums of squares is at the intersection of two different variables for example 223.6 is the cross product sums of squares for SMATHS × MATHS.

The next section of output contains simple summary statistics. In this example the sample size for all the cells of the correlation matrix is the same because there is no missing data. The sample size is therefore only printed in the summary statistics. If there had been different sample sizes for each variable then *n* would have been printed for each correlation in the correlation matrix in the following section.

The final section of output contains the correlation matrix of rows and columns headed by each variable name. Each cell of the matrix, intersection between a row and a column variables contains two values, the bivariate correlation coefficient and the associated p-value. This probability value is the level of significance resulting from a test of the null hypothesis, Prob $>$ |R| under H_0: Rho $= 0$. For example, the value of the correlation between MATHS and SMATHS is $r = 0.89629$. This indicates a positive linear relationship between the two variables. The associated p-value is 0.0004 which provides evidence in support of the alternative hypothesis that the true population correlation is not zero. Notice that a variable correlated with itself is always 1.

Partial Correlation

A partial correlation between two variables adjusts the linear relationship between both variables to take account of a third variable. This is called a **first order partial correlation**. If the RAVEN variable is correlated with both MATHS and SMATHS then the correlation between SMATHS and MATHS is likely to be reduced when the effect of the RAVEN variable is partialled out (adjusted for). The general formula to compute a first order partial correlation is,

$$r_{xy.z} = \frac{r_{xy} - r_{xz}r_{yz}}{\sqrt{(1 - r_{xz}^2)(1 - r_{yz}^2)}} \qquad \textbf{First order partial correlation} - 8.14$$

The partial correlation between SMATHS and MATHS with RAVEN partialled out is given by

$$r_{xy.z} = \frac{0.896 - ((-0.591) \times (-0.694))}{\sqrt{(1 - (-0.591)^2) \times (1 - (0.694)^2)}}$$
$$= 0.4858/0.5808$$
$$= 0.836$$

Interpretation

Notice that the correlation between MATHS and SMATHS has been reduced slightly (from 0.896 to 0.836 when the effect of the RAVEN variable has been partialled out. This indicates that a small portion of the common variance between MATHS and SMATHS is explained by the third variable RAVEN.

SAS code for producing a partial correlation between SMATHS and MATHS partialling out the effect of the RAVEN variable is shown,

```
proc corr data=a pearson csscp ;
  var maths smaths raven;
  partial raven;
run;
```

The relevant section of SAS output resulting from this partial statement is:

Pearson Partial Correlation Coefficients
/ Prob > |R| under Ho: Partial Rho=0 / N = 10

	MATHS	SMATHS	RAVEN
MATHS	1.00000	0.83722	.
	0.0	0.0049	
SMATHS	0.83722	1.00000	.
	0.0049	0.0	
RAVEN	.	.	.

Interpretation

Notice that SAS treats the RAVEN variable as missing in the correlation matrix. The partial correlation for MATHS and SMATHS corresponds with the value computed in the worked example (allowing for rounding error). A researcher may want to test the significance of a difference between two correlations from independent samples. A SAS programme to do this is presented in Figure 16, Appendix A3.

8.4 Independent *t*-test (unrelated two sample procedure)

When to Use

The two-sample independent *t*-test (sometimes called unrelated *t*-test) is most frequently used in survey and experimental (parallel group) designs when an investigator wants to determine whether there is a significant difference between two independent group means. For example, an educational researcher may want to know which of two classroom activities, reading silently or teachers' storytelling is most helpful in improving childrens' word meanings. A teacher compares the vocabulary scores of two independent classroom groups, one which has followed a reading programme including teacher storytelling and the other which followed the same reading programme but had periods of silent reading in the reading corner instead of the storytelling. In another example, as part of a research programme on employee motivation and productivity, a psychologist compares personality scores on Catell's Sixteen Personality Factor Test (16PF) for male and female employees.

In the *t*-test procedure, sample means are used to estimate the unknown population means (parameters). With the two-sample *t*-test a researcher is interested in whether any observed difference in means represents a real difference (not attributable to chance fluctuations) and therefore justifies the inference that the two samples represent two distinct populations with different population means rather than one population. The *t*-statistic (sometimes called a *t*-ratio) is an estimate of the difference between two population means. The significance of this difference is evaluated by calculating the difference between the two means divided by the standard error of this difference. The idea of computing this **ratio** is to compare the variability in the predicted differences in scores, simply the difference between the mean scores for the two groups, to the total variability of all scores (in both samples). Think of it as a proportion of variability predicted compared with total variability. The **standard error of the difference between means** is a measure of this total variability. The standard deviation of a sampling distribution is usually referred to as the standard error of that distribution. Thus the standard deviation of the mean is called the standard error of the mean. The difference between two means also has a sampling distribution which has a mean and a standard deviation, the latter is referred to as the standard error of the difference in means.

The sensitivity of the t-test in detecting differences is dependent upon the total variability in scores (standard error of the difference in means). If the overall variability in scores is minimal then only a small difference between means of the two groups might reflect a consistent and significant difference. However, if there is large overall variability in scores then a larger difference between means is required to attain statistical significance. It is more difficult to detect real differences with heterogeneous groups because more of the variability in individuals' scores may be due to error or other (unmeasured) effects rather than the predicted differences of interest. The implication for research design is that you are more likely to detect a significant difference between groups if overall scores are homogeneous. See also the discussion of power analysis in Chapter 5.

When samples are small ($n < 30$) the sample standard deviation may not be a good estimator of the unknown population standard deviation (with small samples, the sample standard deviation underestimates the population standard deviation more than half the time) and consequently the ratio of the difference between means to the standard error of the difference ($\bar{x}_1 - \bar{x}_2$)/SE diff in means, may not have a normal distribution. This ratio is called a t-statistic and when the variances in both samples are similar, the t-statistic has a probability distribution known as the **Student's t-distribution**.

The shape of the t-distribution changes with sample size, that is there is a different t-distribution for each sample size, so when we use the t-distribution we also need to refer to the appropriate degrees of freedom which is based on the sample size and the number of parameters estimated. As the sample size increases above 30, the t-distribution approaches a normal distribution in shape.

Statistical Inference and Null Hypothesis

We use the t-test to see whether there is a difference between two means, the null hypothesis is therefore, H_0: $\mu_1 - \mu_2 = 0$; this is equivalent to $\mu_1 = \mu_2$. In words, this says that the population means are the same, which is equivalent to saying there is one population and not two. The alternative hypothesis is either non-directional, H_1: $\mu_1 \neq \mu_2$, rejection region $|t| > t_{1-\alpha/2}$ (this means that the absolute value of t is greater than the critical value of t at the 0.025 level of significance, if alpha is 5 per cent) or it may be one-sided, $\mu_1 > \mu_2$ or $\mu_1 < \mu_2$, rejection region $t > t_{1-\alpha}$ or $t < -t_{1-\alpha}$. The sampling distribution of the difference between means is used to test this null hypothesis.

Pooled Variance Estimate of t-ratio (equal variance)

The t-statistic has an exact distribution *only* when the two populations have the same variance. This is called the **homogeneity of variance** assumption. When a pooled estimate of the population variance, σ^2, is used in the calculation of the t-ratio it is referred to as a pooled variance estimate. This is given by the formula:

$$S_p^2 = \frac{(n_1 - 1)S_1^2 + (n_2 - 1)S_2^2}{n_1 + n_2 - 2}$$

Pooled variance estimate – 8.15

This pooled variance estimate is the average of the two separate sample variances weighted by their respective sample sizes. The degrees of freedom associated with the pooled variance estimate of the t-statistic are $n_1 + n_2 - 2$; one degree of freedom is associated with each sample variance (sample variance has $n - 1$ df). The homogeneity of variance assumption is more reasonable with experimental designs because such designs generally assume that groups are equivalent prior to treatment.

Separate Variance Estimate of the Approximate t′-ratio (unequal variance)

When the assumption of homogeneity of variance is unreasonable (procedures for checking are described under the heading Test assumptions) the approximate t-statistic denoted t' is calculated using the separate variance estimates from each sample. The sampling distribution of t' *does not* have a t-distribution and does not have $n_1 + n_2 - 2$ degrees of freedom. The exact sampling distribution has been evaluated but is not generally used. Instead, approximate procedures have been developed for determining the critical values to use with the approximate t' distribution.

One procedure is the Satterthwaite (1946) approximation which is used in many propriety statistical packages. This procedure uses a modified degrees of freedom, estimated from the sample sizes, to approximate the t-distribution. The df for the Satterthwaite (1946) approximation are,

$$df = \frac{\left(\frac{S_1^2}{n_1} + \frac{S_2^2}{n_2}\right)^2}{\frac{1}{n_1 - 1}\left(\frac{S_1^2}{n_1}\right)^2 + \frac{1}{n_2 - 1}\left(\frac{S_2^2}{n_2}\right)^2}$$

df for separate variance estimate – 8.16

This approximation often results in degrees of freedom which are not whole numbers. Associated probabilities cannot therefore be found directly from statistical tables. The p-value has to be interpolated based on tabled entries or a function can be used in computer packages (**TINV** function in SAS) to produce exact p-values. Standard computational procedures such as **PROC TTEST** in **SAS** automatically print equal and unequal variance estimates and exact p-values.

Test Assumptions

The assumptions for the independent *t*-test are:

- The populations from which the samples are selected should have an **approximate normal distribution**. What is meant here is that the sampling distributions of the means are normally distributed. If the sample is sufficiently large then because of the Central Limit Theorem, even if the distribution of the variables are not normal, their sample means will be. If the samples are small and both variables are normally distributed their means will also have an underlying normal distribution. *(Verify the normality assumption by doing a normal probability plot for the two variables. Interpret the plot as described in Chapter 5, section 5.5, checking for normality.)*
- The population variances should be equal, this is called the **homogeneity of variance** assumption. *(Verify assumption of homogeneity by an approximate rule, variances are homogeneous if the ratio of the larger standard deviation (SD) to the smaller standard deviation is less than or equal to two. A folded F-test may be used, the ratio of two sample variances distributed with $n_1 + n_2 - 2$ df but this is affected by non normality of data. This assumption is not necessary if the approximate t'-ratio (separate variance estimate) is used.)*
- Samples are **independent** and selected at random. *(This assumption is related to the research design.)*

In a practical setting these assumptions are not straightforward to apply and as this is one of the most common statistical tests some interpretation and guidance is required.

Guidelines for Practical Use of the t-test

The utility of the independent *t*-test is related to how far these assumptions can be relaxed without invalidating inferences.

Normality assumption. What is important is that sample means are normally distributed in the population. With large sample sizes ($n > 30$ in each sample) this is not a problem. With smaller samples the equality of sample sizes is important. The independent *t*-test is robust against non normality even with small sample sizes ($n < 10$), provided the sample sizes are equal.

Moderately skewed distributions. If both samples are moderately skewed, have similar shape and are approximately equal in size with the smaller sample being about 15 or more, then the *t*-test may be used with caution.

Severely skewed distributions. The *t*-test should only be considered with larger samples, $n_1 + n_2 > 45$ which are approximately equal in size and have similar variances. If these assumptions are not met consider transforming the data, using an alternative sampling distribution, use a nonparametric test or use a different analytic approach. A general discussion about what to do when parametric assumptions are not met is presented at the end of this chapter.

Unequal variances. If the approximate t' (unequal variance estimate) is used then the homogeneity assumption is not critical.

Independence. The sample observations must be independent, this is a critical assumption.

Outlier observations. The independent *t*-test should not be used when there are extreme outlier observations. These observations will greatly influence the means and invalidate any inferences.

Example from the Literature

Christensen and Cooper (1992) examined the research hypothesis that 6–7-year-old children achieve greater proficiency in simple problems of addition when they use cognitive strategies compared with children who do not use them. Study participants included twenty-two girls and eighteen boys from two classes of a suburban public school in Australia. This was a pre-test–post-test design but only pre-test data is analysed here. Students were given a screening pre-test on written and oral problems of addition. Pre-testing confirmed all children had conceptual understanding of addition and that no child utilized cognitive strategies. All children participated in an intervention (involving a variety of instructional activities) over a twelve-week period. Post-testing was completed immediately following the period of intervention. Children were assigned to cognitive strategy and non-cognitive strategy groups *after the intervention* when strategy group could be identified.

Response variables analysed included **written score** (number of correct responses on a written test), **oral latency score** (time interval between initial display of test item and student correct response), **error score** (number of errors on oral test) **retrieval score** (number of items retrieved from memory), and **counting score** (number of items answered by counting). For memory and counting scores it was not specified whether only 'number correct' items were counted.

Table 1 in Christensen and Cooper's paper presents data on mean pre-test and post-test scores for the two groups of students. Part of this table showing pre-test data only, is reproduced as follows:

Table 8.5: *Means, standard deviations and results of significance tests for strategy and non-strategy groups at pretest*

	Strategy group		Non-strategy group			
	Mean	SD	Mean	SD	Test	p
Written	20.05	13.04	12.70	11.07	$t_{38} = 2.04$	.048
Oral latency	5.87	2.07	8.53	2.53	$t_{38} = 3.64$	.001*
Errors	7.70	9.35	5.75	4.66	$t_{38} = 0.83$	.409
Proficient	1.55	2.01	0.60	1.43	$t_{38} = 1.72$	.093
Retrieval	37.70	13.15	21.85	15.36	$t_{38} = 3.51$	.001*
Counting	17.30	13.15	33.15	15.36	$t_{38} = 3.51$	.001*

* Statistically significant

With respect to this pretest data, six research questions were addressed, one question for each response variable. In each case the question is of the form, *Is the average pre-test score for students who are strategy users different to the average pre-test score for students who are non-strategy users?* The population of interest in this study is the population of students who might participate in a twelve-week instructional programme. Implicitly this is the population to which the authors generalize their results.

The authors are in effect posing the question, if the population of potential programme participants were to be randomly assigned to strategy and non-strategy groups, would the two groups differ with respect to pre-intervention competency measures (the six response variables in Table 8.5), even though assignment to groups was not made until after the intervention. The inferences in this section of the analysis relate to two separate populations – a population of cognitive strategy users and a population of non-strategy users. The inferential process addresses the issue of whether the two samples of competency scores (cognitive strategy user sample and non-strategy user sample) represent competency scores from one population of students or alternatively scores from two separate populations of students, a cognitive strategy user population and a non-strategy user population.

The null hypotheses tested are of the form, the average competency score of the population of students who might be exposed to the instructional programme and who are cognitive strategy users (or would become so at follow up) is equal to the average competency score of the population of students who might be exposed to the programme but are non-strategy users (or do not become strategy users at follow up). Put simply this could be stated as, *There are no differences between the pre-intervention competency scores of cognitive strategy and non-cognitive strategy users.*

For the variable Written in Table 8.5 the null hypothesis is $H_0: \mu_1 = \mu_2$ which in words is, the mean *written* pre-test score is equal for the population of cognitive strategy and non-strategy users. The precise nature of the alternative hypothesis is not stated by the authors. However, by knowing the test statistic value which is shown in Table 8.3 (under the heading Test) and the reported p-value of 0.0048, it is possible to determine that the authors were using a non-directional alternative hypothesis and making a two-tailed *t*-test. The degrees of freedom, which are a whole number, suggest that an equal variance estimate of *t* was used.

In testing the statistical hypothesis of equality of means the authors were comparing, for example, the average oral latency score of 5.87 for the cognitive strategy group with the average score of 8.53 for the non-strategy group. The obtained *t*-statistic of 3.64 for this comparison was larger than the non-directional, (two-tailed) critical *t*-value of 3.572 at the 0.001 level. This critical *t*-value of 3.57 is obtained using the SAS function TINV. The table of percentage points of the *t*-distribution shown in Appendix A4 does not have a value for 38 degrees of freedom.

The appropriate SAS code to evaluate the critical *t*-value is:

```
data a;
  t=round(TINV(0.9995,38),.001);
  put t=;
run;
```

As the obtained *t*-value was greater than the critical *t*-value at the 1 per cent level, then the authors were able to reject the null hypothesis and conclude that there were some initial ability differences between groups. They go on to say that the impact of initial ability differences on the results of the study cannot be discarded.

When reviewing reported results where the independent *t*-test procedure has been used, or if considering use of this procedure on your own data, the reader should reflect on the underlying assumptions on which the independent *t*-test is based. Taking the results reported in Christensen and Cooper's paper as an example, the reader might like to consider answers to the following questions:

- Are two independent sample averages being compared?
- Has an element of randomization entered the design, random sampling or randomization to groups?
- Are the groups independent?
- Are the assumptions of homogeneity of variance reasonable?
- Are the data distributions skewed? When a standard deviation is greater than the mean, this suggests the distribution may be skewed.
- Is the chosen alpha level and statistical power reasonable?

If a high level of alpha is selected, for example, 1 per cent, this increases the likelihood of a Type I error (conclude there are differences although no true differences really exist) but decreases the likelihood of a Type II error. That is accepting the null hypothesis when it is false. In this particular example this would mean concluding there are no differences at pre-test when there are differences.

As an exercise evaluate the statistical power of the t-tests in Table 8.5. You should for example, find that for the variable Retrieval with an alpha of 1 per cent, the power equals 81 per cent.

Worked Example

The following data, abstracted from a student's dissertation study on children's strategies for subtraction, is used to illustrate computation of the *t*-statistic for independent samples. Twenty subjects, ten aged 6-years and ten aged 7-years were given a series of test items that required subtraction (when both numbers were less than 10, subtraction of a single digit from a two-digit number and subtraction when both numbers were double digits). Correct answers were totalled for each subject and the subtraction strategy noted. The researcher predicted that there would be a difference in both correct scores and strategy use between the two age groups. In this example subjects' total correct scores are analysed. Data for the 20 subjects is shown in Table 8.6. A non-directional alternative hypothesis is specified and a 5 per cent alpha level is chosen.

Table 8.6: *Subtraction score for thirty test items (total subtractions correct) for 6- and 7-year-old pupils*

Group 1 AGE 6		Group 2 AGE 7	
OBS	SCORE	OBS	SCORE
1	17	11	16
2	13	12	20
3	17	13	24
4	6	14	17
5	13	15	25
6	20	16	20
7	6	17	22
8	19	18	18
9	12	19	11
10	9	20	22
$\bar{X}$ = 13.2		$\bar{X}$ = 19.5	
S^2 (variance)* = 25.733		S^2 (variance) = 17.389	

* The sample variance is calculated using formula 3.1 in Chapter 3

For Age 6, $S^2 = \dfrac{1974 - 1742.4}{9}$ and for age 7, $S^2 = \dfrac{3959 - 3802.5}{9}$

Separate Variance Estimate

To calculate a separate variance estimate for t', three steps are involved, i) find the difference in means between the two groups; ii) calculate the standard error of the difference in means; and iii) evaluate t' which is the ratio of the difference in means (i above) to the standard error of this difference in means (ii above).

1   Difference in means

In this example the difference is $\bar{x}_1 - \bar{x}_2 = -6.3$

2   *Standard error of the difference in means* (separate variance estimate)

The standard error of the difference in means is,

$$\sqrt{\frac{S_1^2}{n_1} + \frac{S_2^2}{n_2}}$$

Standard error of difference in means separate variance estimate – 8.17

The $SE_{\text{diffin means}}$ for the data in Table 8.6 is, $\sqrt{\dfrac{25.733}{10} + \dfrac{17.389}{10}}$

3 t'-ratio

The t'-ratio is evaluated as $(\bar{x}_1 - \bar{x}_2)/SE$ diff in means, which gives the value, $t' = -3.0338$

For the separate variance estimate the degrees of freedom are estimated using equation 8.16,

$$df = \frac{\left(\dfrac{25.733}{10} + \dfrac{17.389}{10}\right)^2}{\dfrac{1}{10-1}\left(\dfrac{25.733}{10}\right)^2 + \dfrac{1}{10-1}\left(\dfrac{17.389}{10}\right)^2}$$

which gives the value df = 17.4

Interpretation

The t'-statistic represents the size of the difference between two groups, the larger the t'-value the greater the size of the difference. In this example, the alternative hypothesis is non-directional, H_1: $\mu_1 \neq \mu_2$, and the rejection region is $|t| > t_{1-\alpha/2}$. To be statistically significant the calculated t'-value needs to exceed the critical t-value, with 17.4 degrees of freedom at the 5 per cent level. Notice that the degrees of freedom is not a whole number and a critical value for 17.4 df is not shown in the t-table in Appendix A4 (Table 3). We can find the critical value by interpolating between the two nearest values namely df = 17 (critical t = 2.110) and df = 18 (critical t = 2.101). The critical value is approximately 2.106 with df = 17.4. Using the TINV function in SAS the exact critical value is also found to be 2.106. See the following SAS code,

```
data a;
 alpha=0.975; ** This is equivalent to a two-tailed test at the 5%
 level**;
 tcrit=round (tinv(0.975,17.4),.001); ** Round statement rounds
 value to**;
 put tcrit=;                          ** 3 decimal places ** ;
run;
```

In this example the observed t'-value of -3.0338 exceeds the critical t-value of 2.106, and we can conclude that the means are significantly different at the 5 per cent level with a two-tailed test. The 7-year-old pupils would seem to have a significantly higher score than the 6-year-old pupils ($t' = -3.0338$, df $= 17.4$, $p < 0.05$).

Pooled Variance Estimate

Three steps are involved in calculating a pooled (equal variance) estimate: i) Check that the sample variances are homogeneous and find the difference in means between the two groups; ii) Calculate the standard error of the difference in means; and iii) evaluate t which is the ratio of the difference in means (i above) to the standard error of this difference in means (ii above).

1   *Difference in means and check for homogeneity*

The first step is the same as for the separate variance estimate, the difference in means is -6.3. Using the approximate rule of thumb for homogeneity of variances, (5.072/4.170 is less than 2) the variances are similar.

2   *Standard error of the difference in means* (pooled variance estimate)

This is evaluated using equation 8.15 for the pooled variance estimate.

$$S_p^2 = \frac{(10 - 1)25.733 + (10 - 1)17.389}{10 + 10 - 2}$$

$$S_p = 4.643$$

3   *t-ratio*

As in the separate variance estimate t is the ratio of the difference in means to the standard error of the difference, $\dfrac{-6.3}{4.643\sqrt{\dfrac{1}{10} + \dfrac{1}{10}}}$,

$$t = -3.034$$

The associated degrees of freedom for a pooled variance estimate is simply $n_1 + n_2 - 2 =$ df $= 18$.

Interpretation

Assuming a two-tailed test because no specific difference was specified by the researcher and a 5 per cent significance level, interpretation is the same as in the previous example except that the degrees of freedom are a whole number and can therefore be looked up in a table of the *t*-distribution. The p-value for a *t* of −3.034 is found by comparing the observed *t*-ratio (*t* = −3.034) to a critical *t*-value with 18 df in Table 3 (Appendix A4). For 18 df and 5 per cent two-tailed the critical *t* is 2.101. Since the observed value exceeds the critical value we can conclude that there is evidence of a significant age difference in correct score for subtraction tasks (*t* = −3.034, df = 18, p < 0.05).

In these two worked examples the separate and pooled variance estimates of the *t*-ratios are similar because the sample variances are not very different. The negative *t*-ratio is attributable to the larger mean being subtracted from the smaller mean (in both examples the mean for 7-year-olds was subtracted from the mean for 6-year-olds). The response variable would be checked for normality in the usual way with a normal probability plot.

Confidence Interval (CI) for Difference in Means

It is useful to present an estimate of the plausible range of population mean differences as well as the result of a hypothesis test. The 95 per cent CI for the difference in means is given by,

$$\bar{x}_1 - \bar{x}_2 +/- t_{1-\alpha/2} s_p \sqrt{\frac{1}{n_1} + \frac{1}{n_2}}$$

Confidence interval difference between means independent samples – 8.18

In this example $t_{1-\alpha/2}$ with 18 df is 2.101 and the 95 per cent CI is 13.2 − 19.5 +/− 2.101(4.643)(0.4472), the lower bound estimate is −10.663 and the upper bound estimate is −1.937.

Interpretation

The difference between the sample mean correct score in 6- and 7-year-old pupils was −6.3 with a 95 per cent CI from −10.663 to −1.937, the equal variance *t*-ratio, two-tailed test, was −3.034, with 18 degrees of freedom and an associated p-value of 0.05. The interval does not include zero which corresponds to a rejection of the null hypothesis (zero difference between means is equivalent to the null hypothesis). The interval width is rather large probably because of the small sample size. We are 95 per cent certain that the mean difference could, with rounding, be as small as −2 or as large as −11 but the most likely value is −6.

Output from a SAS programme for computing a Confidence Interval for the difference between two means for independent samples (see the SAS programme in Figure 17, Appendix A3) is shown in Figure 8.10.

sample size (gp 1)	sample size (gp 2)	mean (gp 1)	mean (gp 2)	variance (gp 1)	variance (gp 2)
10	10	13.2	19.5	25.733	17.389

	Alpha	Critical t-value	Lower Confidence Limit	Upper Confidence Limit
	0.05	2.101	-10.663	-1.937

Figure 8.10: 95 per cent CI for difference between two means

The values in this output correspond with the 95 per cent CI interval width in the worked example.

Computer Analysis

The SAS procedure PROC TTEST performs an independent *t*-test, the following SAS code produced the output shown in Figure 8.11,

```
proc ttest;
  class age;
  var score;
run;
```

The CLASS statement names the classification variable that classifies the data set into two groups; in this example there are two age groups. The VAR statement specifies the response variable that is analysed.

```
                        T-TEST PROCEDURE

Variable: SCORE

AGE          N            Mean              Std Dev           Std Error
- - - - - - - - - - - - - - - - - - - - - - - - - - - - - - - - - - - - - - - -
6           10        13.20000000       5.07280330        1.60416126
7           10        19.50000000       4.16999867        1.31866936

Variances      T       DF      Prob>|T|
- - - - - - - - - - - - - - - - - - - - - -
Unequal     -3.0338   17.4     0.0074
Equal       -3.0338   18.0     0.0071

For H0: Variances are equal, F' = 1.48 DF = (9,9) Prob>F' = 0.5686
```

Figure 8.11: Independent t-test comparing ages 6 and 7 on total score correct for 30 subtraction test items

Interpretation

Look first at the bottom of the output where the result of performing the folded F' test for homogeneity of variance (equal variances) is shown. The p-value indicates that F' statistic is not significant. This means that the variances are not significantly different. Therefore, the results of the equal variance t-ratio are used (pooled variance estimate). Here the p-value associated with a t-value of -3.0338 is 0.0071, which is significant at the 5 per cent level. The results are significant at the 1 per cent level but α (the significance level or probability of incorrectly rejecting the null hypothesis) was set initially to 0.05 so this should be reported; statistical significance should never be based on the results of the test. The null hypothesis of no difference is rejected, and we can conclude that there is a difference in means.

8.5 Paired t-test (related)

When to Use

When two group means are to be compared which are from the same sample, that is, paired measurements for each subject in the sample, the paired t-test (sometimes called dependent t-test) should be considered. Measurements would also be related if two independent samples were matched and then the means of the two samples compared. A paired t-test is often used to analyze the results of a 'before' and 'after' research design. For example, a researcher may want to know whether there is any improvement in vocabulary acquisition scores which could be attributed to the effect of a reading programme. Subjects' vocabulary score would be determined before commencement of the reading programme, and they would be measured again after the programme had been completed. Each subject would have paired vocabulary scores one measure before the programme and one after. The purpose of a repeated measures analysis using the paired t-test would be to determine whether the average change (average of the differences before–after scores) in scores is greater than would be expected due to chance fluctuations alone.

The paired t-test is based on the same idea as the independent t-test, the test statistic is a ratio of mean difference (predicted variability) to the standard error of the difference (overall variability in scores). When the same subjects are used for both measurements the standard error is smaller (a desirable research design feature) and consequently smaller differences in means are likely to be detected. With fewer than five pairs of scores the test is not very sensitive. Large differences in scores are needed to detect a significant difference and this procedure should not be used when the population of differences is non-normal.

Statistical Inference and Null Hypothesis

The sampling distribution of the difference scores (represented by D) is used as the basis for statistical inference in the paired t-test. The mean of the population of difference scores, μ_D, is zero, when the null hypothesis is true. We think of this as a one sample test even though we are comparing two means because we have one population distribution of difference scores. The null hypothesis can be written as $H_0: \mu_D = \mu_1 - \mu_2 = 0$. There are three possible alternative hypotheses:

1   $\mu_D \neq 0$ a non directional test (two tailed), rejection region is $|t| > t_{1-\alpha/2}$.
2   $\mu_D < 0$ directional test (one tailed) rejection region $t > t_{1-\alpha}$ or $t < -t_{1-\alpha}$.
3   $\mu_D > 0$ directional test (one tailed) rejection region $t > t_{1-\alpha}$ or $t < -t_{1-\alpha}$.

Test Assumptions

The paired t-test should be considered when the population of interest consists of difference scores from paired observations; this implies continuous measurement. The following assumptions should be met:

- Paired differences are randomly selected from the population. This usually means that the sample is drawn at random.
- The population of difference scores is approximately normally distributed.
- Observations within a treatment condition are independent of each other.

Example from the Literature

Borzone de Manrique and Signorini (1994) compared two measures, spelling and reading, within groups, using the t-test for paired observations. Scores analysed were percentage correct to allow for comparisons across the spelling and reading tests which had different numbers of items. Two paired t-tests were performed on separate groups of pupils, a group of skilled readers, $n = 19$, (score at the 75th percentile or better on a standardized reading comprehension test) and a group of less skilled readers, $n = 20$.

The authors reported a significant difference between spelling and reading in the less skilled group, $t_{(19)} = 5.24$, p < 0.001, but no difference was found in the skilled group, $t_{(18)} = 1.63$, not significant. The authors concluded that the skilled readers perform similarly on spelling and reading, while the less skilled readers show a clear advantage of spelling over reading.

Although not stated by the authors, this is likely to be a two-tailed test, the null hypothesis being that there is no population difference in mean reading and spelling scores. It is important not to set the alpha level *after* a test statistic has been evaluated and it is presumed that the authors decided a priori on a 1 per cent level of significance. Significant results of exploratory analyses, that is significance tests which were not defined a priori with alpha levels and power considerations, should be interpreted cautiously until other studies confirm similar findings. In the absence of any distributional information about the sample distribution of difference scores the reader should also assume that these are approximately normal. The reader should recall, however, that percentages are often skewed and particular care is needed when checking assumptions for the paired t-test that the difference in percentage correct scores is not severely skewed.

Worked Example

In an example of the paired *t*-test we can consider data from a study on primary school childrens referential communication skills, the study referred to in the worked example (p. 264) on simple linear regression. Researchers were interested in the stability of one of their measures, speaker scores, in particular. They wanted to know whether there was any carry-over effect of testing (whether testing itself influenced scores on the referential communication test). The data presented in Table 8.7 represents a few cases abstracted from the test–retest analysis of the referential communication study which is intended to show whether there is any change in speaker scores over a three-month period.

Table 8.7: *Comparison of test–retest scores for speaker (5-year-old pupils)*

OBS	(OCCASION 1)	(OCCASION 2)	DIFFERENCE (D)
1	14	17	3
2	26	13	-13
3	37	17	-20
4	0	6	6
5	13	13	0
6	0	20	20
7	0	6	6
8	5	19	14
9	0	12	12
10	0	9	9

Mean difference $(\bar{D}) = \dfrac{\Sigma D}{n} = 37/10 = 3.7$

Computation of the paired *t*-statistic involves three steps, 1) calculation of the mean difference; 2) calculation of the standard deviation of the difference scores; and 3) calculation of the standard error of the difference scores. The *t*-statistic is evaluated once again as the ratio of the mean difference 1) above to the standard error of the differences 3) above.

1 *Mean difference*

This is simply the average difference score (occasion 2-occasion 1) = 3.7.

2 *Standard deviation of the differences* (SD_{diff})

The standard deviation of the differences is calculated using the usual formula:

$$SD_{diff} = \sqrt{\dfrac{\Sigma D^2 - \dfrac{(\Sigma D)^2}{n}}{(n-1)}}$$

$$SD_{diff} = \sqrt{\frac{1471 - \frac{(37)^2}{10}}{(10 - 1)}} = 12.175$$

3 *Standard error of the differences*

The standard error of the differences is simply the standard deviation divided by the square root of the sample size, which is $12.175/(\sqrt{10})$, = 3.850.

The *t*-statistic is the mean difference divided by the standard error of the differences, *t* is therefore $(3.7/3.850) = 0.961$. The degrees of freedom are given by $n - 1$, in this example df = 9. One degree of freedom is used in estimating the variance of difference scores in the population which is estimated from the sample mean difference.

Interpretation

The critical value at the 5 per cent significance level from the *t*-table (Table 3, Appendix A4) is 2.262. Since the observed *t*-value of 0.961 is less than this critical value we cannot reject the null hypothesis and therefore we conclude that it is plausible that the mean difference (occasion 2–occasion 1) speaker scores is not significantly different from zero.

Confidence Interval for the Mean Difference (paired measures)

To calculate a 95 per cent CI, $t_{1-\alpha/2}$ is required. With 9 degrees of freedom this value is 2.262. The 95 per cent CI is given by,

$\bar{d}$ +/– $(t_{1-\alpha/2} SE_{diff})$ **95 per cent CI for mean difference (paired data)** – 8.19

which is 3.7 +/– (2.262 × 3.850)

The 95 per cent CI for the population value of the mean difference, 'occasion 2– occasion 1' speaker scores is −5.009, to 12.409.

Interpretation

We can be 95 per cent certain that the difference between occasion 1 and occasion 2 speaker scores falls within the interval −5.009, to 12.409. This confidence interval includes the value zero, which provides a simultaneous test of the null hypothesis. As the value of zero difference falls within the confidence interval, there is no evidence to reject the null hypothesis, and we conclude that there is no significant difference between the mean occasion 1 and occasion 2 speaker scores.

Computer Analysis

SAS code for the *t*-test is,

```
Data a;
   input caseno occ1 occ2 @@;
   diff= occ2 - occ1;
   cards;
1 14 17 2 26 13  3 37 17 4 0 6 5 13 13 6 0 20 7 0 6
8  5 19 9  0 12 10  0  9
;
proc means n mean stderr t prt;
  var diff;
run;
```

The variable 'diff' can be entered in a data step as in this example. The MEANS statement computes the average difference on the specified variable diff. The same analysis can be performed using PROC UNIVARIATE with the variable diff. Output from PROC MEANS is shown in Figure 8.12.

```
      Analysis Variable : DIFF

   N         Mean        Std Error           T          Prob>|T|
   ----------------------------------------------------------------
   10      3.7000000      3.8501082       0.9610119       0.3617
   ----------------------------------------------------------------
```

Figure 8.12: Paired t-test comparing difference scores, post–pre, for speaker test items

Interpretation

The mean difference is 3.7, the same as in the worked example. The margin of error is rather large, 3.850 (Standard error of difference), *t* is 0.961 which has an associated (exact) probability of 0.3617. The mean difference in speaker scores is not statistically significant.

Confidence Intervals for Paired Difference t-test

The following section of SAS code computes the 95 per cent CI for difference in means when samples are paired (related) as follows:

```
data a; set a;
diff= occ2 - occ1;
proc summary data=a ;
   var diff;
   output out=out mean=mean stderr=stderr n=n;
run;
```

```
data b; set out;
  alpha=.05;
  df=n-1;
  tobs=mean/stderr;
  t=round (tinv(1-alpha/2,df),.001);
  lc=round(mean-t*stderr,.001);
  uc=round(mean+t*stderr,.001);
proc print data=b split= '*' noobs;
  var n alpha tobs lc uc;
  title1 'Confidence intervals for difference between paired means';
  label alpha='Alpha'
    n ='Sample size'
    tobs='t-ratio'
    df ='Degrees of Freedom'
    sediff='Standard error'
    lc ='Lower Confidence Limit'
    uc ='Upper Confidence Limit';
run;
```

Output from this SAS code is shown:

Confidence intervals for difference between paired means				
Sample size	Alpha	t-ratio	Lower Confidence Limit	Upper Confidence Limit
10	0.05	0.96101	−5.009	12.409

The interpretation is exactly the same as in the worked example.

8.6 Introduction to Analysis of Variance (ANOVA)

Analysis of variance is a statistical hypothesis testing procedure first developed by Fisher (1953) to analyse data generated by experimental designs. The ANOVA approach enables an investigator to assess the causal influence of two or more independent variables (treatments), and possible interactions of these treatment effects on a single response (outcome) variable. In a classical experimental design to compare different treatments, each treatment is applied to several experimental units, and the assignment of units to treatments is random. In many designs the number of units per treatment are equal and this is then called a **balanced design**. In psychology and education the experimental units are usually individuals. An ANOVA analysis enables causal inferences to be made in experimental designs by partitioning total variation between individuals (experimental units) into separate components, each component representing a different source of variation or treatment effect. It is then possible to identify the relative influence of the different treatments (independent variables) and to compare the between-treatments variation (the observed differences) to differences attributable to chance. Chance differences are any differences among individuals within the various treatment groups due to uncontrolled or unknown variables. This source of variation is conveniently termed **error variance**. The proportion of total variation attributable to treatments when compared with the proportion attributable to error forms the basis of the F-ratio or F-statistic. If the observed treatment effects, that is differences between treatments as summarised by treatment means, account for about the same proportion of variability in the response variable as the chance differences, then it is reasonable to assume that the observed treatment differences are probably just random fluctuations and conclude that there are no differences between treatments (the independent variables). If the proportion of variance accounted for by the between-treatment conditions is large compared with the error variance then this indicates a significant treatment effect which may warrant further investigation to find out which treatment(s) have a significant influence on the response variable.

Consider the vocabulary teaching methods experiment introduced in Chapter 1 (Example 2). The experimental units, in this case pupils, were randomly assigned to one of three treatment groups. One condition was silent reading, another was storytelling and the third was storytelling enhanced by pictures. After the intervention programme pupils' vocabulary acquisition was assessed and the mean scores for each of the three treatment groups were compared.

Analysis of variance methods can also be used with observational data which would include both comparative and survey designs. In comparative designs the impact on a metric response variable of categorical independent variables, representing naturally occurring groups, is assessed. The researcher is looking for the effect of membership of a particular group (independent variable) on the response variable. Variables used to define groups are called **factors**, for example, sex, and the various treatments within a factor are called **levels**, for example, male or female. The researcher looks to see whether there are differences between the means of the treatment groups. This term is used because of the original development of the ANOVA technique for analysis of true experimental designs. The investigator is really examining differences among the means of the levels of a factor, such as difference between mean scores for males and females. Comparative designs differ from true experimental designs because the levels of the independent variables (group membership – male, female) are not randomly assigned (they have already occurred or are natural categories) before their effects on the response variable are observed. Survey designs are similar to comparative designs except that mean differences for population subclasses are examined. The subclasses are described by the researcher, for example, a particular age band of 5–7-year-olds or a particular type of school. Subjects may even be subclassified by their responses after data has been collected for example – cognitive strategy users and non-strategy users might only be defined by the researchers after initial data analysis.

Repeated measurement designs are also frequently analysed using ANOVA techniques. Repeated measures or observations are treated as a factor in the analysis with measurements on one variable at different occasions corresponding to levels of the factor. The same subjects are involved in repeated measures. It is also possible to have mixed or 'split-plot' designs (a term derived from the initial development of the technique with agricultural experiments) where there are two factors, one of which is a repeated measurement where the same subjects are used and on the other where different subjects are used (between-subjects factor). This chapter serves only as an introduction to the analysis of experimental designs. There are many more complex designs requiring sophisticated analytic strategies. The interested reader is referred to Mead (1992) for a comprehensive guide to the principles of experimental design and analysis.

ANOVA and the General Linear Model

Consideration of analysis of variance from the point of view of an underlying **general linear model** means that its relationship to regression can easily be seen; more importantly this approach will form a foundation for the use of more sophisticated techniques such as multivariate analysis of variance (MANOVA – this is used when there are multiple response variables rather than a single response variable as is the case with univariate ANOVA), factor analysis and discriminant analysis. The underlying general linear model helps integrate ANOVA and regression which are often treated as independent analytic strategies. In fact, ANOVA is a special case of multiple linear regression. This common framework also helps the researcher see why ANOVA and regression share many of the same underlying assumptions. Most proprietary computer programmes for statistical analysis present data in a form consistent with the underlying general linear model, and unless you understand commonalities and differences between ANOVA and regression, you will be reduced to learning the meaning of computer output by rote rather than understanding and reporting with insight.

Consider the linear model for the one-factor vocabulary teaching experiment introduced in Chapter 3. It is represented here as an illustration of the general form of the ANOVA statistical model for a one-factor design,

$$y_{ij} = \mu + \alpha_i + \varepsilon_{ij}$$ **Statistical model for one-factor ANOVA – 8.20**

This general linear model describes the observed vocabulary score for the jth individual pupil from the ith treatment, y_{ij}, as the sum of three separate components: i) a response common to all pupils in the target population of interest, μ, hence the term **mean response**. This represents the average score of all pupils in the experiment; ii) a deviation from the mean response for a particular treatment group, α_i. In this experiment there are three treatments, so we have α_1 corresponding to all pupils who receive silent reading, α_2 corresponding to the storytelling only condition, and α_3 corresponding to the storytelling enhanced by pictures condition; iii) a unique deviation from the average treatment response for a particular jth pupil in the ith treatment, ε_{ij}. This is called the error term and in ANOVA is estimated as the deviation of the observed score from the appropriate treatment cell mean.

As an illustration of how the statistical model apportions effects of the independent variables treatment effects, consider a pupil in the silent reading condition who scores 16 on the vocabulary test. This score can be decomposed into the three components: i) the population mean score is 9; ii) the difference between the population mean score and the treatment mean for all pupils in the silent reading condition, say a later treatment mean of 12; and iii) the difference between the pupils score and the contribution of the mean treatment effect. The three components of the pupils score are as follows:

$$16 = \underset{\substack{\text{Population mean} \\ \text{score} \\ 9}}{\mu} + \underset{\substack{\text{Treatment mean} \\ \text{score} \\ 12}}{\alpha_1} + \underset{\substack{\text{Error residual} \\ \text{score}}}{\varepsilon_{ij}}$$

$$16 = 9 + 12 - 9 + 16 - 12$$

One point of difference between ANOVA and regression is in the estimation of the error term. In regression it is estimated as the difference between an observed and a predicted score (based on the linear model) rather than as in ANOVA, the deviation between an observed score and a cell mean. These different procedures can lead to different error estimates and associated degrees of freedom. Interpretation may also be different and this depends upon the assumptions the researcher makes about the relationship between the independent variables and the response variable. Estes (1991) discusses these points with illustrated examples.

Comparison of ANOVA and Regression Models

For the purpose of comparing the structural (statistical) models for ANOVA and regression, a two-factor design is described so that the interaction term in the model can be illustrated and interpretation of this effect discussed. Assume we modify the vocabulary experiment and make it a two-factor fixed effects design, one factor is sex with two levels male, female, and the other factor is treatment with two levels storytelling, and storytelling enhanced by pictures. The investigator wants to see whether there is an added effect of pictures and whether this is the same for both males and females. Sex is clearly a fixed effect (not under the control of the researcher) and treatment can be considered a fixed effect if we assume that the two treatments are not chosen at random from a range of possible treatments and the treatment would be the same in all replications of the experiment.

The statistical model for a Two-way fixed effect ANOVA can be written as,

$$y_{ijk} = \mu + \alpha_i + \beta_j + \alpha\beta_{ij} + \varepsilon_{ijk}$$
$$\text{Pupil} = \text{constant} + \text{teaching} + \text{sex} + \text{teaching} \times \text{sex} + \text{error}$$
$$\text{score} \qquad\qquad\quad \text{method} \qquad\qquad \text{method}$$

Full model for ANOVA 2-way – 8.21

y_{ijk} represents the vocabulary score of the kth pupil, in treatment condition ij, μ is the population mean vocabulary score, α_i is the population treatment effect for the intervention (α_1 = storytelling, α_2 = storytelling + pictures), β_j is the population effect for sex (β_1 = male, β_2 = female), $\alpha\beta_{ij}$ is the **interaction** effect of treatments and ε_{ijk} is the error term for pupil k. The interaction term in the model represents the average effect on the pupils' vocabulary score attributable to a particular combination of teaching method and sex.

The full 2-Way ANOVA statistical model can be rewritten in a regression format,

$$Y_{ijk} = \mu x_0 + \alpha_1 x_1 + \alpha_2 x_2 + \beta_1 x_3 + \beta_2 x_4 + \alpha\beta_{11} x_5 + \alpha\beta_{12} x_6 + \alpha\beta_{21} x_7 + \alpha\beta_{22} x_8 + \varepsilon_{ijk}$$

Each value of x will be either 0 or 1 depending upon the treatment combination. For example, a pupil who was in treatment combination 2 for both factors ($\alpha = 2$ is storytelling + pictures and $\beta = 2$ is female) would have: x_0 set to 1 because the overall mean always has an effect, x_2, x_4 and x_8 would also be set to 1 because they represent the main effects of storytelling + pictures, the main effect of being a female and the interaction effect of being in the storytelling + pictures and female group. The other x's would be set to zero (in the regression framework x is the value of what is called an indicator variable) indicating that the other treatment effects and combinations do not contribute to pupil k's score.

When comparing the ANOVA and regression statistical models a commonality which, on reflection, should be clear is that the response variable is hypothesized to be a weighted combination of independent variables, in regression these weights are called **regression coefficients** and in ANOVA they are called treatment effects. Both models are also linear in their parameters, that is the weighted parameters are assumed to be additive. In ANOVA this is termed the 'additivity' of the model and in regression the term linearity of the model is used.

Significance Tests and Estimation in ANOVA

As in regression analysis, the sums of squares derived from sample data are used to estimate the various components of the ANOVA model. Sums of squares for the overall model are partitioned into component sums of squares representing independent variables, any interactions and error variance. Associated with each source of variance are degrees of freedom, mean squares and F-statistics. These component sums of squares and associated statistics are output in most statistical packages (although the terminology might vary).

The general linear model approach to testing the significance of a linear model (significant model effect) is to compare the fit of two statistical models, a **full model** (sometimes called an effects model) and a **reduced model** (when there is no 'treatment' this is called a means only model). In a One-way ANOVA the full model, where the factor has an effect, is:

$$y_{ij} = \mu + \alpha_i + \varepsilon_{ij}$$

The reduced model which is just the overall mean effect and underlying variation, is

$$y_{ij} = \mu_i + \varepsilon_{ij}$$

y_{ij} is the value for the jth observation for the mean treatment i plus underlying variation.

For a Two-way ANOVA, the effect of any interaction can be evaluated by comparing the full model (Equation 8.21) with a reduced model where the interaction term is deleted.

$$y_{ijk} = \mu + \alpha_i + \beta_j + \varepsilon_{ijk} \qquad \textbf{Reduced model for Two-way ANOVA} - 8.22$$

The interaction sums of squares is evaluated as the difference between the error sums of squares for the full model and the error sums of squares for the reduced model. There are more direct ways of estimating the interaction sums of square but this approach works with both balanced and unbalanced designs (unequal numbers in the cells of the design).

In a One-way ANOVA, for example, the null hypothesis tested is H_0: $\mu_1 = \mu_2 = \mu_3 = \mu_n$, the means of the treatment groups are equal or in model terms, all α_i's are equal. The alternative hypothesis is that the means are not equal. Two measures of variation are used in the test of significance of the overall model: 1) **Sums of squares** describing the variation *between* treatment groups in terms of how different the treatment group means are, and 2) Sums of squares describing variation attributable to individuals *within* the treatment groups (chance variation among individuals). The ratio of the between to within sources of variance (sums of squares), each sums of squares divided by their appropriate degrees of freedom, forms the F-statistic and is an overall test of the model fit. The sums of squares divided by degrees of freedom is called the **Mean Square**. Degrees of freedom (df) are values associated with sums of squares, the total df are partitioned into df associated with each source of variance. If a model fits the data well, then differences among treatment group means will be large in comparison to the differences among individuals. That is the **Mean Square Between** groups MS_b a summary of treatment mean differences, will be larger than the measure of differences among individuals within all groups called the **Mean Square Within** groups. In this situation the effects of the treatment groups will be distinguished from random differences among individuals, and the null hypothesis of equal treatment group means is likely to be rejected. The F-test statistic will be larger than 1 (equivalent to the null hypothesis of equal variation among treatments and individuals – treatment group effects are no more than random fluctuations) and a small p-value will indicate a significant statistical model has been fitted to the data. We would conclude there are differences between treatment group means.

Once a model has been fitted to empirical data and an F-test statistic is found to be significant, then the investigator will need to determine the nature of the differences among treatment means. Even if the overall null hypothesis of equal group means is rejected there may be some means that do not differ from one another. Comparisons among means may be suggested by the data itself and these are called **post hoc comparisons**. Alternatively planned comparisons may have been determined before the analysis and in this case **contrasts** of differences between means are performed following the F-test.

In SAS, One-way ANOVAs can be performed by several procedures two of which are PROC ANOVA, which can only handle balanced designs, and PROC GLM (meaning General Linear Models). Since the latter is the most flexible it is illustrated in this chapter. In PROC GLM *post hoc* comparisons can be performed using the **means** statement and confidence limits for the differences in means for each pairwise comparison can be output using the CLDIFF option. When specific hypothesis tests are suggested prior to data analysis preplanned comparisons can be performed in SAS using the **contrast** and **estimate** statements. The **contrast** statement generates a sums of squares for the contrast and an F-value for testing the null hypothesis of no difference (linear combination of parameters = 0). The **estimate** statement, used in the same way as the contrast statement generates an estimate of the difference in means, the standard error of the difference, a t-test to show whether the estimate of the difference is significantly different from zero and an associated p-value. Confidence intervals can then be constructed for the estimate of the difference in the means.

In the remainder of this chapter, four ANOVA procedures are described: One-way ANOVAs (both unrelated and related); a Two-way ANOVA (2×2) Factorial design (unrelated); and a Two-way ANOVA Split Plot design (mixed, a related and an unrelated factor). Worked examples of a One-way related and unrelated analysis are presented and compared with computer output so that the reader can grasp the general principles of the ANOVA approach in the context of the general linear model. These principles can be extended to Two-way and more complex factorial designs. Calculations by hand for the Two-way analyses are tedious (and prone to error) and are therefore omitted. The researcher is likely to use a proprietary computer package for analyses of more complex designs and emphasis is therefore given to interpretation of computer output for a Two-way factorial and a split plot design. All of these ANOVA procedures and associated hypothesis tests are based on assumptions underpinning, use of the F-test statistic, and underlying assumptions of the general linear model. These assumptions, and ways to verify them, rather than listing them under each ANOVA procedure are presented here as a unified set.

Assumptions for ANOVA

1 The response variable should be a continuous metric, at least at the interval level of measurement (equal intervals).
2 The distribution of the response variable should be approximately normal in the population, but not necessarily normal in the sample.
3 The variance of the response variable should be equal in all population subgroups (treatment groups) represented in the design. This is the homogeneity of variance assumption. *(Verify by plotting residual against predicted values. A random scatter of points about the mean of zero indicates*

constant variance and satisfies this assumption. A funnel shaped pattern indicates nonconstant variance. Outlier observations are easily spotted on this plot.)

4   Errors should be independent. This is the most important assumption for use of the *F*-statistic in ANOVA. To prevent correlated errors subjects should be sampled at random (independent of each other) and subjects' responses should be independent.

Assumptions specific to the general linear model include:

5   Effects should be additive, that is the relationship among the independent variables and the response variable is assumed to be additive. Each independent variable contributes an effect to the response variable independent of all other factors in the model. *(Check the underlying theory if there is one, for example, for some learning theories the response variable might be a multiplicative rather than additive function of independent variables.)*

6   Errors should be unbiased independently and normally distributed with constant variance for significance tests to be valid. In ANOVA the errors or residuals represent deviations of observed scores from cell means. Survey researchers are most likely to encounter problems of response bias which gives rise to biased errors. *(Verify normality of errors by plotting residuals against the normalized score of the rank of the residuals. A straight line plot indicates normality.)*

   (If an investigator is more interested in treatment mean differences than estimate of the treatment means then any bias in errors can be assumed to be constant across all treatments, unless there is reason to believe otherwise.)

ANOVA is moderately robust against violations of normality and homogeneity of variance assumptions but dependencies among subjects or their responses (such as same subjects or repeated measures within subjects) for independent ANOVA invalidates the analysis.

   Hypothesis tests are generally of the form that subgroup means or treatment means are equal. Sample means are used to estimate these fixed population parameters.

8.7   One-way ANOVA *F*-test (unrelated)

When to Use

This procedure is used when an investigator wants to test for differences among the means of two or more independent groups (treatment groups in experimental designs or subgroups in survey and comparative designs). The procedure may be viewed as an extension of the independent *t*-test when there are three or more independent groups. In an unrelated design, different subjects appear in each of the treatment conditions or subgroups. The hypothesis tested by the *F*-statistic is that population subgroup (or treatment group) means are equal. The researcher is often interested in which means differ and in what way. A plot of the subgroup means can be very informative as well as modified *t*-tests on *post hoc* pairwise comparisons of subgroup means. Less frequently in educational research an investigator might specify a particular hypothesis prior to data analysis in which case a *t*-test on the preplanned comparison of interest and an estimate of the mean difference with confidence limits would be appropriate.

Example from the Literature

The efficacy of three different writing courses designed for postgraduate research students, a cognitive strategies approach, a generative writing course and a product-centred approach, is reported by Torrance, Thomas and Robinson (1993). Of 104 students in total who participated in the study, forty-one completed the product-centred course, thirty completed the strategies course and thirty-three completed the generative writing course. At the end of the course a questionnaire was administered which asked five questions about how helpful they thought the course would be with different aspects of the writing process. Each response was scored on a scale from 1, 'not at all helpful' to 5 'very helpful'. Data presented in the authors' original paper is shown in Table 8.8.

Table 8.8: Students' assessment of how helpful the course would be in producing a piece of writing

	COURSE		
	Product-centred	Cognitive strategies	Generative writing
Getting started	4.0(0.87)	4.5(0.78)	4.2(0.81)
In the middle	3.6(1.0)	3.9(0.92)	3.7(1.0)
Finishing off	3.5(0.97)	3.8(1.1)	3.3(1.2)
Developing thinking*	3.7(0.92)	4.5(0.78)	4.2(0.98)
Expressing ideas*	3.1(1.1)	3.8(0.87)	3.8(1.1)

* Differences between courses significant at $p < 0.01$

This is an example of an independent One-way analysis of variance based on survey type data. Mean responses across the three independent subgroups (represented by participants who attended the three different writing courses) are compared. As five questions were asked, there are five one-way ANOVAS (one for each question). The authors reported, however, that there were significant differences for only two of the ANOVAs (two questions) among the three courses, Developing thinking: $F = 7.34$ [df](2,102), $p < 0.001$; and Expressing ideas: $F = 5.40$ [df] (2,98), $p < 0.01$. The two hypotheses tested here were: i) no differences in mean scores across the three courses on students; response to the question about Developing thinking; and ii) the same null hypothesis with respect to Expressing ideas. The degrees of freedom between subgroups is given by the number of groups − 1 = (3 − 1) = 2, the total degrees of freedom would be n − 1, and therefore the error degrees of freedom are given by subtraction, $df_{tot} - df_{between}$. In the authors' original table the sample sizes are not reported for each question mean, but it is evident from the reported degrees of freedom in the two F-tests (102 and 98) that the number of responses for at least two of the questions must have been different.

Once a significant *F*-test had been found, establishing that the three means corresponding to the three writing courses were different, the investigators performed a *post hoc* test, (called a Scheffe test) on pairwise comparisons of which there would be three. The authors reported that these *post hoc* tests indicated that in both cases (developing thinking and expressing ideas), the product-centred course was perceived as being significantly less help than both the cognitive strategies course and the generative writing course (p < 0.05).

Worked Example

In a simplified example taken from a PhD student's project on pupils' understanding of probability and cultural background, pupils' attributions about chance events were determined by asking them to respond to a series of statements, such as 'Getting a 6 on a normal dice depends on knowing how to throw the dice'. Attribution scores for eight pupils from each of three separate religious communities, Christian, Muslim and Jewish (24 pupils in total) are shown in Table 8.9.

Table 8.9: *Attribution scores for three religious groups*

	Christian Religion Group 1	Religious Community Muslim Religion Group 2	Jewish Religion Group 3
	17	22	18
	19	19	13
	18	22	18
	17	19	20
	18	19	12
	15	14	15
	16	15	17
	17	14	18
TOTAL	137	144	131
Mean	17.125	18.000	16.375

Data summarizing ANOVA computations are usually presented in an ANOVA table which identifies the sources of variance, sums of squares and degrees of freedom, means squares and *F*-statistics. (See for example, Figure 8.13.)

Source of variation	Degrees of Freedom (df)	SS	MS (SS/df)	F (MS_{mod}/MS_{error})
Between groups (MODEL)	$k - 1$			
Within individuals (ERROR)	$\sum\limits_{j=1}^{k}(n_j - 1)$			
CORRECTED TOTAL	$N - 1$			

Where:

SS Is the sums of squares
MS Is the mean square, sums of squares divided by the degrees of freedom
F   Is the ratio of MS effect to MS error
k   Is the number of independent groups (treatments or subgroups)
N   Is the total number of observations in the analysis
n_j Is the number of observations in the jth group (subgroup or treatment)

Figure 8.13 Layout of results table for One-way ANOVA

Consider for example the data presented in Table 8.9. The $df_{(between\ groups)}$ is $(3 - 1) = 2$. A degree of freedom is lost because deviations from the overall mean sum to zero. The constraint here is that the deviations of the subgroup means from the overall mean must sum to zero hence 1 df is lost. The degrees of freedom between individuals within groups, what is usually termed $df_{(error)}$, is again given by the constraint that deviations from each subgroup mean sum to zero. Here there are three subgroup means so the df are: $(n_1 - 1) + (n_2 - 1) + (n_3 - 1) = (8 - 1) + (8 - 1) + (8 - 1) = 21$. The error degrees of freedom can be evaluated simply by subtraction, $df_{(error)} = df_{(corrected\ total)} - df_{(between\ groups)} = (24 - 1) - 2 = 21$. The principle of evaluating the degrees of freedom is important to grasp. The corrected total degrees of freedom is simply, number of subjects $-1 = (24 - 1) = 23$.

Steps in Computation

To compute F-ratios the general procedure is 1) Identify the sources of variance and compute sums of squares for each source; 2) apportion degrees of freedom to each source of variance; 3) evaluate the mean squares; and 4) calculate F-statistics and determine probabilities.

Step 1: Compute sums of squares

a) *Sums of squares between groups (conditions or treatments)*
    Computation of sums of squares causes the most confusion in ANOVA calculations. It may help if you realize that the denominator value in a sums of squares calculation is the number of observations on which the total score in the numerator is based.
    Sums of squares between groups, $SS_{(bet)}$, is given by,

$$SS_{(bet)} = \Sigma\left(\frac{T_j^2}{n_j}\right) - \frac{(\Sigma x_i)^2}{N}$$

Sums of squares between subjects – 8.23

where:

T_j = Total score for the jth subgroup (treatment group)

n_j = Number in the jth subgroup (treatment group)

N = Total number of subjects

x_i = Individual score

This equation is appropriate for both balanced and unbalanced designs.

$$SS_{(bet)} = \frac{(137)^2}{8} + \frac{(144)^2}{8} + \frac{(131)^2}{8} - \frac{(412)^2}{24}$$

$SS_{(bet)}$ = 7083.25 − 7072.6667 = 10.5833

b) *Sums of squares within individuals (error sums of squares)*

The error sums of squares, $SS_{(error)}$, is given by

$$SS_{(e)} = \Sigma x_i^2 - \Sigma\left(\frac{T_j^2}{n_j}\right)$$

Sums of squares error – 8.24

Where:

T_j = Total score for the jth subgroup (treatment group)

n_j = Number in the jth subgroup (treatment group)

x_i = Individual score

$$SS_{(e)} = 7224 - \frac{137^2}{8} + \frac{144^2}{8} + \frac{131^2}{8}$$

$SS_{(error)}$ = 7224 − 7083.25 = 140.750

c) *Corrected total sums of squares*

The corrected total sums of squares, $SS_{(ct)}$ is given in the usual way

$$SS_{(ct)} = \Sigma x_i^2 - \frac{(\Sigma x_i)^2}{N}$$

Corrected total sums of squares – 8.25

Where:

x_i = Individual score

N = Total of all subjects

$$SS_{(ct)} = 7224 - \frac{(412)^2}{24}$$

$SS_{(ct)}$ = 7224 − 7072.6667 = 151.333

The reader should note that an easier computation for $SS_{(error)}$ is given by:

$SS_{(error)}$ = $SS_{(ct)}$ − $SS_{(bet)}$ = 151.333 − 10.5833 = 140.750

Step 2: Evaluate degrees of freedom (for explanation see above)

The df for $SS_{(bet)}$ is 2, the df for $SS_{(error)}$ is 21 and the $df_{(ct)}$ is 23.

Step 3: Evaluate mean squares

The mean square for between groups $MS_{(bet)}$ is $SS_{(bet)}/df_{(bet)} = 10.5833/2 = 5.2917$. Mean square error is calculated in exactly the same way, $MS_{(error)} = SS_{(error)}/df_{(error)} = 140.750/21 = 6.7024$.

Step 4: Calculate F-ratios

In this example there is only one *F*-ratio to calculate which is a test of the hypothesis that subgroup mean attribution scores are equal. The *F*-statistic is given as $MS_{(bet)}/MS_{(error)} = 5.2917/6.7024 = 0.7895$ with 2 and 21 degrees of freedom. The degrees of freedom of 2 relates the numerator mean square ($MS_{(bet)}$) and degrees of freedom of 21 corresponds to the denominator df ($MS_{(error)}$). We can now summarize these results in an ANOVA table:

Source of variation	Degrees of freedom	SS	MS	F
Between groups (Model)	2	10.583	5.292	$F = 0.79$; df2,21
Within individuals (Error)	21	140.750	6.702	
Corrected total	23	151.333		

Interpretation

We can look up the significance of the *F*-statistic corresponding to our chosen alpha level of 5 per cent, in Table 7 of Appendix A4. We enter the column at the top of the table with numerator df of 2 and find where this intersects with a row or denominator df of 21. The critical *F*-value in the body of the table is 3.47. The observed *F*-value does not fall beyond this critical value and therefore we cannot reject the null hypothesis of equal means, $F = 0.79$, df 2,21. It therefore appears that pupils in the three religious groups have similar attributions about the concept of probability.

Computer Analysis

The SAS procedure PROC GLM is used to perform an analysis of variance on the data shown in Table 8.9. PROC GLM (general linear models) uses the method of least squares analysis to fit statistical models to data. It is suitable for both balanced and unbalanced designs and can be used for both univariate and multivariate analyses. To perform a One-way ANOVA the following SAS code would be submitted:

```
proc glm data=a;
  class religion;
  model attrib1 = religion;
  output out = new r=res1 p=pred1;
  run;
```

The **class** statement specifies the variable(s) that categorizes the data into subgroups. The **model** statement specifies on the left of the equals sign the response variable(s) and on the right of the sign the independent variables that you want to model. In this example we want to determine the effects of different categories of the independent variable, *religion* (different religions) on the response variable *attrib1* (attribution score). The **output** statement outputs the residuals and predicted values from the fitted statistical model to a data set which is named *new*. The residual and predicted values are named *res1* and *pred1* respectively.

The summary ANOVA table produced by SAS is shown in Figure 8.14. Although there are no missing values in this particular data set, PROC GLM can handle missing data. The GLM procedure actually estimates values for the missing data points from the fitted least squares solution such that the residuals sum to zero.

To check the model assumptions of normality and homogeneity of variance the fitted residuals are ranked using PROC RANK, using the following SAS code.

General Linear Models Procedure
Class Level Information

Class	Levels	Values
Religion	3	1 2 3

Number of observations in data set = 24

General Linear Models Procedure

Dependent Variable: ATTRIB1

Source	DF	Sum of Squares	Mean Square	F Value	Pr > F
Model	2	10.5833333	5.2916667	0.79	0.4671
Error	21	140.7500000	6.7023810		
Corrected Total	23	151.3333333			

R-Square	C.V.	Root MSE	ATTRIB1 Mean
0.069934	15.08095	2.58890	17.1667

Source	DF	Type I SS	Mean Square	F Value	Pr > F
Religion	2	10.5833333	5.2916667	0.79	0.4671

Source	DF	Type III SS	Mean Square	F Value	Pr > F
Religion	2	10.5833333	5.2916667	0.79	0.4671

Figure 8.14: *Analysis of variance from PROC GLM*

```
    *** rank the residuals ***;
proc rank data=new ties=mean normal=blom;
 var res1; ranks norm1;
run;
    *** plot to check the models assumptions ***;
proc plot;
   plot res1*norm1;
   plot res1*pred1;
   title4 'test of normality';
run;
```

The option ties = mean is used so that any tied ranks would take the mean value, and the option normal = blom converts the ranked residuals into normal scores. The variable (norm1) is thus a normalized score of the ranked residuals. A plot of the residuals (res1) against the normalized rank residuals (norm1) should give a straight line plot, and a plot of res1 against pred1 should give a random scatter of points if the assumptions of normality and homogeneity of variance are valid. Output from these plots is shown in Figure 8.15.

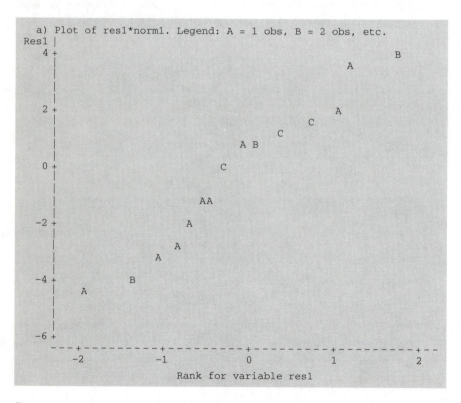

Figure 8.15a: Plot to check ANOVA assumptions

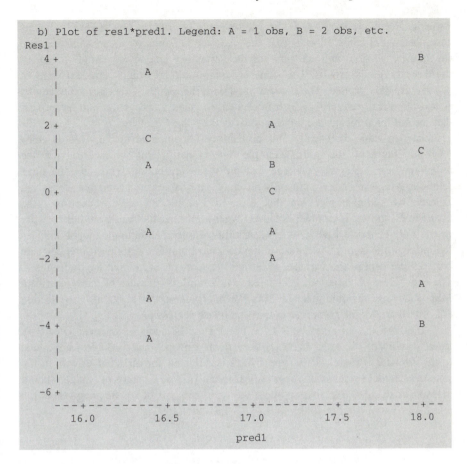

```
  b) Plot of res1*pred1.  Legend: A = 1 obs, B = 2 obs, etc.
Res1 |
  4 +                                                                B
     |                  A
     |
     |
     |
  2 +                                      A
     |              C
     |
     |              A                      B
     |                                                                C
  0 +                                      C
     |
     |
     |              A                      A
     |
 -2 +                                      A
     |
     |                                                                A
     |              A
     |
 -4 +                                                                B
     |              A
     |
     |
     |
 -6 +
     - - - + - - - - - - - - - + - - - - - - - - - + - - - - - - - - - + - - - - - - - - - + - -
          16.0            16.5            17.0            17.5            18.0
                                      pred1
```

Figure 8.15b: Plot to check ANOVA assumptions

Interpretation of Computer Output

To see whether the data meets the necessary assumptions for ANOVA the plots shown in Figures 8.15 a and b should be inspected first. A general linear trend is indicated in the first plot and there is no discernible pattern to the scatter of points in the second plot so the assumptions appear to have been met.

Looking at the first section of output in Figure 8.14, summary information on the variables entered in the model is printed. You should look at the number of observations and the levels of the class variable to check that the model has been specified as you intended.

The next section of output presents results of the analysis of variance in the form of an ANOVA table. You should first examine the degrees of freedom to check they are correct. Under the column heading Source there are three row headings, Model, Error and Corrected Total. The total variation attributable to all the independent variables in the model, (in this case there is only one independent variable, Religion) is given as the Model sums of squares (10.5833333). In this case, the model sums of squares is the same as the sums of squares for Religion (in the next section) and accounts for the variability among the sample means of the three religious groups. The sums of squares for error and corrected sums of squares are also printed. These correspond with the values in the worked example. A test of overall model fit which in this case is also a test of the null hypothesis that the Religion means are equal is provided by the F-statistic, $F = 0.79$, and the associated p-value of 0.4671. This probability is compared to the selected alpha level of 5 per cent, and in this example there is insufficient evidence to reject the null hypothesis, and we conclude that the mean attribution scores for the three religious groups are not significantly different – the same conclusion that we arrived at in the worked example. Note that in the SAS output the exact probability of the obtained F-statistic is printed, however, when reporting the results authors usually give a 5 per cent or a 1 per cent level. Additional information in the output includes R-Square, a measure of variation in the data attributable to group differences here only 6.9 per cent of the variance in attribution scores is accounted for by Religion. The coefficient of variation, CV statistic, is a unitless measure of variation (Root MSE/Response variable mean) $\times$ 100. For interpretation of Root MSE see section 8.2, interpretation of computer output for linear regression.

The SAS output gives both Type I and Type III sums of squares. Type I SS takes account of the order in which the effects (independent variables) are added to the statistical model. The Type III SS is adjusted for all other effects in the statistical model (order is unimportant). Generally Type III sums of squares should be used. A detailed explanation about the types of sums of squares is given in the text *SAS System for Linear Models* (SAS Institute, 1991).

A priori and post hoc Multiple Comparison Procedures

Once a significant F-statistic has been found, the nature of the differences among the means should be investigated. In this example a preplanned hypothesis test was not specified and so an a priori comparison would not be used. Similarly, the F-statistic is not significant so a *post hoc* test would not usually be appropriate. For illustrative purposes, however, both an a priori test to estimate the differences in means between Group 1 and Group 2, and a *post hoc* test for all pairwise comparisons among subgroup means are illustrated. There are a number of multiple comparison tests and the reader is referred to an informative text by Toothaker (1991) on choice of appropriate multiple comparison test procedures.

Preplanned comparisons

When variances are homogeneous and sample sizes are equal then a planned t-test can be computed by substituting the standard error of the difference in the usual t-test with the MS_{error} value from the ANOVA output. The obtained t-statistic is evaluated against degrees of freedom for MS_{error} (in the ANOVA output). Consider for example a preplanned comparison of the difference in means between Group 1 (Christian) and Group 2 (Muslim), the observed difference is −0.875, an investigator wants to know whether this difference is significant. As there are equal sample sizes and variances are not drastically different, the *t*-statistic is given by

$$t = \frac{\bar{x}_1 - \bar{x}_2}{\sqrt{\dfrac{2MS_e}{n}}} = -\frac{0.875}{1.2944} = -0.676$$

where *n* is the number in the group, here 8. A 95 per cent interval for the difference could be estimated.

When sample sizes are unequal or when variances are heterogeneous, individual variances and a Satterthwaite correction for degrees of freedom should be used (see section on *t*-tests). Preplanned comparisons can be handled easily in SAS. If an estimate of the difference in means is required then the statements LSMEANS and ESTIMATE are used. Least square means (LSMEANS) adjust for unequal sample sizes and when we have a balanced design are the same as the ordinary means. To output an estimate of the difference in means between Group 1 and Group 2, an orthogonal contrast because Group 3 is not involved, the following SAS code is entered after the model statement:

```
lsmeans religion /stderr pdiff;
estimate '1-2' religion 1 -1 0;
```

The label 1–2 is given to the selected contrast in the SAS output – see Figure 8.16.

General Linear Models Procedure

Dependent Variable: ATTRIB1

Parameter	Estimate	T for H0: Parameter=0	Pr > |T|	Std Error of Estimate
1-2	-0.87500000	-0.68	0.5064	1.29444785

Figure 8.16: Estimate of the difference between the means of Group 1 and Group 2

Interpretation

The estimate of the difference and the *t*-value (−0.68) are the same as in the previous worked example. We would conclude that there is no significant difference between Christian and Muslims in their mean attribution scores.

Post hoc comparisons

Multiple *t*-tests on a set of means should be discouraged because this will lead to a high **experiment-wise** error rate, that is for all the comparisons made in the analysis of an experiment (or survey) at least one Type I error will be made. If we assume that α' is the Type I error rate for a single comparison then the experiment-wise error rate, $EW\alpha$ is $1 - (1 - \alpha')^c$, where c is the number of orthogonal (independent) comparisons in the experiment. For example, with only two comparisons, and an alpha of 5 per cent, then $EW\alpha$ is about 10 per cent $[1 - (1 - 0.05)^2 = 9.75\%]$. Most *post hoc* multiple comparison procedures adjust for experiment-wise error, this is one reason why multiple ordinary *t*-tests should not be used.

To perform a Newman Keul's *post hoc* procedure, which adjusts for experiment-wise error in all pairwise comparisons, the following SAS code would be entered after the MODEL statement,

```
means religion /snk;
```

Output from this procedure is shown in Figure 8.17:

```
                General Linear Models Procedure
          Student Newman-Keuls test for variable: ATTRIB1
  NOTE:   This test controls the type I experiment-wise error
          rate under the complete null hypothesis but not
          under partial null hypotheses.

              Alpha= 0.05  df= 21  MSE= 6.702381

            Number of Means          2          3
            Critical Range   2.6919532   3.2627471

Means with the same letter are not significantly different.

            SNK Grouping     Mean      N     SET

                 A          18.000      8      2
                 A
                 A          17.125      8      1
                 A
                 A          16.375      8      3
```

Figure 8.17: SAS output for Newman-Keul's multiple comparison procedure

Interpretation

As expected, in this particular analysis there are no significant differences among any of the means.

8.8 One-way ANOVA *F*-test (related)

When to Use

Many research designs in psychology involve subjects in repeated measurements, that is the same (or matched) subjects participate in each of the experimental conditions. Observations or measurements are therefore correlated and treatment effects are analysed using a repeated measures analysis of variance. Another name for this analysis is **within subjects ANOVA** because comparison of treatment effects is within subjects.

In a related ANOVA differences in scores attributable to individuals, (subjects) can be treated as a separate source of variance because the same subjects take part in each of the treatment conditions. This source of variance is called Subjects variance, $SS_{(subj)}$. The other variance components, we would have in a One-way ANOVA are a source of variance attributable to **between** treatment conditions, $SS_{(bet)}$, and error variance which represents differences among subjects **within** each of the treatment conditions, $SS_{(error)}$. Recall that in a One-way unrelated ANOVA we only have two sources of variance: *between* treatments and *within* individuals which is the error variance.

In a related ANOVA the *F*-test of significance is usually constructed on the ratio, $MS_{(bet)}/MS_{(error)}$, the error term is reduced in comparison to what it would be in an unrelated analysis because variance accounted for by subjects has been partitioned separately. In most repeated measurement analyses Subjects are treated as a random effect in the statistical model, the treatment effect is usually considered to be fixed. The distinction between fixed and random effects is of importance when there is more than one factor; this is discussed in section 8.9. In a related ANOVA the $MS_{(error)}$ is not a pure error term because part of the variation within subjects is attributable to the different treatments, and part is due to individual differences. An *F*-test of significance for Subjects is not therefore valid unless we are willing to assume that there is no interaction between subjects and treatments. Ordinarily this is not a problem because the researcher is interested in differences among treatment means and not differences among Subjects.

The assumptions for related ANOVA are the same as for the unrelated analysis with the additional requirements of homogeneity of covariance among population error terms for the different treatments and independence of errors for the different treatment conditions. This assumption is of little concern in a practical setting but the interested reader should consult Winer (1962), Chapter 4.

Example from the Literature

In an experiment designed to investigate the effects of visual interference on visuospatial working memory (Toms, Morris and Foley, 1994) twelve subjects (university undergraduates) were presented with two tasks – one spatial imagery and the other verbal. Subjects performed each task under four conditions (eyes shut; looking at blank screen; looking at a white square; and looking at a changing pattern) the order of conditions was counterbalanced using a Latin square design (for explanation of this design see Winer, 1962). Each condition was presented in a block of four trials. The response variable score was the mean number of correctly recalled sentences per trial in each condition for the spatial and verbal tasks. Data from the authors' paper is presented in Table 8.10:

Table 8.10:   Spatial imagery data

| | Mean number correct per trial | | | |
	Eyes shut	Blank screen	Square	Pattern
Spatial task	6.8	6.7	5.5	5.5
	(1.0)	(0.9)	(1.2)	(0.9)
Verbal task	4.6	4.6	4.4	4.8
	(0.8)	(1.2)	(1.0)	(0.9)

In this example there is one response variable (mean number of correctly recalled sentences) and one repeated measures factor, interference, with four levels corresponding to the four conditions. A One-way repeated measures ANOVA is therefore an appropriate analytic procedure if the researchers want to determine whether there is a significant interference effect-difference among condition means. To do this the researchers need to compare subjects' performance over the four experimental conditions (between treatment groups). Differences between subjects within the conditions is not usually of interest in this design. The treatments are counterbalanced to reduce serial effects (learning) from one treatment to the next. Each subject takes all tasks and conditions and the general idea is to see whether differences between condition means account for more variance than differences between individuals *within* each of the four conditions. Differences in scores among subjects as a whole are treated as a separate source of variance in this design.

The null hypothesis would be that variance between conditions is equal to the variance between individuals within conditions. Should this be true it implies that differences among condition means are no greater than chance variations, or stated another way the condition means are equal. In this design, the total degrees of freedom (df) are the number of measurements −1. Three subjects were assigned to each row of 4 trials (12 measures) and there were 4 experimental blocks giving 48 measures, total df is therefore 47. The degrees of freedom for subjects is given by number of subjects − 1 = (12 − 1) 11, and degrees of freedom for conditions is number of conditions − 1 = (4 − 1) 3. The degrees of freedom for error term is given by $df_{total} - df_{between\ conditions} - df_{subjects}, = (47 - 3 - 11) = 33$.

The authors reported a significant interference effect for the spatial task, $F = 23.1$, df 3,33, $p < 0.0001$. They followed this F-test with a *post hoc* Newman-Keuls test on all pairwise comparisons. This procedure is designed for equal sample sizes. Inspection of these comparisons showed that performance on the square and changing-pattern conditions was significantly poorer than in either of the other two conditions ($p < 0.01$).

Worked Example

A subset of data is taken from an evaluation of a reading recovery programme and used here to illustrate the principles and computational details of a repeated measures analysis. In the recovery programme five children were tested for reading accuracy on three occassions, when they entered the programme (Time 1); two weeks after entry (Time two); and one month after entry (Time 3). All pupils remained in the programme for a period of at least one month. The data is shown in Table 8.11.

Table 8.11: Reading accuracy scores for pupils in the reading recovery programme

Subject	Time 1	Reading Score Time 2	Time 3	Total Score
1	5	7	12	24
2	4	6	15	25
3	4	7	8	19
4	6	7	13	26
5	3	5	6	14
Occasion Totals	22	32	54	GT = 108

Steps in Computation

To compute F-ratios, the usual sums of squares have to be computed, the degrees of freedom determined, and mean square terms calculated.

Step 1: Compute sums of squares

a) Sums of squares *between* treatments (conditions) $SS_{(bet)}$
This term is evaluated using the following formula:

$$SS_{(bet)} = \Sigma\left(\frac{T_s^2}{n_j}\right) - \frac{(\Sigma x_i)^2}{n_t n_s}$$

Sums of squares between subjects (repeated measures) – 8.26

where:
T_s = Total score for all subjects at each measurement occassion
n_j = Number in the jth subgroup (treatment group)
n_t = Number of treatments (conditions)
n_s = Number of subjects
x_i = Individual score

$$SS_{(bet)} = \frac{(22)^2}{5} + \frac{(32)^2}{5} + \frac{(54)^2}{5} - \frac{(108)^2}{3 \times 5}$$
$$SS_{(bet)} = 884.8 - 777.6 = 107.2$$

b) Sums of squares for *subjects* within treatments $SS_{(subj)}$
The subjects sums of squares are given by:

$$SS_{(subj)} = \Sigma\left(\frac{T_{rm}^2}{n_{rm}}\right) - \frac{(\Sigma x_i)^2}{n_t n_s}$$

Sums of squares for subjects (repeated measures) – 8.27

where:

T_{rm} = Total score over repeated measurements for each subject
n_{rm} = Number of repeated measures
n_t = Number of treatments (conditions)
n_s = Number of subjects
x_i = Individual score

$$SS_{(subj)} = \frac{(24)^2}{3} + \frac{(25)^2}{3} + \frac{(19)^2}{3} + \frac{(26)^2}{3} + \frac{(14)^2}{3} - \frac{(108)^2}{3 \times 5}$$

$SS_{(subj)} = 811.333 - 777.600 = 33.733$

c) Corrected total sums of squares $SS_{(ct)}$

The corrected total sums of squares are given in the usual way:

$$SS_{(ct)} = \Sigma x_i^2 - \frac{(\Sigma x_i)^2}{n_t n_s}$$ **Corrected total sums of squares**
(repeated measures) – 8.28

Where:

x_i = Individual score
n_t = Number of treatments (conditions)
n_s = Number of subjects

$$SS_{(ct)} = 948 - \frac{(108)^2}{3 \times 5}$$

$SS_{(ct)} = 948 - 777.6 = 170.40$

d) Error sums of squares $SS_{(error)}$

The error sums of squares are obtained by subtraction,

$$SS_{(error)} = SS_{(ct)} - SS_{(subj)} - SS_{(bet)}$$
$SS_{(error)} = 170.400 - 33.733 - 107.20 = 29.467$

Step 2: Evaluate degrees of freedom

The df for $SS_{(bet)}$ are number of conditions – 1 = 2; df for $SS_{(subj)}$ are the number of subjects – 1 = 4; the df $SS_{(ct)}$ are the total number of scores – 1 = 14; and the df for $SS_{(error)}$ are obtained by subtraction of ($df_{(bet)} + df_{(subj)}$) from $df_{(ct)} = (14 - (2 + 4)) = 8$.

Step 3: Evaluate mean squares

The mean square for between conditions (over the three occasions): $MS_{(bet)}$ is $SS_{(bet)}/df_{(bet)} = 107.2000/2 = 53.6$. Mean square error is calculated in exactly the same way for $MS_{(subj)}$ and $MS_{(error)}$: $MS_{(subj)} = SS_{(subj)}/df_{(subj)} = 33.733/4 = 8.433$; $MS_{(error)} = SS_{(error)}/df_{(error)} = 29.467/8 = 3.6834$.

Step 4: Calculate F-ratios

The main hypothesis of interest is whether there are any differences in reading accuracy over the period in which pupils were in the reading recovery programme, that is whether mean scores differ over time. A test of this hypothesis is given by the F-test statistic which is $MS_{(bet)}/MS_{(error)}$ = 53.6/3.6834 = 14.5518. If we assume no interaction between subjects and measurement occasions, the hypothesis of overall differences among subjects is tested by the F-statistic which is $MS_{(subj)}/MS_{(error)}$ = 8.433/3.6834 = 2.2895.

Interpretation

The F-statistics are interpreted as usual (see previous worked example). For the between conditions effect, the critical value of F at the 5 per cent level with 2 and 8 df is 4.46. Since the obtained F of 14.55 (rounded) is larger than this we can reject the null hypothesis and conclude that there are significant differences in reading accuracy over the three measurement occasions; $F = 14.55$; df 2,8; $p < 0.05$. For subjects, the critical F-value is 3.84, since the observed value of 2.29 is less than this we can conclude that overall, differences among subjects are not statistically significant. Results of these tests can be presented in a summary table as follows:

Table 8.12: Summary table for One-way repeated measures ANOVA

Source of variation	Degrees of freedom	SS	MS	F
Between occasions	2	107.200	53.60	F = 14.55; df 2,8
Subjects	4	33.733	8.433	F = 2.29; df 4,8
Error	8	29.467	3.6834	
Corrected total	14	170.400		

Computer Analysis

The following SAS code performs a One-way repeated measures ANOVA on the data presented in Table 8.11.

```
data a;
   input subj t1 t2 t3;
   cards;
1  8 7 4
2  7 8 5
3  9 5 3
4  5 4 6
5  6 6 2
6  8 7 4
;
```

```
data b; set a;
    drop t1-t3;
    time=1; score=t1; output;
    time=2; score=t2; output;
    time=3; score=t3; output;
proc glm data=b;
  class subj time;
  model score= subj time ;
run;
```

Data is usually in the format of one case per line, which has a case number or some other subject identification followed by the response variable score for each of the measurement occasions (see data after the *cards* statement). To create a single response variable *score* for use in PROC GLM a data step is used to rearrange the data. This new variable score is the reading accuracy score at each measurement occasion (time 1, time 2 and time 3 in Table 8.11). To associate each score with its measurement occasion a variable *time* is created. The PROC GLM procedure analyses the response variable score with subject and time as the independent variables. For an explanation of the MODEL statement refer to the description given in the section on computer analysis for an unrelated One-way ANOVA. SAS output for this analysis is shown in Figure 8.18.

```
                    General Linear Models Procedure
                       Class Level Information

                    Class     Levels      Values

                    Subj        5        1 2 3 4 5
                    Time        3        1 2 3

              Number of observations in data set = 15

                    General Linear Models Procedure
Dependent Variable: SCORE
Source          DF    Sum of Squares    Mean Square    F Value    Pr > F

Model            6     140.933333        23.488889       6.38     0.0100
Error            8      29.466667         3.683333
Corrected
Total           14     170.400000

          R-Square           C.V.            Root MSE          SCORE Mean

          0.827074         26.65557          1.91920            7.20000

Source          DF    Type I SS         Mean Square    F Value    Pr > F

Subj             4     33.733333          8.433333       2.29     0.1481
Time             2    107.200000         53.600000      14.55     0.0022

Source          DF    Type III SS       Mean Square    F Value    Pr > F

Subj             4     33.733333          8.433333       2.29     0.1481
Time             2    107.200000         53.600000      14.55     0.0022
```

Figure 8.18: Output for One-way repeated measures analysis of variance

It is often informative to inspect any differences in means visually, a plot of the mean reading accuracy scores for each measurement occasion is given by the following SAS code:

```
*** To produce plot of means by treatment occasion ***;
proc sort;by time;
run;
proc means mean noprint data=b;
    var score;
    by time;
output out=means mean=score;
run;

proc plot data=means;
    plot score*time;
run;
```

Interpretation of Computer Output

The usual plots to check for underlying assumptions should be performed before detailed examination of the results. The SAS output is interpreted in exactly the same way as described in the section on unrelated One-Way ANOVA, the only difference here is the partitioning of a separate source of variance attributable to Subjects. Also note, The Model sums of squares is equivalent to the total of the sums of squares for Subject and Time.

As before, the first section of output in Figure 8.18 contains summary information on the variables entered in the model. Here the variables subject and time are analysed, the summary information shows there are five subjects, three occasions for time and a total of fifteen observations.

The next section of output presents results of the analysis of variance, again an investigator should first check that the degrees of freedom are correct. The sums of squares for the model and error are presented first and then the model sums of squares is partitioned into separate sources of variance, subject and time. A test of overall model fit is given by the first F-value of 6.38 which is significant at the 1 per cent level ($p = 0.01$). This indicates that the sources of variance specified in the statistical model have a significant effect on reading accuracy scores. F-statistics for the effects of individual sources of variance are given in the following section of the output. We can conclude that the mean reading accuracy score differs over the three measurement occasions, $F = 14.55$; df 2,8; $p < 0.05$ and there is no significant subject effect. Overall individual differences among subjects are not significant at the 5 per cent level. The statistics in the SAS output and the substantive conclusions are the same as in the worked example.

An investigator having identified a significant time effect may want to inspect this further by examining any possible trends in the means. Clearly if this was a design intention it would be preferable to have more than three repeated measures. One method to describe a trend is to use polynomials (non-linear relationships) of varying degree in a regression analysis. The treatment levels would correspond to the X variable and the treatment group means would be the Y variable in a regression of Y on X. A further design implication is that the various treatment levels should correspond to a sensible measurement scale, i.e., equal steps along an ordered scale. We would pick equal time intervals in this example.

A linear (first degree) model would be fitted first to see whether there was any linear relationship. Polynomial terms would then be fitted e.g., quadratic (second degree) and cubic (third degree). *F*-tests can then be performed to detect the significance of linear and higher order trends. The reader is referred to Chapter 3 in Winer (1962) for a worked example.

8.9 Two-way ANOVA 2 × 2 Factorial (unrelated) Two factors with two levels for each factor

When to Use

When a survey or experimental design has two independent variables (factors) and every level of one factor is paired with every level of the other factor this is called a factorial design and can be analysed by a 2 × 2 Factorial ANOVA. In this design different subjects appear in each combination of different levels of the factors, hence the term **unrelated**. In a 2 × 2 design there are two factors each with two levels giving four cells. Results can therefore be analysed by examining main effects of each factor, (ignoring the effect of the other factor) and by looking for **interaction** effects. Often a factorial analysis is performed because an investigator believes there will be a significant interaction between the two independent variables. In an unrelated 2 × 2 factorial design there is only one score per subject (experimental unit) and if the design is balanced there will be an equal number of subjects (and scores) in each of the four cells of the design.

In this analysis the total variance between subjects is partitioned into three separate components, a sums of squares for each factor, SS_{F1}, SS_{F2}, and an interaction sums of squares $SS_{F1 \times F2}$. Any differences between subjects within each combination of treatment conditions is counted as a source of error variance. The interaction sums of squares can be calculated, using a pocket calculator, by calculating the sums of squares for all four cells in the design (based on the totals of all four cells) and then subtracting the sums of squares for each single factor (based on the totals of only two cells). A computer analysis evaluates the interaction term by first fitting a full statistical model and then comparing the estimated values with a reduced model with the interaction term deleted. One final problem that researchers occasionally encounter with factorial designs is the choice of an appropriate error term for the denominator of the *F*-test when a random effects or mixed effects (fixed and random factor) model is fitted. Choice of error terms and how to specify these in your analysis is described in the section on computer analysis.

Example from the Literature

In an experimental study on ways to improve the clarity of journal abstracts Hartley (1994) designed a study to examine the effects of changes in type-size, layout and language on the perceived clarity of published abstracts. In one of four studies to see whether formal language is more appropriate for overseas students a 2×2 unrelated factorial (unbalanced) design was used, one factor being the *abstract* which was presented in original vs. revised condition (2 levels) and the other factor was *student*, British students vs vs. Overseas students (2 levels). Data were analysed using a Two-way ANOVA for unrelated measures.

Data represented in Table 8.13 is taken from Table 5 of the author's original paper.

Table 8.13: *Mean cloze (comprehension) scores (out of 20) for British and overseas postgraduate librarianship students on the original and revised version of abstract A*

| | | ABSTRACT | |
		Original version	Revised version
British students	M	7.6	10.5
	SD	0.8	2.3
	N	5	10
Overseas students	M	3.6	6.8
	SD	3.3	2.7
	N	5	7

Hypotheses tested by the author include: i) main effects for Abstract, that is the means for the two abstract groups will be equal, ignoring the effects of students; ii) main effects for students; and iii) interaction effects, that is whether the effects of one variable depend on the level of the other, for example, one hypothesis might be no different among students for revised abstract.

The author reported two significant main effects. A main effect is the effect of one factor ignoring the effect of the other. In this example the significant main effect for revision of abstract indicated that participants did better with the revised abstracts than with the original versions, $F = 7.58$, df = 1,23, p = 0.01. Degrees of freedom for the factor abstract is, number of conditions $- 1$, $(2 - 1 = 1)$, and the degrees of freedom for error are given by $df_{total} - df_{Factor\ 1} - df_{Factor\ 2} - df_{interaction}$ which is evaluated as $(27 - 1) - (1) - (1) - (1) = 23$. The degrees of freedom for the interaction term are: $df_{interaction} = df_{F1} \times df_{F2} = (1 \times 1) = 1$. The main effect can be seen by examining the body of the table, the differences in means between original and revised versions of the abstract are evident ignoring the main effect of student. The main effect of student is also significant, British students had higher scores than overseas students, ignoring the effect of abstract, $F = 13.83$, df = 1,23, p = 0.001. The author reported no significant interaction effect.

The author did not report any tests of the ANOVA assumptions even though sample sizes were small, cells were unbalanced and the variance in one cell is much smaller than the variances in the other three cells.

Computer Analysis

When analysing any two-factor design it is important to distinguish between **fixed** and **random** effects. The error term, the denominator in the F-test, is dependent upon whether a factor is fixed or random. For example, in a two-factor design where both factors are random (unusual in education), both main factors would be tested against the interaction term, for example $F_{F1} = MS_{(F1)}/MS_{(F1 \times F2)}$, however, the interaction effect would be tested against the error term (e.g., $F_{F1 \times F2} = MS_{(F1 \times F2)}/MS_{(error)}$. With a fixed effects design the F-statistic would be found for all effects by dividing by $MS_{(error)}$ in the usual way. In a mixed design with both fixed and random effects (common in education) both the random factor and the interaction term are tested against the usual error term, but the fixed factor is tested against the $MS_{(interaction)}$ term.

Data for the following analysis is taken from the study on pupils' understanding of probability and cultural background that was described briefly in section 8.7. The additional factor here is sex of respondent. One of the religious groups has also been changed so we now have Christian and Sikh as the two levels of the other factor. The data is shown in Table 8.14.

Table 8.14: Data for 2 × 2 factorial ANOVA

Variable Religion (REL)	Male (code = 0)			Female (code = 1)		
Christian	17	19	22	18	15	19
(code = 2)	19	18	13	14	12	15
Sikh	18	17	22	16	17	15
(code = 5)	19	18	20	14	17	18

The following SAS code is used to perform a 2 × 2 factorial analysis of variance on the data shown in Table 8.13. Pre-planned significance tests as well as estimates of the differences in means between: i) males and females, (ESTIMATE '0 − 1' SEX 1 −1) and ii) Christians and Sikhs (ESTIMATE '5 − 2' REL −1 1) are also output.

```
proc glm data=a;
  class sex rel;
  model attrib1 = sex rel sex*rel;
  lsmeans sex rel/ stderr pdiff;
  means sex rel/ deponly;
  estimate '0-1' sex 1 -1;
  estimate '5-2' rel -1 1;
  output out = new r=res1 p=pred1;
  run;
```

Output from this analysis is shown in Figure 8.19. The *lsmeans* statement produces least-square means for the response variable attrib1 split on the independent variables *religion* and *sex*. The standard error of the lsmean is also produced (code is stderr) along with a test of the null hypothesis that the lsmeans are equal (code is pdiff). The *means* statement produces means instead of lsmeans (in this example they are both the same). Use of the *estimate* statement is described in section 8.7 under the heading 'A priori and *post hoc* multiple comparison procedures'.

```
                General Linear Models Procedure
                   Class Level Information

                  Class     Levels     Values

                   sex        2          0 1

                   rel        2          2 5

           Number of observations in data set = 24
```

Dependent Variable: ATTRIB1

Source	DF	Sum of Squares	Mean Square	F Value	Pr > F
Model	3	47.0000000	15.6666667	3.00	0.0547
Error	20	104.3333333	5.2166667		
Corrected Total	23	151.3333333			

R-Square	C.V.	Root MSE	ATTRIB1 Mean
0.310573	13.30487	2.28400	17.1667

Source	DF	Type I SS	Mean Square	F Value	Pr > F
sex	1	42.6666667	42.6666667	8.18	0.0097
rel	1	4.1666667	4.1666667	0.80	0.3821
sex*rel	1	0.1666667	0.1666667	0.03	0.8599

Source	DF	Type III SS	Mean Square	F Value	Pr > F
sex	1	42.6666667	42.6666667	8.18	0.0097
rel	1	4.1666667	4.1666667	0.80	0.3821
sex*rel	1	0.1666667	0.1666667	0.03	0.8599

Least Squares Means

Sex	Attrib1 lsmean	Std Err lsmean	Pr > |T| HO: lsmean=0	Pr > |T| HO: lsmean1=lsmean2
0	18.5000000	0.6593347	0.0001	0.0097
1	15.8333333	0.6593347	0.0001	

Rel	Attrib1 lsmean	Std Err lsmean	Pr > |T| HO: lsmean= 0	Pr > |T| HO: lsmean1=lsmean2
2	16.7500000	0.6593347	0.0001	0.3821
5	17.5833333	0.6593347	0.0001	

```
                    General Linear Models Procedure
        Level of            -------- ATTRIB1 --------
        SEX        N          Mean                  SD

         0         12      18.5000000          2.39317211
         1         12      15.8333333          2.03752672

        Level of --------           ATTRIB1 --------
        REL        N          Mean                  SD

         2         12      16.7500000          2.95803989
         5         12      17.5833333          2.15146180

                    General Linear Models Procedure
  Dependent Variable: ATTRIB1
                                   T for H0:                  Std Error of
   Parameter      Estimate      Parameter=0     Pr > |T|        Estimate

    0 - 1       2.66666667         2.86          0.0097        0.93244005
    5 - 2       0.83333333         0.89          0.3821        0.93244005
```

Figure 8.19: Output for 2 × 2 Factorial ANOVA on the data shown in Table 8.14

Interpretation of Computer Output

The ANOVA results section of the output is interpreted in the usual way (see interpretation of One-way unrelated ANOVA). When interpreting main effects and interactions a quick approximation of the importance of these effects is indicated by the relative size of the sums of squares. In this example the variable *sex* has by far the largest sums of squares. The F-ratios should be inspected for significance and main effects should always be examined first followed by lower- to higher-order interactions. Here there is a significant main effect for sex, $F = 8.18$; df 1,20; $p < 0.05$; but no significant effect for religion.

The interaction term signifies dependence and therefore has no sensible meaning without first considering the main effects. In this example interactions effects are small and none significant, only the results of main effects should therefore be reported. Should the interaction have been significant, the main effects would have to be interpreted with caution.

The next section of output contains information about means and can be used for plotting simple effects (effect of one variable at one level of the other). These plots can be very informative when there is a significant interaction. We can conclude from the ANOVA table that there is a significant difference in the mean attribution scores for males and females and this difference does not appear to depend upon religion. The final section of this output relates to the preplanned hypothesis tests and estimates of the differences in mean attribution scores between males and females and between the Christians and Sikhs. The results indicate that whereas there is a significant difference between males and females, there is no significant difference between the religious groups.

8.10   Split-Plot ANOVA

When to Use

The split-plot design is quite common in educational and psychological research. Split-plot ANOVA should be considered when measures on a response variable are continuous, when two independent groups of subjects are given two or more tests (treatments) and each subject takes all tests (treatments – the repeated measures). The usual ANOVA assumptions should be met. Often the type of subjects in a design are of particular interest and the investigator wants to compare the effects of treatments for different subcategories, such as sex, age groups, or different types of learning difficulty. In this case different subjects are required hence the between subjects factor. However, the same subjects in a subgroup will appear in the different treatment conditions or different measures over time if the design is intended to examine differences between pre-test, post-test and delayed post-test mean scores.

Example from the Literature

Teacher researchers have shown that a substantial proportion of teachers report high levels of occupational stress, the main stressors being work conditions, pupils' behaviour, staff relationships and pressure of time. In a study to investigate the relationship between teachers' cognitive style and stress, Borg and Riding (1993) surveyed 212 secondary school teachers in Malta. The investigators performed a split-plot ANOVA to determine whether there was any interaction between teachers' perception of four stressors (pupil misbehaviour, poor staff relationships, poor working conditions, time pressure), the within subjects factor, and cognitive style between subjects factor (wholists vs. analytics). They reported a highly significant within-subjects factor, teacher perception of stress, $F = 20.31$, df 3,312, $p < 0.001$, which indicated that teachers' stress factor perceptions differed. No *post hoc* tests were reported, but the authors commented that the most stressful factor for the group of teachers was pupil misbehaviour. A significant interaction between stress and cognitive style was also reported, $F = 3.13$, df3,312, p = 0.026. The authors examined plots of simple effects and concluded that 'Analytic thinkers reported greater stress than wholists for "pupil misbehaviour" and "working conditions" but the converse was true for "poor staff relations" and "time pressure".' The authors reported no significant between-subjects effect (for the wholist-analytics comparison).

Data referred to in an earlier section taken from a student's thesis study on augmentation and children's vocabulary acquisition is used to illustrate computer analysis of a split-plot ANOVA. Children were read a story based on a folktale containing target words on which they would be tested. The target words did not occur naturally in the story; they replaced easier words, such as 'pinnacle' for 'top'. The fourteen target words consisted of eight nouns, three adjectives and three verbs.

Each pupil was tested individually on three occasions: one week before the story was read to them by the teacher, (Time 1); shortly after the storytelling by the teacher (Time 2); and two weeks after the storytelling (Time 3). In the test situation a choice of six alternative words was provided, one of which was similar in meaning to the target word. A score of 1 was given for each correct answer. Boys and girls were treated as a between-subjects factor in the analysis. Data from ten subjects is shown in Table 8.15.

Table 8.15: *Vocabulary acquisition data for split-plot analysis*

Factor (Sex)	Subjects	Before story (Time1)	Factor (Time) Shortly after story (Time2)	Delayed post-test (Time3)
Male	S1	5	8	6
(code = 1)	S2	4	8	6
	S3	3	5	5
	S4	6	10	9
	S5	3	6	5
Female	S6	6	5	7
(code = 0)	S7	4	4	4
	S8	5	6	5
	S9	4	5	5
	S10	3	4	5

Three main hypotheses were tested:

- whether there was a difference between males and females;
- whether there was a difference in vocabulary score between the testing occasions (Time1 to Time3);
- whether there was an interaction between sex and time.

Computer Analysis

The sources of variance in a split-plot design can be partitioned first into sums of squares **between-subjects** and sums of squares **within-subjects**. Then the within-subjects sums of squares can be further partitioned into sums of squares for treatment effects (in this example *time*), sums of squares for the interaction of between-subjects by treatment factor (*time*sex* in this example), and the **within-error** sums of squares which is actually the sums of squares for treatment by subjects within the between subjects factor, (*time*subj(sex)*). The between-subjects partition of the data has its own sums of squares error term, subjects within the between-subjects factor, (*subj(sex)*) which is independent of the within-subjects effects. This partitioning of the sums of squares for the data shown in Table 8.15 is illustrated in Figure 8.20.

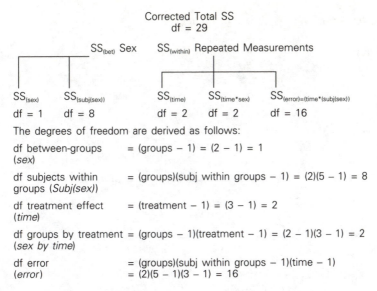

The degrees of freedom are derived as follows:

df between-groups (*sex*)	$= (\text{groups} - 1) = (2 - 1) = 1$
df subjects within groups (*Subj(sex)*)	$= (\text{groups})(\text{subj within groups} - 1) = (2)(5 - 1) = 8$
df treatment effect (*time*)	$= (\text{treatment} - 1) = (3 - 1) = 2$
df groups by treatment (*sex by time*)	$= (\text{groups} - 1)(\text{treatment} - 1) = (2 - 1)(3 - 1) = 2$
df error (*error*)	$= (\text{groups})(\text{subj within groups} - 1)(\text{time} - 1)$ $= (2)(5 - 1)(3 - 1) = 16$

Figure 8.20: *Partitioning of sums of squares in a 2 × 2 split-plot design*

The data if collected in the usual way (one line per case with each repeated time measurement on the same line) is first rearranged using a data step. For an explanation, see under the heading Computer Analysis for the related ANOVA. PROC GLM is then used to produce the ANOVA output see the following SAS code:

```
data a;
   input subj sex t1 t2 t3;
   cards;
 1  1  5  8   6
 2  1  4  8   6
 3  1  3  5   5
 4  1  6  10  9
 5  1  3  6   5
 6  0  6  5   7
 7  0  4  4   4
 8  0  5  6   5
 9  0  4  5   5
10  0  3  4   5
 ;
data b; set a;
   drop t1-t3;
   time=1; score=t1; output;
   time=2; score=t2; output;
   time=3; score=t3; output;
proc glm data=b;
  class sex subj time;
  model score= sex subj(sex) time sex*time;
  test h=sex e=subj(sex);
run;
```

Output from this code is shown in Figure 8.21.

```
                    General Linear Models Procedure
                       Class Level Information

             Class    Levels              Values

             sex         2        0 1
             subj       10        1 2 3 4 5 6 7 8 9 10
             time        3        1 2 3

            Number of observations in data set = 30

                    General Linear Models Procedure
Dependent Variable: SCORE
```

Source	DF	Sum of Squares	Mean Square	F Value	Pr > F
Model	13	76.7000000	5.9000000	15.06	0.0001
Error	16	6.2666667	0.3916667		
Corrected					
Total	29	82.9666667			

R-Square	C.V.	Root MSE	SCORE Mean
0.924468	11.66148	0.62583	5.36667

Source	DF	Type I SS	Mean Square	F Value	Pr > F
sex	1	9.6333333	9.6333333	24.60	0.0001
subj(sex)	8	39.3333333	4.9166667	12.55	0.0001
time	2	17.8666667	8.9333333	22.81	0.0001
sex*time	2	9.8666667	4.9333333	12.60	0.0005

Source	DF	Type III SS	Mean Square	F Value	Pr > F
sex	1	9.6333333	9.6333333	24.60	0.0001
subj(sex)	8	39.3333333	4.9166667	12.55	0.0001
time	2	17.8666667	8.9333333	22.81	0.0001
sex*time	2	9.8666667	4.9333333	12.60	0.0005

Tests of Hypotheses using the Type III MS for subj(sex) as an error term

Source	DF	Type III SS	Mean Square	F Value	Pr > F
sex	1	9.63333333	9.63333333	1.96	0.1991

Figure 8.21: Output for univariate split-plot ANOVA on the data shown in Table 8.15

Interpretation of Computer Output

The first section of output contains the usual summary information which should be checked to ensure the model fitted is correct. Here there are two levels for the between subjects factor (sex), three repeated measurements over time, ten subjects and a total of thirty observations. The corrected total degrees of freedom and the partitioning into between and within sources should then be checked. Considering next the overall model fit this is significant, $F = 15.06$; df 13;16 p < 0.0001 indicating that the independent variables have a significant effect. Notice that the model sums of squares (and df) are equivalent to the total of the sums of squares for: (sex), (subj(sex)), (time), and (sex*time) indicating the additive nature of ANOVA. Considering the first hypothesis, whether there is a significant main effect of sex, the observed F-statistic, obtained from the bottom of the SAS output, is $F = 1.96$; df1,8; p $= 0.199$ which indicates that the null hypothesis cannot be rejected. It is therefore concluded that there is no difference between males and females in their mean vocabulary scores. The reader should note that an F-value for the effect of *sex* is printed in the body of the ANOVA table but this is based on an inappropriate error term. The output at the bottom of the table reminds the analyst that the requested denominator for the F-test has been used, 'Tests of Hypotheses using the Type III MS for *subj(sex)* as an error term'. The Type III sums of squares are used by default but Type I, II or IV can be requested.

A significant difference is found among the three means for the pre-, post- and delayed-post-tests, (Time in the analysis) $F = 22.81$; df2,16; p < 0.001 suggesting there may be a possible trend in the data. These means should be plotted but with only three measurement points in time it probably would not be worth examining the data for trends using polynomial terms. Finally, group by repeated measures interaction, sex*time, is significant, $F = 12.60$; df $= 2,16$; p < 0.001. This indicates that male and female vocabulary scores differ depending upon the measurement occasion. Plots of the simple effects that is the effects of one variable at individual levels of the other variable, (for example, a plot of mean vocabulary scores, Y-axis against measurement occasion, X-axis for males and females separately) are likely to be informative.

8.11 What Can Be Done when Assumptions of Homogeneity of Variance and Normality of Residuals Are Not Met?

This is an issue that most researchers face at some time or another but is generally not discussed in introductory statistical texts.

First, to deal with the two sample problem of unequal variances when the assumption of normality is reasonable, a modified *t*-test should be used called the Satterthwaite approximation procedure. This was described in the section on *t*-tests; for more detailed discussion the reader is referred to Winer (1971).

When the assumption of normality is also violated then the answer is to perform a rank transformation on the raw scores and then use the modified Satterthwaite *t'*-test on the ranks of the scores instead of the scores themselves. This procedure will to a large extent eliminate the effects of both non-normality and unequal variances. Zimmerman and Zumbo (1993) provide a very readable account with straightforward practical guidance about what to do in this situation.

When more than two means are compared the same principles can be applied, for example, use of PROC GLM on the ranked scores and non-parametric procedures such as those described in Chapter 7. Alternatively, other data transformations should be considered, such as log transform or square root. The purpose of data transformation is usually to obtain scores which have improved normality and homogeneity of variance characteristics. However, the reader should be aware that transformation of data to change the variance of a distribution or restore normality will also affect the shape of the distribution. For example, homogeneity of variance may be achieved but a distribution may then be skewed. Another consequence resulting from data transformation is the possibility of induced non-linearity. With reference to the arcsine transformation there is no general agreement as to when this transformation is appropriate (Milligan, 1987), and when the null hypothesis is false the transformation can reduce the power of a statistical test.

A third strategy, seldom mentioned, is to perform the analysis but then to make nominal adjustments to the statistical significance and power of a test, see Horton (1978) for discussion of this alternative.

Concluding Remarks

Generally ask yourself the following questions when interpreting results: Does this make sense? Is it what I might have expected? Is there an alternative interpretation or explanation? Statistical significance should be distinguished from educational or clinical significance. If a clinical or educational effect is reported consider the magnitude of the effect, the 'effect size' and the statistical power. Consider also whether reported results are exploratory or confirmatory and if survey data is reported, pay particular attention to non-sampling errors when interpreting findings. Statistical analysis should be used to gain insight into data and not as an end itself or to lend respectability to a poorly designed study. Too much or over-sophisticated statistical analysis should be avoided, as one statistician is reported to have commented, any data set will confess if you interrogate it long enough.

Appendix

Appendix A1   Data

Table 1:   Data set for 114 First Class Honours Graduates (Chapter 3)

OBS	SUB	SEX	CASENO	DEGP	ASCORE1	NUMV	AGEY
1	Phys.Sci/5	F	302	I/5	7	3	18.7500
2	Phys.Sci/5	M	303	I/5	14	3	18.7500
3	Phys.Sci/5	M	320	I/5	15	3	18.2500
4	Phys.Sci/5	M	321	I/5	12	3	20.3333
5	Phys.Sci/5	M	329	I/5	11	3	19.0000
6	Phys.Sci/5	M	330	I/5	9	4	18.7500
7	Phys.Sci/5	M	331	I/5	14	4	19.0833
8	Phys.Sci/5	M	367	I/5	20	4	18.6667
9	Phys.Sci/5	F	368	I/5	20	4	19.8333
10	Phys.Sci/5	M	369	I/5	20	4	19.0000
11	Phys.Sci/5	F	370	I/5	10	3	18.5000
12	Phys.Sci/5	F	371	I/5	12	3	18.5833
13	Phys.Sci/5	M	374	I/5	18	4	18.8333
14	Phys.Sci/5	F	375	I/5	13	3	19.5833
15	Phys.Sci/5	F	376	I/5	11	3	21.0833
16	Phys.Sci/5	M	377	I/5	15	3	18.6667
17	Phys.Sci/5	M	378	I/5	13	3	18.7500
18	Phys.Sci/5	F	379	I/5	13	3	18.1667
19	Phys.Sci/5	F	380	I/5	8	3	18.9167
20	Phys.Sci/5	M	381	I/5	11	3	19.3333
21	Phys.Sci/5	M	382	I/5	10	3	18.2500
22	Phys.Sci/5	F	402	I/5	13	3	19.0000
23	Phys.Sci/5	M	408	I/5	12	3	19.0000
24	Phys.Sci/5	M	435	I/5	13	3	18.5833
25	Phys.Sci/5	M	441	I/5	14	3	18.9167
26	Phys.Sci/5	M	442	I/5	20	4	18.8333
27	Phys.Sci/5	M	443	I/5	11	3	18.3333
28	Phys.Sci/5	M	444	I/5	20	4	19.4167
29	Phys.Sci/5	M	445	I/5	15	3	18.0833
30	Phys.Sci/5	M	446	I/5	19	4	18.9167
31	Phys.Sci/5	M	447	I/5	13	4	18.6667
32	Phys.Sci/5	M	448	I/5	15	3	19.0000
33	Phys.Sci/5	M	449	I/5	19	4	18.2500
34	Phys.Sci/5	F	450	I/5	16	4	18.6667
35	Phys.Sci/5	M	451	I/5	20	4	18.8333
36	Phys.Sci/5	M	456	I/5	20	4	19.0833
37	Phys.Sci/5	M	457	I/5	19	4	18.1667

Table 1: Cont'd

OBS	SUB	SEX	CASENO	DEGP	ASCORE1	NUMV	AGEY
38	Phys.Sci/5	M	458	I/5	19	4	19.0000
39	Phys.Sci/5	M	459	I/5	14	3	19.5000
40	Phys.Sci/5	F	460	I/5	18	4	18.9167
41	Phys.Sci/5	M	461	I/5	19	4	18.5833
42	Phys.Sci/5	M	462	I/5	17	4	19.4167
43	Phys.Sci/5	M	463	I/5	20	4	18.2500
44	Phys.Sci/5	M	464	I/5	19	4	19.0833
45	Phys.Sci/5	M	465	I/5	20	4	18.7500
46	Phys.Sci/5	M	466	I/5	14	3	19.0833
47	Phys.Sci/5	M	467	I/5	15	3	18.8333
48	Phys.Sci/5	M	468	I/5	13	3	18.2500
49	Phys.Sci/5	M	469	I/5	15	4	18.3333
50	Phys.Sci/5	M	470	I/5	20	4	18.1667
51	Phys.Sci/5	M	471	I/5	13	3	18.3333
52	Phys.Sci/5	M	472	I/5	15	3	18.7500
53	Phys.Sci/5	M	473	I/5	15	3	19.5000
54	Phys.Sci/5	F	474	I/5	13	4	18.7500
55	Phys.Sci/5	M	475	I/5	14	3	18.9167
56	Phys.Sci/5	F	476	I/5	15	3	17.8333
57	Phys.Sci/5	F	477	I/5	20	4	18.4167
58	Phys.Sci/5	M	542	I/5	19	4	18.5833
59	Phys.Sci/5	M	548	I/5	16	4	19.0833
60	Phys.Sci/5	M	549	I/5	18	4	18.5000
61	Phys.Sci/5	M	550	I/5	15	3	18.3333
62	Phys.Sci/5	M	551	I/5	15	3	18.5833
63	Engineer/7	M	782	I/5	18	4	18.4167
64	Engineer/7	M	800	I/5	10	4	18.5833
65	Engineer/7	M	804	I/5	12	3	19.3333
66	Engineer/7	M	805	I/5	18	4	18.6667
67	Engineer/7	M	806	I/5	20	4	19.2500
68	Engineer/7	M	807	I/5	18	4	19.5833
69	Engineer/7	M	808	I/5	14	4	20.9167
70	Engineer/7	M	809	I/5	15	3	18.7500
71	Engineer/7	M	810	I/5	12	3	18.4167
72	Engineer/7	F	836	I/5	17	4	18.1667
73	Engineer/7	M	837	I/5	19	4	19.5833
74	Engineer/7	M	859	I/5	20	4	19.0000
75	Engineer/7	M	860	I/5	13	4	20.7500
76	Engineer/7	M	861	I/5	13	3	18.2500
77	Engineer/7	M	863	I/5	13	3	18.7500
78	Engineer/7	M	886	I/5	11	4	19.4167
79	Engineer/7	M	887	I/5	20	4	19.5000
80	Engineer/7	M	888	I/5	15	3	19.4167
81	Engineer/7	M	889	I/5	17	4	19.5833
82	Engineer/7	M	891	I/5	13	3	19.5833
83	Engineer/7	M	893	I/5	14	4	19.0000
84	Engineer/7	M	894	I/5	14	3	20.3333
85	Engineer/7	F	895	I/5	16	4	19.5000
86	Engineer/7	M	896	I/5	13	3	18.5833
87	Engineer/7	M	897	I/5	14	3	20.5833
88	Engineer/7	M	898	I/5	15	3	20.6667

Table 1: Cont'd

OBS	SUB	SEX	CASENO	DEGP	ASCORE1	NUMV	AGEY
89	Engineer/7	M	934	I/5	19	4	20.0833
90	Engineer/7	M	935	I/5	10	3	20.5833
91	Engineer/7	M	937	I/5	19	4	20.3333
92	Soc.Sci/9	F	1119	I/5	16	4	19.0000
93	Soc.Sci/9	M	1154	I/5	15	3	18.5000
94	Soc.Sci/9	F	1155	I/5	18	4	19.2500
95	Soc.Sci/9	M	1158	I/5	10	2	16.7500
96	Soc.Sci/9	M	1172	I/5	15	4	18.5000
97	Soc.Sci/9	M	1230	I/5	8	2	19.5000
98	Soc.Sci/9	F	1231	I/5	11	3	19.0833
99	Soc.Sci/9	M	1232	I/5	10	3	18.2500
100	Soc.Sci/9	F	1273	I/5	20	4	19.7500
101	Soc.Sci/9	M	1352	I/5	13	3	18.5833
102	Soc.Sci/9	M	1497	I/5	12	3	20.0833
103	Soc.Sci/9	M	1498	I/5	11	3	19.4167
104	Soc.Sci/9	M	1502	I/5	20	4	21.7500
105	Soc.Sci/9	M	1503	I/5	11	3	19.9167
106	Soc.Sci/9	F	1504	I/5	15	3	18.0833
107	Soc.Sci/9	F	1505	I/5	12	3	18.8333
108	Soc.Sci/9	M	1506	I/5	11	3	27.1667
109	Soc.Sci/9	M	1507	I/5	15	3	19.6667
110	Soc.Sci/9	F	1508	I/5	18	4	19.2500
111	Soc.Sci/9	M	1668	I/5	9	3	20.1667
112	Soc.Sci/9	M	1677	I/5	14	3	24.2500
113	Educat/15	F	2251	I/5	13	3	20.6667
114	Educat/15	F	2272	I/5	20	4	19.5833

Table 2: Raw data on 227 school children's mathematical self-concept and mathematical achievement as presented originally for analysis

```
1113144124123    22114143444425    43214122224428    64324423414310
2114134553218    23114454321416    44213123913322    65324421411318
3113234423445    24114345415414    45214234423427    66324252115514
4114324514515    25214152222328    46215444222426    67325112425419
5111114123322    26214223245510    47213352354222    68325411245508
6111134511118    27214113323418    48214224422416    69324232423318
7114132324413    28215244224415    49215253443314    70325151255518
8114234324526    29214232314419    50324345411524    71325554232422
9114124122419    30214122114509    51323143323222    72324124311416
10114222121413   31214224324424    52324313414419    73324153234312
11114123311411   32214255414422    53324444524509    74324552435513
12113134353426   33214154352216    54324125424321    75325254414418
13114133222422   34215244112413    55324225222414    76333231454516
14114133212421   35214223322424    56324234424316    77334232223414
15114234213419   36214234231411    57324143131325    78334213323412
16114223344524   37215012211421    58324234214415    79335134221420
17114251344427   38214233423424    59324113525412    80434144233416
18114332424323   39214134344516    60325252344317    81434243435319
19114232314516   40213154244412    61324234424415    82434294314312
20114234522423   41214154354318    62324153253516    83434252534214
21113134453317   42214233322416    63324354454223    84434151342110
```

```
 85434223211212    121524153454320    157743292304206    193864232122424
 86434214614421    122524253335317    158744344412212    1948625.41.34.
 87434214212415    123634112122410    159743232422204    195863314553301
 88433324354410    124635234221408    160744445132116    196864233123403
 89434122424209    125634232323414    161743215314310    197864232144300
 90434221444414    126633454444413    162744424022403    198955524414404
 91434111115410    127634332322414    163744221121008    199955252425505
 92434153325113    128633154352406    164744454254109    2009531254553.
 93434114324408    129634132223310    165744414414405    2019554453254.
 94434222424412    130634232223414    166744352333301    20295...24.5400
 95434123322409    131635352253205    167744324314308    203954241151208
 96433123414419    132634152454312    168743353424409    204954122213312
 97433125111314    133634211414411    169744432344411    205954352425402
 98433235434412    134632404534410    170744212353305    206955111125501
 99525142334416    135634344514510    171744124425111    2079555115410.
100524234334316    136634331312310    172743124352206    2089543124543.
101524142123218    137635443214314    173744242454405    209953443434300
102524244243324    138634323324308    174744442452302    210954111125239
103525134131319    139633244313412    175744121414310    211954223151110
104523153113414    140633224244206    17674423.12220     212954112343305
105523313343316    141633124424408    177744234342301    213954444544100
106524232324418    142634242224410    178744114311105    2149542432143.
107524253444321    143634132225317    179744432222306    215954454352407
108524154354418    144633131224514    180745242324310    216953334544411
109525211444413    145634333414412    181744422051109    217953245424200
110524111313512    146744252342310    182743243353208    218954212424205
111524445222417    147744445224508    183744232212309    219954532424301
112524234422415    148744213225310    184744124224405    2209543434554.
113525454322419    149744242544405    185744231214410    221954.422444.
114523324223426    150744224333300    186744124254508    222954241425306
115524221.24420    151744047334302    187864134444403    223955245414209
116524214242417    152745414355304    188864.253254.     224951415152501
117524232324411    153744454255405    189864130031404    2259533.1125403
118523250324316    154744121300010    190864155310103    226955452552504
119523224314318    155744244324508    191864442.422.     227954214424205
120524222322321    156744212324205    192862324233102
```

352

Appendix A2　Statistical Notation

Statistics makes use of algebraic notation to express mathematical operations.

1　*Notation for variables and values*

Generally a variable is denoted with a particular upper case Latin letter, for example, X. An individual value of that variable is represented by a lower case letter and a subscript, such as x_i. Here i is the **subscript** which denotes the ith value for the variable X.

For example, look at this set of 5 anxiety scores:

$$5 \quad 4 \quad 7 \quad 9 \quad 8$$

If you wish to refer to a single score from this set without specifying which one, you could can refer to x_i, where i can take on any value between 1 and 5. The first score (5) would be referred to as x_1, the second x_2, and so on. A general form of notation for this example would be (x_i; $i = 1, 2, \ldots n$). This means in the set of n values of the variable X, a single value x_i may extend over a range of values from 1 to n.

2　*Summation*

In statistics we are often required to sum a set of values. The upper case Greek letter sigma (Σ), means add up or sum what follows. So, Σx_i is read sum over all x_i. To be perfectly correct, the notation for summing all n values of x_i (from $i = 1, 2, \ldots n$) is:

$$\sum_{i=1}^{n} x_i$$

This means sum all of the x_i's from $i = 1$ to $i = n$. To keep things simple, when the suffix i assumes all values in the range we use Σx_i or simply Σx. The **range** of values to be summed is indicated above and below sigma. So, with respect to the five anxiety scores,

$$\sum_{i=2}^{5} x_i = x_2 + x_3 + x_4 + x_5 = 28$$

Rules of summation:

Σx_i^2, is read as sum of all the squared values of x_i, that is $5^2 + 4^2 + 7^2 + 9^2 + 8^2$. This is equal to 235. However, $(\Sigma x_i)^2$ means sum all the values of x_i and then square this value $(5 + 4 + 7 + 9 + 8)^2$. This equals $33^2 = 1089$.

Note $\Sigma x_i^2 \neq (\Sigma x_i)^2$. The general rule, which always applies, is to perform operations within parentheses before performing operations outside parentheses.

3   *Order statistics*

Should you want to specify the order of a set of values this is denoted by adding small brackets around the subscript i, that is (i). In general form this would be $x_{(1)}, x_{(2)} \ldots x_{(n)}$ where $x_{(1)}$ would be the smallest value in a set, i.e., rank of 1, $x_{(2)}$ would be the second smallest value in a set, i.e., rank of 2 and so on. This implies that $x_{(1)} \leq x_{(2)} \leq \ldots x_{(n)}$ where $\leq$ means less than or equal to. For the set of 5 anxiety scores,

$$x_{(1)} = 4, \; x_{(2)} = 5, \; x_{(3)} = 7, \; x_{(4)} = 8, \text{ and } x_{(5)} = 9$$

Appendix A3   SAS Programs

```
************************************************************************;
**  Filename:  CHECK.JOB                                           **;
**                                                                 **;
**  Purpose:   Use this check job to identify out-of-range and     **;
**             missing numeric data (character data is ignored).   **;
**                                                                 **;
**  Created: 16 March 1995                                         **;
**                                                                 **;
**  Input file:  SEE NOTES                                         **;
**  Output file: NONE                                              **;
**                                                                 **;
**  Notes:                                                         **;
**                                                                 **;
**  1.  You need on the 'a' disk the following files:              **;
**      check.job (this file)                                      **;
**      main.dat - the data file to be checked                     **;
**                                                                 **;
**  2.  Rename the data file you want to check as main.dat         **;
**                                                                 **;
**  3.  You will need to write a format statement for your own     **;
**      data. This means after the input statement in the          **;
**      next section of SAS code you should write in your own      **;
**      variable list. If a character variable is included in      **;
**      your data list it should be followed by a $ and a space,   **;
**      then the name of the next variable. All character          **;
**      variables will be ignored in the data check program.       **;
**      All variable names should be TYPED IN UPPER CASE.          **;
**                                                                 **;
**  4.  You will need to change the lines of SAS code after the    **;
**      data limits statement to correspond to the variables       **;
**      and ranges for each numeric variable in main dataset.      **;
**      All variable names should be TYPED IN UPPER CASE. Do       **;
**      not include CASEID in the list of variables after          **;
**      the data limits statement.                                 **;
**                                                                 **;
************************************************************************;

options pagesize=65;
data main;
    infile 'a:main.dat';

**  EDIT THE NEXT LINE (see 2. above)                              **;

    input CASEID 1-3 CLASS 4 SET 5 ATTB1 6 ATTB2 7 ATTB3 8 ATTB4 9
          SELFC1 10 SELFC2 11 SELFC3 12 SELFC4 13 SCORE 14-15;
data limits;

**  EDIT THE NEXT FEW LINES (see 3. above)                         **;

  input vname $ min max;
  cards;
```

```
    CLASS   1 9
    SET     1 6
    ATTB1   1 5
    ATTB2   1 5
    ATTB3   1 5
    ATTB4   1 5
    SELFC1  1 5
    SELFC2  1 5
    SELFC3  1 5
    SELFC4  1 5
    SCORE   0 30
;

**  Transpose data main.dat creating one variable containing    **;
**  all variables in the data set                               **;

proc transpose data=main out=new;
   by caseid;

proc sort data=new;
   by _name_ caseid;

proc sort data=limits;
   by vname;

**  Merge this data set new with limits data set               **;

data new;
    merge new (rename= (_name_=vname col1=varval)) limits
(in=inlim);
   by vname;
        if inlim;
        if varval ne . then do;
          if varval < min then lessmin = caseid;
          else if varval > max then gtmax = caseid;
        end;
        else misdat = caseid;

**  Delete observations with no values outside limits/missing data **;

   if sum (lessmin,gtmax,misdat) =. then delete;
run;

proc print data = new label;
   by vname;
   id vname;
   var lessmin misdat gtmax;
   label  vname   = 'variable name'
          lessmin = '<min'
          misdat  = 'missing'
          gtmax   = '>max';
   title 'Out of Range Values and Missing Data by Caseid';
run;
```

Figure 1: SAS program to check missing and out-of-range values

```
**********************************************************************;
**  Filename: POWER1.JOB                                           **;
**                                                                 **;
**  Purpose:  Calculates statistical power and sample size for     **;
**            the difference between two proportions               **;
**            (independent groups)                                 **;
**                                                                 **;
**            ALSO USED FOR TWO-GROUP TWO-PERIOD CROSS OVER        **;
**            DESIGNS                                              **;
**                                                                 **;
**  Calculations are based on Machin, D. and Campbell, M.J. (1987). **;
**                                                                 **;
**  Created:  16 March 1995                                        **;
**                                                                 **;
**  Input file:   NONE (see notes)                                 **;
**  Output file:  NONE (see notes)                                 **;
**                                                                 **;
**  Notes:    Data is entered after the cards statement Enter      **;
**            power alpha pie1 pie2 and each separated by a space  **;
**            -9 is used for the parameter to be estimated, only   **;
**            one -9 should be entered per line (i.e., 3 parameters **;
**            are entered and 1 is estimated) only POWER or        **;
**            N can be estimated.                                  **;
**                                                                 **;
**            Pie1 and pie2 are the two proportions (pie1 is the   **;
**            smallest).                                           **;
**            This is a two-sided test, for a 1-sided test change  **;
**            alpha/2 to alpha in the 2nd line of code after the   **;
**            data                                                 **;
**                                                                 **;
**********************************************************************;

data a;
    input power alpha pie1 pie2 n;
    cards;

0.80  0.05  0.07  0.12  -9

;
data a; set a;
   pza=abs(probit(alpha/2));        /* pza=significance level as a z
                                        score ie        5%=1.96*
                      */
   diff= (abs (pie1-pie2))**2;
pieval= ((pie1*(1-pie1)) + (pie2*(1-pie2)));

   if n=-9 then do;                 /* Find n

        flag = 1;
        pz=probit(power);           /* pz=cumulative z value for given
                                        power */
        function= (pz + pza)**2; /* function=power function        */
        n=ceil((function*pieval)/diff);
   end;
```

```
   else if power=-9 then do;        /* Find power              */
        flag=2;
        function= (n*diff)/pieval;
        pz=sqrt(function) -pza;
        power=round(abs(probnorm(pz)),.01);
   end;
                                     /* Print out results       */
title1 'Comparison of two Proportions (independent groups)';
   proc print split = '*';
        where flag=1;               /* found n                 */
        id power;
         var alpha pie1 pie2 n;
        label n='CALCULATED VALUE* OF N (PER GROUP)';
         title3 'Finding number of subjects (n)';
   run;

   proc print split='*';
        where flag = 2;             /* found power             */
        id alpha;
         var pie1 pie2 n power;
        label power='CALCULATED VALUE*OF POWER';
         title3 'Finding the power';
   run;
```

Figure 2: *SAS program POWER1 for power and sample size calculations, difference between two proportions (independent groups)*

```
*********************************************************************;
**  Filename:   POWER2.JOB                                        **;
**                                                                **;
**  Purpose:    This job calculates statistical power and sample  **;
**              sizes for comparison of two means independent     **;
**              groups.                                           **;
**                                                                **;
**              Calculations are based on Machin, D. and Campbell,**;
**              M.J. (1987).                                      **;
**                                                                **;
**  Created:    16 March 1995                                     **;
**                                                                **;
**  Input file:  NONE (see notes)                                 **;
**  Output file: NONE (see notes)                                 **;
**                                                                **;
**  Notes:                                                        **;
**  1.  Data is input after the cards statement. Enter power alpha**;
**      diff sd and n separated by spaces either POWER or n should**;
**      be set to -9 (value to be estimated).                     **;
**                                                                **;
**  2.  Sd is the pooled standard deviation derived from both     **;
**      samples.                                                  **;
**                                                                **;
**  3.  Diff is the difference in sample means to be detected.    **;
**                                                                **;
**  4.  This is a two-sided test, for a one-sided test change     **;
**      alpha/2 to alpha in the second line of code after the data.**;
```

```
**  5.  If sample sizes are unequal the harmonic mean, n, of n₁    **;
**      and n₂ should be used. This is evaluated as                **;
**      2(n₁ n₂)/(n₁ + n₂). Alternatively, two power               **;
**      estimates can be determined, one for each n.               **;
**                                                                 **;
*********************************************************************;

data a;
    input power alpha diff sd n;
    cards;

0.910  0.05  1.5   1.2   -9
0.80   0.05  5     10    -9

;

data a; set a;
  pza=abs(probit(alpha/2));    /* pza=significance level as a z
                                  score ie 5%=1.96                  */

  if n=-9 then do;             /* Find n                            */
  flag=1;
  pz=probit(power);            /* pz=cumulative z value for given
                                  power                             */
  function=(pz+pza)**2;        /* function=power function           */
  n=ceil((function*2*(sd**2))/(diff**2));
  end;

  else if power=-9 then do;    /* Find power                        */
      flag=2;
      function=(n*diff**2)/(2*(sd**2));
      pz=sqrt(function)-pza;
      power=round(abs(probnorm(pz)),.01);
    end;
                               /* Print out results                */

title1 'COMPARISON OF TWO MEANS (UNPAIRED DATA)';

  proc print split='*';
      where flag=1;            /* found n                           */
      id power;
       var alpha diff sd n;
      label n='CALCULATED VALUE* OF N PER GROUP';
       title3 'Finding number of subjects (n) per group';
  run;

  proc print split='*';
      where flag=2;            /* found power                       */
      id alpha;
       var diff sd n power;
      label power='CALCULATED VALUE*OF POWER';
       title3 'Finding the power';
  run;
```

Figure 3: SAS program POWER2 for power and sample-size calculations, comparison of two means (independent groups)

```
**********************************************************************;
**  Filename:  POWER3.JOB                                          **;
**                                                                 **;
**  Purpose:   This job calculates statistical power and sample    **;
**             sizes for comparison of two means (paired data).    **;
**                                                                 **;
**  Calculations are based on Machin, D. and Campbell, M.J. (1987).**;
**                                                                 **;
**  Created:   16 March 1995                                       **;
**                                                                 **;
**  Input file:  NONE (see notes)                                  **;
**  Output file: NONE (see notes)                                  **;
**                                                                 **;
**  Notes:     Data is input after the cards statement.            **;
**             Sd is the pooled standard deviation derived from both **;
**             samples.                                            **;
**                                                                 **;
**********************************************************************;
data a;
    input power alpha diff sd n;
    cards;

 -9    0.001  0.6   3.676  828
0.80   0.05   0.8  20.715   -9
;
data a; set a;
  pza=abs(probit(alpha/2));          /* pza=significance level as a  */
                                     /* z score i.e. 5%=1.96         */

  if n=-9 then do;                   /* Find n                       */
         flag=1;
         pz=probit(power);           /* pz=cumulative z value for    */
                                     /* given power                  */
         function=(pz + pza)**2;     /* function=power function      */
         n=ceil((function*(sd**2))/(diff**2));
  end;

  else if power=-9 then do;          /* Find power                   */
         flag=2;
         function=(n*(diff**2))/(sd**2);
         pz=sqrt(function) -pza;
         power=round(abs(probnorm(pz)),.01);
    end;
                                     /* Print out results            */
title1 'COMPARISON OF TWO MEANS (PAIRED DATA)';

    proc print split='*';
         where flag=1;               /* found n                      */
         id power;
          var alpha diff sd n;
         label n='CALCULATED VALUE* OF N';
          title3 'Finding number of subjects (n)';
    run;
```

```
proc print split='*';
    where flag=2;                    /* found power              */
    id alpha;
     var diff sd n power;
    label power='CALCULATED VALUE*OF POWER';
     title3 'Finding the power';
run;
```

Figure 4: SAS program POWER3, sample size and power calculations for comparison of two means for paired data

```
**********************************************************************;
**  Filename:  CHI.JOB                                            **;
**                                                                **;
**  Purpose:   Chi-square test (one-sample/two-sample and r x K   **;
**             sample                                             **;
**                                                                **;
**             Tests whether there is an association between two  **;
**             category variables (test of independence) or whether **;
**             distribution of proportions in the k-populations   **;
**             with respect to the categorical response variable  **;
**             are different (test of homogeneity)                **;
**                                                                **;
**  Created: 16 April 1995                                        **;
**                                                                **;
**  Input file:  NONE (Data entered in programme)                 **;
**  Output file: NONE                                             **;
**                                                                **;
**  Notes:  Data is entered after the cards statement.            **;
**                                                                **;
**********************************************************************;

data chi;
    input row col celln @@;
    cards;                      /* Data entered on next line        */

1  1  21  1  2  27  2  1  10  2  2  69
;
proc freq data=chi;
   weight celln;
   table row*col / nopercent chisq;
 title 'Chi square test for gender (row var) and understanding(col var)';
 run;
```

Figure 5: Program for Chi-square analysis

```
**********************************************************************;
**  Filename: FISHER.JOB                                          **;
**                                                                **;
**  Purpose:   Fisher's exact test                                **;
**                                                                **;
**             Tests whether there is a difference in proportions **;
**             between two groups in a 2 x 2 table.               **;
```

```
**  Created:   16 April 1995                                            **;
**                                                                      **;
**  Input file:  NONE (Data entered in program)                        **;
**  Output file: NONE (see notes)                                       **;
**                                                                      **;
**  Notes: Data is entered after the cards statement                   **;
**                                                                      **:
***********************************************************************;

data fisher;
    input row $ col $ count @@;
    cards;

1  1  3  1  2  1  2  1  3  2  2  3
;
proc freq data=fisher;
   weight count;
   table row*col / nopercent chisq;
title 'Fisher's exact test';
run;
```

Figure 6:   Program for Fisher's exact test

```
***********************************************************************;
**  Filename:  PROPORT.JOB                                             **;
**                                                                      **;
**  Purpose:   Proportions test                                         **;
**                                                                      **;
**             Tests whether there is a difference between two         **;
**             independent proportions and provides a confidence        **;
**             interval for the difference.                             **;
**                                                                      **;
**  Created:   16 April 1995                                            **;
**                                                                      **;
**  Input file:  NONE (Data entered in programme)                      **;
**  Output file: NONE (see notes)                                       **;
**                                                                      **;
**  Notes:    Data is entered after the data statement                 **;
**                                                                      **:
***********************************************************************;

data a;         **  Enter 5 data values on following 5 lines           **;

    n1=110;     **  n1 is sample size for sample 1                     **;
    n2=108;     **  n2 is sample size for sample 2                     **;
    x1=96;      **  x1 is relevant count for sample 1                  **;
    x2=72;      **  x2 is relevant count for sample 2                  **;
    CI=95;      **  Required confidence interval, for example, 95,     **;

    p1=x1/n1;
    p2=x2/n2;

    alpha=1 - (ci/100);
sediff=sqrt((p1*(1-p1))/n1 + ((p2*(1-p2))/n2));
```

```
y=probit(alpha/2);
y=abs(y);
LOWERCI = ROUND (((p1 - p2) - (y*sediff)),.01);
UPPERCI = ROUND (((p1 - p2) + (y*sediff)),.01);
proc print;
run;
```

Figure 7: Program for proportions test (with confidence interval for difference)

```
*****************************************************************************;
**   Filename:  COCHRAN.JOB                                             **;
**                                                                      **;
**   Purpose:   Cochran's Q test                                        **;
**                                                                      **;
**              Tests whether there is a difference between two or      **;
**              more treatments in a repeated measures design when      **;
**              the response variable is binary, 1 (success) 0          **;
**              (fail).                                                 **;
**                                                                      **;
**   Created:   16 April 1995                                           **;
**                                                                      **;
**   Input file:  NONE (Data entered in programme)                      **;
**   Output file: NONE (see notes)                                      **;
**                                                                      **;
**   Notes:    The number of treatment groups (repeated measures) is    **;
**             entered sequentially (separated by a space) after the    **;
**             input statement e.g. t1 t2 t3 . . . tn.                  **;
**             Data is entered after the cards statement, one           **;
**             subject per row, each value (either 1 or 0)              **;
**             separated by a space.                                    **;
**             Subjects (lines of data) with all 1's or 0's should      **;
**             be excluded (not entered in the data step).              **;
**                                                                      **;
*****************************************************************************;
data a;
                ** On next line enter vars t1 t2 etc after input **;
                ** statement                                     **;
                ** see notes above                               **;
  input t1 t2 t3;
  cards;         /* Enter data on following lines one subject    */
                 /* per line                                     */
                 /* see notes above                              */
1 0 1
1 1 0
0 1 0
1 0 0           /*
1 1 0
1 0 1
1 0 1
0 0 1
;
                ** Do not edit beyond this line                  **;
%macro cochran;
```

```
**  Find number of groups and store in macro var j **;

      %global j;
Proc transpose data=a out=trans;
run;
   data _null_;
       if 0 then set trans nobs=count;
          call symput ('j', left (put(count,8.)));
          stop;
       run;

data a;
set a end = eof;
   n+sum(of t1 - t&j);                   ** Find n                **;
   sumr2 + (sum(of t1 - t&j)**2);        ** Find sum r squared **;

      %do i=1 %to &j;
         c&i + t&i;                      ** Find totals for c  **;
         if eof then do;
            c2&i=c&i**2;
         end;
      %end;

   if eof then do;
         sumc2=sum(of c21-c2&j);         ** sum c squared          **;
         ** find cochran q **;
         q= ((&j-1)*(&j*sumc2-(n**2)))/((&j*n)-sumr2);
         numobs = _n_;                   ** find no. of observations **;
      output;
     end;
** evaluate q **;

data _null_;
  set a;

rowcol = &j * numobs;                    ** number of cells        **;

file print;

  put @25 'Cochran Q Test Results'//;

  if rowcol < 24 then do;
     put @15 'CAUTION - the number of cells is less than 24' / ;
  end;

  conscv5 = (&j - 1)*3.84;    ** 5% conservative critical value   **;
  conscv1 = (&j - 1)*6.63;    ** 1% conservative critical value   **;
  libdf = &j - 1;             ** liberal df                       **;

  lib = 1 - round(probchi(q,libdf),.001);   ** find p-value **;
  q = round(q,.001);
```

```
  put @20 'Cochran Q test value =' q //;
  put @20 'p-value with liberal df:'  /;
    put @20 'df = ' libdf /;
    if lib <= 0.01 then
                put @20 'p <= 0.01 (p-value = 'lib')'//;
    else if lib <= 0.05 then
                put @20 'p <= 0.05 (p-value = 'lib')'//;
    else        put @20 'Not significant at 5% level (p-value = 'lib')'//;

  put @20 'p-value with conservative critical value:' /;
  if q > conscv1 then
            put @20 'p <= 0.01'//;
  else if q > conscv5 then
            put @20 'p <= 0.05'//;
  else      put @20 'Not significant at 5% level';

run;

%mend cochran;
%cochran;
```

Figure 8: Program for Cochran's Q test (with conservative and liberal critical values)

```
******************************************************************************;
**  Filename:  RUNS.JOB                                                    **;
**                                                                         **;
**  Purpose:   Calculates statistical significance for number of          **;
**             observed runs in a sequence of observations. Data          **;
**             should be dichotomous.                                      **;
**                                                                         **;
**             Provides a test of the null hypothesis that the            **;
**             pattern of occurrence of observations is random.           **;
**                                                                         **;
**             This procedure uses a large sample approximation for **;
**             the sampling of U, (the number of runs) and the            **;
**             number of observations in either of the two groups         **;
**             should be > 20.                                             **;
**                                                                         **;
**  Created:   MAY 23 1995                                                 **;
**                                                                         **;
**  Input file:  NONE (see notes)                                          **;
**  Output file: NONE                                                      **;
**                                                                         **;
**  Notes:     Four data values are entered:                              **;
**                                                                         **;
**             SAMPLE SIZE (N), NUMBER OF RUNS (U), and the number **;
**             of observations in category 1 (CAT1) and category 2 **;
**             (CAT2)                                                      **;
**                                                                         **;
**             P-values for one and two-tailed tests are output           **;
**                                                                         **;
******************************************************************************;

data a;         ** Enter, after the cards statement, the values for  *;
                ** N, U, CAT1, CAT2, in this order. Each value should*;
```

```
                    ** be separated by a space. In this example N=35,    *;
                    ** U=16, CAT1=21, and CAT2=14                         *;

      input n u cat1 cat2;
      cards;
      35 16 21 14
       ;

                  ** DO NOT EDIT BEYOND THIS LINE**;
  data a; set a;
    label
     p1='One-tailed test p-value'
     p2='Two-tailed test p=value';

    a = 2*(cat1*cat2);

    if u < (a/(n+1)) then adj=0.5;
      else if u > (a/(n+1)) then adj=-0.5;

    b= (u+ (adj - (a/n))) - 1;
    c= (a*(a - n));
    d= ((n*n)*(n - 1));
    e= sqrt(c/d);
    z= abs(b/e);
    p=round(1-(probnorm(z)),.0001);
    p1=p;
    p2=2*p1;

  proc print label;
     var z p1 p2;
  run;
```

Figure 9: *Program for one-sample runs test for randomness*

```
*****************************************************************************;
**   Filename:  WILCOXSR.JOB                                              **;
**                                                                        **;
**   Purpose:   Wilcoxon signed ranks test                                **;
**                                                                        **;
**              Provides a test of the null hypothesis that the           **;
**              median of the population differences is zero.             **;
**              It is used to test the differences between pairs of       **;
**              related observations or matched pairs of subjects.        **;
**                                                                        **;
**              This procedure is an approximate test for large           **;
**              samples (where n > 25) using z-scores.                    **;
**                                                                        **;
**   Created:    JUNE 17 1995                                             **;
**                                                                        **;
**   Input file:  NONE (see notes)                                        **;
**   Output file: NONE                                                    **;
**                                                                        **;
**   Notes:  The pair of observations for each subject are entered,       **;
**           the first observation and then the second for each           **;
**           subject                                                      **;
**                                                                        **;
*****************************************************************************;
```

```
data a;

 input first second @@;

cards;                                    /* edit the next line */
4 2 3 1 5 3 2 2 3 1 5 1 1 1 4 3 3 4 4 2
;

*** DO NOT EDIT BELOW THIS LINE ***;

data a; set a;
  diff = abs(first-second);
  signdiff = first-second;
  if diff= 0 then delete; ** delete abs differences of zero **;

proc rank data=a out=b;
 var diff;
 ranks rankdiff;
run;

proc print data=b split='*';
  var first second diff signdiff rankdiff;
label
    first= 'first*value'
   second= 'second*value'
     diff= 'absolute*difference'
 signdiff= 'difference'
 rankdiff= 'ranked*differences';
 title 'Wilcoxon signed ranks test';
run;

data b; set b end=eof;
 retain n t 0;
 if signdiff > 0 then t=t+rankdiff;
 n=n+1;
 if eof then output;

data b; set b;
 se=sqrt((n*(n+1))*((((2*n) +1))/24));
 expect = (n*(n+1))/4;
 z=abs((t-expect)/se);
 p=round(1-(probnorm(z)),.0001)*2;

 proc print data=b label;
 id n;
var t expect se z p;
label p       = 'p-value (2-tailed test)'
      expect = 'expected value'
      n      = 'No. of subjects'
      t      = 'observed value (T)'
      z      = 'z score';
title3 'Summary Statistics';
run;
```

Figure 10:   Program for Wilcoxon Signed Ranks test

```
****************************************************************************;
**  Filename:  KRUSK-W1.JOB                                              **;
**                                                                       **;
**  Purpose:   Kruskal-Wallis test                                       **;
**             Using a dataset containing each response for each         **;
**             subject.                                                  **;
**             Also does multiple comparison tests between               **;
**             the groups.                                               **;
**                                                                       **;
**  Created:   8 June 1995                                               **;
**                                                                       **;
**  Input file:  NONE (data entered in program)                          **;
**  Output file: NONE (see notes)                                        **;
**                                                                       **;
**  Notes:       Data is entered after the cards statement,              **;
**               inputing the group value and response value             **;
**               for each subject                                        **;
**                                                                       **;
**               The alpha level is entered for multiple comparison      **;
**               tests after the data (see comment in the program)       **;
**                                                                       **;
**               NOTE: group values must be numbered consecutively       **;
**               from 1                                                   **;
**                                                                       **;
****************************************************************************;

data a;
  input group response @@ ;
  cards;
1 22 1 26 1 27 1 22 1 18
2 31 2 30 2 21 2 17 2 21
3 13 3 16 3 21 3 17 3 12
;

%macro kw;

%let alpha= 0.1;  ***** ENTER ALPHA LEVEL ON THIS LINE *****;

*****************************************************;
*** DO NOT EDIT THE PROGRAM BEYOND THIS LINE ****;

proc datasets;
  delete comps;
 run;

****************************;
**** kruskal-wallis test ****;
****************************;

proc npar1way data=a wilcoxon;
  class group;
  var response;
title 'Kruskal-Wallis test - worked example';
run;
```

```
*********************************;
* post hoc pairwise comparisons *;
*********************************;
** rank the data **;

proc rank data=a out=b;
 var response;
 ranks rankresp;
run;

**** find the mean rank for each group and number in each group ****;

proc sort data=b; by group;
proc means data=b noprint;
 by group;
 var rankresp;
 output out=rank mean=meanrank n=num;

**** find total number of subjects ****;

data numsub;
 set a end=eof;
  if eof then do;
     totnum=_n_;
      output;
  end;

**** find the total number of groups ****;

   %global totgp;
   data _null_;
      if 0 then set rank nobs=count;
      call symput ('totgp',left(put(count,8.)));
      stop; run;

data rank;
  if _n_ = 1 then do;
        set numsub;
      end;
    set rank;

**********************************************************;
****** carry out comparisons for each pair of groups *****;
**********************************************************;

%do i = 1 %to &totgp-1;

  %do j = &i+1 %to &totgp;

    data gp1(rename=(meanrank=mrank1 num=num1))
        gp2(rename=(meanrank=mrank2 num=num2));
     set rank;
     if group = &i then output gp1;
        else if group = &j then output gp2;
```

```
      data ranks(keep=gp1 gp2 num1 num2 prob sig se crit diffrank);
        merge gp1 gp2;

      **** calculate the statistics for the comparison ****;

      se = sqrt(((totnum*(totnum+1)/12) * (1/num1 + 1/num2)) );
      gp1 = &i; gp2 = &j;
      diffrank = abs(mrank1 - mrank2);
      prob= &alpha/(&totgp*(&totgp-1));
      crit = abs(probit(prob));

      if diffrank >= crit*se then sig= 'yes';
        else sig = 'no';

      proc append base=comps data=ranks;
       run;

      %end;
    %end;

***** print out the results *****;

proc print split='*';
 id gp1;
 var gp2 num1 num2 diffrank se crit prob sig;
 label gp1     = 'First*group'
       gp2     = 'Second*group'
       num1    = 'No. of*subjects*(gp 1)'
       num2    = 'No. of*subjects*(gp 2)'
       diffrank= 'Abs. diff*in mean*ranks'
       se      = 'SE of*diff.'
       prob    = 'Adjusted*alpha'
       crit    = 'critical*Z value'
       sig     = 'sig. at*adjusted*alpha';
 title3 'Post hoc multiple comparison tests between the groups';
 title5 'Significance is based on an initial alpha of &alpha (two-tailed test)';
 title6 'but adjusted for the number of pairwise comparisons tests';
 run;

%mend kw;

%kw;
```

Figure 11: *Program for Kruskal-Wallis test and pairwise multiple comparisons*

```
*****************************************************************************;
**  Filename:  KRUSK-W2.JOB                                              **;
**                                                                       **;
**  Purpose:   Kruskal-Wallis test uses data in the form of             **;
**             frequencies for each response                            **;
**                                                                       **;
**  Created:   8 June 1995                                              **;
```

```
**  Input file:   NONE (data entered in program)              **;
**  Output file:  NONE (see notes)                            **;
**                                                            **;
**  Notes:        Data is entered after the cards statement.  **;
**                A line is input for each combination of group and **;
**                response, that is, on each line the group value,  **;
**                response value and number of subjects with the    **;
**                response is entered.                        **;
**                                                            **;
*****************************************************************************;

data a;
   input group response totsubj;
   cards;
1 5 0
1 4 11
1 3 3
1 2 1
1 1 1
2 5 5
2 4 32
2 3 5
2 2 4
2 1 0
3 5 1
3 4 20
3 3 10
3 2 3
3 1 3
4 5 2
4 4 14
4 3 3
4 2 2
4 1 1
5 5 6
5 4 7
5 3 5
5 2 0
5 1 1
6 5 10
6 4 76
6 3 15
6 2 4
6 1 1
;

*** create one observation per subject, ***;
*** using the frequency variable totsubj ***;

data a(drop=totsubj);
   set a;

do i = 1 to totsubj;
   output;
end;
```

```
******************************;
**** kruskal-wallis test *****;
******************************;

proc npar1way data=a wilcoxon;
  class group;
  var response;
title 'Kruskal-Wallis test - looking at type of student and perceived success';
run;
```

Figure 12: Program for Kruskal-Wallis test for data in the form of frequencies (contingency table)

```
*******************************************************************************;
**   Filename:   FRIEDX.JOB                                                 **;
**                                                                          **;
**   Purpose:    Friedman's ANOVA by ranks test using a dataset            **;
**               containing each response for each subject. Also           **;
**               does multiple comparison tests between the groups.        **;
**                                                                          **;
**   Created:    8 June 1995                                               **;
**                                                                          **;
**   Input file:  NONE (data entered in program)                          **;
**   Output file: NONE (see notes)                                        **;
**                                                                          **;
**   Notes:       Data is entered after the cards statement.              **;
**                Inputing the subject number, condition value and        **;
**                response for each subject (the response can be          **;
**                either the response value or the rank value).           **;
**                                                                          **;
**                The alpha level is entered for multiple comparison      **;
**                tests after the data (see comment in the program)       **;
**                                                                          **;
**   Note:        condition values must be numbered consecutively         **;
**                from 1                                                    **;
**                                                                          **;
*******************************************************************************;

data a;
 input subject cond $ rank @@;
 cards;
1 1 3.5  1 2 2  1 3 1  1 4 3.5
2 1   4  2 2 3  2 3 2  2 4 1
3 1   3  3 2 2  3 3 4  3 4 1
4 1   4  4 2 1  4 3 2  4 4 3
5 1   4  5 2 1  5 3 3  5 4 2
6 1   4  6 2 2  6 3 1  6 4 3
;

%macro fr;

%let alpha= 0.1;  ***** ENTER ALPHA LEVEL ON THIS LINE *****;

****************************************************;
*** DO NOT EDIT THE PROGRAM BEYOND THIS LINE ****;
```

```
proc datasets;
  delete comps;
 run;


*****************************;
**** Friedmans ANOVA test****;
*****************************;

proc freq;
  tables subject*cond*rank / noprint cmh;
 run;
title 'Friedmans ANOVA by ranks test - worked example';
run;


********************************;
* post hoc pairwise comparisons *;
********************************;

** rank the data      **;
** in case not ranked **;

proc sort data=a; by subject;

proc rank data=a out=b;
 by subject;
 var rank;
 ranks rankresp;
run;

**** find total number of subjects ****;

proc transpose data=a out=numsub;
 by subject;
 var rank;
run;

  data numsub;
    set numsub end=eof;
     if eof then do;
        totnum = _n_;
        output;
     end;

**** find the sum of the ranks for each cond ***;

    proc sort data=b; by cond;

    proc means data=b noprint;
     by cond;
     var rankresp;
     output out=rank sum=sumrank;
 run;
```

```
**** find the total number of groups ****;

    %global totgp;
    data _null_;
        if 0 then set rank nobs=count;
        call symput ('totgp',left(put(count,8.)));
        stop; run;

data rank;
   if _n_ = 1 then do;
           set numsub;
         end;
      set rank;

*************************************************************;
****** carry out comparisons for each pair of groups *****;
*************************************************************;

%do i = 1 %to &totgp-1;

   %do j = &i + 1 %to &totgp;

     data gp1(rename=(sumrank=srank1))
          gp2(rename=(sumrank=srank2));
       set rank;
       if cond =&i then output gp1;
          else if cond = &j then output gp2;

     data ranks(keep=gp1 gp2 prob sig se crit diffrank);
       merge gp1 gp2;

     **** calculate the statistics for the comparison ****;

     se = sqrt((totnum*&totgp*(&totgp+1))/6);
     gp1 = &i; gp2 = &j;
     diffrank = abs(srank1 - srank2);
     prob = &alpha/(&totgp*(&totgp-1));
     crit = abs(probit(prob));

     if diffrank >= crit*se then sig = 'yes';
       else sig = 'no';
     proc append base=comps data=ranks;
       run;

     %end;
   %end;

***** print out the results *****;

proc print split='*';
  id gp1;
```

```
var gp2 diffrank se crit prob sig;
label gp1    = 'First*group'
      gp2    = 'Second*group'
      diffrank= 'Abs. diff*in sum of*ranks'
      se     = 'SE of*diff.'
      prob   = 'Adjusted*alpha'
      crit   = 'critical*Z value'
      sig    = 'sig. at*adjusted*alpha';
 title3 'Post hoc multiple comparison tests between the groups';
 title5 "Significance is based on an initial alpha of &alpha (two-
tailed test)";
 title6 'but adjusted for the number of pairwise comparisons tests';
run;


%mend fr;


%fr;
```

Figure 13: Program for Friedman's ANOVA by ranks and pairwise multiple comparisons

---

```
goptions vsize=6.5 hsize=7.0 device=win target=winprtm;

proc gplot data=outreg;
  axis1 value=(f=simplex) label=(f=simplex justify=right
'Standardized Maths Score')
   order=90 to 140 by 10;
   axis2 label=(f=simplex 'Teacher estimate of maths ability')
order= 0 to 10 by 1
   value=(f=simplex);
   legend1 label =(f=simplex 'KEY:') value=(f=simplex) frame;
   plot smaths*maths / frame
   legend = legend1
   vaxis=axis1 haxis=axis2 hminor=0;
   symbol1 c= black v=circle i=R;
   title1 f=simplex h=1 'FITTED LEAST SQUARES REGRESSION LINE FOR
PREDICTION OF STANDARDIZED';
   title2 f=simplex h=1 'MATHS ABILITY SCORE FROM TEACHER ESTIMATE OF
MATHS ABILITY';
 run;

 proc gplot data=outreg;
   axis1 value= (f=simplex) label= (f=simplex justify=right
   'Standardized Maths Score')
   order=90 to 140 by 10;
   axis2 label= (f=simplex 'Teacher estimate of maths ability')
order= 0 to 10 by 1
   value=(f=simplex);
   legend1 label=(f=simplex 'KEY:') value=(f=simplex) frame;
   plot smaths*maths / frame
   legend = legend1
   vaxis=axis1 haxis=axis2 hminor=0;
   symbol1 c=black v=circle i=RLCLI95;
```

```
      title1 f=simplex h=1 'FITTED LEAST SQUARES REGRESSION LINE FOR
   PREDICTION OF STANDARDIZED';
      title2 f=simplex h=1 'MATHS ABILITY SCORE FROM TEACHER ESTIMATE OF
   MATHS ABILITY';
      title3 f=simplex h=1 'WITH 95% CONFIDENCE LEVEL FOR INDIVIDUAL
   PREDICTED VALUES';
   run;

proc gplot data=outreg;
   axis1 value=(f=simplex) label=(f=simplex justify=right
   'Standardized Maths Score')
   order=90 to 140 by 10;
   axis2 label=(f=simplex 'Teacher estimate of maths ability')
order= 0 to 10 by 1
   value=(f=simplex);
   legend1 label=(f=simplex 'KEY:') value=(f=simplex) frame;
   plot smaths*maths / frame
   legend=legend1
   vaxis=axis1 haxis=axis2 hminor=0;
   symbol1 c=black v=circle i=RLCLM95;
      title1 f=simplex h=1 'FITTED LEAST SQUARES REGRESSION LINE FOR
   PREDICTION OF STANDARDIZED';
      title2 f=simplex h=1 'MATHS ABILITY SCORE FROM TEACHER ESTIMATE OF
   MATHS ABILITY';
      title3 f=simplex h=1 'WITH 95% CONFIDENCE LEVEL FOR MEAN PREDICTED
   VALUES';
   run;
```

Figure 14: SAS code for plotting i) fitted linear regression line; ii) 95 per cent confidence interval for mean response; and iii) 95 per cent prediction interval (individual response) PC version of SAS

```
**********************************************************************;
**  Filename:  CORR95CI.JOB                                       **;
**                                                                **;
**  Purpose:   95 per cent CONFIDENCE INTERVAL FOR PEARSONS r     **;
**             CORRELATION                                        **;
**                                                                **;
**  Created: 10 JULY 1995                                         **;
**                                                                **;
**  Input file:  NONE (Data entered in program)                   **;
**  Output file: NONE                                             **;
**                                                                **;
**  Notes:     Data is entered after the DATA statement           **;
**             Enter pearsons r on first line                     **;
**             Enter sample size on second line                   **;
**                                                                **;
**********************************************************************;
DATA A;
   r =0.896;                   *ENTER pearsons r *;
   n =10;                      *ENTER sample size *;

   **** DO NOT EDIT THE PROGRAM BEYOND THIS LINE ****;
```

```
** find Fishers z **;
z= 0.5*(log((1+r)/(1-r)));

** find two quantities, z1 and z2 ***;
z1 = z- (1.96/sqrt(n-3));
z2 = z+ (1.96/sqrt(n-3));

** find the 95% confidence intervals **;
lower = round((exp(2*z1) -1)/(exp(2*z1) +1),.001);
upper = round((exp(2*z2) -1)/(exp(2*z2) +1),.001);
proc print split ='*';
 id r;
 var n lower upper;
 label   r = 'Pearsons*r'
         n = 'sample size'
    lower = 'lower 95%*confidence*limit'
    upper = 'upper 95%*confidence*limit';
 title '95% confidence interval for pearsons r correlation';
run;
```

Figure 15: Program for 95 per cent confidence interval for Pearson correlation

---

```
*****************************************************************************;
** Filename:  CORRDIFF.JOB                                               **;
**                                                                        **;
** Purpose:   DIFFERENCE BETWEEN TWO INDEPENDENT CORRELATAIONS 'r' **;
**                                                                        **;
** Created:   10 JULY 1995                                                **;
**                                                                        **;
** Input file:  NONE (Data entered in programme)                          **;
** Output file: NONE                                                      **;
**                                                                        **;
** Notes:     This is a one-tailed test of the alternative               **;
**            hypothesis that the larger correlation r1 is               **;
**            significantly different from the smaller                    **;
**            correlation r2                                              **;
**                                                                        **;
**            Data is entered after the DATA statement:                   **;
**                                                                        **;
**            Enter in the program r1, r2, on first line                 **;
**            followed by N1 and N2 on the next line                     **;
**                                                                        **;
*****************************************************************************;

DATA A;                     *BEGIN DATA STEP;
  r1 = .92;    r2 = .82;    *ENTER TWO CORRELATIONS HERE r1 is the
                             largest;
  N1 = 60;     N2 = 50;     *ENTER CORRESPONDING SAMPLE SIZES HERE;

 **** DO NOT EDIT THE PROGRAM BEYOND THIS LINE ****;

  A=LOG(1+R1); B=LOG(1-R1); C=A-B;
  D=LOG(1+R2); E=LOG(1-R2); F=D-E;
```

```
FZ1= ROUND(.5*(C),.001); *THIS COMPUTES FISHER Z TRANSFORM;
FZ2= ROUND(.5*(F),.001);

G=1/(N1-3); H=1/(N2-3); I=G+H;

SEZDIFF=ROUND(SQRT(I),.001);

Z=(FZ1-FZ2)/SEZDIFF;
Z=ROUND(Z,.001);
NORMPROB=ROUND(1 - PROBNORM(Z),.001);
FILE PRINT;

PUT 'FISHER Z TRANSFORM FOR R1= ' FZ1;
PUT 'FISHER Z TRANSFORM FOR R2= ' FZ2;
PUT 'STANDARD ERROR OF DIFFERENCE BETWEEN Z COEFFICIENTS = 'SEZDIFF;
PUT 'Z DEVIATE FOR DIFFERENCE BETWEEN CORRELATIONS= ' Z;
PUT 'ONE TAILED TEST, (R1>R2) PROBABILITY FOR Z DEVIATE = 'NORMPROB;
RUN;
```

Figure 16: Program for testing significance of a difference between two Pearson correlations obtained from independent samples

```
********************************************************************;
*   Filename:    CIDIFF.JOB                                       *;
*                                                                 *;
*   Purpose:     CONFIDENCE INTERVAL MEAN DIFFERENCE FOR TWO      *;
*                INDEPENDENT SAMPLE MEANS                         *;
*                                                                 *;
*   Created:     10 JULY 1995                                     *;
*                                                                 *;
*   Input file:  SEE NOTES                                        *;
*   Output file: NONE                                             *;
*                                                                 *;
*   Notes:       DATA NEEDS TO BE ENTERED                         *;
*                CHANGE 3 VALUES IN THE PROGRAM:                  *;
*                i) data set name, ii) response var to be         *;
*                analysed and iii) class var, (the var used       *;
*                to allocate subjects to groups                   *;
*                                                                 *;
********************************************************************;

****ENTER YOUR DATA USING EITHER THE CARDS STATEMENT, AN EXTERNAL  *;
****   DATA FILE e.g. INFILE INPUT etc, or a LIBNAME STATEMENT  ******;

proc summary data=all nway; *** Change 'All' to your Data set name *;
   var score;                 *** EDIT response var to be analysed  *;
   class age;                 *** EDIT class var which is the       *;
                        *** classification var for the two groups*;

            *** DO NOT EDIT BELOW THIS LINE ***;

   output out=out mean=ymean var=variance n=n;

data b; set out;
   n2=n;
   n1=lag(n);
```

```
        y2=ymean;
        y1=lag(ymean);
        variance=round(variance,.001);
        v2=variance;
        v1=lag(variance);
        alpha= .05;
        ndiff=n1+n2;
        ydiff= y1-y2;
        poolvar= ((n1-1)*v1+ (n2-1)*v2)/(ndiff-2);
        sediff=sqrt(poolvar*(1/n1 + 1/n2));
        t=round (tinv(1-alpha/2,ndiff-2),.001);
        lc=round(ydiff-t*sediff,.001);
        uc=round(ydiff+t*sediff,.001);

proc print data=b split='*' noobs;
    where t ne .;
    var n1 n2 y1 y2 v1 v2 alpha t lc uc;
    title1 'Confidence interval for difference between means';
    label alpha='Alpha'
            t = 'Critical*t-value'
          y1 = 'mean*(gp 1)'
          y2 = 'mean*(gp 2)'
          n1 = 'sample*size*(gp 1)'
          n2 = 'sample*size*(gp 2)'
          v1 = 'variance*(gp 1)'
          v2 = 'variance*(gp 2)'
          lc = 'Lower Confidence Limit'
          uc = 'Upper Confidence Limit';
run;
```

Figure 17: Program for confidence intervals for difference between two independent sample means

Table 1:   The normal distribution (Z deviates)

Probability values in the body of the table correspond to a given Z score. This Z score (deviate) represents the proportion of the total area under the normal curve that is beyond (to the right of) the given Z score. The probability values are thus appropriate for a **one-tailed** test. These probabilities should be doubled for a two-tailed test.

The left hand column gives values of Z to one decimal place, the top row gives values of Z to the second decimal place. For example, the probability of a Z score ≥ 1.96, for a one-tailed test, is p=0.025. For a two-tailed test the same Z score would have a probability, p=0.05.

Z	0.00	0.01	0.02	0.03	0.04	0.05	0.06	0.07	0.08	0.09
0.0	0.5000	0.4960	0.4920	0.4880	0.4840	0.4801	0.4761	0.4721	0.4681	0.4641
0.1	0.4602	0.4562	0.4522	0.4483	0.4443	0.4404	0.4364	0.4325	0.4286	0.4247
0.2	0.4207	0.4168	0.4129	0.4090	0.4052	0.4013	0.3974	0.3936	0.3897	0.3859
0.3	0.3821	0.3783	0.3745	0.3707	0.3669	0.3632	0.3594	0.3557	0.3520	0.3483
0.4	0.3446	0.3409	0.3372	0.3336	0.3300	0.3264	0.3228	0.3192	0.3156	0.3121
0.5	0.3085	0.3050	0.3015	0.2981	0.2946	0.2912	0.2877	0.2843	0.2810	0.2776
0.6	0.2743	0.2709	0.2676	0.2643	0.2611	0.2578	0.2546	0.2514	0.2483	0.2451
0.7	0.2420	0.2389	0.2358	0.2327	0.2296	0.2266	0.2236	0.2206	0.2177	0.2148
0.8	0.2119	0.2090	0.2061	0.2033	0.2005	0.1977	0.1949	0.1922	0.1894	0.1867
0.9	0.1841	0.1814	0.1788	0.1762	0.1736	0.1711	0.1685	0.1660	0.1635	0.1611

Table 1: Cont'd

	0.00	0.01	0.02	0.03	0.04	0.05	0.06	0.07	0.08	0.09
1.0	0.1587	0.1562	0.1539	0.1515	0.1492	0.1469	0.1446	0.1423	0.1401	0.1379
1.1	0.1357	0.1335	0.1314	0.1292	0.1271	0.1251	0.1230	0.1210	0.1190	0.1170
1.2	0.1151	0.1131	0.1112	0.1093	0.1075	0.1056	0.1038	0.1020	0.1003	0.0985
1.3	0.0968	0.0951	0.0934	0.0918	0.0901	0.0885	0.0869	0.0853	0.0838	0.0823
1.4	0.0808	0.0793	0.0778	0.0764	0.0749	0.0735	0.0721	0.0708	0.0694	0.0681
1.5	0.0668	0.0655	0.0643	0.0630	0.0618	0.0606	0.0594	0.0582	0.0571	0.0559
1.6	0.0548	0.0537	0.0526	0.0516	0.0505	0.0495	0.0485	0.0475	0.0465	0.0455
1.7	0.0446	0.0436	0.0427	0.0418	0.0409	0.0401	0.0392	0.0384	0.0375	0.0367
1.8	0.0359	0.0351	0.0344	0.0336	0.0329	0.0322	0.0314	0.0307	0.0301	0.0294
1.9	0.0287	0.0281	0.0274	0.0268	0.0262	0.0256	0.0250	0.0244	0.0239	0.0233
2.0	0.0228	0.0222	0.0217	0.0212	0.0207	0.0202	0.0197	0.0192	0.0188	0.0183
2.1	0.0179	0.0174	0.0170	0.0166	0.0162	0.0158	0.0154	0.0150	0.0146	0.0143
2.2	0.0139	0.0136	0.0132	0.0129	0.0125	0.0122	0.0119	0.0116	0.0113	0.0110
2.3	0.0107	0.0104	0.0102	0.0099	0.0096	0.0094	0.0091	0.0089	0.0087	0.0084
2.4	0.0082	0.0080	0.0078	0.0075	0.0073	0.0071	0.0069	0.0068	0.0066	0.0064
2.5	0.0062	0.0060	0.0059	0.0057	0.0055	0.0054	0.0052	0.0051	0.0049	0.0048
2.6	0.0047	0.0045	0.0044	0.0043	0.0041	0.0040	0.0039	0.0038	0.0037	0.0036

Table 1: Cont'd

z	0.0	0.01	0.02	0.03	0.04	0.05	0.06	0.07	0.08	0.09
2.7	0.0035	0.0034	0.0033	0.0032	0.0031	0.0030	0.0029	0.0028	0.0027	0.0026
2.8	0.0026	0.0025	0.0024	0.0023	0.0023	0.0022	0.0021	0.0021	0.0020	0.0019
2.9	0.0019	0.0018	0.0018	0.0017	0.0016	0.0016	0.0015	0.0015	0.0014	0.0014
3.0	0.0013	0.0013	0.0013	0.0012	0.0012	0.0011	0.0011	0.0011	0.0010	0.0010
3.1	0.0010	0.0009	0.0009	0.0009	0.0008	0.0008	0.0008	0.0008	0.0007	0.0007
3.2	0.0007	0.0007	0.0006	0.0006	0.0006	0.0006	0.0006	0.0005	0.0005	0.0005
3.3	0.0005	0.0005	0.0005	0.0004	0.0004	0.0004	0.0004	0.0004	0.0004	0.0003
3.4	0.0003	0.0003	0.0003	0.0003	0.0003	0.0003	0.0003	0.0003	0.0003	0.0002
3.5	0.0002	0.0002	0.0002	0.0002	0.0002	0.0002	0.0002	0.0002	0.0002	0.0002
3.6	0.0002	0.0002	0.0001	0.0001	0.0001	0.0001	0.0001	0.0001	0.0001	0.0001
3.7	0.0001	0.0001	0.0001	0.0001	0.0001	0.0001	0.0001	0.0001	0.0001	0.0001
3.8	0.0001	0.0001	0.0001	0.0001	0.0001	0.0001	0.0001	0.0001	0.0001	0.0001
3.9	0.0000	0.0000	0.0000	0.0000	0.0000	0.0000	0.0000	0.0000	0.0000	0.0000
4.0	0.0000	0.0000	0.0000	0.0000	0.0000	0.0000	0.0000	0.0000	0.0000	0.0000

Source: The entries in this table were computed by the author.

Table 2: χ^2*distribution*

For a particular degree of freedom (df) and at a given level of
significance (e.g., 0.05, 0.01 etc), the observed value of χ^2 is
significant if it is greater than or equal to the value shown in the
body of the table.

DF	0.10	0.05	0.02	0.01	0.001
1	2.706	3.841	5.412	6.635	10.828
2	4.605	5.991	7.824	9.210	13.816
3	6.251	7.815	9.837	11.345	16.266
4	7.779	9.488	11.668	13.277	18.467
5	9.236	11.070	13.388	15.086	20.515
6	10.645	12.592	15.033	16.812	22.458
7	12.017	14.067	16.622	18.475	24.322
8	13.362	15.507	18.168	20.090	26.124
9	14.684	16.919	19.679	21.666	27.877
10	15.987	18.307	21.161	23.209	29.588
11	17.275	19.675	22.618	24.725	31.264
12	18.549	21.026	24.054	26.217	32.909
13	19.812	22.362	25.472	27.688	34.528
14	21.064	23.685	26.873	29.141	36.123
15	22.307	24.996	28.259	30.578	37.697
16	23.542	26.296	29.633	32.000	39.252
17	24.769	27.587	30.995	33.409	40.790
18	25.989	28.869	32.346	34.805	42.312
19	27.204	30.144	33.687	36.191	43.820
20	28.412	31.410	35.020	37.566	45.315

Table 2: Cont'd

DF	0.10	0.05	0.02	0.01	0.001
21	29.615	32.671	36.343	38.932	46.797
22	30.813	33.924	37.659	40.289	48.268
23	32.007	35.172	38.968	41.638	49.728
24	33.196	36.415	40.270	42.980	51.179
25	34.382	37.652	41.566	44.314	52.620
26	35.563	38.885	42.856	45.642	54.052
27	36.741	40.113	44.140	46.963	55.476
28	37.916	41.337	45.419	48.278	56.892
29	39.087	42.557	46.693	49.588	58.301
30	40.256	43.773	47.962	50.892	59.703
50	63.167	67.505	72.613	76.154	86.661
75	91.061	96.217	102.243	106.393	118.599
100	118.498	124.342	131.142	135.807	149.449

Source: The entries in this table were computed by the author.

Table 3: t-distribution

For any particular degree of freedom (df) and at a given level of
significance, the observed t-value is significant if it is greater than
or equal to the value shown in the body of the table.

Level of significance for a one-tailed test

	0.050	0.025	0.010	0.005	0.0005
	Level of significance for a two-tailed test				
	0.100	0.050	0.020	0.010	0.001
DF					
1	6.314	12.706	31.821	63.657	636.619
2	2.920	4.303	6.965	9.925	31.599
3	2.353	3.182	4.541	5.841	12.924
4	2.132	2.776	3.747	4.604	8.610
5	2.015	2.571	3.365	4.032	6.869
6	1.943	2.447	3.143	3.707	5.959
7	1.895	2.365	2.998	3.499	5.408
8	1.860	2.306	2.896	3.355	5.041
9	1.833	2.262	2.821	3.250	4.781
10	1.812	2.228	2.764	3.169	4.587
11	1.796	2.201	2.718	3.106	4.437
12	1.782	2.179	2.681	3.055	4.318
13	1.771	2.160	2.650	3.012	4.221
14	1.761	2.145	2.624	2.977	4.140
15	1.753	2.131	2.602	2.947	4.073
16	1.746	2.120	2.583	2.921	4.015
17	1.740	2.110	2.567	2.898	3.965
18	1.734	2.101	2.552	2.878	3.922

Table 3: Cont'd

		0.100	0.050	0.020	0.010	0.001
DF						
19		1.729	2.093	2.539	2.861	3.883
20		1.725	2.086	2.528	2.845	3.850
21		1.721	2.080	2.518	2.831	3.819
22		1.717	2.074	2.508	2.819	3.792
23		1.714	2.069	2.500	2.807	3.768
24		1.711	2.064	2.492	2.797	3.745
25		1.708	2.060	2.485	2.787	3.725
26		1.706	2.056	2.479	2.779	3.707
27		1.703	2.052	2.473	2.771	3.690
28		1.701	2.048	2.467	2.763	3.674
29		1.699	2.045	2.462	2.756	3.659
30		1.697	2.042	2.457	2.750	3.646
31		1.696	2.040	2.453	2.744	3.633
32		1.694	2.037	2.449	2.738	3.622
33		1.692	2.035	2.445	2.733	3.611
34		1.691	2.032	2.441	2.728	3.601
35		1.690	2.030	2.438	2.724	3.591
40		1.684	2.021	2.423	2.704	3.551
45		1.679	2.014	2.412	2.690	3.520
50		1.676	2.009	2.403	2.678	3.496
60		1.671	2.000	2.390	2.660	3.460
∞		1.645	1.960	2.326	2.576	3.291

Level of significance for a two-tailed test

Source: The entries in this table were computed by the author.

Table 4: Critical value of U in the runs test for testing randomness

The two counts, n_1 and n_2 in the two categories of the binary variable should be ≤ 20.

To determine the LOWER critical value of U we enter the table with n_1 and n_2, if the observed value of U is ≤ the lower of the two values shown in the body of the table U is significant at the 0.05 level.

To determine the UPPER critical value of U we enter the table with n_1 and n_2, if the observed value of U is ≥ the larger of the pair of values shown in the body of the table then U is significant at the 0.05 level.

Any value of U for n_1 and n_2 which: i) is equal to either of the pair of critical values in the body of the table or ii) is smaller than the lowest figure in the pair or larger than the largest figure in the pair, is significant at the alpha = 0.05 level.

Each cell below shows the pair of critical values as *lower , upper* (only the lower value is shown where no upper critical value applies; "–" indicates neither value applies).

n_2＼n_1	2	3	4	5	6	7	8	9	10	11	12	13	14	15	16	17	18	19	20
2	–	–	–	–	–	–	–	–	–	–	2	2	2	2	2	2	2	2	2
3	–	–	–	–	2	2	2	2	2	2	2	2	3	3	3	3	3	3	3
4	–	–	–	2,9	2,9	2	3	3	3	3	3	3	3	3	4	4	4	4	4
5	–	–	2,9	2,10	3,10	3,11	3,11	3	3	4	4	4	4	4	4	4	5	5	5
6	–	2	2,9	3,10	3,11	3,12	3,12	4,13	4,13	4,13	4,13	5	5	5	5	5	5	6	6
7	–	2	2	3,11	3,12	3,13	4,13	4,14	5,14	5,14	5,14	5,15	5,15	6,15	6	6	6	6	6
8	–	2	3	3,11	3,12	4,13	4,14	5,14	5,15	5,15	6,16	6,16	6,16	6,16	6,17	7,17	7,17	7,17	7,17
9	–	2	3	3	4,13	4,14	5,14	5,15	5,16	6,16	6,16	6,17	7,17	7,18	7,18	7,18	8,18	8,18	8,18

Appendix

Table 4: Cont'd

Each cell gives the lower / upper critical value (— = not defined).

n_2 \\ n_1	2	3	4	5	6	7	8	9	10	11	12	13	14	15	16	17	18	19	20
10	2/—	2/—	3/—	3/—	4/13	5/14	5/15	5/16	6/16	6/17	7/17	7/18	7/18	7/18	8/19	8/19	8/19	8/20	9/20
11	2/—	2/—	3/—	4/—	4/13	5/14	5/15	6/16	6/17	7/17	7/18	7/18	8/19	8/19	8/20	9/20	9/20	9/21	9/21
12	2/—	2/—	3/—	4/—	4/13	5/14	6/16	6/16	7/17	7/18	7/19	8/19	8/20	8/20	9/21	9/21	9/21	10/22	10/22
13	2/—	2/—	3/—	4/—	5/—	5/15	6/16	7/17	7/18	7/19	8/19	8/20	9/20	9/21	9/21	10/22	10/22	10/23	10/23
14	2/—	2/—	3/—	4/—	5/—	6/15	6/16	7/17	7/18	8/19	8/20	9/20	9/21	9/22	10/22	10/23	10/23	11/23	11/24
15	2/—	3/—	3/—	4/—	5/—	6/—	6/16	7/18	8/18	8/19	8/20	9/21	9/22	10/22	10/23	11/23	11/24	11/24	12/25
16	2/—	3/—	4/—	4/—	5/—	6/—	6/16	7/18	8/19	8/20	9/21	9/21	10/22	10/23	11/23	11/24	11/25	12/25	12/25
17	2/—	3/—	4/—	4/—	5/—	6/—	7/17	8/18	8/19	9/20	9/21	10/22	10/23	11/23	11/24	12/24	12/25	12/26	13/26
18	2/—	3/—	4/—	5/—	5/—	6/—	7/17	8/18	8/19	9/20	9/21	10/22	10/23	11/24	11/25	12/25	12/25	13/26	13/27
19	2/—	3/—	4/—	5/—	6/—	6/—	7/17	8/18	9/20	9/21	10/22	10/23	11/23	11/24	12/25	12/26	13/26	13/27	13/27
20	2/—	3/—	4/—	5/—	6/—	6/—	7/17	8/18	9/20	9/21	10/22	10/23	11/24	12/25	12/25	13/26	13/27	13/27	14/28

*Table 4 is taken from table G of Siegel, S. and Castellan, N.J. (1988) Nonparametric Statistics for the Behavioral Sciences, 2nd edition, published by McGraw-Hill and reproduced with the kind permission of the authors and publisher.

Table 5: Wilcoxon matched-pairs signed-ranks test rank sum total statistic critical values

Number of pairs = N	Level of significance for 1-tailed test		
	0.025	0.010	0.005
	Level of significance for 2-tailed test		
	0.05	0.02	0.01
6	0	–	–
7	2	0	–
8	4	2	0
9	6	3	2
10	8	5	3
11	11	7	5
12	14	10	7
13	17	13	10
14	21	16	13
15	25	20	16
16	30	24	20
17	35	28	23
18	40	33	28
19	46	38	32
20	52	43	38
21	59	49	43
22	66	56	49
23	73	62	55
24	81	69	61
25	89	77	68

Appendix

Table 6:   Critical values for the Kruskal-Wallis ANOVA by ranks statistic h

Sample sizes			α				
n_1	n_2	n_3	.10	.05	.01	.005	.001
2	2	2	4.25				
3	2	1	4.29				
3	2	2	4.71	4.71			
3	3	1	4.57	5.14			
3	3	2	4.56	5.36			
3	3	3	4.62	5.60	7.20	7.20	
4	2	1	4.50				
4	2	2	4.46	5.33			
4	3	1	4.06	5.21			
4	3	2	4.51	5.44	6.44	7.00	
4	3	3	4.71	5.73	6.75	7.32	8.02
4	4	1	4.17	4.97	6.67		
4	4	2	4.55	5.45	7.04	7.28	
4	4	3	4.55	5.60	7.14	7.59	8.32
4	4	4	4.65	5.69	7.66	8.00	8.65
5	2	1	4.20	5.00			
5	2	2	4.36	5.16	6.53		
5	3	1	4.02	4.96			
5	3	2	4.65	5.25	6.82	7.18	
5	3	3	4.53	5.65	7.08	7.51	8.24
5	4	1	3.99	4.99	6.95	7.36	
5	4	2	4.54	5.27	7.12	7.57	8.11
5	4	3	4.55	5.63	7.44	7.91	8.50
5	4	4	4.62	5.62	7.76	8.14	9.00
5	5	1	4.11	5.13	7.31	7.75	
5	5	2	4.62	5.34	7.27	8.13	8.68
5	5	3	4.54	5.71	7.54	8.24	9.06
5	5	4	4.53	5.64	7.77	8.37	9.32
5	5	5	4.56	5.78	7.98	8.72	9.68
Large samples			4.61	5.99	9.21	10.60	13.82

Note: The absence of an entry in the extreme tails indicates that the
distribution may not take on the necesary extremes values.
Table 6 is taken from table O of Siegel, S. and Castellan, N.J. (1988)
Nonparametric Statistics for the Behavioral Sciences, 2nd edition,
published by McGraw-Hill and reproduced with the kind permission of
the authors and publisher.

Table 7: Critical values of the F-distribution at various levels of probability (0.05, 0.025 and 0.01)

For any combination of V1 (numerator df) and V2 (denominator or error df) the observed value of the F statistic is significant at the chosen alpha level if it is equal to or larger than the critical F value shown in the body of the table.

Alpha = 0.05

V2						V1					
	1	2	3	4	5	6	7	8	12	24	50
1	161.4	199.5	215.7	224.6	230.2	234.0	236.8	238.9	243.9	249.1	251.8
2	18.51	19.00	19.16	19.25	19.30	19.33	19.35	19.37	19.41	19.45	19.48
3	10.13	9.55	9.28	9.12	9.01	8.94	8.89	8.85	8.74	8.64	8.58
4	7.71	6.94	6.59	6.39	6.26	6.16	6.09	6.04	5.91	5.77	5.70
5	6.61	5.79	5.41	5.19	5.05	4.95	4.88	4.82	4.68	4.53	4.44
6	5.99	5.14	4.76	4.53	4.39	4.28	4.21	4.15	4.00	3.84	3.75
7	5.59	4.74	4.35	4.12	3.97	3.87	3.79	3.73	3.57	3.41	3.32
8	5.32	4.46	4.07	3.84	3.69	3.58	3.50	3.44	3.28	3.12	3.02
9	5.12	4.26	3.86	3.63	3.48	3.37	3.29	3.23	3.07	2.90	2.80
10	4.96	4.10	3.71	3.48	3.33	3.22	3.14	3.07	2.91	2.74	2.64
11	4.84	3.98	3.59	3.36	3.20	3.09	3.01	2.95	2.79	2.61	2.51

Table 7: Cont'd

Alpha = 0.05

V1

V2	1	2	3	4	5	6	7	8	12	24	50
12	4.75	3.89	3.49	3.26	3.11	3.00	2.91	2.85	2.69	2.51	2.40
13	4.67	3.81	3.41	3.18	3.03	2.92	2.83	2.77	2.60	2.42	2.31
14	4.60	3.74	3.34	3.11	2.96	2.85	2.76	2.70	2.53	2.35	2.24
15	4.54	3.68	3.29	3.06	2.90	2.79	2.71	2.64	2.48	2.29	2.18
16	4.49	3.63	3.24	3.01	2.85	2.74	2.66	2.59	2.42	2.24	2.12
17	4.45	3.59	3.20	2.96	2.81	2.70	2.61	2.55	2.38	2.19	2.08
18	4.41	3.55	3.16	2.93	2.77	2.66	2.58	2.51	2.34	2.15	2.04
19	4.38	3.52	3.13	2.90	2.74	2.63	2.54	2.48	2.31	2.11	2.00
20	4.35	3.49	3.10	2.87	2.71	2.60	2.51	2.45	2.28	2.08	1.97
21	4.32	3.47	3.07	2.84	2.68	2.57	2.49	2.42	2.25	2.05	1.94
22	4.30	3.44	3.05	2.82	2.66	2.55	2.46	2.40	2.23	2.03	1.91

Table 7: Cont'd

23	1.88	2.01	2.20	2.37	2.44	2.53	2.64	2.80	3.03	3.42	4.28
24	1.86	1.98	2.18	2.36	2.42	2.51	2.62	2.78	3.01	3.40	4.26
25	1.84	1.96	2.16	2.34	2.40	2.49	2.60	2.76	2.99	3.39	4.24
26	1.82	1.95	2.15	2.32	2.39	2.47	2.59	2.74	2.98	3.37	4.23
27	1.81	1.93	2.13	2.31	2.37	2.46	2.57	2.73	2.96	3.35	4.21
28	1.79	1.91	2.12	2.29	2.36	2.45	2.56	2.71	2.95	3.34	4.20
29	1.77	1.90	2.10	2.28	2.35	2.43	2.55	2.70	2.93	3.33	4.18
30	1.76	1.89	2.09	2.27	2.33	2.42	2.53	2.69	2.92	3.32	4.17
40	1.66	1.79	2.00	2.18	2.25	2.34	2.45	2.61	2.84	3.23	4.08
50	1.60	1.74	1.95	2.13	2.20	2.29	2.40	2.56	2.79	3.18	4.03
60	1.56	1.70	1.92	2.10	2.17	2.25	2.37	2.53	2.76	3.15	4.00
120	1.46	1.61	1.83	2.02	2.09	2.18	2.29	2.45	2.68	3.07	3.92
150	1.44	1.59	1.82	2.00	2.07	2.16	2.27	2.43	2.66	3.06	3.90
200	1.41	1.57	1.80	1.98	2.06	2.14	2.26	2.42	2.65	3.04	3.89
250	1.40	1.56	1.79	1.98	2.05	2.13	2.25	2.41	2.64	3.03	3.88
500	1.38	1.54	1.77	1.96	2.03	2.12	2.23	2.39	2.62	3.01	3.86

Table 7: Cont'd

Alpha = 0.025

V2 \ V1	1	2	3	4	5	6	7	8	12	24	50
1	647.8	799.5	864.2	899.6	921.9	937.1	948.2	956.7	976.7	997.3	1008
2	38.51	39.00	39.17	39.25	39.30	39.33	39.36	39.37	39.41	39.46	39.48
3	17.44	16.04	15.44	15.10	14.88	14.73	14.62	14.54	14.34	14.12	14.01
4	12.22	10.65	9.98	9.60	9.36	9.20	9.07	8.98	8.75	8.51	8.38
5	10.01	8.43	7.76	7.39	7.15	6.98	6.85	6.76	6.52	6.28	6.14
6	8.81	7.26	6.60	6.23	5.99	5.82	5.70	5.60	5.37	5.12	4.98
7	8.07	6.54	5.89	5.52	5.29	5.12	4.99	4.90	4.67	4.41	4.28
8	7.57	6.06	5.42	5.05	4.82	4.65	4.53	4.43	4.20	3.95	3.81
9	7.21	5.71	5.08	4.72	4.48	4.32	4.20	4.10	3.87	3.61	3.47
10	6.94	5.46	4.83	4.47	4.24	4.07	3.95	3.85	3.62	3.37	3.22
11	6.72	5.26	4.63	4.28	4.04	3.88	3.76	3.66	3.43	3.17	3.03
12	6.55	5.10	4.47	4.12	3.89	3.73	3.61	3.51	3.28	3.02	2.87

Table 7: Cont'd

	6.41	4.97	4.35	4.00	3.77	3.60	3.48	3.39	3.15	2.89	2.74
13	6.41	4.97	4.35	4.00	3.77	3.60	3.48	3.39	3.15	2.89	2.74
14	6.30	4.86	4.24	3.89	3.66	3.50	3.38	3.29	3.05	2.79	2.64
15	6.20	4.77	4.15	3.80	3.58	3.41	3.29	3.20	2.96	2.70	2.55
16	6.12	4.69	4.08	3.73	3.50	3.34	3.22	3.12	2.89	2.63	2.47
17	6.04	4.62	4.01	3.66	3.44	3.28	3.16	3.06	2.82	2.56	2.41
18	5.98	4.56	3.95	3.61	3.38	3.22	3.10	3.01	2.77	2.50	2.35
19	5.92	4.51	3.90	3.56	3.33	3.17	3.05	2.96	2.72	2.45	2.30
20	5.87	4.46	3.86	3.51	3.29	3.13	3.01	2.91	2.68	2.41	2.25
21	5.83	4.42	3.82	3.48	3.25	3.09	2.97	2.87	2.64	2.37	2.21
22	5.79	4.38	3.78	3.44	3.22	3.05	2.93	2.84	2.60	2.33	2.17
23	5.75	4.35	3.75	3.41	3.18	3.02	2.90	2.81	2.57	2.30	2.14
24	5.72	4.32	3.72	3.38	3.15	2.99	2.87	2.78	2.54	2.27	2.11
25	5.69	4.29	3.69	3.35	3.13	2.97	2.85	2.75	2.51	2.24	2.08
26	5.66	4.27	3.67	3.33	3.10	2.94	2.82	2.73	2.49	2.22	2.05
27	5.63	4.24	3.65	3.31	3.08	2.92	2.80	2.71	2.47	2.19	2.03
28	5.61	4.22	3.63	3.29	3.06	2.90	2.78	2.69	2.45	2.17	2.01

Table 7: Cont'd

Alpha = 0.025

V1

V2	1	2	3	4	5	6	7	8	12	24	50
29	5.59	4.20	3.61	3.27	3.04	2.88	2.76	2.67	2.43	2.15	1.99
30	5.57	4.18	3.59	3.25	3.03	2.87	2.75	2.65	2.41	2.14	1.97
40	5.42	4.05	3.46	3.13	2.90	2.74	2.62	2.53	2.29	2.01	1.83
50	5.34	3.97	3.39	3.05	2.83	2.67	2.55	2.46	2.22	1.93	1.75
60	5.29	3.93	3.34	3.01	2.79	2.63	2.51	2.41	2.17	1.88	1.70
120	5.15	3.80	3.23	2.89	2.67	2.52	2.39	2.30	2.05	1.76	1.56
150	5.13	3.78	3.20	2.87	2.65	2.49	2.37	2.28	2.03	1.74	1.54
200	5.10	3.76	3.18	2.85	2.63	2.47	2.35	2.26	2.01	1.71	1.51
250	5.08	3.74	3.17	2.84	2.62	2.46	2.34	2.24	2.00	1.70	1.49
500	5.05	3.72	3.14	2.81	2.59	2.43	2.31	2.22	1.97	1.67	1.46

Table 7: Cont'd

Alpha = 0.01

	V1										
V2	1	2	3	4	5	6	7	8	12	24	50
1	4052	5000	5403	5625	5764	5859	5928	5981	6106	6235	6303
2	98.50	99.00	99.17	99.25	99.30	99.33	99.36	99.37	99.42	99.46	99.48
3	34.12	30.82	29.46	28.71	28.24	27.91	27.67	27.49	27.05	26.60	26.35
4	21.20	18.00	16.69	15.98	15.52	15.21	14.98	14.80	14.37	13.93	13.69
5	16.26	13.27	12.06	11.39	10.97	10.67	10.46	10.29	9.89	9.47	9.24
6	13.75	10.92	9.78	9.15	8.75	8.47	8.26	8.10	7.72	7.31	7.09
7	12.25	9.55	8.45	7.85	7.46	7.19	6.99	6.84	6.47	6.07	5.86
8	11.26	8.65	7.59	7.01	6.63	6.37	6.18	6.03	5.67	5.28	5.07
9	10.56	8.02	6.99	6.42	6.06	5.80	5.61	5.47	5.11	4.73	4.52
10	10.04	7.56	6.55	5.99	5.64	5.39	5.20	5.06	4.71	4.33	4.12
11	9.65	7.21	6.22	5.67	5.32	5.07	4.89	4.74	4.40	4.02	3.81
12	9.33	6.93	5.95	5.41	5.06	4.82	4.64	4.50	4.16	3.78	3.57

Table 7: Cont'd

Alpha = 0.01

	V1										
V2	1	2	3	4	5	6	7	8	12	24	50
13	9.07	6.70	5.74	5.21	4.86	4.62	4.44	4.30	3.96	3.59	3.38
14	8.86	6.51	5.56	5.04	4.69	4.46	4.28	4.14	3.80	3.43	3.22
15	8.68	6.36	5.42	4.89	4.56	4.32	4.14	4.00	3.67	3.29	3.08
16	8.53	6.23	5.29	4.77	4.44	4.20	4.03	3.89	3.55	3.18	2.97
17	8.40	6.11	5.18	4.67	4.34	4.10	3.93	3.79	3.46	3.08	2.87
18	8.29	6.01	5.09	4.58	4.25	4.01	3.84	3.71	3.37	3.00	2.78
19	8.18	5.93	5.01	4.50	4.17	3.94	3.77	3.63	3.30	2.92	2.71
20	8.10	5.85	4.94	4.43	4.10	3.87	3.70	3.56	3.23	2.86	2.64
21	8.02	5.78	4.87	4.37	4.04	3.81	3.64	3.51	3.17	2.80	2.58
22	7.95	5.72	4.82	4.31	3.99	3.76	3.59	3.45	3.12	2.75	2.53
23	7.88	5.66	4.76	4.26	3.94	3.71	3.54	3.41	3.07	2.70	2.48
24	7.82	5.61	4.72	4.22	3.90	3.67	3.50	3.36	3.03	2.66	2.44

Table 7: Cont'd

25	7.77	5.57	4.68	4.18	3.85	3.63	3.46	3.32	2.99	2.62	2.40
26	7.72	5.53	4.64	4.14	3.82	3.59	3.42	3.29	2.96	2.58	2.36
27	7.68	5.49	4.60	4.11	3.78	3.56	3.39	3.26	2.93	2.55	2.33
28	7.64	5.45	4.57	4.07	3.75	3.53	3.36	3.23	2.90	2.52	2.30
29	7.60	5.42	4.54	4.04	3.73	3.50	3.33	3.20	2.87	2.49	2.27
30	7.56	5.39	4.51	4.02	3.70	3.47	3.30	3.17	2.84	2.47	2.25
40	7.31	5.18	4.31	3.83	3.51	3.29	3.12	2.99	2.66	2.29	2.06
50	7.17	5.06	4.20	3.72	3.41	3.19	3.02	2.89	2.56	2.18	1.95
60	7.08	4.98	4.13	3.65	3.34	3.12	2.95	2.82	2.50	2.12	1.88
120	6.85	4.79	3.95	3.48	3.17	2.96	2.79	2.66	2.34	1.95	1.70
150	6.81	4.75	3.91	3.45	3.14	2.92	2.76	2.63	2.31	1.92	1.66
200	6.76	4.71	3.88	3.41	3.11	2.89	2.73	2.60	2.27	1.89	1.63
250	6.74	4.69	3.86	3.40	3.09	2.87	2.71	2.58	2.26	1.87	1.61
500	6.69	4.65	3.82	3.36	3.05	2.84	2.68	2.55	2.22	1.83	1.57

Source: The entries in this table were computed by the author.

References

Audit Commission for Local Authorities and the National Health Service in England and Wales (1992) *Getting in on the Act, Provision for Pupils with Special Educational Needs: The National Picture*, London, HMSO.

Bartholomew, D.J. (1995) 'What is statistics?', *Journal Royal Statistical Society*, A 158, Part 1, 1–20.

Bartram, D. (1990) 'Reliability and validity', in Beech, J.R. and Harding, L. (Eds) *Testing People: A Practical Guide to Psychometrics*.

Bernadin, H.J. and Bownas, D.A. (1985) (Eds) *Personality Assessment in Organizations*, New York, Praeger.

Birkes, D. and Dodge, Y. (1993) *Alternative Methods of Regression*, London, Wiley.

Blair, R.C. and Higgins, J.J. (1985) 'Comparison of the power of the paired samples t-test to that of Wilcoxon's signed-ranks test under various population shapes', *Psychological Bulletin*, **97**, 1, 119–28.

Blasingame, M. and McManis, D. (1977) 'Classification, relative thinking, and transitivity performance by retarded individuals', *American Journal of Mental Deficiency*, **82**, 1, 91–4.

Boneau, C.A. (1960) 'The effects of violations of assumptions underlying the t-test', *Psychological Bulletin*, **57**, 49–64.

Booth, C. (1889–1902) *Labour and Life of the People of London*, 17 volumes, Macmillan, London.

Borg, M.G. and Riding, R.J. (1993) 'Teacher stress and cognitive style', *British Journal of Educational Psychology*, **63**, 271–86.

Borzone de Manrique, A.M. and Signorini, A. (1994) 'Phonological awareness, spelling and reading abilities in Spanish-speaking children', *British Journal of Educational Psychology*, **64**, 429–39.

Boser, J. and Poppen, W.A. (1978) 'Identification of teacher verbal response roles for improving student-teacher relationships', *Journal Educational Research*, **72**, 2, 90–9.

Boyle, G.J. and Houndoulesi, V. (1993) 'Utility of the school Motivation Analysis Test in predicting second language acquisition', *British Journal of Educational Psychology*, **63**, 500–12.

Bradley, J.V. (1984) 'The complexity of nonrobustness effects', *Bulletin of the Psychonomic Society*, **22**(3), 250–3.

British Psychological Society (1990) *Psychological Testing: A Guide*, British

Psychological Society (BPS) Steering Committee on Test Standards, Professional Affairs Board, Leicester, BPS.

BUROS, O.K. (1978) *The VIIth Mental Measurement Year Book*, Highland Park, NJ, Gryphon Press.

CAMILLI, G. and HOPKINS, K.D. (1978) 'Applicability of chi-square to 2×2 contingency tables with small expected cell frequencies', *Psychological Bulletin*, **85**, 1, 163–7.

CATTELL, R.B., EBER, H.W. and TATSUOKA, M.M. (1970) *Handbook for the Sixteen Personality Factor Questionnaire* (16PF), Champaign, IL, IPAT.

CHATFIELD, C. (1984) *The Analysis of Time Series*, 3rd edn., London, Chapman and Hall.

CHATFIELD, C. (1985) 'The initial examination of data' (with discussion), *Journal Royal Statistical Society*, A, **148**, 214–53

CHATFIELD, C. (1993) *Problem Solving a Statistician's Guide*, London, Chapman & Hall.

CHATFIELD, C. (1995) 'Model uncertainty, data mining and statistical inference' (with discussion), *Journal Royal Statistical Society, Series A (Statistics in Society)*, **158**, 3, 419–66.

CHRISTENSEN, C.A. and COOPER, T.J. (1992) 'The role of cognitive strategies in the transition from counting to retrieval of basic addition facts', *British Educational Research Journal*, **18**, 1, 37–44.

CIECHALSKI, J.C. (1988) 'A basic program for computing the Kruskal-Wallis H', *Educational and Psychological Measurement*, **48**, 707–9.

CLIFFE, M.J. (1992) 'Symptom-validity testing of feigned sensory or memory deficits: A further elaboration for subjects who understand the rationale', *British Journal of Clinical Psychology*, **31**, 2, 207–9.

CLAY, M.M. (1990) 'The reading recovery programme, 1984–88: Coverage, outcomes and educational board district figures', *New Zealand Journal of Educational Studies*, **25**, 61–70.

CONOVER, W.J. (1980) *Practical Non-Parametric Statistics*, 2nd edn., New York, Wiley.

COOK, D.C. and CAMPBELL, D.T. (1979) *Quasi-experimentation: Design and Analysis Issues for Field Settings*, Boston, MA, Houghton Mifflin.

COPE, P., INGLIS, B., RIDDELL, S. and SULHUNT, O. (1992) 'The value of inservice degrees: Teachers' long-term perceptions of their impact', *British Educational Research Journal*, **18**, 3, 297–307.

CRONBACH, L.J. (1990) *Essentials of Psychological Testing*, 5th edn., New York, Harper & Row.

CULLINGFORD, C. (1994) 'Children's responses to television advertising: The magic age of 8', *Research in Education*, **51**, 79–84.

DAGENAIS, F. and MARASCIULO, L.A. (1981) 'Perception of the success of integration in multiracial high school among social groups defined by social interaction', *Journal of Educational Research*, **75**, 78–86.

DELLATOLAS, G., MOREA, T., JALLON, P. and LELLOUCH, J. (1993) 'Upper limb injuries and handedness plasticity', *British Journal of Psychology*, **84**, 201–5.

DELUCCHI, K.L. (1983) 'The use and misuse of the chi-square: Lewis and Burke revisited', *Psychological Bulletin*, **94**, 1, 166–76.

DOCUMENTA GEIGY (1970) *Scientific Tables*, 7th edn., Basle.

DOWSWELL, T. and HEWISON, J. (1995) 'Schools, maternal employment and child health care', *British Educational Research Journal*, **21**, 15–29.

DRACUP, C. (1995) 'Hypothesis testing: What it really is', *The Psychologist*, August, 359–62.

EBEL, R.L. and FRISBIE, D.A. (1986) *Essentials of Educational Measurement*, Englewood Cliffs, NJ, Prentice-Hall.

EFRON, B. (1995) 'The statistical century', *RSS News*, **22**, 5, 1–2.

ELKIND, D. (1961) 'Children's concepts of right and left: Piaget replication study IV', *Journal of Genetic Psychology*, **99**, 269–76.

ELLIOTT, J.A. and HEWISON, J. (1994) 'Comprehension and interest in home reading', *British Journal of Educational Psychology*, **64**, 2, 203–20.

ESTES, W.K. (1991) *Statistical Models in Behavioral Research*, New Jersey, Lawrence Erlbaum Associates, Inc.

FISHER, R.A. (1935) 'The logic of inductive inference', *Journal Royal Statistical Society, Series A*, **98**, 39–54.

FISHER, R.A. (1953) *The Design of Experiments*, 6th edn., Edinburgh and London, Oliver & Boyd.

FULLJAMES, P., GIBSON, H.M. and FRANCIS, L.J. (1991) 'Creationism, scientism, christianity and science: A study in adolescent attitudes', *British Educational Research Journal*, **17**, 2, 171–90.

GABRIEL, K.R. and LACHENBRUCH, P.A. (1969) 'Non-parametric ANOVA in small samples: A Monte Carlo study of the adequacy of the asymptotic approximation', *Biometrics*, **25**, 593–6.

GARDINER, J.M. (1989) 'A generation effect in memory without awareness', *British Journal of Psychology*, **80**, 163–8.

GARDNER, M.J. and ALTMAN, M.J. (1989) 'Statistics with confidence: Confidence intervals and statistical guidelines', London, British Medical Journal.

GUILFORD, J.P. and FRUCHTER, B. (1973), 'Fundamental statistics in psychology and education', New York, McGraw-Hill.

GUSTAFSON, D.H., KESTLY, J.J., LUDKE, R.L. and LARSON, F. (1973) 'Probabilistic information processing: Implementation and evaluation of a semi-PIP diagnostic system, *Computational Biomedical Research*, **6**, 355–70.

HART, P.M., WEARING, A.J. and CONN, M. (1995) 'Conventional wisdom is a poor predictor of the relationship between discipline policy, student misbehaviour and teacher stress', *British Journal of Educational Psychology*, **65**, 27–48.

HARTLEY, J. (1994) 'Three ways to improve the clarity of journal abstracts', *British Journal of Educational Psychology*, **64**, 331–43.

HAYS, W.L. (1981) *Statistics*, 3rd edn., New York, Holt, Rinehart & Winston.

HEARN, J.C. and GRISWOLD, C.P. (1994) 'State-level centralization and policy innovation in US postsecondary education', *Educational Evaluation and Policy Analysis*, **16**, 2, 161–90.

HENRY, G.T. (1990) 'Practical sampling', *Applied Social Research Methods Series*, **12**, London, Sage.

HOPKINS, K.D. and WEEKS, D.L. (1990) 'Tests for normality and measures of skewness and kurtosis: Their place in research reporting', *Educational and Psychological Measurement*, **50**, 717–29.

HORTON, R.L. (1978) *The General Linear Model*, New York, McGraw-Hill International.

JOHNSTON, R.S., RUGG, M.D. and SCOTT, T. (1987) 'The influence of phonology on good and poor readers when reading for meaning', *Journal of Memory and Language*, **26**, 57–8.

KENDALL, M.G. (1948) *Rank Correlation Methods*, London, Griffin.

KESELMAN, H.J. and ROGAN, J.C. (1977) 'An evaluation of some non-parametric and parametric tests for multiple comparisons', *British Journal of Mathematical Statistical Psychology*, **30**, 125–33.

KLINE, P. (1990) 'Selecting the best test', in BEECH, J.R. and HARDING, L. (Eds) *Testing People: A Practical Guide to Psychometrics*, Windsor, NFER-Nelson.

KORNBROT, D.E. (1990) 'The rank difference test: A new and meaningful alternative to the Wilcoxon signed ranks test for ordinal data', *British Journal of Mathematical and Statistical Psychology*, **43**, 241–64.

KYRIACOU, C. (1992) 'Active learning in secondary school mathematics', *British Journal of Educational Research*, **18**, 3, 309–18.

LEWIS, D., and BURKE, C.J. (1949) 'The use and misuse of the chi-square test', *Psychological Bulletin*, **46**, 6, 433–89.

LIPSEY, W.M. (1990) *Design Sensitivity Statistical Power for Experimental Research*, London, Sage.

LITTLE, R.J.A. and RUBIN, D.B. (1987) *Statistical Analysis with Missing Data*, New York, Wiley.

MACHIN, D. and CAMPBELL, M.J. (1987) *Statistical Tables for the Design of Clinical Trials*, Oxford, Blackwell Scientific Publishers.

MACKAY, T.A. and BOYLE, J.M. (1994) 'Meeting the needs of pupils with learning difficulties: What do primary and secondary schools expect of their educational psychologists?', *Educational Research*, **36**, 2, 187–96.

MANLEY, B.F.J. (1986) *Multivariate Statistical Methods*, London, Chapman and Hall.

MARASCUILO, L.A. and DAGENAIS, F. (1982) 'Planned and post hoc comparisons for tests of homogeneity where the dependent variable is categorical and ordered', *Educational and Psychological Measurement*, **42**, 777–81.

MARSH, A.J. (1995) 'The effects on school budgets of non-statemented special educational needs indicators within a common funding formula', *British Educational Research Journal*, 99–115.

MARTIN, M. and NORWICH, B. (1991) 'The integration of research findings on classroom management into a programme for use in teacher education', *British Educational Research Journal*, **17**, 4, 333–51.

MEAD, R. (1992) The design of experiments: Statistical principles for practical application.

MESSICK, S. (1989) 'Validity', in LINN, R.L. (Ed.) *Educational Measurement*, 3rd edn., New York: ACE/Macmillan.

MILLIGAN, G.W. (1987) 'The use of the Arc-Sine transformation in analysis of variance', *Educational and Psychological Measurement*, **47**, 563–73.

MORRIS, L.J., FITZ-GIBBON, C.T. and LINDHEIM, E. (1987) *How to Measure Performance and Use Tests*, London, Sage.

MOSTELLER, F. and TUKEY, J.W. (1977) *Data Analysis and Regression*, Reading, MA, Addison-Wesley.

MURPHY, R. and TORRANCE, H. (1988) *The Changing Face of Educational Assessment*, Milton Keynes, Open University Press.

MYERS, J.L., DICECCO, J.V., WHITE, J.B. and BORDEN, V.M. (1982) 'Repeated measurements on dichotomous variables: Q and F tests, *Psychological Bulletin*, **92**, 2, 517–25.

NEWELL, K.M. and HANCOCK, P.A. (1984) 'Forgotten moments: A note on skewness and kurtosis as influential factors in inferences extrapolated from response distributions', *Journal of Motor Behavior*, **16**, 320–35.

ONOCHA, C. and OKPALA, P. (1990) 'Classroom interaction patterns of practising and pre-service teachers of integrated science', *Research in Education*, **43**, May 23–31.

OPEN UNIVERSITY PRESS (1986) *Statistics in Society*, Course text MDST 242, Unit A1., Open University Press, Milton Keynes.

PATIL, K.D. (1975) 'Cochran's Q test: Exact distribution', *Journal American Statistical Association*, **70**, 186–9.

PEERS, I.S. (1994) 'Gender and age bias in the predictor-criterion relationship of A levels and degree performance, a logistic regression analysis', *Research in Education*, **52**, 23–41.

PEERS, I.S. and JOHNSTON, M. (1994) 'The influence of learning context on the relationship between A-level attainment and final degree performance: A meta-analytic review', *British Journal of Educational Psychology*, **64**, 1–18.

PILLINER, A. (1979) 'Norm-referenced and criterion referenced tests: An evaluation', in *Issues in Educational Assessment*, Edinburgh, Scottish Education Department.

RAUDENBUSH, S.W., EAMSUKKAWAT, S., DI-IBOR, I., KAMALI, M. and TAOKLAM, W. (1993) 'On-the-job improvements in teacher competence: Policy options and their effects on teaching and learning in Thailand', *Educational Evaluation and Policy Analysis*, **15**, 3, 279–97.

REGIS, D., BISH, D. and BALDING, J. (1994) 'The place of alcohol education: Reflections and research after Eiser *et al.*' (1988), *Educational Research*, **36**, 2, 149–56.

RIDDELL, S., BROWN, S. and DUFFIELD, J. (1994) 'Parental power and special educational needs: The case of specific learning difficulties', *British Educational Research Journal*, **20**, 3, 327–44.

ROBERTSON, C. (1991) 'Computationally intensive statistics' in LOVIE, P. and LOVIE, A.D. (Eds) *New Developments in Statistics for Psychology and the Social Sciences*, London, Routledge, 49–80.

ROBINSON, A. and ROBINSON, M.E. (1983) 'Mental mapping and the co-ordination of perspectives in young children', *Research in Education*, **30**, 39–51.

ROKER, D. and BANKS, M. (1993) 'Adolescent identity and school type', *British Journal of Psychology*, **84**, 297–300.

ROOPNARINE, J.L., AHMEDUZZAMAN, M., DONNELY, S., GILL, P., MENNIS, A., ARKY, L., DINGLER, K., MCLAUGHLIN, M. and TALUKDER, E. (1992) 'Social-cognitive play behaviors and playmate preferences in same-age and mixed-age classrooms over a 6-month period', *American Educational Research Journal*, Winter, **29**, 4, 757–76.

SAS INSTITUTE, INC. (1990) SAS *Procedures Guide*, Version 6, 3rd edn., Cary, NC, SAS Institute Inc.

SAS INSTITUTE, INC. (1991) SAS *System for Linear Models*, 3rd edn., Cary, NC, SAS Institute Inc.

SAS INSTITUTE, INC. (1993a) SAS/INSIGHT *User's Guide*, Version 6, 2nd edn., Cary, NC, SAS Institute Inc.

SAS INSTITUTE, INC. (1993b) SAS *Language Reference Version 6*, 1st edn., Cary, NC, SAS Institute Inc.

SACHDEVA, D. (1975) 'Some useful applications of the sign test', *Psychological Reports*, 36, 55–8.

SATTERTHWAITE, F.E. (1946) 'An approximate distribution of estimates of variance components, *Biometrics Bulletin*, **2**, 110–14.

SCHLOTZHAUER, S.D. and LITTELL, R.C. (1987) SAS *System for Elementary Statistical Analysis*, Cary, NC, SAS Institute Inc.

SCOTT, W. (1955) 'Reliability of content analysis: The case of nominal scale coding', *Public Opinion Quarterly*, **19**, 3, 321–25.

SIEGEL, S. and CASTELLAN, N.J. (1988) 'Nonparametric statistics for the behavioral sciences', 2nd edn., New York, McGraw-Hill.

SINGER, J.D. and WILLETT, J.B. (1993) 'It's about time: Using discrete-time survival analysis to study duration and timing of events, *Journal of Educational Statistics*, **18**, 2, 155–95.

SKAALVIK, E.M. and RANKIN, R.J. (1994) 'Gender differences in mathematics and verbal achievement, self-perception and motivation', *British Journal of Educational Psychology*, **64**, 419–28.

SPECTOR, P.E. (1993) SAS *Programming for Researchers and Social Scientists*, London, Sage.

SWATTON, P. and TAYLOR, R.M. (1994) 'Pupil performance in graphical tasks and its relationship to the ability to handle variables, *British Educational Research Journal*, **20**, 2.

SWED, F.S. and EISENHART, C. (1943) 'Tables for testing randomness of grouping in a sequence of alternatives', *Annals of Mathematical Statistics*, **14**, 83–6.

TABACHNICK, B.G. and FIDELL, L.S. (1989) *Using Multivariate Statistics*, New York, Harper Collins.

TIKU, M.L. TAN, W.Y. and BALAKRISHNAN, N. (1986) *Robust Inference*, New York, Dekker.

TOMS, M., MORRIS, N. and FOLEY, P. (1994) 'Characteristics of visual interference with visuospatial working memory', *British Journal of Psychology*, **85**, 131–44.

TOOTHAKER, L.E. (1991) *Multiple comparisons for researchers*, London, Sage.

TORRANCE, M., THOMAS, G.V. and ROBINSON, E.J. (1993) 'Training in thesis writing: An evaluation of three conceptual orientations', *British Journal of Educational Psychology*, **63**, 170–84.

WALSH, B.F. and TOOTHAKER, L.E. (1974) 'An empirical comparison of the ANOVA F-test, Normal scores test and Kruskal-Wallis test under violation of assumptions', *Educational and Psychological Measurement*, **34**, 789–99.

WINER, B.J. (1962) *Statistical Principles in Experimental Design*, New York, McGraw-Hill.

WINER, B.J. (1971) *Statistical Principles in Experimental Design* (2nd edn.), New York, McGraw-Hill.

YATES, F. (1934) 'Contingency tables involving small numbers and the χ^2 test', *Journal of the Royal Statistical Society Supplement*, **1**, 217–35.

ZAR, J.H. (1972) 'Significance testing of the Spearman rank correlation coefficient', *Journal of the American Statistical Association*, **67**, 578–80.

ZIMMERMAN, D.W. (1993) 'A note on nonindependence and nonparametric tests', *Perceptual and Motor Skills*, **76**, 407–12.

ZIMMERMAN, D.W. and ZUMBO, B.D. (1993) 'Rank transformations and the power of the student *t*-test and Welch *t´*-test for non-normal populations with unequal variances', *Canadian Journal of Experimental Psychology*, **47**, 3, 523–39.

Index

DESIGN:	COUNT DATA				CONTINUOUS DATA	
One. Sample	*Binomial/Nominal*		*Rank*		*Normal*	
Research Q: *Association/ relationship*	One sample χ^2 test of Independence (6.1) Phi Coefficient and Cramer's Phi (6.1)		Spearman's rank order r_s correlation (7.2)		Pearson correlation r (8.3)	
Difference	Binomial test difference *between* 2 proportions (or %) (6.2)		One sample Runs test (7.3)		—	
Research Q: *Prediction* (independent variable is continuous)	—		—		Linear Regression (Response variable is continuous (8.2))	
Two. Sample	*Independent*	*Related*	*Independent*	*Related*	*Independent*	*Related*
Research Q: *Comparison/ differences*	Fisher's exact test (6.3) Proportions test* (6.4)	Sign test (6.5)	Wilcoxon M-W test (7.4)	Wilcoxon Signed Ranks test (7.5)	*t*-test (8.4)	*t*-test (8.5)
Association (class variable is discrete forming groups)	r × 2 sample χ^2 test of homogeneity (6.1)	—	—	—	—	—
Multiple Samples (groups) *1 Independent variable* (factor)						
	Independent	*Related*	*Independent*	*Related*	*Independent*	*Related*
Research Q: *Differences between groups* (class variable is discrete forming groups)	—	—	Kruskal-Wallis One-way ANOVA (7.6)	Friedman ANOVA by Ranks (7.7)	One-way ANOVA (unrelated) (8.7)	One-way ANOVA (related) (8.8)
Multiple Samples (groups) *More than 1 independent variable* (factors)						
Research Q: *Differences between groups* (class variable is discrete forming groups)		Cochran's Q test for > 2 proportions (6.7)	—	—	Two-way ANOVA (unrelated)((8.9)	Two-way ANOVA split-plot† (8.10)
Association (class variable is discrete forming groups)	r × k χ^2 test (6.6)	—	—	—	—	—

* Can be independent or related; (6.1) indicates Chapter and section in text; † Independent and related

Decision chart for choosing a statistical test